THE MOVIES

THE

MOVIES

THE SIXTY-YEAR STORY OF

THE WORLD OF HOLLYWOOD AND

ITS EFFECT ON AMERICA. FROM

PRE-NICKELODEON DAYS TO THE PRESENT

BY RICHARD GRIFFITH

AND ARTHUR MAYER

BONANZA BOOKS, NEW YORK

AN ACKNOWLEDGMENT TO The Museum of Modern Art FILM LIBRARY

When, in 1935, the trustees of The Museum of Modern Art founded the Museum's Film Library, they opened to the student and to the film public a new field of study and enjoyment. Through the Film Library it became possible, for the first time, to examine and to analyze the record of achievement of this newest of the modern arts.

Certainly the present book could not have been written and compiled without access to the Library's collections of motion pictures, "stills," books, magazines, and memorabilia. The authors wish to thank the members of the Museum staff for much intelligent help—in particular, John Adams, Assistant Curator of the Film Library, who secured many rare stills for the book in this country and abroad and who guided us in our search through the more than 500,000 stills which constitute the Library's own collection; Eileen Bowser, Research Assistant in the Film Library, for both researching and checking the factual material; René d'Harnoncourt, Director of the Museum, and Monroe Wheeler, Directors of Exhibitions and Publications, for consultation and advice.

RG and AM

to **ANNIE** and **LILLIE**, our best critics and severest friends

FURTHER ACKNOWLEDGMENTS

THE page layouts and picture arrangements in this book are the work of Paul Jensen, of whose skill and enthusiasm the authors are deeply appreciative. Ann Warren Griffith typed, proofread, and indexed the manuscript, and made many valuable editorial suggestions, as did Lillie Mayer. We also wish to thank the following individuals and organizations at the right for help in locating and securing pictorial material:

The Academy of Motion Picture Arts and Sciences
John E. Allen
Joseph Aurrichio, RKO
Frederick Bullock, 20th Century-Fox
Rodney Bush, 20th Century-Fox
Roger Caras
James Card, George Eastman House
Culver Service
Det Danske Filmmuseum, Copenhagen
William K. Everson
Filmhistoriska Samlingarna, Stockholm
Nat Gartsman, Warner Brothers
Phillip Gerard, Universal
Miss Bernice Gobel, Columbia
Mrs. Oscar Godbout
Mrs. Judith Greene
Miss Terry Hamill, United Artists
Joseph Homler, M-G-M
Miss Tess Klausner, Paramount
Robert MacGregor, Theatre Arts Books
Mrs. Estelle Nathan, Universal
George Pratt, George Eastman House
Martin Quigley, Jr., Quigley Publications
Sidney Rechetnik, Warner Brothers
Miss Bea Ross, Republic
Miss Franziska Schacht, New York Public Library
Miss Hortense Schorr, Columbia
Silas Seadler, M-G-M
John Springer, RKO
Al Stern, RKO
Miss Norah Traylen, British Film Institute
Max Youngstein, United Artists

SELECTED BIBLIOGRAPHY

Barry, Iris, *D. W. Griffith: American Film Master,* The Museum of Modern Art, New York, 1940.

Barry, Iris, *Let's Go to the Movies,* Payson and Clarke, New York, 1927.

Cooke, Alistair, *Douglas Fairbanks: the Making of a Screen Character,* The Museum of Modern Art, New York, 1940.

Cooke, Alistair, ed., *Garbo and the Night Watchmen,* Faber, London, 1937.

deMille, William C., *Hollywood Saga,* Dutton, New York, 1939.

Griffith, Richard, *The World of Robert Flaherty,* Duell, Sloan and Pearce, New York, 1953.

Hampton, Benjamin B., *A History of the Movies,* Covici-Friede, New York, 1931.

Hecht, Ben, *A Child of the Century,* Simon and Schuster, New York, 1954.

Jacobs, Lewis, *The Rise of the American Film,* Harcourt, Brace, New York, 1939.

Mayer, Arthur, *Merely Colossal,* Simon and Schuster, New York, 1953.

Ramsaye, Terry, *A Million and One Nights,* Simon and Schuster, New York, 1926.

Rosten, Leo, *Hollywood: the Movie Colony, the Movie Makers,* Harcourt, Brace, New York, 1940.

Rotha, Paul, and Griffith, Richard, *The Film Till Now,* Funk and Wagnalls, New York, 1950.

Seldes, Gilbert, *An Hour with the Movies and the Talkies,* Lippincott, Philadelphia, 1929.

Talmey, Allene, *Doug and Mary and Others,* Macy-Masius, New York, 1927.

Vidor, King, *A Tree Is a Tree,* Harcourt, Brace, New York, 1953.

Zukor, Adolph, and Kramer, Dale, *The Public Is Never Wrong,* Putnam, New York, 1953.

Photoplay Magazine

Picture Play Magazine

CONTENTS

PREFACE

A MORE UNLIKELY pair of collaborators for a book about the movies than the authors of this volume could scarcely be found. One of them is, or thinks he is, a thoroughly commercial character who drifted into the picture industry purely by chance and remained in it because he found it pleasurable and profitable. The other is, or at least is frequently so regarded, an unworldly purist who, as a small boy thirty-five years ago, fell in love with the flickers and grew up to become the chronicler of their lightning development. One thing, however, we two had in common: the conviction that of the machines which have changed our lives in the twentieth century, only the internal-combustion engine rivals the movie camera in the scope of its influence. The movie was born at the beginning of what Frederick Lewis Allen called "the big change," the biggest change in human history, the industrialization of much of mankind in less than half a century. The movie has been the mirror of that change, and in mirroring it became the agent of change as well. Other mass media have played their parts in constructing the image of mechanized civilization, but the movie did it first and did it most vividly. Future historians, when they search the ruins of our vanished life, will look not only for manuscripts but for motion pictures—if we have the sense to preserve them.

This conception we sold to our simple-minded publishers as the basis for a book, along with the idea that such a book must necessarily be profusely illustrated with stills of our favorite films and performers. The project, however, had a substantial flaw. It would have taken a book twice as long as this to correlate what was happening on the American screen with what was happening on the American scene, and one even longer than that to include a tithe of the stills which we thought it close to criminal to discard. The mayhem involved in selection has been considerable. Reluctantly we had to abandon any idea of discussing most of the great foreign pictures which at critical moments fertilized and reinvigorated domestic production. Sadly, and only after long discussion, we excluded cartoons, even the most delectable of Disney and the craftsmen of the UPA; these masters have created a cinematic world of their own and deserve a book of their own. The vast field of documentary films, except when they reached mass audiences, as in wartime, was also obviously beyond our scope. And we have dealt with post-World War II picture developments in briefer compass than their importance justifies, suspecting that time must elapse before we or anybody can have sufficient perspective to appraise them.

Whatever preconceptions we brought to it, we found ourselves dominated in the making of this book by one overriding feeling—the fun we've had in more than three decades of moviegoing—and it is this that we have tried to render here. Reliving that fun was also fun, but fun of a different and rather special kind, one we hope the reader is now about to experience. The quality of it is indicated by an observation by Iris Barry, founder of the Museum of Modern Art Film Library, who earlier and better than anyone else understood what makes people of all kinds love the movies. "To the average adult today, his own past can be most quickly recaptured or recalled through the medium of old phonograph discs and old films. But to hear the discs and see the films again is not to recall one's past; that is achieved better by pure recollection of past music and past movies. Actually to hear and see again what pleased one so much in music or in photographic imagery is, rather, to get a sharp critical slant on one's own past. That was what one enjoyed ten years ago; this is what seemed the most exciting or beautiful thing in one's adolescence. *Cabiria* and *Male and Female* and "I Must Have That Man" have not changed: it is we who have changed and the world we live in."   RICHARD GRIFFITH
                                                             ARTHUR MAYER

New York
March 1957

THE BIRTH OF THE MOVIES

Thomas Alva Edison

WHITE MAGIC

The nineteenth century was rushing toward its close, propelled by steam and electricity. The railroad, the steamship, the telegraph, the telephone, the phonograph, and the internal combustion engine took their places in human life in bewildering succession, but the American people never tired of exclaiming, "What hath God wrought?" even though they were more inclined to attribute most of these marvels to Thomas A. Edison. The barbarous human past was dead, and with it all superstitious beliefs and forebodings. "White Magic," the miracle of science was called in the 1890s, and it was to be the successor to those dark, abandoned superstitions. It led straight to Utopia, everybody agreed, and no one mentioned Pandora and her box.

Edison himself, the high priest of the new gospel, had invented the phonograph in 1876 and shortly thereafter began to try to contrive its visual equivalent. By 1889, he and George Eastman had perfected the frame-lined celluloid strip which set pictures in motion. Having solved the basic problem, he had little interest in going further. He regarded the invention as a toy and did not respond to the urging of his associates that he try to find a way of projecting these one-inch film images from the confines of a small box onto a screen large enough to be looked at by a theater audience. But, always the practical man, he made his invention available to the first outlet which appeared. Beginning in 1892, "moving pictures" could be seen in places originally called Penny Arcades or Peep Shows, which soon became known as Kinetoscope Parlors.

The Kinetoscope Arcade, San Francisco, c. 1899. Penny arcades for a while also featured "Kinetophones" which enabled the spectator to hear music or "sound effects."

THE KINETOSCOPE

Penny arcades were for the poor and the young. They were storerooms with wide entrances decked with circus posters and lurid stills, forerunners of the garish movie advertising of later years. Phonographs had been installed in them early, and now sound and picture were crudely harnessed together to provide such naïvely comic or pornographic bits of life as "What the Bootblack Saw" or "How Bridget Served the Salad Undressed." (A trend manifested itself from the beginning: the risqué and slapstick were immediately popular, while "Surf at Dover" or "Beavers at Play" brought in meager returns.) To see these scraps of film, you dropped a penny in a slot, looked into an aperture like that of a stereoscope, and ground a crank. A light flashed on, and for a minute you watched Fatima wiggle her torso or a small boy squirt the garden hose on a well-dressed gentleman. You can see them today, in the flea circuses of the world,

and now they are disarmingly redolent of an age of innocence. Then, they were glimpses of a far *less* innocent world than the poor and the young knew from their own experience.

The Kinetoscope was as far as Edison considered it expedient to take his new invention. Pleased with the flood of pennies that flowed in from the peep-show parlors, he feared that if he were to project his images so that more than one person could see them at a time, the audience would soon be exhausted. But the pull of "living pictures" magnetized a host of would-be Edisons here and abroad. By 1895, the Kinetoscope had a lively imitative competitor in the Mutoscope, and strenuous efforts were being made by a score of mechanically minded men to combine the Kinetoscope principle with that of the magic lantern, so as to throw a larger-than-life-size picture on a sheet or on some other white surface.

THE MOVIES
ACHIEVE
THE SCREEN

Prodded by the many imitators who threatened to reap the rewards of his ingenuity, Edison finally sanctioned the projection of his tiny film images on the rudimentary equivalent of today's theater screen. The first public performance under his aegis was held on April 23, 1896, in the famed Koster and Bials' Music Hall in New York. Next morning, the *Times* reported: ". . . an unusually bright light fell upon the screen. Then came into view two precious blond persons of the variety stage, in pink and blue dresses, doing the umbrella dance with commendable celerity. Their motions were all clearly defined."

These "wonderfully real and singularly exhilarating" scenes were mostly moving photographs of standard vaudeville acts, and vaudeville houses, then in their heyday, became the first home of the movies. For a time the new invention took the place of the star turn. There was something marvelous and magical about even routine acts when they were blown up by the camera to ten times life size—and when they involved the onlooker in a new physical experience. The distance between the movie viewer and what happens on the screen is in a state of perpetual flux. He is either drawn into the midst of the action or the action comes toward or recedes away from him. In 1896, this was a new and godlike experience.

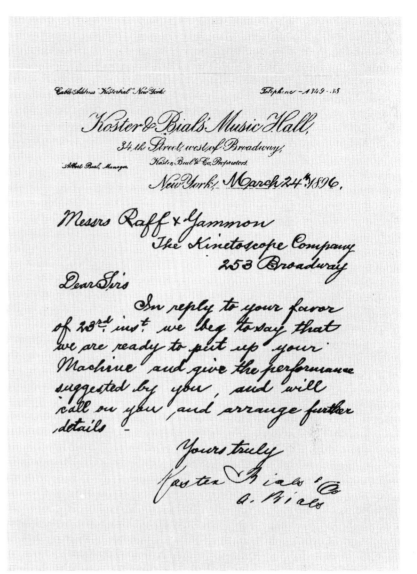

The turning of a historic page: Koster and Bials' letter inviting the managers of the Kinetoscope Company to put on the first public showing of motion pictures.

Fatima, the sensation of the 1896 Chicago World's Fair, was filmed in her famous *danse du ventre,* to general shock. The compassionate censors of those early days, not wanting to deprive audiences of the lady altogether, simply blotted out the offending portions of her Egyptian shimmy.

SCIENTIFIC AMERICAN

(Entered at the Post Office of New York, N. Y. as Second Class matter.)

A WEEKLY JOURNAL OF PRACTICAL INFORMATION, ART, SCIENCE, MECHANICS, CHEMISTRY, AND MANUFACTURES.

Vol. LXXVI.—No. 16.]
Established 1845.

NEW YORK, APRIL 17, 1897.

[$3.00 A YEAR.
Weekly.

Fig. 1.—THE DARK ROOM AND REEL FOR DEVELOPING FILMS.

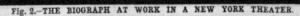

Fig. 2.—THE BIOGRAPH AT WORK IN A NEW YORK THEATER.

Fig. 3.—INTERIOR OF THE "MUTOSCOPE."

A year after the first projection of movies, the *Scientific American* was satisfying the curiosity of mechanically minded Americans about the workings of the movie marvel.

Cripple Creek Barroom, 1898. This authentic-looking vignette of the Old West was actually produced in Edison's "Black Maria" studio in Menlo Park, New Jersey.

THE FIRST MOVIES

The American Mutoscope and Biograph Company was Edison's first important rival, the Mutoscope being a peep-show machine similar to the Kinetoscope, while the Biograph was a projector operating on principles nearly identical with Edison's but artfully varied to circumvent his patents. On the page opposite, the cumbrous Biograph camera photographs the Pennsylvania Limited running "at sixty miles an hour," while the equally ponderous Biograph projector throws it on the screen. Audiences of 1896 shrieked in fear when they saw the train speeding upon them. It was an experience not repeated until the advent of Cinerama and 3-D in 1953.

Audiences soon grew used to snippets of faked "news" and faked adventure, wonderful as they seemed at first. By 1900, moving pictures were relegated to the closing act on the bill in the vaudeville houses where they were shown. A scientific toy in the eyes of its own inventor, a "chaser" to the variety tycoons, the film seemed headed for the limbo of outworn novelties.

GEORGES MELIES

The movies received their next impetus from a man as typical of the era of White Magic as Edison himself. Georges Melies, proprietor of the Théâtre Robert-Houdin in Paris, was a popular magician and specialist in legerdemain and electromagnetic marvels. He saw the movie as a mechanical extension of magical illusion, with which he could achieve effects never before conceived. Buying a camera from the father of the French movie, Louis Lumière, Melies set about filming anything that moved, for the sheer miracle of animation. He soon discovered something still more miraculous. As he filmed a truck passing down a street, his camera jammed. By the time he had set it in motion again, the truck had passed on and a hearse succeeded it. When projected on a screen, this bit of film showed the truck turn into a hearse. Movie magic had been born.

Within a few years Melies invented or stumbled upon double exposure, stop motion, fast and slow motion, animation, fades, dissolves, almost the entire repertory of the trick film as it exists now. In 1900 he did something of even greater significance. He filmed the old fairy tale *Cinderella*. Though the film, less than 1000 feet long, was little more than picture-book illustration, it had a beginning, middle, and end. It told a story.

Melies' imaginative films astonished and delighted movie-goers the world over. He flung himself into the work of writing scenarios, designing and painting scenery, drilling his little corps of artists and helpers, and appearing himself in the rich succession of "transformations, tricks, fairy tales, apotheoses, artistic and fantastic scenes, comic subjects, war pictures, fantasies and illusions" which his letterhead offered. But this versatile and ingenious pioneer was no businessman. He sold prints of his films instead of renting them, and he became a victim of the illegal duping prevalent in the early movie days. In 1914 the war ended his career as a producer; in 1925 he lost his theater, destroyed all the films in his possession and vanished.

Four years later, he was recognized hawking newspapers in the Paris streets, and for a brief moment he was photographed and feted as the founding father of the French movie industry. Then friends bought him a little toy and candy stand at the Gare Montparnasse. When he became too old to sell toys, he was made a Chevalier of the Legion of Honor and was admitted to the old actors' home at Orly. Here he spent the last years of his life, receiving such visitors as called to pay their respects to a pioneer of the world's most lucrative art, and hoping to be again actively employed in film-making. He died, still hoping, on January 22, 1938.

Innumerable science-fiction films were made by Melies. *An Impossible Voyage,* 1904 (left), and *A Trip to the Moon,* 1902, were the most notable. His pictures both satirized and celebrated scientific progress. Caption of this scene is: "Tableau 17: To the summit of the Jungfrau at full speed."

← A French family group at the height of the era of "white magic." Georges Melies, right, *en famille* at Garches, France, 1892.

→

Le Rêve de Shakespeare, 1907, known in English as *Shakespeare Writing Julius Caesar,* with Melies as the dramatist envisioning Caesar's assassination. In Melies' films the sets were backdrops painted by the director himself. He seems here to have Rome as already in ruins.

Long - Distance Wireless Photography, 1907. Hardly had Marconi invented the "wireless" when Melies produced this burlesque in which a whiskered inventor displays his radioed photo of three damsels, who symbolically float above. The girls are from the Folies Bergère, which Melies used in some capacity in nearly all his films.

In imitation of Melies, Edwin S. Porter made many films for the Edison Co., such as *Dream of a Rarebit Fiend,* a trick movie of 1906.

Thomas L. Tally's Los Angeles "Electric Theatre" was speedily imitated throughout the world. This one was probably in Robert Dooner's fairground in South Wales, Britain.

The definitive edition of the movie showplace finally became known by the generic name of Nickelodeon. Here are the Warner brothers standing in front of one.

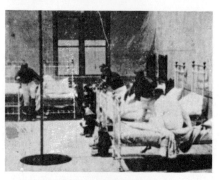
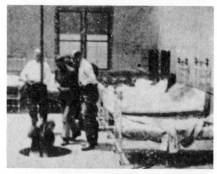

Life of an American Fireman, 1903, by Edwin S. Porter.

THE NICKELODEON AGE

THE STORE SHOWS

Before 1900, screen-projected movies were practically a monopoly of the vaudeville theaters and even in them had lost favor. But in the first year of the century, the nation's vaudeville actors formed a union and struck for higher wages. The managers, refusing to recognize the union, either closed their theaters or ingeniously kept their houses open by presenting programs consisting solely of motion pictures. Projection manufacturers found themselves swamped with orders as vaudeville managers clamored for equipment. With the end of the strike, however, the cumbersome machines abruptly became a drug on the market. Manufacturers were overstocked, and the eager buyers of yesterday were prepared to sell their machines secondhand at any price.

At bargain prices, though, a new market appeared. Penny arcade owners of the Nineties had seen their peep-show movies eclipse cooch dancers and flea circuses as the most popular attractions of their motley emporia. When films projected on the large screen outdistanced peep shows, they longed to compete, but equipment had been as scarce as it was costly. Now, with projectors going begging, came the opportunity of the penny-ante boys.

In Los Angeles, Thomas L. Tally set up a movie show in the rear of the amusement parlor he owned. He converted skeptics by cutting a hole in the partition which separated the darkened projection room from the rest of the arcade, so that doubting Thomases could see for themselves that life-sized pictures were being shown in the rear. So successful was this device that he soon jettisoned his other ventures, turned his arcade into an auditorium, and advertised 'The Electric Theater. For Up-to-Date High-Class Motion Picture Entertainment Especially for Ladies and Children.'

Tally's success—and it was sensational—attracted a horde of followers from the fringes of show business—ex-barkers, hawkers, pitchmen, and medicine-show men, as well as the owners of the peep shows where the infant movie had first found a home. They shared two things in common: a hunch that an untapped, unsophisticated public was avid for low-priced entertainment, and a lack of cash with which to capitalize on that hunch. They knew that the theater and vaudeville magnates were convinced that movies had already exhausted their brief popularity, but they hoped that they could exploit the vestiges of the movies' fame among the lowly by renting unused stores and equipping them with projection machines, a screen, and some chairs. The "store shows" were usually family enterprises, managed, staffed, and cleaned up by papa, mama, and the boys. They were dank, noisome places, repulsive to the elect. But there were plenty of the unelected, and they kept coming.

THE MOVIES LEARN TO TELL STORIES

Till Edwin S. Porter's *Life of an American Fireman*, U. S. movies still consisted of "topical views"—tidbits of nature study, brief comic interludes, and nearly as brief scenes from stage successes (Joseph Jefferson as Rip Van Winkle, Sarah Bernhardt enacting the duel scene from *Hamlet*). But, taking his cue from Melies, Porter captured the popular imagination by introducing narrative and thus gave the movies a fresh lease on life. Georges Melies had told stories on the screen in the manner of the theater, but an Edison film by Edwin S. Porter was the first to arrive at a cinematic form of narration. It shows a fire chief sitting in his office dreaming (in what was then called a "dream balloon") of his wife at home. We cut to a close shot (the first known) of a street-corner fire alarm and to another of a hand setting off the alarm. We cut again to another distant scene, that of the firemen jumping from bed, sliding down the firehouse pole, and starting toward the fire. The remaining frames of this short film detail the rescue of a woman and child from a burning home. Today, film scholars dispute the order and the meaning of these frames, the argument turning on whether Porter merely anticipated or actually invented the principal device of screen narrative, cross-cutting, which enables the director to annihilate space and time.

Porter had begun his career as an itinerant cameraman for the Edison Company. *The Life of an American Fireman* and *The Great Train Robbery* made him the foremost director of the Nickelodeon Age, and even after the advent of D. W. Griffith he remained a leading figure in the industry. In 1915, his fortune made, he retired, but the crash of 1929 wiped out his wealth, and Porter spent his old age as a minor employee of an appliance corporation, a modest spectator of the growth of an industry to which he had given the initial creative push.

1 The telegraph operator's daughter prays for her father, bound and sandbagged by the train robbers.

2 The robbers force the engineer to uncouple the locomotive.

3 They make their escape into the woods.

4 Spending their ill-gotten gains in a saloon, the robbers force a tenderfoot to dance.

5 At the end of the film, for no reason connected with the story, one of the characters draws his pistol and fires at the audience.

THE FIRST

More famous than any American picture except *The Birth of a Nation* and possibly *Gone with the Wind*, *The Great Train Robbery* has lingered in the national consciousness as the first real movie. In it, Edwin S. Porter merely extended and refined the storytelling principles he had used in *Life of an American Fireman*. But this was a story of crime and the Far West (it was actually filmed in New Jersey), and these favorite themes of American popular entertainment acquired a new potency in the new and flexible medium of the screen. *The Great Train Robbery* became a classic overnight. For

Uncle Tom's Cabin

1 A super-production of 1903: the background is painted, the steamboats are toys, the water is real.

2 Eliza shakes a defiant fist at Simon Legree.

3 Death of Little Eva. Aunt Sally bows her head, Uncle Tom his knee, while the angel gathers up the departed.

4 Death of Uncle Tom, with Little Eva beckoning him to heaven.

REAL MOVIES

years newly opened nickelodeons invariably billed it as their initial attraction, just as years later, with the coming of the talkies, theaters which had closed to be wired for sound always reopened with Al Jolson's *The Singing Fool.*

As soon as the movies learned to tell stories, they began to film the classics. Porter himself brought *Uncle Tom's Cabin* to the screen in what, for the nickelodeon era, had all the earmarks of a modern super-production. The tableaux, backdrops, and painted light of this delicious film breathe forth the odor of the nineteenth-century popular theater.

5 After the death of Uncle Tom, a symbolic tableau of Lincoln promises the freeing of the slaves.

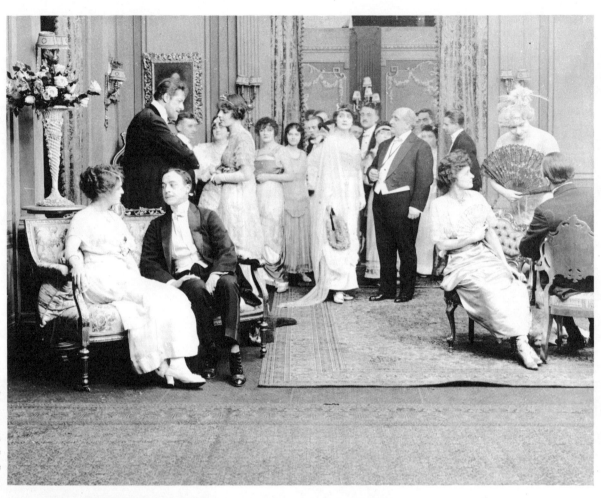

The Reception, Edison, *c.* 1911. Though the close-up had been invented by 1902, most directors insisted on arranging action in the manner of the stage, with all the characters shown full length and considerable floor space between them and the camera.

FILMS OF THE NICKELODEON AGE

With a lively partisanship unknown today, films of the nickelodeon era tore into current issues as they came along. Labor vs. capital, votes for women, graft, political chicanery, race discrimination—all found reflection on the screen. Production was con-

The Suffragette, Edison, *c.* 1912. Films of the period ridiculed the "unwomanly woman" who wanted to vote. Here one of them tells the dog to keep watch on her husband and see that he minds the baby and gets dinner while she is out speech-making.

Romeo and Juliet, Vitagraph, 1908. Early film-makers made municipal architecture do duty for classical or medieval settings, as amateurs do today. Here the death of Mercutio is staged against the background of the Central Park Mall in New York.

trolled by wealthy men, but they were not as yet aware of the power of the films to influence human thought and conduct, while directors and writers were ready and willing to supply situations and solutions satisfactory to their humble audiences.

The murder of Stanford White by Harry K. Thaw on the Madison Square Garden roof re-enacted for the Biograph Mutoscope and rushed to the nickelodeons a few hours after the shooting occurred.

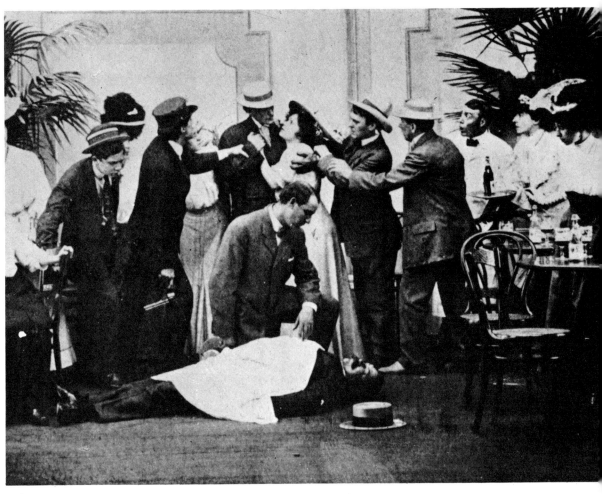

13

PERSONAL—"Young French Nobleman, recently arrived, desires to meet wealthy American girl, object, matrimony; will be at Grant's Tomb at 10 this morning, wearing boutonniere of violets."

A subtitle from the 1904 film, *How the French nobleman got a wife through the New York* Herald *Personal columns.*

FILMS OF THE NICKELODEON AGE

Magic remained a mainstay of the movies' appeal in the Nickelodeon Age. Descendants of Melies, forerunners of Disney and Clair, the merrymakers of these deliberately mad films took their audiences on flights of fancy which today's producers think themselves too sophisticated to attempt.

The Disintegrated Convict, 1907. A convict, hiding from police

Roosevelt in Africa, 1910. Theodore Roosevelt was a "natural" for the movies. An enterprising producer, Col. William N. Selig, hired a vaudeville actor bearing a slight resemblance to "T.R.," and while the ex-President was on safari in Africa, made a movie of a lion hunt in his Chicago studio. The public accepted it as genuine.

The Fighting Roosevelts, 1919. A year after his death, Roosevelt was the hero of a film which perpetuated the legend of the

in a barrel, escapes them by changing into a striped hose.

weakling bespectacled Easterner who, hardened by the Wild West, became the nation's leading exponent of the strenuous life.

Gertie the Dinosaur, 1909. One of the first animated films, drawn by Winsor McCay, famous cartoonist of the period.

LADIES AND CHILDREN
ARE CORDIALLY INVITED
TO THIS THEATRE
NO OFFENSIVE PICTURES
ARE EVER SHOWN HERE

Ladies K
yo

The Bijou Dream (Rochester, New York, *c.* 1909) usurped the entire ground floor of a commercial building, but its proudest boast remained, "Admission 5c."

THE NICKELODEON AND ITS PATRONS

Nickelodeons like the Bijou Dream in Rochester sprang up in storerooms, hotel ballrooms, disused lecture halls, any place that could be improvised into the semblance of a theater. Carrying on the tradition of the visiting Lyceum lecturer or touring stock company, managed as often as not by local people, they gradually developed into community centers which met an entertainment need that could be filled in no other way. Concert singers, Wild West shows, and stock companies reached small American towns only once or twice a year, and even then only the comfortably off could afford to attend them. But the nickelodeon was a local fixture whose price was within reach of all. Its cheapness and ready access were something new under the sun. "The telegraph, the telephone, the electric light," says Benjamin B. Hampton, pioneer movie financier and producer, ". . . had created a sensation but they had not entered into the lives of millions of people. The common man and his family still used kerosene lamps; none but the well-to-do had telephones; and the telegram was a form

of communication seldom known in the average household except to announce serious illness or death. But this new thing—this 'living picture' affair—was not a prosaic tool to reduce labor or to save time; it was not an instrument to create more comfort and luxury for the well-to-do. It was a romantic device to bring entertainment to the common people."*

Soon the nickelodeons became a home away from home for the whole family. Local advertisers found the screen a profitable billboard. Slides familiarly instructed patrons in the elementary courtesies and neatnesses. Baritones and tenors led the audience in song, while scenes illustrating the lyrics were thrown on the screen. And always there were the movies themselves—still "flickers," "galloping tin-types" yet, but bringing new sights and new thoughts to people whose imaginative world had been bounded by the village, slum, or farm.

* A History of the Movies, by Benjamin B. Hampton, Covici-Friede, 1931.

"Hello, Central, Give Me Heaven," says the little girl whose mother lives there. A nickelodeon song slide.

"Trust Him Not, the Gypsy Fortune Teller Said." J. D. Cress was the author of this, the above, and many other songs popular in the nickelodeons.

17

PART II
8 PAGES

THE ST. LOUIS REPUBLIC.

WANT AD
SECTION

102d YEAR.

SUNDAY MORNING, FEBRUARY 6, 1910.

PRICE FIVE CENTS

ST. LOUIS'S HIGH-CLASS MOVING-PICTURE THEATRES

Newspapers ignored the nickelodeons until they began to take advertising space. Then they suddenly discovered—as in the above story from the St. Louis *Republic*—that: "Electricity, that mysterious force about which we still know so little, has been harnessed by man and now drives the motors that connect with the machinery, and for a consideration of 5 or 10 cents a visitor may now enter a luxuriously upholstered hall, brilliantly illuminated, and while sitting spellbound by the rapidly shifting scenes that transport him in imagination to tropical climes, he may ravish his soul with fine orchestral effects from deep-toned instruments whose wonderful voices pour forth upon the air the melodies of New York's famous songsters or St. Louis' leading musicians." What press agent ever went further?

Had any of the owners of the motion picture trust walked past the Crystal Hall on Fourteenth Street one day in 1914, they would have been confirmed in their contempt for the commodity they produced. The theater's poster artist had transformed—probably in all innocence—the Italian import *Tigris* to *Tigress, The Mysterious Criminal.*

THE NICKELODEON AND ITS PATRONS

In contrast to the small-town store shows, nickelodeons in New York and other big cities grew out of penny arcades in many cases, and they looked as dark, dirty, and smelly as penny arcades and flea circuses look to us today. Their first patrons were often tramps and drunks; the respectable shuddered away from them and murmured against them. It began to be said that something ought to be done about policing them or maybe banning them altogether. But the city nickelodeons thrived. Even more than in rural America, they were the only entertainment available to the poor.

Especially were they the chief entertainment of the hordes of immigrants from southern and eastern Europe who poured into the metropolis in the early 1900s. Barred from the theater by their ignorance of English, they could follow the one-reel picture dramas of the nickelodeons, learning much about American life and values in the process, and piecing out their English as they gradually related the subtitles to the action. Observing this, some of the more farsighted social workers of the period began to think that the despised "poor man's show" might become his university as well.

By the end of the Nickelodeon Age, even the city nickelodeons were safe and comfortable places which the most fastidious might (and some surreptitiously did) attend without offense. Exhibitors began to clamor for longer films with better stories and acting, knowing that audiences would pay more if they got more, but their clamor went unheeded. The real powers of the new industry, the producers, refused to believe that anybody would ever shell out more than a nickel to see a movie. They didn't think the pictures they made were worth even a plugged one.

THE MEN WHO OWNED THE BUSINESS

High above the "mob" which attended nickelodeons and the "gypsies and bunco artists" who ran them sat the mighty Thomas Alva Edison and his eight associates in the Motion Picture Patents and the General Film companies. They were not offended when the movies were called a "plaything for children of all ages" or a "cheap show for cheap people." They fully agreed and they did not care, so long as the nickels of the cheap people continued to flow into their coffers.

Edison's initial indifference to the possible profits of his invention had opened the way for numerous small operators to enter production. By 1907, the gross income from film production exceeded that of the legitimate theater and vaudeville combined, and the Wizard belatedly thought of the profits he was losing. At first he tried to sue his competitors for violation of his basic patents, but all claimed patents of their own, and the Edison Company seemed in danger of spending a decade in the courts with no certainty of the outcome. His advisers then suggested that he invite his more "substantial" competitors to join with him in forming a company in which each would acknowledge the validity of the others' claims. Accordingly, the leading American companies of the day, Vitagraph, Selig, Essanay, Kalem, Biograph, Lubin, and Kleine, together with two important French concerns, Pathé and Melies, joined Edison in forming the Motion Picture Patents Company. In January 1909, the ten partners announced that they alone owned the right to photograph, develop, and print motion pictures, that they alone could do so under the patent laws of the U.S., Great Britain, France, Germany, and Italy, and that no license to do so would ever be issued to anyone else.

Having declared a monopoly on production, the combine speedily sought to extend its stranglehold to distribution and exhibition. It formed the General Film Company, which was to be its instrument of control over the wholesaling and retailing of pictures. The leading film exchanges were acquired and the exhibitors were informed that they could continue to operate only at the pleasure of General Film. Since the manufacturers controlled production, exhibitors could book only films made by the members of Motion Picture Patents; since they controlled the manufacture of projectors, exhibitors needed a license from General Film in order even to show the motion pictures of General Film itself. And that license cost each of them two dollars a week fifty-two weeks a year. This license fee was to net the General Film Company an income of $1,250,000 per year.

The nine producers whom Edison had so generously taken to his bosom could not believe their good luck. Their lawyers advised them that Motion Picture Patents and General Film constituted between them an "airtight trust," but that the beauty of it was that they could not be prosecuted under the Sherman Act because their monopoly was firmly based on patent protection. Their competitors were eliminated, their business standardized, and, best of all, the "riff-raff" of exhibitors far below them in the industry structure would have to pay them to continue to exist. The license fee was the hallmark of their impregnable position, or so they thought.

It proved, however, the rock on which the trust broke. The nickelodeon operators reacted to it much as the colonists of 1760 reacted to the Stamp Act. Legal it might or might not be, but it was taxation without representation, and they needed only leadership to declare their independence.

Making movies for ten cents a foot was lots of fun. A jovial meeting of the Motion Picture Patents Company—Thomas A. Edison surrounded by (left to right) Albert Smith, Vitagraph; George Scull, Edison; George Kleine, Kalem; Edison; Siegmund Lubin, Lubin; H. N. Marvin, Biograph; J. Stuart Blackton, Vitagraph; Frank Marion, Kalem.

THE FIGHTING INDEPENDENTS

The nickelodeon operators found leadership in William Fox and Carl Laemmle, two exhibitors who had climbed into the distributing end of the business by operating "exchanges." Exchanges were at first literally just that: offices where exhibitors met to barter prints of films they had already used for others their patrons had not yet seen. When renting instead of buying films became the rule, the exchanges developed into wholesaling outlets, buying films in job lots from producers and renting them individually to nickelodeons. They were the middlemen between manufacturers and consumers, and as such had to be brought into the closed system General Film was creating. But when General Film announced that it was buying the leading independent exchanges and that those it did not condescend to buy out must get out, Laemmle and Fox refused either to sell or to quit. They proclaimed the right to run their businesses as they pleased, and to hell with the patent laws.

Their position seemed hopeless. Lately risen from obscurity, they lacked the capital which General Film with its vast resources could array against them in the form of lawsuits, injunctions, and boycotts. All they had on their side was the resentment of exhibitors against the trust and their willingness to flout its requirements whenever they could get away with it. But that turned out to be all they needed.

Fox at first contented himself with ignoring the Patents Company, although eventually he fought and won a lawsuit against the trust. But Laemmle declared open war. He created the character of "General Flimco," and in a series of cartoons contrasted the trust's wealth and greed with the plight of the small exhibitor. When the trust threatened to boycott exhibitors who dealt with him, Laemmle printed the threatening letters as evidence that General Film was a coercive monopoly. When the trust, as a precaution against exhibitors' "going independent," added to its exhibition contract a "3rd Condition" requiring the payment of the hated weekly license fee in advance and on a yearly basis, Laemmle declaimed, "Read that '3rd Condition' again. Take it home and play it on your pianola. Play it upside down, sidewise, before and behind. Tell, when you're all through, tell me what you think of it!!!" When the trust cut off his exchanges' supply of films, he began to make them himself, significantly calling his producing firm The Independent Motion-Picture Company. And all the time he harped on the frustration of exhibitors, horse-traders all, at the trust's rule that all films, good and bad, should be paid for at ten cents a foot.

"Ten cents a foot" was indeed as good a war cry for Laemmle as "two dollars a week," and this the moguls completely failed to understand. The corporation lawyers, big-business executives, and financiers who controlled the trust believed that their films as well as everybody else's were shoddy stuff fit only for illiterates, and what was the use of trying to improve them? They were too far removed from their audiences to sense what exhibitors and exchange men knew at first hand—that this motley rabble of "immigrants, children, chambermaids, and streetcar conductors" wanted better films. As more and better independent films came on the market, more and more exhibitors were willing to pay high for them and unwilling to abide by the trust's ten cents a foot and two dollars a week. Long before General Film was abolished by judicial decision in 1915, it had become a hollow shell.

William Fox parlayed a small nickelodeon into a $20,000,-000 producing and distributing corporation by working even while he ate.

Carl Laemmle smilingly returning from his annual visit to his German birthplace many years after his defeat of the General Film Company.

Come Out of It, Mr. Exhibitor!

Bitterly sore because they have

seen me pass them in the race for supremacy and become the largest and best film renter in the world, several film exchanges are now making an attack on me. They haven't any more nerve than the Lord gave little kittens, so they confine their attacks to personal letters, marked "confidential." And what do you think the frightful charge is that they lay against me? Picking pockets? No, worse than that. Robbery? No, worse than that. Murder? No, far worse than that. Then what on earth is this horrible accusation? Listen, here it is: They say "Laemmle is a hot-air advertiser." Isn't it awful? Doesn't it curdle the very gizzard of your soul? Do they charge that my films are not good? No, because they know that you know better. They know that you know that I am now the greatest film renter in the world solely because of quality. And who are the people who charge me with "hot-air advertising?" Why, they are simply the folks who used to be a big power in the film field until I jumped into the game less than three years ago and put the kibosh on them. Since I turned independent, I have increased my business 90 per cent. It is the most terrific demonstration of faith ever given by the exhibitors of America to any renter. They have taken my word that the independent films are masterpieces of photography, ingenious in conception and perfect in execution. They have taken my word that the license game is but a trick of the Trust, and a most palpable trick at that. If any one writes you a letter, lying about me, please ask him why he hasn't the nerve to come out in the open. Ask him to lay his finger on any one single blot in my whole career as a renter. Ask him if he is doing as much for the exhibitors as I am. Ask him who it is that has given the Trust some jolts that it will never forget. Ask him if he really thinks it is possible to give a better service than the Laemmle offices are giving. And then ask him if hot-air advertising alone would build up the greatest film renting business in the world in less than three years' time. Meanwhile ask yourself this one question: "Am I going to pay $2 a week every week I am in the business for the right to run my own theater and use my own goods?"

CARL LAEMMLE, President

THE LAEMMLE		**FILM SERVICE**
Headquarters: 196-198		Lake Street, CHICAGO
MINNEAPOLIS MINN.		**SALT LAKE CITY** UTAH
PORTLAND ORE.		**OMAHA** NEB.
EVANSVILLE IND.		**WINNIPEG** CAN.
DENVER COLO.		**MONTREAL** CAN.

THE FIGHTING INDEPENDENTS

Carl Laemmle encouraged exhibitors to defy the trust by ridiculing it. His weekly full-page advertisements in the *Moving Picture World* impressed the humbler nickelodeon operators with the heights to which one of their number had risen, at the same time that they rubbed salt in the wound of the humiliating license fee. Laemmle's ads usually began, "Good Morrow! Have you paid $2 for a license to pick your teeth this week?" and ended, "By the way, have you paid $2 for a license to kiss your wife?" When the trust brought two hundred and forty court actions against him, he entered a countersuit claiming "Relief from Multiplicity of Suits."

THE DEVELOP-MENT OF NARRATIVE

The Wild Duck.

LOOK—how beautiful he is!
Swift his flight as a bullet
As he comes in from the sea in the morning.
For the wind is from the sea in the morning.
See! He is bound for the hilltops,
The gold hilltops, the gold hilltops.
There he will rest 'neath the flowers,
The red flowers—the white and red,
The poppy—the flower of dreams,
The crimson flower of dreams.
There must he rest in the morning.
Happy wild duck! Happy wild duck!
For the wind is from the sea in the morning.

So will he rest 'neath the roses,
The red roses, the love roses,
And their petals will fall around him,
Sweet and warm around him,
Closer and closer around him,
Warmer and warmer around him,
Till even in the day-time the stars shall be shining.
Happy wild duck! Happy wild duck!
For the wind is from the sea in the morning.
There by the roses bloom the lilies, the flowers of peace,
The white flowers of peace,
Red and white together, red and white and red,
Waving and blowing together,
Blooming and waving together
On the gold hilltops in the morning,
For the wind is from the sea in the morning.

Ah me! but the wind soon changes in these parts,
Ah me! Ah me!
It was not so in the old days.
Look, look, ah, look, see, even now it is changing out, out
      to the sea!
Look, look, above the hilltops,
With eyes turned back to the mainland,
And tired wings wearily beating, but vainly,
For the wind blows out to the sea in the evening.
Poor little wild duck! Poor little wild duck!
Look, there is crimson, warm on his breast!
Look, red drops fall from his breast!
Poor little wild duck! Poor little wild duck!
In the evening,
For the wind is out to the sea in the evening.

Look! He is falling, falling out to the sea.
Ah, there is mist on the sea!
There is always mist on the sea in the evening.
Perhaps his nest is beyond, I know not;
Perhaps it is built of the mist, I know not.
Only with tired wings wearily beating,
And eyes turned back to the mainland,
To the red and white and red,
Waving and blowing together,
Blooming and blowing together,
He is falling out, out to the sea.
Poor little wild duck! Poor little wild duck!
In the evening when the wind blows out to the sea!
Ah me! Ah me! Ah me!
In the evening when the wind blows out to the sea.
                              DAVID WARK GRIFFITH.

This early poem by D. W. Griffith, published in
Leslie's Weekly in 1907, foreshadows the literary
style of his later subtitles.

D. W. GRIFFITH

In 1907 most films were still produced as though they were plays. Each scene began with the entrance of the actors and lasted unbroken until their exit. The players were always shown full size and at a fixed distance from the camera. The action consisted of their movements and gesticulations, greatly exaggerated to compensate for the absence of dialogue. By now, crude subtitles attempted to do duty for speech, but the motion picture still looked to most people like a shadowy carbon of the living theater. No one knew how to break its umbilical cord to the older medium.

The man who did break it, and so brought to birth a new art, was an unlikely choice for his historic role. Like all stage people of the time, David Wark Griffith regarded the movies with contempt—nor was he particularly proud of his career as journeyman actor in touring stock companies, interrupted of necessity by work as a subscription salesman, ore shoveler, hop picker, and day laborer. When, as a youth of twenty-two, he had joined the Meffert Stock Company in Louisville, Kentucky, he had assumed the name of Lawrence Griffith. He thought he owed it to his heritage to reserve his right name for more respectable enterprises.

His heritage was one familiar enough—of high traditions, past glories, and present straits. His family had held property and position in Maryland and Kentucky for a hundred years, and his father, Col. Jacob Wark Griffith was a member of the Kentucky legislature and a hero of the Confederacy; but after the Civil War the Griffith fortunes had declined. The family home, at the time of David Wark Griffith's birth on January 23, 1875, was heavily mortgaged. At his father's death ten years later, there was less than nothing left. The family moved into Louisville and young David helped out by working as cashboy in a dry-goods store, where he was embarrassed to be seen by his father's more prosperous friends.

Col. Griffith was unquestionably visionary and improvident, but his son idolized him and absorbed from him, along with a militant "Southron" tradition, a love of literature and an ambition to write. When in 1897 he embarked on an acting career he looked upon it only as a stopgap until he should establish himself as a novelist and playwright. But ten years later the sum of his writing achievements was a few published stories and poems and an unsuccessful play, and when marriage to a young actress pushed him into seeking steady employment outside the theater, his future seemed bleak indeed.

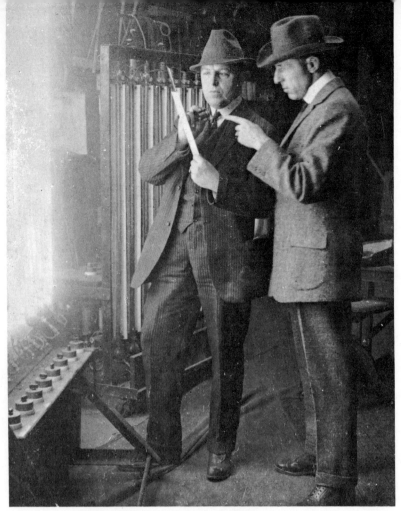

G. W. Bitzer and D. W. Griffith.

"AMERICAN BIOGRAPH"

"Duping" made the piracy of films an easy practice in the business chaos of the early Nickelodeon Age. To prevent rivals from removing the main title from a film, making a duplicate negative, and releasing prints of it as their own work, the leading companies formed the practice of inserting a symbol or trade name into every possible scene, tacked up on the wall or otherwise conspicuously displayed. One such trade symbol, the famous "AB" of the American Mutoscope and Biograph Company, came to have actual cash value. Joseph Wood Krutch recalls that, as a boy in Tennessee, he and his companions wandered from one nickelodeon to another looking for a display of the "AB" symbol, signifying that it was "Biograph night" at the theater. No one knew who made films or who played in them, but the nickelodeon public came to realize that Biograph films were somehow superior to other productions.

It was D. W. Griffith's contribution to motion-picture narrative that gave Biograph its lead. As a stage actor and proud Southerner, he was ashamed at being reduced to this low form of occupation, and even when Biograph offered him a chance to direct, he said to his wife, "In a way it's very nice,

but, you know, we can't go on forever and not tell our friends and relatives how we are earning our living." He was also far from sure that he could master this new knack of "canning" drama on film. Before he would undertake the direction of his first film, *The Adventures of Dollie* (1908), H. N. Marvin, vice-president of Biograph, had to reassure him that if he failed as a director he could continue with the company as writer and actor.

Before work began on *The Adventures of Dollie,* it was thought advisable that the new director should be given some advice by the most experienced hand at the studio. G. W. "Billy" Bitzer had joined the firm in 1896 as an electrician and had risen to be head cameraman and trouble shooter. "The cameraman was the whole works at that time," Bitzer wrote in 1940, "responsible for everything except the immediate handling of the actors. It was his say not only as to whether the light was bright enough but make-up, angles, rapidity of gestures, etc., besides having enough camera troubles of his own. I agreed to help Griffith in every way. He needed a canvas covering for a gypsy wagon. I would get that—in fact, all the props. I also offered to condense the script and lay out the opportunities it had so that he would be able to understand it. I had divided off half a dozen columns on the back of a laundry-shirt cardboard and headed the columns with titles—Drama, Comedy, Pathos, Pretty Scenes—and wrote in what I thought he should stress. Judging the little I had caught from seeing his acting, I didn't think he was going to be so hot."

Bitzer could not know that theirs was to be the most famous creative partnership in film history, but he soon found that this apparently unpromising novice was a "human short-circuit type" whose energy and initiative earned him the grudging respect and then the admiration of the studio hacks. "He was very grateful for the tips I gave him. All through the following sixteen years that I was at his side he always was not above taking advice, yes, even asking for suggestions and ideas. He always said to me, 'Four eyes are better than two.'"

Before Griffith was given the direction of *The Adventures of Dollie,* Biograph had fallen upon evil days. The company was selling fewer than twenty prints of each subject and the management was worried. By the end of the next year, during which Griffith had directed every Biograph production—more than a hundred one-reel films—the quality of the Biographs had improved so noticeably that exhibitors were clamoring for them. The studio, and gradually the entire industry, realized that a man had arrived in their midst who knew how to make these cheap, unconvincing pictures express ideas and arouse emotion.

CLOSE-UPS
AND LONG SHOTS

D. W. Griffith made his first radical innovation in a now lost film, *For Love of Gold*, 1909, when he departed from the old "one scene–one shot" method by demanding a change of camera position in the middle of a scene. In moving the camera closer to the actors, he had invented the "full shot," in which only the upper half of the player's body was shown. Biograph was shocked; the studio managers believed people would think the camera work amateurish and that this scene had been included in the film by mistake. But audiences, pleased at being able to read the actors' thoughts in their expressions, unmistakably endorsed the new method. Despite studio opposition, in the next four years Griffith moved his camera nearer and nearer to the players. In this close approach to the action, the stereotyped gestures and "artistical attitudes" inherited from the theater were unnecessary. Moreover, for this new kind of acting, stage training was not important and could even prove a handicap. The intense light needed for close-ups grew harder and harder on the human face, and Griffith began to gather round him young boys and girls on whose round cheeks time had not yet marked a single line. Only two of them, Blanche Sweet and the sixteen-year-old veteran Mary Pickford, had had stage experience. Robert Harron had been a studio errand boy, Mabel Normand a model, and Mae Marsh a movie-struck fan.

Under Griffith's intense rehearsal, these malleable young people registered exactly the expressions he wanted from them, often without knowing the plot of the film or even the content of the scene of which they were a part. Clearly it was he, not they, who was responsible for the effect of their work. And it was equally clear, as the results of these methods became apparent, that the movie was not a speechless copy of the stage but a new and uncharted medium of expression.

When Griffith began to take close-ups not only of his actors' faces but also of objects and other details of the scene, he demonstrated that it was the "shot" and not the actor which was the basic unit of expression of the motion picture. When to the full shot and the close-up he added the extreme long shots of *Ramona*, 1909, he had completed the "long shot–mid shot–close shot" combination which remains today the classic approach to the material in any motion-picture scene. When to these discoveries he added that of a method of assembly and composition of these lengths of film taken at varying distances from the action, the basis of modern technique had been established.

Lines of White on a Sullen Sea, 1908, directed by Griffith for Biograph, with Linda Arvidson (Mrs. D. W. Griffith).

The Lonedale Operator, 1911, directed by Griffith for Biograph, with Blanche Sweet, Frank Grandon.

Fighting Blood, 1911, directed by Griffith for Biograph, with Blanche Sweet.

BIOGRAPH MASTERPIECES

Long after the rise of the feature film, people remembered the "Griffith Biographs" with affection (for years they were regularly revived and became the staff of Biograph's declining days). Elderly people today, who were young enough then not to mind the social stigma that attached to attending nickelodeons, remember how exciting it was to go to the movies in those days. As, almost from week to week, Griffith introduced technical novelties and expanded and refined his narrative style, as he turned the camera on social problems, far lands, and distant epochs, seeing each successive film was a new and thrilling adventure, and to thoughtful people a thought-provoking one. When Vachel Lindsay published his *Art of the Moving Picture* in 1914, the respectable press was astonished that a poet should take the movies seriously, but the audiences of the despised nickelodeons had known for years that they were witnesses at the birth of a new experience.

By now Griffith also knew that the movie was a new form of storytelling radically unlike the traditional ones, and that few people besides himself sensed its possibilities. He began to take pride in his work and to intensify his experimentation. The type copy of his third contract with Biograph was made out to Lawrence Griffith, but "Lawrence" is altered to David in pen, and the fourth contract, signed the next year, 1911, is made out directly to David Wark Griffith. The degree of success and self-expression he had attained not only recon-

ciled him to working in motion pictures but also to admitting it.

All that now restricted the fluid narrative technique he had developed was the brevity of films. In 1911, Biograph had reluctantly permitted him to advance from the one- to the two-reel length, but beyond two reels—twenty minutes of screen time—the company refused to go. Longer films would cause eyestrain, they would weary audiences, said the lords of Biograph; what they really meant was that nickelodeon patrons could not appreciate and therefore did not deserve an improved product. But Griffith could not attain in the two-reel length the humanity and impressiveness which were now his goals, and his bitterness increased as imported

Man's Genesis, 1912, with Robert Harron, Mae Marsh. This "psychological study founded upon the Darwinian Theory" portrayed a Stone Age battle between "Weak-hands" and "Brute-force" which "Weak-hands" wins by inventing the ax.

The Musketeers of Pig Alley, 1912, with Lillian Gish. Social problems had always interested Griffith, and he turned his attention to the East Side slums in this little masterpiece, an ancestor of the gangster films of later decades.

European films of three, four, and even five reels began to appear in the United States and steal the spotlight from him. Finally he could bear his frustration no longer. He took his company to the town of Chatsworth, California, far from other movie units operating out of Los Angeles, and farther still from the Biograph home office in New York, and there in great secrecy made the four-reel spectacle film *Judith of Bethulia* in 1913. *Judith* was the first example of movie gigantism, but when Griffith returned to New York with it in triumph, he found himself not only in disgrace with the Biograph executives but also outclassed by the new flood of foreign spectacles and the sudden craze for "Famous Players in Famous Plays."

The Fade-Out

To basic film grammar Griffith and Bitzer contributed many punctuation devices, notably the fade-out, which they hit upon by accident. Bitzer mounted a large iris diaphragm on the front of his camera, to which he had added a handle. While he was photographing, the weight of the handle gradually closed the iris, and when the shot was projected a ring of shadow blotted out the action. "This was just what we needed," Bitzer wrote. "The climax of all these films was the kiss. We couldn't hnger over the embrace, for then the yokels in the audience would make catcalls. We couldn't cut abruptly—that would be crude. The fade-out gave a really dignified touch; we didn't have a five-cent movie any more."

THE FEATURE FILM ARRIVES

The trust refused to let Griffith and other directors move toward quality and length, but nothing restrained the independents. The man who became their leader and soon a veritable trust in himself was a deceptively inconspicuous little exhibitor named Adolph Zukor, who had waited for his chance at the big time for years and took it by importing the French feature film *Queen Elizabeth,* so obviously an august and respectable production that the trust was forced to license him to show it in America. Its success was immediately followed by the even greater vogue of a colossal Italian version of *Quo Vadis?.* Actually these elaborate productions, theatrical and even operatic in technique, were technically and aesthetically far behind the one-reel American movies of the preceding five years. They were, however, initially shown in legitimate theaters on Broadway to upper-income groups who, knowing nothing of the progress of the movies in America, were impressed by their

exotic air of tradition and prestige. And they abruptly awakened the magnates of the legitimate theater from their scornful indifference to the "nickel show." If imported films like these could be shown in legitimate theaters at stage prices, then the Broadway producers' own backlogs of old plays could be filmed at great profit with little trouble. For the first time the independents found a ready hearing in Broadway offices. Zukor again led the way by announcing that he was forming a corporation to produce "Famous Players in Famous Plays," beginning with James O'Neill in 1913 in his greatest success, *The Count of Monte Cristo.*

Even now, the old-line trust companies held back. They were sure the "feature fad" would be only temporary, just as they had been sure that the "movie craze" itself would not last. They would continue to make two-reelers as long as there was a demand. The dwindling market lasted about four more years—till the last of the nickelodeons ex-

Quo Vadis?, 1913. George Kleine, one of the more progressive members of the trust, imported this twelve-reel Italian spectacle which opened at the Astor Theatre on April 21, 1913. This first version of the Sienkie-wicz perennial was as wooden as it was gigantic, but its "uncommon elegance" kept it running at the Astor for 22 weeks at the record admission charge of $1.50, and the following summer "road companies" were showing it throughout the United States in theaters usually devoted to stage attractions. *Quo Vadis?* proved that the movies had arrived at respectability—as long as they came from Europe and dealt with traditional subjects. Don't ask us to explain the hammer and sickle.

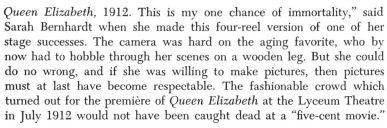

Queen Elizabeth, 1912. This is my one chance of immortality," said Sarah Bernhardt when she made this four-reel version of one of her stage successes. The camera was hard on the aging favorite, who by now had to hobble through her scenes on a wooden leg. But she could do no wrong, and if she was willing to make pictures, then pictures must at last have become respectable. The fashionable crowd which turned out for the première of *Queen Elizabeth* at the Lyceum Theatre in July 1912 would not have been caught dead at a "five-cent movie."

pired. By then the heads of the trust had retired, many of them millionaires in spite of themselves.

Biograph made one attempt to maintain its leadership. While continuing to produce one- and two-reelers, it also contracted with the famous theatrical firm of Klaw and Erlanger to photograph its stage successes in five reels, for summer showings in legitimate theaters across the country. D. W. Griffith naturally expected to be given the direction of this ambitious new project, but he was ordered to continue to produce two-reel films. The big Klaw and Erlanger specials would be filmed by "stage experts." "If you stay with Biograph," he was told, "it will be to make the same kind of short pictures you have in the past. You will not do that. You've got the hundred-thousand-dollar idea in the back of your head."

No, Griffith would not do that—not continue what both he and his employers had always considered hack work when at last the vision of a new art and a new public was before him. Harry Aitken, president of the Mutual Film Corporation, lured him with a contract for a thousand dollars a week, supervision of the entire product of the company, and the privilege of making two independent pictures a year. On October 1, 1913, Griffith left Biograph for Mutual.

The fate of the Biograph–Klaw and Erlanger photographed plays illustrated the results of the trust's attempt to compromise with the new era. The legitimate theaters to which they were offered for off-season showing refused to play speechless copies of dramas which they had played in past seasons in the flesh. The nickelodeons refused to pay high rentals for plays and players known only to legitimate audiences. Eventually the K. and E. productions were cut down from five reels to three and sold for what they could get in competition with the regular fare of the nickelodeons. They got little or nothing.

Lillian Gish, heroine of *The Birth of a Nation*.

Tantalizing glimpses such as this from the production location of *The Clansman* made all Hollywood wonder what

THE FEATURE CRAZE

The picture business seethed with excitement after the success of *Quo Vadis?*. Now every ambitious young man wanted to make features. The bonds of the old trust system were burst beyond repair and the young hopefuls had their way. With little or no capital, often against the direct orders of their superiors, they somehow put together five- and six-reel pictures to which their audiences responded enthusiastically. The diehards were bewildered. The safe, sane "manufacturing" business was being transformed before their eyes into a nonesuch somewhere between art and speculation—and transformed by the public itself. No one could deny the reality of the feature craze when the stream of nickels and dimes from the store shows was joined by the torrent of quarters and dollars from Broadway.

Griffith was stung anew at being outclassed not only by the European imports but also by the bright youngsters who were making their *Traffic in Souls* and *Spoilers* and *Sea Wolves* and taking them to market. He was the prisoner of his partial success: Mutual could pay him his high salary only if he turned out pictures fast. But while he super-

vised potboilers he was marshaling his forces. Most of the Biograph stock company had followed him to Mutual, and he now made special efforts to persuade his reluctant cameraman, Billy Bitzer, to join him in his bid for fame and independence. Said Bitzer, "Among the inducements Mr. Griffith pictured to me was one in which he said, 'We will bury ourselves in hard work out at the Coast for five years and make the greatest pictures ever made, make a million dollars and retire, and then you can have all the time you want to fool around with your camera gadgets, and I shall settle down to write.' Now I thought, How can he be so sure of that when even now in the pictures we had, we never did know whether we had a bestseller until it went out?"

But Griffith in the end proved persuasive. He was on fire with an idea for the "greatest picture ever made," which, Bitzer said, "changed D. W. Griffith's personality entirely. Where heretofore he was wont to refer in starting on a new picture to 'grinding out another sausage' and go at it lightly, his attitude in beginning on this one was all eagerness. He acted like here we have something worth

Griffith was up to. Here he directs Sherman's march on Atlanta helped by G.A.R. veterans as "technical experts."

Mae Marsh, the "little pet sister" of *The Birth of a Nation.*

while. Personally I did not share his enthusiasm. I had read the book and figured that a Negro chasing a white girl was just another sausage after all and how would you show it in the South?"

The "something worth while" was the Rev. Thomas E. Dixon's *The Clansman,* which, as novel and barnstorming play, had enjoyed success for years. Griffith remembered that in 1907 he had been hired and then fired as leading man in another of the Rev. Dixon's melodramas, *The One Woman,* but the clergyman had been watching his ex-actor's career ever since *The One Woman,* and showed his confidence in him by selling the screen rights to *The Clansman* for $2,500 and 25 per cent of the profits. The two men had much in common; Southerners both, they worked harmoniously throughout the production of the film. When it was finished and shown to Dixon, he exclaimed, "It's too big to be called *The Clansman.* Let's call it *The Birth of a Nation.*"

Griffith combined the plot of *The Clansman* with that of another Dixon novel, *The Leopard's Spots,* for his scenario—only there was never a scenario for this or Griffith's other important films. "He car-

ried the ideas in his head," says Lillian Gish, "or I should say in his heart. As the son of 'Roaring Jake' Griffith he firmly believed that the truth of the Civil War and Reconstruction had never been told, and he was quite ready to tell, through this new medium of the silent screen, the story he believed in above all else in the world. I am sure it seemed more real to him than the World War which was then taking place."

The Clansman was to be one of the two independent productions which Griffith's contract with Mutual permitted him to make. While nominally supervising Mutual productions, he was secretly arranging to hire thousands of extras, horses, costumes. As the picture grew, its size horrified his backers. Harry Aitken invested $25,000 of Mutual's money in it, but his board of directors insisted that he personally underwrite the investment. The cast and technicians chipped in, often going without salary. "Griffith reached everywhere for money," says Terry Ramsaye. "His struggles are reminiscent of Bernard Palissy, the sixteenth-century ceramic artist, burning his very home to keep the fires of his furnace going."

"War's peace" is the subtitle preceding this scene.

The Battle of Antietam, Billy Bitzer at the camera, lower left corner. Bitzer modeled his photography on the work of Matthew Brady, wheedling the Brady prints from a librarian, who parted with her precious collection for a box of chocolates. The orthochromatic film of those days aided the illusion of nineteenth-century photography.

As Lillian Gish leaves the hospital in *The Birth of a Nation*, Griffith inserted a bit in which a sentry sighs wistfully over Miss Gish's beauty as she passes. The scene created a sensation and audiences of 1915 demanded to know who the man was who played the sentry. He had been picked out of the extra ranks, and by the time Griffith sent for him he had disappeared forever

THE BIRTH OF A NATION

No doubt Griffith wanted to make his battle scenes surpass in scope and spectacle all that had been shown on the screen before, but even greater was his urge to show the Civil War as his father had described it and as the whole South had cherished it in legend for three generations. The war is sketched in this film, but sketched with the sensitive selectivity, almost, of a nostalgic remembering.

The battle scenes, and the whole of *The Birth of a Nation*, were shot by only one camera and one cameraman, G. W. Bitzer. It was necessary for

Bitzer to stick to his camera while lying flat on the ground when Griffith thought a shot of horses leaping directly over the camera would be a great effect. World War I had put a premium on blue-blooded horseflesh, and Griffith had to content himself with nags of lower pedigree. In his old age Bitzer wrote, "Well, nothing to do but put the camera on the ground and if they come too close maybe it would be easy to roll out of the way off to one side. Mr. Griffith, who always stood near the camera, would shoo them off somehow. After the

The Little Colonel Returns

The returning Little Colonel (right) sees his fire-ravaged home for the first time. Women of the South tried to hide their poverty from returning menfolk by wearing "Southern ermine," made by dotting cotton with coal dust and sewing it on their old dresses. Here Henry B. Walthal detects Mae Marsh's innocent deception. The highest point of emotion in *The Birth of a Nation* "was made profound and universal," wrote Gilbert Seldes, "because the face of the principal player was not shown. . . . From behind the door, as the soldier enters, comes the arm of his mother drawing in her son with an immemorial gesture, taking to her heart his sorrows and the sorrows still to come."

leaders passed, the dust became thick, and, sensing the cameraman's danger, Mr. Griffith rushed wildly in, waving his arms and yelling madly, thus preventing all but one of the horses from smashing into the camera on the ground, not, however, before he had kicked in the side of the wooden camera. It was soon repaired with some tape and we were taking another run.

"Just the same, there were times when I wished that Mr. Griffith didn't depend on me so much, especially in battle scenes. The fireworks men shoot-ing smoke bombs over the camera—most of them exploding outside camera range—and D. W. shouting, 'Lower, lower, can't you shoot those damn bombs lower?' 'We'll hit the cameraman if we do,' answered the fireworks brigade, and bang! one of them whizzed past my ear. The next one may have gone between my legs for all I knew. But the bombs were coming into the camera field so it was okay. As I write this, looking at my hand, it still shows the blue powder specks from the battlefield of *The Birth of a Nation*."

A rather jocose Lincoln (Joseph Henabery) tells club-footed Austin Stoneman (Ralph Lewis) that he will not treat the Confederacy as a conquered province. Though he appears in relatively few scenes, Lincoln is an important figure in *The Birth of a Nation*, especially important to the fabric of Southern belief which it expresses. When the news of his assassination reaches Cameron Hall, Col. Cameron sadly exclaims: "The South has lost its best friend!" the implication being that had he lived the Confederate states would have been allowed to resume their former position in the Union. The blame for the evils of Reconstruction Griffith placed on Senator Charles Sumner of Massachusetts and the leader of the Republican radicals, Thaddeus Stevens. Both men were powerfully concerned lest the Republican party lose power if the white South was at once allowed to send representatives to Congress. But neither profited from Reconstruction or personally participated in its administration. Stevens died before the full force of the Reconstruction Acts could be felt. But the Hon. Austin Stoneman who is Stevens in *The Birth of a Nation* visits South Carolina to enjoy to the full the triumph of his policies and lives to witness their consequences.

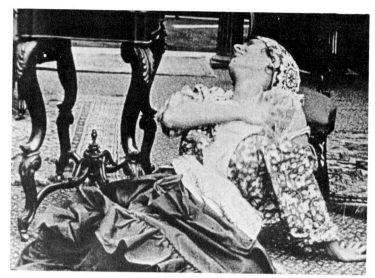

The real Thaddeus Stevens lived for years with a Negro woman, but in spite of his equalitarian ideas never married her because this would have excluded him from Washington society. Austin Stoneman in *The Birth of a Nation* has a mulatto housekeeper who is, by implication, his mistress. Stevens' personal relationship with Negroes obviously seemed more important to Dixon and Griffith than his political affiliations. To Southerners like these two, sex, not economics, lay at the core of the race question. Their horror of miscegenation made it impossible for them to believe that Sumner and Stevens acted from moral motives, and they therefore believed them to be monsters of hypocrisy. Early in the film, Senator Sumner (who is given his real name in the picture) calls on Stoneman. The mulatto housekeeper, who opens the door, hopes that the Senator will treat her as an equal, but he snubs her roundly and passes to the next room where Stoneman is announcing his plans to make his protégé, Silas Lynch, governor of South Carolina, and says he will "crush the white South under the heel of the black South." When Sumner comes out and asks for his hat, the housekeeper haughtily drops it on the floor (above), forcing Sumner to stoop for it. After he leaves, the housekeeper tears her bodice to ribbons and disarranges her hair. The following scene (right) is without subtitles but seems to mean that the disheveled housekeeper convinces Stoneman that Sumner tried to rape her.

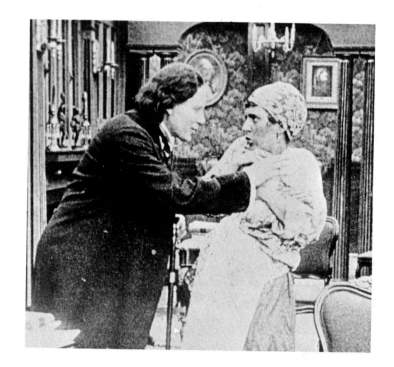

Col. Cameron is turned from the polls by Negro soldiers and white carpetbaggers. The Negroes—except the few who remain loyal to their recent owners—are shown as apelike morons, both foolish and vicious.

The Little Colonel (Henry B. Walthal) refuses the handshake of the mulatto Silas Lynch (George Siegmann), while Austin Stoneman and his daughter (Lillian Gish) look on enraged.

THE IMPACT OF THE BIRTH OF A NATION

The Birth of a Nation opened at the Liberty Theatre in New York on March 3, 1915, at $2 admission. The sensation it created was without precedent and has never been duplicated. People had not known that they could be so moved, so roused, by what is, after all, only a succession of pictures passing across a screen. Everything depends, they discovered, on the order and the manner of that passing. All that Griffith had been striving for in the six years since he had begun directing at Biograph was now actual achievement; almost single-handed he had created a new art form, independent of the spoken word. His picture went on to a success whose dimensions can never be accurately calculated, since Griffith and his backers sold distribution rights to small companies here and abroad for a flat fee rather than a rental or royalty. Even on this unbusiness-like basis, it had by 1939 grossed for its owners $18,000,000 and netted $5,000,000, and it has continued to be shown intermittently ever since. Its initial earnings rocked Wall Street, evoked a press

A PLEA FOR THE ART OF THE MOTION PICTURE

We do not fear censorship, for we have no wish to offend with improprieties or obscenities, but we do demand, as a right, the liberty to show the dark side of wrong, that we may illuminate the bright side of virtue—the same liberty that is conceded to the art of the written word —that art to which we owe the Bible and the works of Shakespeare.

In an effort to stem the rising tide of protest, Griffith inserted this plea as a foreword to the film and published a pamphlet (top), a quaint but not ineffective defense of the screen's right to deal with controversial subjects.

The Ku Klux Klan threatens death to the would-be rapist of Flora, sister of the Little Colonel (right). Triumph of the Klan (far right). Lillian Gish and Miriam Cooper lead the procession after their rescue from Silas Lynch and his Negroes. Griffith portrayed the Little Colonel as the inventor of the Ku Klux Klan, in a scene which emphasized the power of white sheets over the imagination of Negroes. *The Birth of a Nation* movingly revealed the extent of the white South's allegiance to the Klan, which at its height had more than 700,000 members. As a result, the revived Ku Klux Klan of 1915-27 continually claimed Griffith's approval and sought his active support.

interest which the movies had never before been able to attract, and brought comment even from governmental figures. After it was shown at the White House, the first movie ever to be screened there, President Wilson was said to have commented, "It is like writing history with lightning, and my one regret is that it is all so terribly true."

This quote was important to Griffith. He had poured into *The Birth of a Nation* all that he believed and had been taught about the South's degradation and humiliation in the Reconstruction period—a period which had seen the collapse of his own family's fortunes. He felt impelled to bear witness, to tell the North and the world of the sorrows that had been brought upon his land and his people in a period which coincided with his own childhood. Yet he wished to be fair. He would document his charges. He culled from Woodrow Wilson's American histories and those of others actual incidents of Reconstruction days which supported the dark story he told. That there was another side to that story he would not or could not admit. He expressed bewilderment at the storms of protest it evoked when Negroes and the friends of Negroes realized what this much-discussed film was saying about them.

A storm it was. The mildest comment was George Foster Peabody's "It distressed me to see such exceptional ability of organization directed into the wrong channels," and the shrewdest, A. E. Pillsbury's "It gambles on the public ignorance of our own history." Judge Braithwaite charged, "It is not only the hate of the South against the Negro but against the North. It is shown in the figure of Sumner." The elderly Moorfield Storey, who had been Sumner's secretary in his youth, calmly pointed to the chronological inaccuracies of the film: "The Ku Klux Klan had really run its course before the colored voters exercised any substantial power," and continued more cholerically, "Unless the only immorality is sexual immorality, this play tends to corrupt public morals and should be suppressed, as it certainly would be if instead of libeling the weakest among our fellow citizens, it were in like manner to attack a body of great political strength." In view of all this, the White House hastened to disavow its accolade.

It remained for President Charles W. Eliot of Harvard to express the ultimate in remote-control judgment: "I have not seen this play, [but] I want to say that it presents an extraordinary misrepresentation of the birth of this nation."

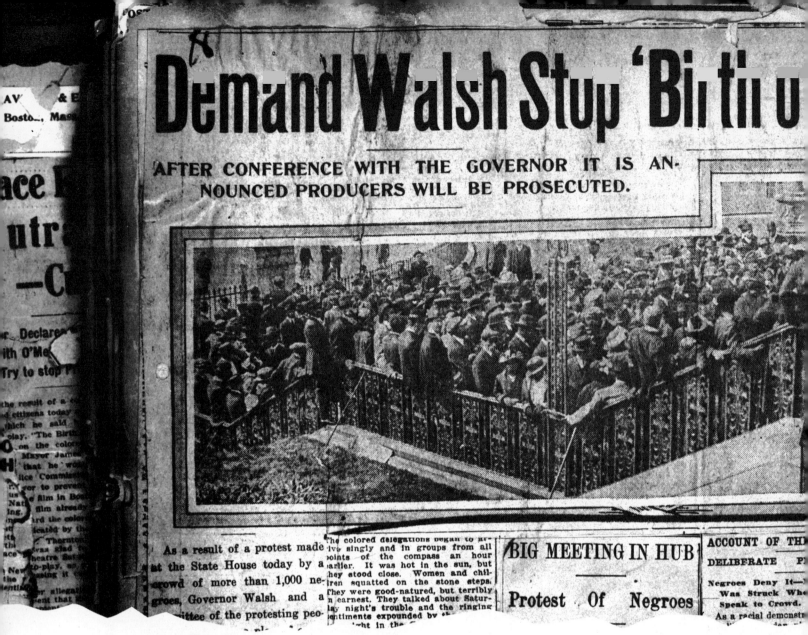

Demand Walsh Stop 'Birth of

AFTER CONFERENCE WITH THE GOVERNOR IT IS AN-
NOUNCED PRODUCERS WILL BE PROSECUTED.

As a result of a protest made at the State House today by a crowd of more than 1,000 negroes, Governor Walsh and a committee of the protesting peo-

The colored delegations began to arrive singly and in groups from all points of the compass an hour earlier. It was hot in the sun, but they stood close. Women and children squatted on the stone steps. They were good-natured, but terribly in earnest. They talked about Saturday night's trouble and the ringing sentiments expounded by the night in the

BIG MEETING IN HUB

Protest Of Negroes

ACCOUNT OF TH

DELIBERATE P

Negroes Deny It—
Was Struck Whe
Speak to Crowd.
As a racial demonst

For weeks before *The Birth of a Nation* opened in Boston, mysterious rumors spread about the film, and after it was first shown crowds stormed the theater and the Boston State House to get the performances stopped. The Rev. Thomas Dixon

The Mother and the Law, 1914. Before *The Birth of a Nation* was released Griffith had begun a new film attacking factory owners who pose as philanthropists but who subtract their benefactions from the wages of the workers.

GRIFFITH'S ANSWER

Observing from afar the tumult over *The Birth of a Nation*, Booker T. Washington remarked, "The managers of this play encourage and even skillfully initiate opposition on account of the advertising the play receives when attempts are made to stop it." That was the dilemma of the liberal leaders who deplored the film. Most of them were against any attempt to censor it. They were content to attack it —but their attacks only brought it greater notoriety and patronage. Moreover, they were aware that the South *had* suffered wrongs in Reconstruction, that there was wrong and right on both sides, and that for the good of the nation the best comment on the whole episode was a healing silence. Jane Addams and Lillian Wald in a joint statement said that the picture was made at a time "too near the period it depicts to be given without danger of inciting hate, hostility, prejudice, and sectionalism." Albert Bigelow Paine, the biographer of Wilson and

was on hand for the occasion and observed, "The silly legal opposition they are giving will make me a millionaire if they keep it up. . . . [We knew] that if we could get it by in Boston we would be able to go anywhere else in the country."

Taft, and, incidentally, of Lillian Gish, remarked, with an historian's faint distaste, "It is within the facts, but it is not within the proprieties."

Griffith himself remained bewildered, if perhaps secretly delighted, at the vituperation poured on the head of a young man previously unknown to the national leaders who now pronounced him the devil's advocate. He protested that he loved the Negro. The Negroes replied that they did not want his love if they had to take *The Birth of a Nation* with it. Unskilled in controversy, Griffith was easily worsted in the newspaper battles. Perhaps he sensed that he was in danger of making himself ridiculous as well as of making enemies in high places. But his sense of injury remained. If he could not successfully answer his critics through the press and pamphleteering, he would turn to the medium of which even his critics acknowledged him the master.

Griffith barred all visitors from the sets of *The Mother and the Law*. As the walls of Babylon began to tower over Sunset Boulevard, Hollywood marveled: what could they have to do with a modern story about industrial unrest?

INTOLERANCE

What had loomed over the bungalows of Sunset Boulevard was the palace of Belshazzar, King of Babylon, setting for the Feast of Belshazzar on the eve of Cyrus of Persia's conquest of the city. Griffith's opulent and untutored imagination festooned this vast set with Egyptian bas-reliefs and Hindu elephant gods as well as Babylonian bearded bulls. To take it all in, he sent Bitzer and his camera aloft in a captive balloon, slowly drawn back to earth in the first equivalent of the modern crane shot. Until Douglas Fairbanks' castle set for *Robin Hood* in 1922, it remained the largest backdrop for a movie scene, and neither has ever been topped.

The attacks on *The Birth of a Nation* had resolved Griffith to turn *The Mother and the Law* into an epic sermon, a mighty purge for hypocrisy through the ages, called *Intolerance*. The slums of today, Renaissance France, Belshazzar's Babylon, and the Crucifixion itself should all speak of man's inhumanity to man in the name of virtue. Hollywood was awed as Griffith flung up halls in which men looked like flies, walls on which an army could march. Extras were hired in regiments. When Griffith's backers faltered, he bought them out with long-term notes which he did not finish paying off until the early Twenties. The picture reached a length of 400 reels, with no end in sight, but Griffith went grimly on. "If I approach success in what I am trying to do in my coming picture," he said, "I expect an even greater persecution than that which met *The Birth of a Nation*."

The Modern story. Robert Harron gives the eye to Miriam Cooper, moll of gangster Walter Long.

The Babylonian story. Seena Owen as the Princess Beloved; Alfred Paget as Belshazzar.

The French story. Margery Wilson, today's teacher of charm by mail, and Eugene Pallette.

"THE ONLY FILM FUGUE"

In adding three more stories to that of *The Mother and the Law* to make up the film *Intolerance*, Griffith, as *Variety* said, departed "from all previous forms of legitimate or film construction. . . ." In *Pippa Passes*, *Judith of Bethulia*, and *Home Sweet Home* he had made four-part films. Now the attraction he felt for this form led him to attempt something entirely new. He told all four stories simultaneously, uniting them by the constantly repeated shot of Lillian Gish rocking a cradle, an image derived from Walt Whitman's "Out of the cradle, endlessly rocking." In Griffith's own words: "The stories begin like four currents looked at from a hilltop. At first the four currents flow apart, slowly and quietly. But as they flow, they grow nearer and nearer together, and faster and faster, until in the end, in the last act, they mingle in one mighty river of expressed emotion."

As such, *Intolerance* is, in Terry Ramsaye's words, "the only film fugue," and as such it entirely failed of public favor. In spite of the splendor of its spectacle, in spite of its incredible cast—among those who played minor roles were Constance Talmadge, Monte Blue, Bessie Love, Alma Rubens, Ruth St. Denis, Carmel Myers, Colleen Moore, Carol Dempster, and Douglas Fairbanks—audiences were cold to it. Two years after its release, Griffith, realizing the inevitable, released the modern and Babylonian episodes as two separate films, but even their receipts did relatively little to relieve him of the burden of debt with which *Intolerance* had saddled him.

Many reasons have been advanced for the failure of this great and unique film. The commonest and most probable is that audiences found it simply too overwhelming, that they could not follow, or become emotionally involved in, these stories which wove in and out of one another with such awesome speed. It has also been suggested that the pacifism which was a leading motif of *Intolerance* was hardly the note to strike in a year when America was preparing to enter World War I.

No one has ever imitated the formal idea on which *Intolerance* was based, but its spectacle has been in Cecil B. De Mille's mind ever since, and but for it Eisenstein might never have made *Potemkin*, Chaplin *The Gold Rush*, or Von Stroheim *Greed*. Equivocal, inconclusive, naïve, *Intolerance* yet marks the furthest advance of screen art.

The Nazarene story. Howard Gaye as Jesus, Erich von Stroheim as the shorter of the two Pharisees.

". . . Out of the cradle, endlessly rocking, uniter of here and hereafter . . ." Lillian Gish as the Woman Who Rocks the Cradle.

Babylon's war engines make a sally through the great gate of Bel.

The Princess Beloved sends a love-message to Belshazzar, all of two feet away, in a little cart drawn by doves.

THE MASTER

Between 1909 and 1916, David Wark Griffith created the art of screen narrative almost single-handed. After *Intolerance*, there was no significant addition to film syntax until the advent of sound and of the wide screen, both mechanical rather than artistic innovations, although of course they affect the art. Acknowledging his influence, Cecil B. De Mille recently said that there is something of Griffith in every film made since his day. His contemporaries regarded him with awe, called him "The Master," and predicted an unlimited future for him after what was thought of as the temporary and accidental failure of *Intolerance*. Yet this "enigmatic and somewhat tragic figure" never fully succeeded in delivering what he had to say through the medium of which he was the virtual creator. His dream of picturing a vast screen mosaic of the American and French revolutions and the birth of modern liberty was incompletely realized; neither *Orphans of the Storm*, 1922, nor *America*, 1924, achieved the impact of *The Birth of a Nation*.

Beset by financial troubles, he was forced to turn out potboilers which boiled the pot less and less frequently. His last important film, the little masterpiece *Isn't Life Wonderful?*, 1924, revealed the source of his difficulties. The incisive realism of this study of the effects of economic inflation in Germany had small appeal to a nation hell-bent on pleasure. The 1920s, engrossed in a sort of witch hunt against everything "Victorian," regarded Griffith suddenly as dated. Why did he insist on filming social problems, why was he so obsessed with "patriotic" themes at a time when patriotism was all but a dirty word? Hard pressed for money, Griffith tried to obey his critics, but his attempts at Jazz Age films seemed the fumbling efforts of an amateur compared to the work of De Mille and his disciples. Though still nominally the dean of his profession, Griffith in the later Twenties was given the sort of respect we accord the dead.

His revenge is Time's. As fashion follows fashion with ever-accelerating speed, as the films of the Twenties and Thirties begin to look flat and superficial, Griffith's greatness emerges. His faults—flowery language, black-and-white morality, naïve cultural pretensions—we no longer judge by today's standards. Now they belong to the past, to a period in which their romanticism is appropriate. Now we can see beyond them to the profound humanity of Griffith's films—see also what we have meantime lost, a direct, naked, firsthand approach to character, psychology, and emotion. Griffith's camera searched the human countenance for "the motions of the spirit" itself.

The informality of early film making encouraged casual droppers-in. The boy to Griffith's right is today's Ben Alexander of "Dragnet" fame.

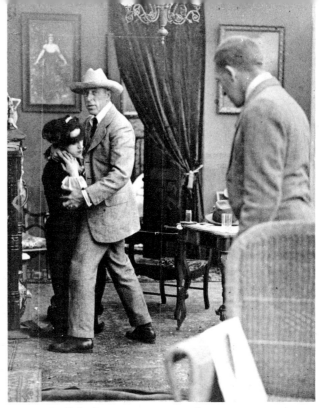

D. W. Griffith demonstrates to Walter Long the correct way to strangle Miriam Cooper.

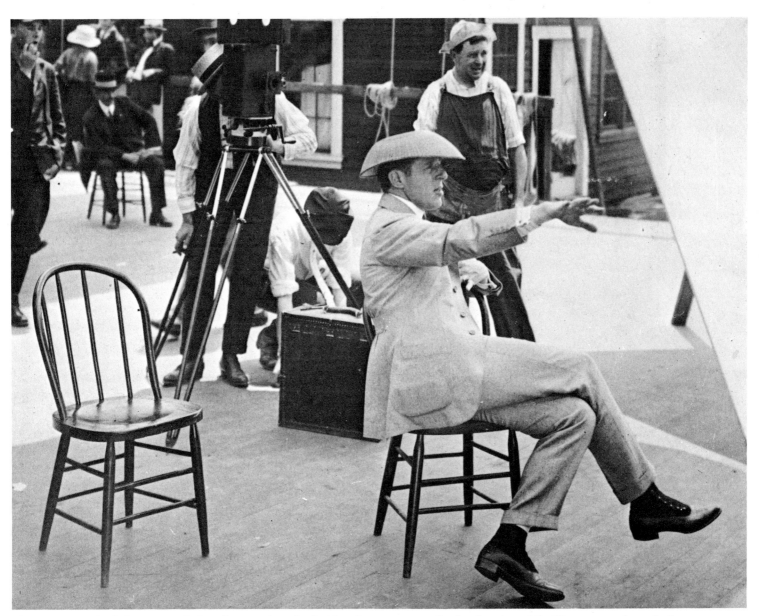

The master at the helm. In suede-top shoes and coolie hat he directs a scene for *Intolerance*, while Bitzer peers through the camera.

Florence Lawrence

THE STAR SYSTEM

Early in 1908 Carl Laemmle electrified the industry, as was his regular custom, by publishing this advertisement (left) in the *Moving Picture World*. It purported to answer a story published in the St. Louis newspapers to the effect that Florence Lawrence, known to nickelodeon fans as the "Biograph girl," had been killed in a streetcar accident. Laemmle denounced the story as a vile slander designed by the film trust to camouflage the fact that Miss Lawrence had left Biograph's bed and board for the more uplifting surroundings of Laemmle's own company. Actually, Laemmle had planted the original story himself and his "reply" to it was designed solely to dramatize the fact that he had lured the then most popular personality in motion pictures away from her original employers: the "Biograph girl" had become the "Imp girl."

Laemmle's ad was only a minor incident in his energetic campaign to demoralize the General Film Company and blacken its name with exhibitors, but his coup portended much. The trust had refused to give out the names of its players, partly because it wished to standardize the business of film manufacture as much as possible, and partly because it rightly feared that players grown famous would also be players grown costly. But the public refused to be frustrated. When no answers came to floods of letters demanding to be told the names of favorite players, nickelodeon patrons took to such nicknames as the "Biograph girl," "the little girl

THE
FORMATIVE
YEARS

with the golden curls," and so forth. (In Britain, nickelodeon operators cheerfully satisfied the curiosity of fans by making up names for American actors: Mabel Normand was known there as "Muriel Fortescue.")

As soon as the independents realized that the public disliked the trust's policy of refusing to give out the names of players, they promptly publicized the names of their own, and in doing so lured valuable actors, eager for recognition and money, away from the trust, which was finally forced to reverse itself, disclose the identity of its stars, and pay them better.

The phenomenon of star worship among stage-struck youths and maidens was not unfamiliar to the entertainment world, but now, for the first time, millions of men, women, and children lovingly discussed film players as though they were members of their own families. From then on, not acting ability or even altogether looks, but something indefinable and uniquely cinematic called "personality" became the key to success. On the day Miss Lawrence moved her make-up kit from Biograph to Imp, the star's salary became the most important single-item in the budgets of most pictures.

Since the star system was the public's own creation, the first stars were players who had stood out from the anonymous ranks of the original studio "stock companies." Comparatively few had stage experience. Other qualifications were more important. Besides youth, they had to have a considerable degree of intelligence, adaptability, and stamina. The breakneck manufacture and release of two one-reel pictures every week required that they be able to play heroines one day, and maids, dowagers, or vamps the next. But most important was a strong and well-defined personality. Invariably what made them stars was some physical attribute or personal mannerism—John Bunny's jovial bulk, Mary Pickford's golden curls and sweet

smile, Maurice Costello's urbanity, Clara Kimball Young's yearning eyes.

What mattered was the possession of some quality, not always at first glance the most conspicuous quality, which people could identify with or admire. The making of a movie star turned out to be a process of spotting this quality and bringing it to the fore, and it mattered little what the quality was: beauty, docility, menace, even ordinariness. The process is still followed. What Alistair Cooke wrote in 1940 about the making of a screen personality was true at the beginning and is still true:

"The most profitable screen heroine that a studio can create . . . is a heroine whose beauty is so overwhelming that it allows her own character never to come into play and therefore never to be called in question. We do not fret over the lack of social purpose, charity, humor, or anything else in such perfections of the type as Greta Garbo, Hedy La Marr, Marlene Dietrich. But nothing is so irritating as the mildly pretty blonde whose beauty is barely acceptable in the first few feet of film and who subsequently has no other charm to offer. Those who fall between these extremes are the majority of stars who combine good looks and certain typical whimsicalities or personal traits of humor, temper, sarcasm—some single quality that is entertaining because it is effective to dramatize. Most movie-goers seem to prefer this compromise formula as a steady diet, probably because it offers superior beauty to any they are personally familiar with, but is at the same time linked up—by the chosen personality characteristic—with a life they know. Thus Jean Arthur's husky downrightness and loyalty, Claudette Colbert's tongue-in-cheek, Carole Lombard's air of honest-to-goodness exasperation, Ginger Rogers' natural acceptance of hard facts: these are the individual characteristics of current favorites who were all originally consigned to a career of solemn prettiness."

47

Constance Talmadge before she joined the Griffith company.

Norma Talmadge as a teen-age leading lady at Vitagraph.

Maurice Costello, balding and graying father of Helene and Dolores Costello, was a movie matinee idol from 1910 to 1917. In contrast to their juvenile leading ladies, male stars of the early period were often on the mature side.

John Bunny. People named their babies after this aged comedian, seen here as Cupid. Until his death in 1915, Bunny co-starred with the equally popular and famous Flora Finch as erring husband and shrewish wife in a series of one-reel comedies.

Francis X. Bushman and Beverly Bayne, the first screen "love team," kept their marriage secret lest it deflate the illusions of their fans. (*Romeo and Juliet,* 1916)

Bessie Barriscale, seen here with Rosetta Maristini, alternately played sweet maidens and sultry vamps.

Charles Ray, perennial hick of scores of Thomas H. Ince's rural dramas. (*String Beans,* 1919)

FAMOUS PLAYERS
IN FAMOUS PLAYS

Those early movie mimes who were also professional stage actors welcomed the anonymity imposed by the trust. To work in pictures was to belong to the theatrical underworld, and no one wanted it known that poverty or unsuccess had forced him to this shabby expedient. But when the public craze for picture personalities brought fame and fortune to former prison guards, hat-check girls, and sandhogs, the prima donnas of Broadway suddenly changed their tune. After all, Adolph Zukor had already imported Sarah Bernhardt in *Queen Elizabeth,* and if the owner of the world's most golden voice was willing to act in silence, it must be acceptable for mere American stars to do like-

The famed Mrs. Leslie Carter brought her production of *Du Barry* to the screen exactly as it was produced on the stage—only without voices.

wise. Besides, William A. Brady and Dan Frohman had lent their names to the Zukor enterprise, and David Belasco was permitting the filming of his backlog of stage successes by Famous Players. When Geraldine Farrar signed with Samuel Goldwyn at $10,000 a week, the gold rush was on. Writers dreamed of selling their old turkeys and rejects for fabulous sums; stars saw themselves earning big money for work that would be, really, little more than a summer vacation in California. Pictures were still "Galloping Tintypes" to Broadway, a butt for jokes and nothing but the thinnest kind of substitute for the "legitimate" theater—but who could resist so much easy money?

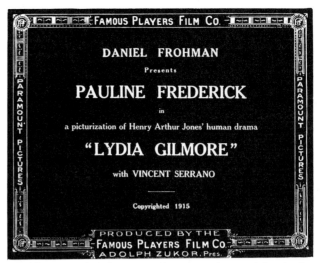

To add tone to his "Famous Players in Famous Plays" idea, Adolph Zukor got Daniel Frohman to "present" his "picturizations" of stage dramas.

To enhance the connection between his film version of *A Good Little Devil* and the original stage production, Zukor introduced the film with a scene showing the author, David Belasco, seated in his study pondering the play, while the ghosts of the characters he is creating appear in double exposure. Mary Pickford and Ernest Truex are materializing at the right.

"Watching director Arthur Hopkins trying to knead Maxine Elliott's beautiful face into the semblance of an expression" afforded amusement during the making of *The Eternal Magdalene* at the Goldwyn studio in 1918.

Zukor's first American presentation under the Famous Players banner was a stagey production with a corpulent James O'Neill of *The Count of Monte Cristo*, 1913.

Mrs. Fiske's fascinating, sinister stage performance as Becky Sharp became, in the movie *Vanity Fair*, 1915, a distressing example of an elderly lady being kittenish.

FAMOUS PLAYERS -- THE FLOPS

Movie producers, conscious of their own humble origins and relative inexperience, were sure that the newcomers from Broadway would sweep the field. Even the picture players did not think they could stand "genuine" professional competition and apprehensively awaited eclipse. Nothing of the sort happened. On the stage, beauty and drama are created by suggestion, illusion; but the intimacy of the camera demands the genuine article. Deprived of their vocal assets, the stage players fell back on a pantomimic technique designed to be visible to the last row of the theater balcony but which, magnified on the screen, appeared dangerously close to caricature—and no one dared suggest to the distinguished performers that their methods might be modified. But when movie extra Monte Blue was called upon to double for Sir Herbert Beerbohm-Tree, when the ankles of a film pretty were substituted, in close-up, for the piano legs of a stage lady, the original picture people took heart. And when the first "Famous Players in Famous Plays" were released, the wave of rumor and surmise which had been seeping through the studios was fully confirmed. They were catastrophic flops. The movie public wanted no part of these aging hams. It wanted the favorites it had chosen for itself.

The case of Mary Garden is typical. Miss Garden followed her rival, Geraldine Farrar, to the Goldwyn studio at $10,000 a week for two pictures. The first, naturally, was to be a "picturization" of her greatest operatic success, *Thaïs*. As the picture had no other reason for being than its star, it consisted of little more than a series of shots of Miss Garden in the statuesque poses of opera tradition and, as a result, was a close approach to a motionless motion picture. The movie public scorned this cold stranger, trying to vamp like their Theda Bara. It was decided that for her second picture a "modern" story might put Miss Garden over more successfully. But *The Splendid Sinner* was modern only in the details of its costume and décor. The story had Miss Garden a Parisian wanton who leaped upon a table and madly played the violin to the rich moths clustered around the flame of her sex appeal. Such abandon could not go on and leave her "sympathetic" in the finale, so she atoned as a Red Cross nurse in a uniform which fitted her as snugly as cunning could contrive. But Nurse's intellectual face did not agree with the sweet compassion written into the subtitles, and Mr. Goldwyn and his backers had another load of grief on their hands.

Mary Garden's operatic hauteur lent small conviction to her role as an abandoned minx in *The Splendid Sinner*, 1918.

Pauline Frederick's eloquent face and intelligent acting made her a favorite with mature and discriminating audiences long after she had passed her first youth.

FAMOUS PLAYERS -- THE SUCCESSES

A few of the stage invaders made a permanent place for themselves on the screen. Those who did so made the grade because they threw themselves into the new, raw business of making pictures with the same zest as the humbler movie pioneers. Behind "Madam Geraldine Farrar of the Metropolitan Opera" was a vital American beauty who looked upon each new opportunity as a challenge. The studio employees who expected an icy diva were confronted instead with an eager movie actress who would face physical danger for the good of the picture, who asked innumerable questions about the camera, and herself figured out her own best "angles." Pauline Frederick was if anything more effective on screen than on stage. Her ability to project emotion with her eyes, her hands, even the set of her shoulders, made her one of the great movie actresses. Alla Nazimova, from the Crimea via Broadway, had definite theories about acting for the silent camera. She thought it comparable to the ballet. Her stylized acting and exotic beauty earned her considerable popularity until she insisted on producing, with her own money, such highbrow plays as *A Doll's House* and *Salome*. All who survived the camera test did so not because of their skill and experience but because they had sharply defined screen personalities.

Charles Ray and Frank Keenan in *The Coward*, 1915. Keenan was too old to simulate youth when he came from Broadway and found a place as a character player.

Lew Cody and Fannie Ward in *Our Better Selves*, 1919. Miss Ward's ageless beauty withstood harsh movie lighting even though she was well advanced in years.

Three brothers, William, Franklyn, and Dustin Farnum had played romantic costume roles on the stage. They switched to the screen by donning movie cowboy clothes.

Geraldine Farrar and Wallace Reid in Cecil B. De Mille's *Carmen*, 1915.

Alla Nazimova and Henry Kolker in *Billions*, 1920. Nazimova's "bizarre" beauty made her the popular stereotype of Continental sophistication as long as she restrained her yearning for the higher things of life.

55

America's Sweetheart—she really was. But this unsmiling early photograph shows a Mary the public never knew.

"LITTLE MARY"

For twenty-three years, Mary Pickford was the undisputed queen of the screen. For fourteen of these years she was the most popular woman in the world. She was literally what she was billed: America's Sweetheart.

Why? It becomes increasingly difficult to answer the question. How far we have come from an instinctive understanding of her appeal is indicated by Alistair Cooke's remark that Miss Pickford was "the girl every young man wanted to have—for his sister." She was not. She was the girl every man wanted to have, or wished he'd had, for himself. On the screen her prettiness was often disfigured by a smudged face, tattered dresses, and pigtails, for she mostly played children—or, rather, girls in that misty mid-region between sexless childhood and buxom womanliness which seems to have had a strong and specific appeal to many American males of the early century. To hold her lead, she always had to play Little Mary, a girl on the verge of puberty, innocent to the point of idiocy of any acquaintance with the facts of life. Yet always hovering in the wings was a male admirer, frequently elderly (her biggest hits included *Daddy Long Legs* and *Poor Little Rich Girl*), and the implication dangled that someday, beyond the final fade-out, perhaps . . .

What was it that set Miss Pickford apart from all her contemporaries, imitators, and competitors? The answer can only be a guess. But her sweetness and light were tempered by a certain realism. Inevitably she played that almost-forgotten character, Pollyanna—but played her not so much saccharinely as vigorously. In spite of her creed, the Glad Girl knew that it was no cinch to make everything come out right. Nothing could have been more in tune with an era which combined limitless optimism with a belief that what was called "git up and git" was necessary to make optimism come true.

The real Mary Pickford had put git up and git before optimism. Born Gladys Smith, she was drilled by her mother in the knowledge that the little family's future depended on the professional exploitation of her good looks. The results of such experiences, so young, are indicated by a conference between the star and Adolph Zukor, after two years' work for him had demonstrated her supremacy at the boxoffice. "You know, Mr. Zukor," she said, "for years I've dreamed of making $20,000 a year before I was twenty. And I'll be twenty very soon now." Zukor learned to recognize this approach. Before long he was paying her $100,000 a year, then half a million. She knew, and he knew that she knew, that he needed her pictures as a bait to lure exhibitors into booking his less desirable features and to establish and consolidate his company's position at the top of the heap. The clincher in her successful bids for more and more money was always that she was worth it.

Finally came the moment when she asked for more than even she was worth. To get it, she was banking on her knowledge that Zukor dared not lose her to his competitors. His last-ditch stratagem to eliminate her as a factor in his war with them was described by an intimately concerned onlooker, William C. de Mille:

"With compassionate eye and throbbing voice, Mr. Zukor told Mary that she was tired, that she had been working much too hard for many years and needed a long rest. No line must ever be allowed to mar her beautiful face, nor should that face ever appear on any screen save Paramount's. Just think what Mary and Paramount had meant to each other these last few years! The thought of her going to another company, where perhaps she would not be so well loved, hurt the kindly Mr. Zukor in his deepest and most sensitive feelings. So, just for friendship and *auld lang syne*, he would give her one thousand dollars every week for five years on condition that she would take a complete rest during that period and not bother her pretty little head about pictures at all.

"Mary's large, soulful, and expensive eyes opened wide as she regarded her generous benefactor with feeling. She was much touched and deeply moved. If the thought occurred to her that, from Paramount's point of view, it was well worth $260,000 to eliminate her for five years as a competitor, she brushed it aside as unworthy. She, too, knew what friendship meant, and her affection for dear, considerate Mr. Zukor was fully as deep as his for her. But, after all, she was only a young girl just on the threshold of what might prove to be a successful career. She was a little tired, perhaps, but not quite tired enough to take a five-year vacation, at the end of which she would undoubtedly be five years older.

"Timidly, in her innocent, childlike way, she explained all this to the man who was so anxious to protect her from the hard life of professional exertion. Tempting as his offer was, she would rather work for $675,000 per annum than rest for $52,000. It desolated her to think of leaving Paramount, where she had been so happy and contented, but, after all, duty was a much nobler goal than mere happiness; so unless Mr. Zukor could see his way clear to meet these terms . . . The poor child could say no more; she was a young artist and they kept forcing her to talk about money."

Nine members of Fred Karno's London troupe, with their wives and children, shortly before their departure for America. The young man, third from the left, with the arrow pointing to his straw hat, is Charles Chaplin. The other arrow points to the youthful Stan Laurel.

Charlie Chaplin in *The Tramp*, 1915.

"THE LITTLE FELLOW"

They were dreadfully poor. Charlie's parents were third-string strolling players. His father died early of alcoholism; his mother was often in asylums, either through drink or because of periodic mental illness. Whenever this happened, Charlie and his brothers had to shift for themselves on the streets of London. Robert Flaherty used to tell the story of one of these times: "It was a rainy winter night. Charlie, who was about eleven, had no place to sleep and was sheltering under an overhanging roof. A solid-looking man came by, took a look at the boy, and asked him what he was doing there. Charlie told his story. The man stroked his chin for a moment and said, 'Well, I've a bit to eat at my place. I've only one room, but you're welcome to stay the night if you don't mind sleeping on the floor.' They went to the man's furnished room, where Charlie slept on a pallet at the foot of his host's bed. Next morning when he woke, the man had gone, but Charlie found a note saying, 'If you've no place to sleep tonight, come here.' Charlie had to avail himself of his friend's help for many nights, but always in the morning the man had gone to his work. Charlie became curious about what that work might be. One morning he managed to wake early. The man was taking out of the closet and measuring in his hands a long, strong rope with a noose at the end of it. He was the common hangman."

Out of such experiences came the greatest comedian in the world. Chaplin came to America in
1913 with Fred Karno's "A Night in an English
Music Hall" troupe. One of Mack Sennett's backers
saw him, signed him to a contract at $150 a week,
and shipped him west to the Sennett studio. It
seemed at first that the studio had gained just another show-wise vaudevillian. But before the end
of his first year with Sennett, the figure of "Charlie"
had begun to emerge. His "funny" walk was based
on a recollection from childhood of the pathetic
shuffle of an old drunk who used to hold horses
outside a London tavern. His insouciance and tattered elegance perhaps reflected the brave front
which actors from time immemorial have assumed
as they enter the manager's office. But no one had
ever seen, before the camera showed it to them,
a smile of such angelic innocence, coupled with a
surprising streak of meanness, violence, and a
certain deliberate vulgarity.

This equivocal, significant figure first became the
favorite of children. By the time their elders discovered the little man with the derby, the cane, and
the oversized shoes, the Chaplin craze was in full
swing. At the end of his year with Sennett, the
comedian accepted a year's contract with Essanay
at $1,000 a week. At the end of that year, 1915, he
demanded and received from the Mutual Film

Corporation $10,000 a week 52 weeks a year. The
news of these financial pole vaults invariably
reached Mary Pickford when she was discussing
with Adolph Zukor, as she did so frequently, the
desirability of canceling her current contract in
favor of one more rewarding to her and more costly
to him. For more than four years, from 1914 to
1918, if Charlie got a raise, Mary had to have a
bigger one, and vice versa. Five years earlier this
pair had both been obscure players. Now the astro-
nomical sums they were receiving advertised to a
world (and a Wall Street) barely conscious of pictures that the movies had become big business. They
advertised, also, that the star system was the most
important single factor in motion pictures. Mary
and Charlie *were* their pictures, and their pictures
needed nothing more to sell them to every exhibitor
and virtually every movie patron in the land.

When Chaplin signed his $10,000-a-week contract
with Mutual, he asked for and was given $100,000
advance on salary. His brother Sidney remonstrated
at his demands, pointing out that they had no way
of knowing whether the company could stand the
unprecedented financial strain its new star was putting on it. Chaplin replied, "Well, even if the bubble
bursts—and I agree it probably will—they can't
take the hundred thousand away from me."

He's still got it.

Charles Chaplin, Mary Pickford, D. W. Griffith, and Douglas Fairbanks.

"DOUG" AND THE BIG FOUR

Douglas Fairbanks was the most conspicuous of the invading "Famous Players" who survived the camera test, but his survival was a near thing, almost an accident. He was signed by Triangle on the basis of his modest reputation as a minor star of polite comedy on the stage, and sent to Hollywood in 1915 to appear in one of Triangle's first releases, *The Lamb*. The regular studio personnel were in the first flush of resentment over the high salaries paid the stage favorites; perhaps it is too much to call it sabotage, but certain it is that Fairbanks was murk-photographed in this first film, and that he had been given an ashen make-up which made him look ten years older than his thirty-two years. Perhaps he was oblivious of this, perhaps he was retaliating in his own way, but throughout the making of the picture he was the hail-fellow-well-met, giving his colleagues mighty slaps on the back and indulging his private penchant for athletics and acrobatics all over the set, often at the expense of the shooting schedule. These antics so pained D. W. Griffith, who was supervising the picture, that he told Fairbanks that if he had any future with the movies it would be with Mack Sennett. But two observers intervened. Anita Loos, a script writer hardly out of her

teens, but who had won Griffith's confidence in their three years of association, pointed out to the great man that this jolly, jumping-jack, off-screen Fairbanks was a far more interesting personality than the polite comedian they had signed. Miss Loos proposed that she and her husband, director John Emerson, be turned loose to see what could be done with the private personality of Douglas Fairbanks in pictures made for the public screen.

The remarkable series of comedies which Miss Loos wrote for Fairbanks established him as a popular figure only slightly below the level of Mary, Charlie, and William S. Hart. He was not the figure we chiefly remember today, the wealthy producer-star of expensive cloak-and-dagger fantasies. The Loos-Emerson Fairbanks was a happy-go-lucky fellow, a prophet of optimism, of "100 per cent Americanism" (as then understood), and, above all, of normalcy. The Loos scripts had him demolish all the current preoccupations which most people disliked or did not understand—psychiatry, Couéism, hypochondria, the craze for European royalty. He was Mr. Average Man with the powers of Superman. And that was important: his triumphs at the end of every picture were the triumphs of clean liv-

Douglas Fairbanks leaping from a tree to a window in *The Iron Mask,* 1929.

Douglas Fairbanks supporting Charles Chaplin and Mary Pickford at the time of the formation of United Artists, 1919.

ing, noble ideals—and muscles of steel. But all this, sugary as it sounds, worked a spell (it still does when you see his pictures) not only with the provincial Americans at whom it was aimed but all over the world. A French critic wrote, "Douglas Fairbanks is a tonic. He smiles and you feel relieved."

Behind the stage star and the grinning athlete there seems to have been a third Douglas Fairbanks, an ambitious one. At any rate, a certain pattern emerges from subsequent events. Fairbanks' star was rising fast, but others still eclipsed it. Then, in 1919, he married Mary Pickford. The union of Doug, the all-American male, with Little Mary, America's Sweetheart, had a sentimental logic which thrilled the fans of both, which was nearly everybody. By another kind of logic, the marriage raised Fairbanks to a place by Mary's side and equated his official popularity with hers. Soon he made another move. At the suggestion of B. P. Schulberg, he pointed out to his wife and to Charlie Chaplin that the enormous salary raises they were successfully demanding were making the margin of profit on their films dangerously low, and that there might come a time when, despite their popularity, they would actually constitute liabilities to their employers. Why not form—with him and D. W. Griffith, who was also getting too expensive for his own good—a company to produce and distribute their own pictures, enabling them to keep all the profits for themselves? In 1919, the United Artists Corporation was formed.

United Artists was the logical conclusion to the star system. When he heard of it, Richard Rowland, head of Metro, commented, "The lunatics have taken charge of the asylum." But the head keeper in this case was no loony. Though only one of four partners, and at first the least powerful, Fairbanks took the most active part in the affairs of the company. In the mid-Twenties, he enticed Joseph M. Schenck to head the administrative affairs of the corporation, bringing with him Norma and Constance Talmadge, who were quickly followed by Gloria Swanson, John Barrymore, and Buster Keaton. In the Thirties, when things were looking bad, Fairbanks brought in Darryl Zanuck. And when D. W. Griffith ceased to be a productive contributor, Fairbanks quietly eased him out of the partnership. So long as he was alive, United Artists made a profit.

Louise Lovely

Mary Pickford

Rubye de Remer

King Baggott

Harold Lockwood

Carlyle Blackwell

62

THE HEROINE

The first requirement for the movie heroine was that she be sweet, preferably as sweet as the high priestess of them all, Mary Pickford, and if possible with a replica of Miss Pickford's golden curls. She should be fond of children and animals (she was customarily introduced to audiences in a shot showing her sitting on the lawn playing with puppies, kittens, or bunnies). That she should be pure went so without saying that it was never referred to except by the color of her dress—white—or at a moment when her purity was menaced, as it constantly was. Intelligence or lack of it was irrelevant, but it helped if her name could symbolize her leading characteristic: the early screen was dotted with Blanche Sweets, Arline Prettys, and Louise Lovelys. It was also helpful if her name was exotic, like Violet Mersereau and Muriel Ostriche, or aristocratic, which was why Olga Cronk was metamorphosed into Claire Windsor and Lucille Langehanke into Mary Astor. Probably this trend reached its climax when Erich von Stroheim introduced as the heroine of his *Foolish Wives* a lady whose lineage was reputedly so high that she must never be referred to except as Miss Dupont.

THE HERO

He, of course, had to be as strong as the heroine was gentle. A proper hero must also be silent, kind, noble, generous, patriotic, pious, slow to anger yet quick to avenge his honor, and horse-loving. Bearing such a heavy load of virtues, it is a wonder that he ever had time to be tempted into sin, but he frequently was—and, unlike the heroine, who never found resisting sin any effort at all, it was all right for the hero to be tempted, as long as he didn't do anything about it. If he did, if he fell, the audience was on notice that at least three reels would now be consumed in remorse, penance, and atonement before he could hope to see an answering light in the heroine's eyes. And even then—well, one asked oneself, how could a sweet, lovely girl like that let any man touch her who had . . . All such thoughts ended in three dots in those days.

It was not important that the hero's name be high-sounding. A man could survive even names like Carlyle Blackwell and J. Warren Kerrigan if there was nothing, absolutely nothing about him of the sissy. The American movie hero of the early silent period was a virile, red-blooded, go-getting, rough-and-ready, he-man, Sunday-school teacher.

THE MOVIE FAMILY

By the time the star system had established itself, there had also emerged a sort of formula movie family or standard *dramatis personae*. With rare variation, these obligatory characters were The Hero, The Heroine, Mother, The Villain, and The Vamp.

Arline Pretty, Dustin Farnum

Lois Wilson, J. Warren Kerrigan

MOTHER

"Why must all American movie mothers be white-haired and tottering even though their children are mere tots? Does the menopause not operate in the United States?" asked Iris Barry, film critic of the London *Daily Mail,* in 1926. The answer to Miss Barry might have been that in American movies, Mother more often than not was old before her time. Her figure might be flawless, her face unlined, but gray-haired at least she must be, to brand her as a martyr, worn out by toil, her fingers worked to the bone in the service of callous husbands and unfeeling children. What deep vein of sentimentality and repressed guilt she touched in the American soul it is hard now to say, but Mother was a figure of supreme importance in the silent drama, symbolizing not only self-sacrifice but rectitude, authority, and an apron-strings world to which many perhaps longed to return. Father was by no means so important. In most movies he was either a figure of dread or of little consequence, almost obliterated by hand-wringing, tear-stained Mom. Increasingly he was obliterated.

Pauline Frederick came to specialize in agonized mothers of erring sons. *Her Honor, the Governor,* 1916, with Carrol Nye.

THE VILLAIN

When Ben Hecht came to Hollywood to write scripts at the invitation of Herman Mankiewicz, his host gave him some friendly advice: "I want to point out to you that in a novel a hero can lay ten girls and marry a virgin for a finish. In a movie this is not allowed. The hero, as well as the heroine, has to be a virgin. The villain can lay anybody he wants, have as much fun as he wants cheating and stealing, getting rich and whipping the servants. But you have to shoot him in the end. When he falls with a bullet in his forehead, it is advisable that he clutch at the Gobelin tapestry on the library wall and bring it down over his head like a symbolic shroud."

Mr. Hecht was so appalled at this counsel that he wrote his first movie, *Underworld,* 1927, entirely around the villain.

The movie villain was more than a scapegoat for the phobias of the audience—fear of foreigners, the aristocracy, the Big City. They projected onto him all their own secret desires for luxury, skullduggery, and unlimited illicit sex. Occasionally villains reformed at the end of the picture, but it was much more satisfactory, as Mankiewicz says, to shoot them. Audiences found it hard to believe that anybody enjoying such a life as the villain led would ever give it up voluntarily.

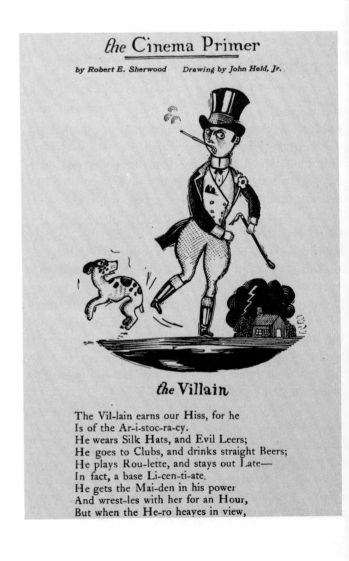

the Cinema Primer

by Robert E. Sherwood Drawing by John Held, Jr.

the Villain

The Vil-lain earns our Hiss, for he
Is of the Ar-i-stoc-ra-cy.
He wears Silk Hats, and Evil Leers;
He goes to Clubs, and drinks straight Beers;
He plays Rou-lette, and stays out Late—
In fact, a base Li-cen-ti-ate.
He gets the Mai-den in his power
And wrest-les with her for an Hour,
But when the He-ro heaves in view,

The archetypal mother, Mrs. Mary Carr, a brisk young matron adept at simulating advanced age.

Mother also yearned over mementoes of faithless or deceased children. Bessie Emerick in *The Black Stork*, 1917.

A screen villain must be recognizable as such at first glance. James Mason, above, was much in demand.

Nobody was better at menacing virtue than Walter Long, as he is here with Constance Talmadge, in *Desire*, 1923.

Cleopatra, 1918.

Gold and the Woman, 1916. Another of Miss Bara's wealthy

THE VAMP

When Frank J. Powell set out to film the stage play *A Fool There Was,* he sought an unknown actress to play the aggressive *femme fatale* who ruins men and tosses them aside. He found her in dark-haired, big-eyed Theodosia Goodman, an extra player from Ohio. This "circumspect and demure" girl was at once whisked out of sight and an entirely new personality was manufactured for her. She was renamed Theda Bara, which the publicity office insisted was an anagram for "Arab Death." She was alleged to be the daughter of a French father and an Egyptian mother, to be a seeress and inscrutably but frightfully evil. A dead-white limousine at-

tended by "Nubian" footmen drove her to the Chicago hotel where she gave an unforgettable interview in a dim room hung in black velvet and filled with incense fumes. The amused press gave her a very rough time about her supposed Egyptian background, but she stood the ordeal bravely until every reporter and photographer had left. Then little Miss Goodman tore the velvet hangings from a window and gasped, "Give me air!"

The campaign, apparently the first designed artificially to create a movie star, was successful. *A Fool There Was* made Miss Bara famous overnight, gave the word "vampire" and its derivatives "vamp" and "baby vamp" to the language, and offered the sublime subtitle, "Kiss me, my fool," which was quoted for a generation. Thereafter Miss Bara was

Theda Bara and the skeleton of one of her victims.

Miss Bara in an uncharacteristic lighter moment.

admirers learns that the future bodes him no good.

wicked through forty subsequent films in four years. Constantly photographed with skulls and with snakes, she became the public's permanent symbol of evil. Attempts to let her play sympathetic roles were as unsuccessful with audiences as attempts to let Mary Pickford play grown-up, romantic roles. Vamp she was and must remain, until the public tired of pictures which seemed increasingly like carbon copies of one another.

After completion of her lucrative contract with William Fox in 1918, Miss Bara, unable to understand the distinction between fame and popularity, waited for further offers. None came. On the strength of her movie name, Al Woods starred her on the stage in a drama of the supernatural, *The Blue Flame,* which amused Broadway sophisticates

for months, much as the Cherry Sisters had. Finally an independent producer brought her back to the screen in a version of *The Unchastened Woman,* of which Sally Benson wrote: "When I realized that this was Theda Bara's comeback picture, and not just one of her old releases, I could hardly believe my eyes." This was in 1925. After that, Miss Bara's occasional roles in short comedies burlesquing the vamp parts she used to play in deadly seriousness only confirmed Hollywood's belief that "they never come back." Wealthy, married to a successful director, Charles Brabin, Miss Bara took up charity work and became something of a social wheel in Los Angeles. But, almost till her death in 1955, she advertised that she was "at liberty" in the Hollywood casting directory.

THE VAMPFOLLOWERS

the Vampire

A Fool there was, and he paid his Coin
To a dark-eyed Dame, from the Ten-der-loin.
He took her out to a West Coast Town,
Dressed her up in a Form-fit Gown,
Filled her Eyes with Bel-la-Don-na,
And said, "Now, Kid, for-get your Hon-na,
For, Hence-forth, you're a scar-let Scamp—
A reg-u-lar, red-lipped, black-souled Vamp."
She signed his Con-tract, for she was Meek,
He made her Fa-mous with-in a Week;
And when I tell you his Pro-fits, you'll
A-gree that, per-haps, he wasn't a Fool.

Theda Bara's success brought an army of vamps to the screen. For five years the movies were overrun with female wickedness, but by 1918 the reign of the vamp was over. She had become unbelievable. The vamp films depended on public acceptance of two rigid conventions. First, that a vamp was at all times automatically, completely irresistible to all males. At the crook of her beckoning finger, a man, any man, would leave his wife, fireside, and job for the purpose of being putty in her hands. This was an absolute law which had to be accepted even when optical evidence suggested that the vamp in question was not so supremely above the ordinary

Louise Glaum's press agent declared that the vampire's leopard coat was "purchased in an Oriental market place."

The Kiss of a Vampire, 1916, with Virginia Pearson and Ke

Barbara La Marr, "the girl who was too beautiful." Her sultry vamping gained her stardom in the Twenties, until death cut short her career.

in beauty and sensual appeal. The other convention was that the vamp was moved by some mysterious force of evil which caused her to revel in the destruction of her victims for the sake of destruction itself. While she accepted, indeed demanded, money from her men, she did not spend it on luxury or save it against the day when she would be too old to vamp. She just wanted to ruin her victims and then laugh at them. She was *bad*.

Such motivation could be accepted only by very unsophisticated people with the narrowest experience of life. For a few years the vamp depended on suspension of disbelief among rustics, the urban poor, and the young. But the movies themselves were mass-producing sophistication on the grandest scale known in human history, and audiences were acquiring wide knowledge of life beyond their own social spheres. By the 1920s, vamps were no longer the central figures of films but sideline "villainesses." Compared to the new Woman of the World created by Cecil B. De Mille, the vamp seemed a crude and old-fashioned figure. Soon her tradition was swallowed up in the new ego-ideal exemplified for American womanhood by Pola Negri and Greta Garbo—the *femme* who is *fatale,* all right, but chiefly to herself.

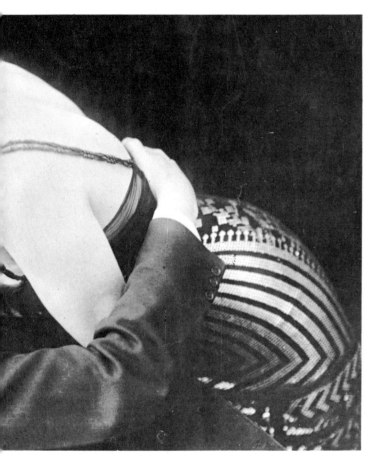

er. The woman was the sexual aggressor in vampire films.

After the success of Theda Bara, Valeska Suratt transferred her vamping activities from stage to screen.

Virginia Pearson, posed here with the obligatory skull, was William Fox's second-string Theda Bara.

The screen's greatest comedienne. Mabel Normand's comedy was mostly a matter of a wry and delicate knowl-edge of life and human beings. Of all Mack Sennett's gifted pupils, only she and Chaplin became creative artists in their own right.

COMEDY

Mack Sennett at the peak of his success in 1926.

MACK SENNETT

Screen comedy began as short, knockabout improvisations. But in 1911, Mack Sennett, a former plumber's helper, wandered into the Biograph studio where D. W. Griffith was at work inventing screen narration. Sennett at once applied the principles of Griffith's discoveries in camera work and cutting to comedy. Two years later, at the head of the famous Keystone Company, he was busy creating his own private world, and in the process shaking the real world with earthquakes of mirth.

The Sennett world is inaccurately remembered today. Slapstick is in a decline, and the antics of the Three Stooges bear little relation to the ordered madness and harmless violence which Sennett made so funny. The principal feature of this master comedian's world was that nothing in it had normal consequences. Frenzied beatings caused the pain of a pinprick, hundreds of bullets produced no fatalities. In this slightly off-center caricature of the world of ordinary experience, people could do things that in real life would have the most catastrophic effects. They are the things we all wish to do, without daring to—hence the primary appeal of Sennett's work.

Nothing was sacred to Sennett and his studioful of irreverent comedians. To the primitive humors of undress and obesity he added wild ridicule of virtue, authority, romantic love, religion itself. In Sennett's world all lawyers were shysters, all pious people hypocrites, all sheriffs both stupid and venal, and in that world everybody was caught with his pants down. His mysterious knack, and it remains a mystery, was that of creating satire as sharp as a needle while simultaneously extracting the sting. Policemen all over the world guffawed as heartily as their neighbors at the Keystone Cops. Perhaps it was just the broad extravagance of such caricature that enabled him to commit his outrages with never a protest from foreign governments, organized religion, labor unions, or Rotary clubs. Deeper than that, Sennett's work said: Whatever we pretend, we're all what we are, and we're all alike. Let's take the masks off for a moment.

Ben Turpin.

Louise Fazenda, Mack Sennett, and Teddy, the Sennett trick do

Sheriff Polly Moran, Ben Turpin, Heinie Conklin (with snee

A GALLERY OF GROTESQUES

Sennett enriched the screen with a great gallery of grotesques—the cadaverous Slim Summerville, the huge Mack Swain and Fatty Arbuckle, cross-eyed Ben Turpin, pop-eyed Ford Sterling, gangling Louise Fazenda, and dozens of others. The tender passion received anything but tender treatment from Sennett: pretty girls mooned over elderly gentlemen, matrimony was a comic predicament, and it was not unusual for the villain to get the girl. His actors were recruited from the ranks of vaudevillians and circus clowns to whom payday fifty-two times a year made his studio the only Eden they had known since childhood. Their heavy eyebrows, enormous mustaches, and dead-white faces gave to the Keystone universe that touch of unreality that Sennett needed.

Slim Summerville and Louise Fazenda heat up the thermometer.

Roscoe Arbuckle, Buster Keaton in *Good Night Nurse*, 1918.

Blackface was still a respectable form of humor in 1913: Ford Sterling, Polly Moran, Guy Woodward in *The Hunt*.

Chester Conklin and Mack Swain.

An assignation in a film entitled *Curses! They Remarked*, 1914.

In the Clutches of a Gang, c. 1913. Sennett's finest: Ford Sterling at the desk; Al St. John, Hank Mann, and Roscoe Arbuckle in the line-up.

A Misplaced Foot, 1913. Mabel Normand to Minta Durfee. Blackberry pie was more effective than custard.

Gloria Swanson in a Sennett comedy of 1916.

SLAPSTICK AND GIRLS

Cops, pies, and bathing belles are all that remain in public memory of the Sennett era. They didn't compose the whole range of his delicate art, but they do illustrate its leading tendencies. Cops, like all authorities, are congenital idiots, a pie the most degrading way of puncturing dignity, and the bathing beauties, alone uncaricatured in the Sennett world, the only sure good thing in life.

Chester Conklin and vintage Sennett beauties, c. 1913.

SENNETT'S IMITATORS

His Last Laugh, c. 1916, with Mary Thurman. Everybody imitated Sennett and mostly trailed him, but here a rival decorator and costumer score a comic victory.

Making a Living, 1914. Chaplin as a Mephisthophelean nobleman in one of the many roles he played before he developed the Tramp character.

A Woman, 1915. One of Chaplin's several female impersonations.

CHARLES CHAPLIN

When Mack Sennett's backers, Kessel and Bauman, signed Charlie Chaplin and sent him out to the studio, Sennett was not much impressed. An obscure Cockney vaudevillian had come to join his troupe of equally obscure small-timers, that was all. For weeks he played snaky counts, sharpers, any odd parts that came along. Then Chaplin invented the Tramp. In costume and gait, this was just another of the funny-looking men in which the Sennett studio abounded. But out of the eyes of the Tramp looked a soul.

The Vagabond, 1916. The Tramp searches his pockets for a toothpick.

CHAPLIN BECOMES
THE TRAMP

After his year with Sennett, Chaplin adopted the Tramp character permanently. Now writing and directing his own films, he provided in a series of one- and two-reel comedies a chronicle of his hero's adventures so fundamentally continuous that one distributor in the Near East spliced together all the short films and called the resulting feature *Charlie's Life*. These episodes from the biography of a vagabond appealed at first to children in the millions, then to everybody. His films were shown from New Guinea to the Arctic, his name was known to savage peoples who had never heard of the founders of the world's great religions. He became in two short years the universal folk-hero of the modern world. Intellectuals lured into the movie houses in search of the source of his fame found that this world hero was a homeless tramp whose shabby elegance and careless poverty bespoke a spirit equal to life's cruelest and most humiliating blows. They found in him as many things as have been found in Hamlet. They found him sly, cruel, pretentious, disdainful, crude, witty. They found a touch of madness in him, and a bottom of hard common sense. And behind this urban lover of nature, this hopeless, hoping lover who snapped his fingers at the universe, there was something that hurt.

A choice group of Sennett headliners: Mabel Normand, Charles Chaplin, Ford Sterling, Chester Conklin.

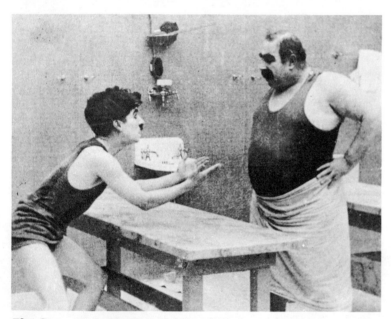

The Bank, 1916. Edna Purviance and Chaplin.

The Cure, 1917. Charlie and his masseur.

A Night in a London Music Hall, 1913.

Sunnyside, 1919. Charlie's first fans were armies of children.

The Perils of Pauline, 1914. Scenes from this famed serial look comparatively tame in relation to those which were to come after it, but it was the spark which set off the serial craze and did much to confirm the movie-going habit.

What Happened to Mary, 1912, with Mary Fuller, Miriam Nesbit, Marc McDermott. The first movie serial was not one story but a series of related stories.

The Million-Dollar Mystery, 1914. The sun, passing through a magnifying glass, is burning off Marguerite Snow's bonds, as Donald Gallagher looks on.

SERIALS

TO BE CONTINUED NEXT WEEK

The movie serial was a by-product of one of America's most sensational newspaper circulation battles. In 1913 the Chicago *Tribune*, fighting desperately with blackjacks as well as black headlines to maintain its local prestige against six hungry rivals, concluded that the nickels of nickelodeon patrons were as good at the bank as those of more cultured readers.

Some unknown genius, possibly City Editor Walter Hovey, later immortalized in *The Front Page*, came up with the notion that it would be profitable to synchronize the weekly publication of a thrill-packed serial with the appearance of a screen version in the nickelodeons. The idea, like many other supposedly startling innovations, was not wholly original. About a year before, McClure's *The Ladies' World* had, as a promotion stunt, arranged for the release in the theaters of a series of two-reel films simultaneously with its publication of a group of short stories known as *What Happened to Mary*. Each story was a self-contained unit only loosely tied in with the other installments by the appearance of the same characters.

The *Tribune's* *The Adventures of Kathlyn*, however, was a continued story which established the unfailing formula for all succeeding movie serials: the maximum of excitement and the minimum of plausibility. Every episode ended on a high note of tension and suspense, nicely calculated to induce any audience to come back the following week to see how the heroine could possibly escape from the horrible predicament into which the villain had lured her. Written by Harold McGrath, produced by Selig, with Kathlyn Williams in the leading role, *The Adventures* was a smashing success. The *Tribune* announced a circulation increase of 10 per cent, and even exhibitors, habitually reticent for fear of increased film rentals, admitted that business was good.

For the next three years the nation was swept by an epidemic of newspaper-sponsored serials each seeking to out-sensationalize its predecessor. The *Tribune's* second entry was *The Million-Dollar Mystery*. The name was chosen first and the story line worked out later. It starred Florence LaBadie and James Cruze, then an unknown actor. The

twenty-three chapters cost approximately $125,000, played in about 7,000 theaters, and grossed nearly $1,500,000—all fabulous figures for those days; it returned to its stockholders 700 per cent on their investment—fabulous for any day.

The serials were a godsend to the movies in their awkward age of transition from two-reelers to features. The old-line companies which feared to embark on the production of the expensive long pictures seized upon the serial as a perfect compromise, and audiences took to their hearts this thrilling hybrid fruit of machine-age culture.

THE TRIAL OF THE ORACLE

The Perils of Pauline

There is not one exhibitor in any part of the country who is not a booster for the "Perils of Pauline." It has paid for itself in many instances on the showing of the first episode, leaving the returns from all the others as clear profit. What would you not pay for a series that forces you to turn people away from your door every time you show it. What would you not give to be able to show one that is so popular your patrons call up and ask that you issue reserved seat tickets for the evenings it is to be shown as they wanted to buy for the full series in advance. Yet this has happened in several instances. Some of the exhibitors have advertised that on the days the "Perils of Pauline" are to be shown the prices will be advanced. They had to do this to protect themselves. Do you need any better evidence of the immense pulling power of this picture?

Pauline Pulls People—She's A Gold Mine

THE ECLECTIC 110 West 40th Street   FILM COMPANY New York City

"Pauline Pulls People—She's A Gold Mine," says this trade advertisement. The suspense of serials brought whole families back to the theaters week after week and thus built up the movie audience.

Ruth Roland in *The Timber Queen*, 1923.

Maurice Costello and Ethel Grandin in *The Crimson Stain Mystery*, 1916.

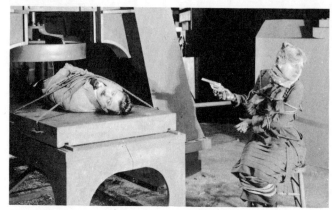

Colt Albertson, Lillian Walker in *$1,000,000 Reward*, 1919.

ACTION - - ACTION - -

The serial craze made movie acting a perilous if lucrative profession. Serial kings and queens had to dangle from airplanes, sink into quagmires, leap from burning buildings, suffer imprisonment, torture, and peril from flood and fire. Action was the keynote of the serial, and in this kind of movie the star's ability to swing from a window ledge to a tree was more important than acting or beauty. The day of the professional stunt man or stunt woman had not arrived, and though doubles were sometimes used by the more timid players, most of the top serial stars actually performed the super-

Hero about to be run over by wagon.

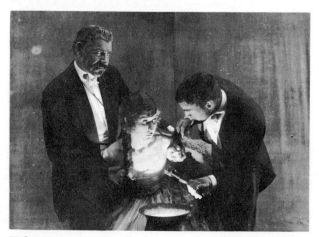

Helen Greene in *The Perils of Our Girl Reporters*, 1916.

The Mysteries of Myra, 1916, with Howard Estabrook,

Charles Lutchison, Anne Luther in *The Great Gamble*, 1919.

ACTION

human physical feats for which they were adored by the public. The two most popular serial queens, Ruth Roland and Pearl White, prided themselves on never using doubles for their thrilling stunts, even though their anxious producers would have much preferred to provide doubles rather than risk the lives of such valuable "properties." Audiences tended to confuse the private lives of Miss Roland and Miss White with what they saw on the screen, an illusion which producers fostered by giving their screen characters their actual names—*Ruth of the Rockies, Pearl in Peril.*

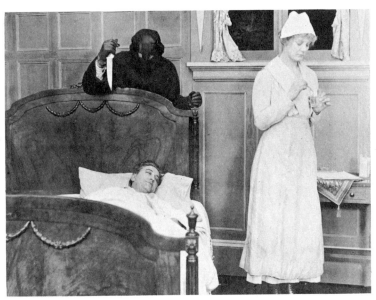

The Great Secret, 1917. Other exact details unknown.

Tom Mix in *3 Jumps Ahead*, 1923.

Natalie Kingston and Milton Sills in *Framed*, 1927.

featured a secret society bent on world domination.

Ruth Roland, Jenny biplane, and friends.

Buck Jones and Silver Buck

Riding Through Nevada, 1943.

WESTERNS

BRONCHO BILLY

When Frank Capra returned to Hollywood in 1945, after four years of Army service, he said, "You can't help being afraid you've lost your touch. I keep wishing I could sneak off and do a couple of quickie Westerns, just to make sure I still know how." The great director wanted to do his finger exercises in the basic movie form. The simple formula of the Western remains the foundation for all the complex storytelling rhetoric the movies have since developed. Whatever the plot is saying, Westerns move. That fact has kept them the staple movie cycle from *The Great Train Robbery* till today.

The first Western movies were descendants of the Wild West shows and dime novels which flooded the world in the days after Col. "Buffalo Bill" Cody began the international exploitation of his adventures on the Western plains. These one-reelers consisted of little more than a chase and a fight, and they were shot in the New Jersey woods and along the Palisades by men who didn't know a bowie knife from a bolo. The actors were equally innocent of life as lived beyond Times Square. One of D. W. Griffith's first movie jobs was playing an extra in a Western. His comment to his wife: "It's not so bad, you know, five dollars for simply riding a horse in the wilds of Fort Lee on a cool spring day."

The first Western star was a peculiar figure indeed. Born Max Aronson in Little Rock, Arkansas, in 1882, he adopted the stage name of Gilbert M. Anderson for his mostly unsuccessful career as a vaudeville actor, then drifted into

working for Edwin S. Porter in the days of *The Great Train Robbery*. By 1907 he had formed a partnership with George K. Spoor of Chicago in the Essanay Company, the name formed from their two initials. The Edison Company had already begun its series of lawsuits against its early competitors, and Anderson found it prudent to move half of Essanay to the West Coast. There, in a studio at Niles, California, he began producing the more than 375 one-reel Westerns centering around his own screen character, "Broncho Billy."

The appeal of "Broncho Billy" is difficult to understand today. This stolid, rather portly figure hardly suggests a product of Western life, and when he began in films Anderson could not even sit on a horse; he was thrown during the first day's work on *The Great Train Robbery*. Later on he finally learned to ride. "But I was never anything more than a competent rider," he said in 1948. "I used doubles for the sensational stunts. And as for marksmanship, heck, in those movies a blank used to turn a corner and kill a man."

Anderson does not think that today's Westerns have changed much. "They're just like I used to make, except that they talk a little. Most of them are mediocre. They all have the same formula—two guns, bullets, 'pardner,' a boy with a crooning voice, horses, and a sheriff. It's one big stew out of the same stewpot." Anderson did more than escape the Edison lawyers by moving to California. On location there, the real West loomed up behind the tinpot action of the one-reel Western and overwhelmed it.

Broncho Billy

Trailin' West, 1936

THE WESTERN BACKDROP

Against the great natural background of the Far West, in itself dramatic, the Western developed from melodrama toward epic. From 1911 till today, the majesty of plains, deserts, and mountains has given an importance beyond itself to the feeblest Western. Whatever plot is spinning, the background reminds us that these films are part of the national drama of the winning of the wilderness. But this was not yet apparent to the America of the Teens. It was, rather, overcultivated old Europe which first saw the Western for what it was and

what it meant. In 1919 the great French critic and film director Louis Delluc pointed out the part played in these films by their background and their physical material: ". . . bare gray plains, mountains as steep and luminous as the screen itself, horses and men in all their brute strength, the tremendous intensity of a life so simple that it has all the room in the world for beauty and harmony and contrast, and lends an incomparable spark of humanity to the simple sentiments like love and revenge which spring from it."

Westward Ho! 1935

Brigham Young, 1940

The French critic Louis Delluc wrote in 1923: "I think that Rio Jim [as William S. Hart was known in France] is the first real figure established by the cinema . . . and his life the first really cinematic theme, already a classic—the adventures of an adventurer in search of fortune in Nevada or the Rocky Mountains, who holds up the mail coach, robs the mails, burns the rancher's house, and marries the sheriff's daughter."

The Gun Fighter, 1916

THE GOOD BAD MAN

The greatest of all Western stars was also the most authentic. William S. Hart was brought up in the "real" West. Born in Newburgh, New York, he was taken by his father to Minnesota and Wisconsin when those states were still inhabited by the Blackfeet and Sioux who had fought Custer in the Indian wars. At six, the boy Bill could speak Sioux and by the time he reached adolescence he had worked as a plowboy and ranch hand, learning to protect himself against the daily dangers of life in a country where knowledge of the terrain and instant readiness for self-defense were conditions of survival. Before he reached manhood, he had come to think of frontier life as the most natural and healthy, and the frontier code an iron law.

When the Harts returned to the East, Bill succumbed to an unaccountable urge to become an actor. From the early 1890s to 1914 he barnstormed the country as leading man to stars like Julia Arthur and Modjeska. Most successful at first in Shakespearean roles, he eventually found his metier in a series of plays of Western life (*The Virginian, The Squaw Man*). This was greatly to his liking. He enjoyed re-creating the experiences of his childhood and instructing Broadway dramatists and thespians in them. But the proscenium was limiting, and when producer Thomas H. Ince invited him to join the famous stage players then trekking to California, he welcomed the chance.

When Hart entered films in 1914, the familiar pattern of the Western film had been established by "Broncho Billy" Anderson and indeed appeared to have exhausted its initial popularity. To Hart, this theatrical version of the frontier was ridiculous and unreal. He determined to put the genuine article on the screen, and in the many two-reel films in which he starred for Ince a new portrait of the frontier appeared, and a new protagonist.

William S. Hart as Messala in the 1899 stage production of *Ben Hur.* Before he became a movie actor, Hart specialized in stage spectacles and in Shakespeare.

91

Hart, that "severe yet impassioned figure," not only felt strong emotions but expressed them with all stops out.

Despite his differences from them, the Good Bad Man displayed all the tricks and traits of the standard Western heroes. Here he condescendingly allows his horse, Pinto Ben, to show his affection.

TWO-GUN BILL HART

William S. Hart created his character, the Good Bad Man, out of his own memories and experiences. In the majority of his pictures, he was an outlaw who underwent moral reformation of a kind, yet stayed outside the law. In this he embodied two conflicting tendencies of the Old West. Murder was not a major crime on the prairies and in the Rockies because rudimentary frontier justice, and often life itself, rested on quick trigger fingers. But horse-stealing, claim-jumping, or consorting with the Indians as a "renegade" were despised because they were *social* crimes—indirect threats to the whole community. Hart, the outlaw, was sympathetic because he always supported the basic code.

To his audiences the Good Bad Man was not only a sympathetic but an enviable figure. Americans of the early twentieth century had been steeped in the traditions of the frontier and fully understood the sliding-scale morality of the Hart films. The West was opened by men whose tenacity in the face of hardship was matched by a boyish desire for adventure for its own sake. As the new country developed, this latter quality became an anachronism and soon *only* an outlaw could live what formerly was the normal life of all men on the frontier. In Hart's films, which represent the halfway stage in this transition, the Good Bad

Evil Louise Glaum lured and sweet Bessie Love redeemed Bill Hart in dozens of films. Top, *The Return of Draw Egan*, 1924; above, *The Aryan*, 1916.

But, good or bad, vamp or heroine, both got the same treatment.

Man was still a glamorous character, secretly envied by all who were irked by civilized restraint. But by 1910-1920 he had to meet a tragic end. The characters *inside* the film might admire him, but the morality of a now-settled country could not permit an outlaw to escape scot-free.

Probably no such pictures as William S. Hart's Westerns will ever be made again. The formula of today's Western is nearly as stylized as that of Restoration comedy. Its purpose is not to portray a way of life but to gratify the escape impulse once served by dime novels and gaslight melodrama. Hart's films were made not primarily to gratify that impulse. They were produced by a man who understood the frontier code and was able to furnish it out in authentic detail. His pictures were not only more accurate psychologically but achieved much wider and more lasting impact than any subsequent Western film or star can boast. People of all sorts found themselves strangely stirred by the conflict between Hart's behavior and his character. It was a conflict to which they felt linked, a cultural inheritance from the "lost, wild America" of the day before yesterday.

Nowhere is Hart's difference from today's conventional Western hero better seen than in his treatment of women and sex. A final clinch may be al-

lowed contemporary cowboys, if the horse is present as a chaperon, but their main concern with their heroines is to rescue them from other men, not for themselves but for the noble cause of virginity. Hart expected all women to be like Louise Glaum, the seductive villainess of many of his films; his relations with them were a working arrangement involving money and sex, no questions asked, no answers given. When to his surprise he encountered innocence in the person of Bessie Love or Margery Wilson, he either ran from them as jail bait or attempted—and often accomplished—seduction, followed by remorse and a tragic death of atonement. There were many tragic endings in Hart's films, unthinkable as that would be today, and Louis Delluc and other European intellectuals were fascinated by their resemblance to the simplicity of classic tragedy, with Louise Glaum as a new Clytemnestra and Miss Love another Electra. The European reception of Westerns was conditioned by the Continental popularity of James Fenimore Cooper, and the French especially thought of Hart and his women as contemporary American types. Despite this confusion of nineteenth- with twentieth-century America, the French were the first to see that the Hart films were epic in style and that their material was truly cinematic.

As audiences responded to Hart's realistic Westerns, he extended their range to include every aspect of the old frontier days he knew and loved. His West was both drab and sinister. It pulsated with menace and passion. Men lied and betrayed and fought and killed. But they also loved and sacrificed.

Hart as Black Deering in *The Toll Gate*, 1920, an outlaw who, in his own words, "ain't never been any good" and doesn't intend to be. Yet he saves Anna Q. Nilsson's child from drowning at the risk of his freedom. On the frontier even outlaws supported the basic code.

Today's Western heroes surge up to the bar and then order sarsaparilla. This is what Hart thought of anything less potent than redeye.

Hart's Western saloons were as genuine as the real thing, and as unglamorous.

WILD AND WOOLLY

Many of the exteriors in Hart's films have the look of a Brady photograph. The characters in them were hard-bitten desperadoes of every national variety who had come to the frontier for no good. Often they were played by men Hart gathered from the last frontiers of Arizona and the Yukon. (Right, *Travellin' On*, 1921.)

The Narrow Trail, 1917. "The plot is nothing extraordinary, but this film contains a little masterpiece: the fight between the two men in the night. . . . In the center of a half-blinded and horrified crowd, the two figures circle. To follow them the camera draws back, moves nearer, rises higher: . . . The naked bodies, slippery with blood, take on a sort of phosphorescence. Two mad creatures are at grips, trying to kill each other. They look as though they were made of metal. Are they kingfishers or seals or men from the moon, or Jacob with the angel? Is it not some Buddha, this great naked figure which falls to its knees and dies there like a thousand little fishes in a lake of mercury? M. Ince may be proud of himself, for a spectacle such as this seems in recollection to equal the world's greatest literature."—Jean Cocteau.

"M. Ince" would certainly have been surprised.

FIGHTS

FIGHTING IS FUN -- IN THE MOVIES

Sir Winston Churchill's readiness to battle on the beaches and in the hills is matched by that of the movies, which are invariably prepared to fight on any provocation or pretext anywhere, any time, and in any manner. Men fight, women fight, children fight. They fight with fists, fingernails, feet, and firearms. They fight in doublet and hose, stripped to the buff, in the glamorous uniforms of the Northwest Mounted and the less glamorous ones of Alcatraz. They fight on mountain tops and under the seas; in fast-moving planes, motor boats, sleek black sedans; in bars, barges, bedrooms, and balconies adjoining said bedrooms; on horseback, on stairways, in quicksands, under tables, on tables, over tables. The good Lord apparently designed cliffs especially for individuals fighting to a finish, but man, with equal ingenuity, provided cellars for good old-fashioned free-for-alls. Any place is good enough.

With the passage of time and the continued advancement of the medium, fights have grown longer, fiercer, and, like some old Japanese drama, immutable to the last detail. The fighter felled by a blow that would kill an ox, rises promptly, like Antaeus refreshed by contact with Mother Earth; the apparent victor about to leap upon his victim encounters a terrific kick that sends him reeling backward; hero and villain alike stretch for the pistol only a few inches from their grasp, while the heroine simulates terror on the sidelines. No Western worthy of the name has fewer than three fights —one to get the picture well started, one in the middle to pick it up, and one in the last reel for a grand finale. But murder mysteries, spectacles, and smart society dramas are also well sprinkled with the thud of flying fists and some occasional happy eye-gouging.

Why do movie characters fight so much? Sometimes to promote skullduggery, sometimes to protect virtue in distress, but always and obviously to make life easier for members of the Screen Writers Guild. A poke in the nose or a half nelson is a lot less exhausting, for the author if not for the actor, than a scintillating line of dialogue. To topple over a host of pursuers by a giant swing on a chandelier requires dexterity on the part of the performer but not of the writer.

And if life is thus simplified for the author, so is it for the audience. They know that a swordsman like Douglas Fairbanks, Sr., can easily resist the onslaught of a dozen high-born Frenchmen. A peaceful stripling like Richard Barthelmess can be relied on to demolish the local bully eventually. Gangsters armed to the teeth, champions defending their titles against youthful contenders, Mexicans, Germans, Indians, Italians, and, nowadays, Russians, all uniformly bite the dust. In a world where all is chaos and confusion, film fights represent the only certainty, the ultimate security. Villainy can never be victorious. The good man is always the best man.

Soldiers, boxers, and other real-life hard guys snicker at fight scenes in movies. They know that the handsome actor who plays the hero has a double for the in-fighting. They observe and remark on the fact that the heavy mayhem is apt to take place in long shots, while in close-up punches are visibly pulled. Thanks to the self-betrayal of the movies in their endless search for publicity, the man in the street is well aware that it is possible and easy for the film editor in his cutting room to fake a shattering blow by cutting from one camera position to the other, and in fact that the fist may belong to an actor who never met the owner of the chin he connected with. He knows that the chairs which break over the victim's head are made of yucca, a wood almost as light as paper, and that the window through which the hero crashes is made of glass as thin as a Christmas tree ornament. He is aware that the fearsome break-bone sounds of fists on flesh and blackjacks on skulls are added by the sound-effects man, *ex post facto*. He knows all this. But just the same he sits forward in his seat when the fight scene comes on and the hero faces half a hundred men single-handed. After all, if Audie Murphy could be a one-man army, maybe you could be, or I, or even that guy on the screen.

The Spoilers, 1914
William Farnum, Tom Santschi.

The Spoilers, 1922
Milton Sills, Noah Beery.

THE SPOILERS

The classic movie fight of all time was the battle between William Farnum and Tom Santschi in the 1914 version of Rex Beach's *The Spoilers*. These fisticuffs lasted a full reel, and every subsequent movie fight has been compared unfavorably to them, while the actors in the three later versions of *The Spoilers* have been faced with the problem of how to surpass not only their immediate predecessors but also the legendary melee of 1914.

The Spoilers, 1930. When the third version was made, Santschi and Farnum were engaged by Paramount to advise William Boyd and Gary Cooper how to restage the famous battle.

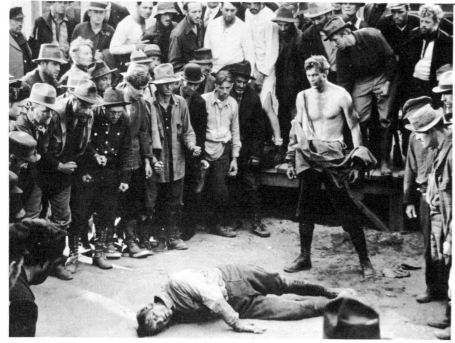

The Spoilers, 1930
William Boyd, Gary Cooper.

The Spoilers, 1942
Randolph Scott, John Wayne.

THEY FIGHT...

North of Nevada, 1924.

Lone Hand Saunders, 1926.

...on balconies

...on cliffs

But wherever
they fight,
the hero can
lick the mob
single-handed.

James Kirkwood in *Luck of the Irish*, 1920.

The Sea Beast, 1926. John Barrymore in an early *Moby Dick.*

Reno, 1924.

...on ships

...in geysers

Douglas Fairbanks in *The Black Pirate,* 1926.

THE NEVER-ENDING FIGHT

Through the years, Charles Starrett and Dick Curtis have fought each other in more than two dozen films. Fights are still regarded as indispensable to the movies. Three of the biggest hits of the past few years, *From Here to Eternity*, *Guys and Dolls*, and *Shane*, climaxed in "epic" brannigans. But some say today's boys don't pack the wallop of the old-timers.

Song of the Prairie, 1945.

Singing Guns, c. 1945.

Hidden Trails, c. 1945.

Shotgun Rider, c. 1945.

Frank Sinatra in *From Here to Eternity*, 1953.

Jean Simmons in *Guys and Dolls,* 1955.

Martin and Osa Johnson, pioneer movie explorers, toast each other in ginger ale at the completion of *Simba,* 1927.

THE WORLD BEFORE YOUR EYES

THE SILENT DRAMA

At the head of the movie page conducted by Robert E. Sherwood in the old *Life* magazine stood, in the Teens and early Twenties, a drawing showing the Muse of the Cinema holding a crystal globe, while on either side stretched a panorama of all peoples, times, and climes. It was in this way that people first thought of the movies—as a Magic Carpet which could take them to the ends of the earth, range through all epochs of history, give them the eyes of a worm or a bird—in short, realize the old dream of omniscience. In particular, it could realize the dream of travel. Movie cameras had become standard equipment for explorers and globe-trotters by the early 1900s, and literally hundreds of travel films began to pour through the theaters. But feature-length "travelogues," to survive in the theaters, had to have a popular quality, usually stemming from the personalities of their makers. Of these, the most successful were Mr. and Mrs. Martin Johnson, whose hold on their audiences came from their casual air of being any American husband and wife on tour. Beginning with *Cannibals of the South Seas,* 1912, the Johnsons made innumerable pictures, and after her husband's death, Osa Johnson summed up their career with a compilation from all their films called *I Married Adventure,* 1940.

Such films continue to be made and shown for that mysterious and enduring breed, the armchair traveler. Indeed, today, on our Cinerama screens, they are more popular than ever before. But the conventional movie audience soon tired of them. It was wonderful to be whisked from Paris to Shanghai in a split second, but actual Paris, actual Shanghai, turned out to be far less exciting than most movie-goers had imagined. So they had to be replaced with those familiar dream worlds, Wicked Paris and the Mysterious East. The cameras returned from the ends of the earth and set to work to duplicate Paris and Shanghai in Hollywood. The duplicates were marvels of accuracy, but these meticulous re-creations were used as backdrops before which were enacted old myths.

All the locale stereotypes with which we are familiar today had established themselves in the movies by World War I, and have continued down the years as the necessities of mass-production have dictated. Sometimes one stereotype moves forward and dominates the rest, registering with seismographic accuracy some subterranean shift in popular feeling—the Sands of the Desert in the Twenties, Low Life during the depression. "We must identify ourselves with what we are," wrote Cesare Zavattini, the author of such Italian realist films as *Paisan* and *Bicycle Thief*. "The world is full of people thinking of myths." But the camera, the most marvelous means yet known of re-creating actual events, has become, by popular dictate, a device for re-creating on a colossal scale the most primitive dreams of man.

From Martin Johnson's *Congorilla,* 1932.

THE FROZEN NORTH

The popularity of Jack London, James Oliver Curwood, and Rex Beach made the Frozen North a natural stereotype locale; the stories of all three authors have been filmed over and over. The Royal Northwest Mounted Police also provided and still provide an agreeable change of scene for the Western star too monotonously identified as a lone rider from Texas or Nevada. Sex, too, has its place amid the ice and snow, thanks to those long winter nights.

THE DESERT SANDS

The white simplicity of desert sands merging with a vast sky irresistibly compelled directors of desert films to complete the composition by mustering an array of horsemen on the horizon. If a palm frond projected into the frame, so much the better. Art-minded cameramen often carried a tree branch with them just in case.

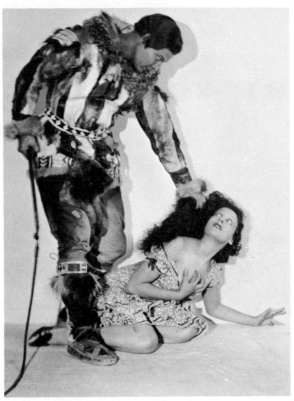

Lenore Ulric made her talkie debut as an Eskimo temptress in *Frozen Justice*, 1929.

A location shot from *Mount McKinley*, 1924.

Beau Sabreur, 1928. "The long line of Touaregs, about to pounce on the Great Oasis."

THE MYSTERIOUS EAST

Defying Rudyard Kipling, East and West met constantly in screen dramas of the Mysterious East. Met and mingled, but rarely blended. Miscegenation or some hint or threat thereof hung over these films like a miasma, but it was usually unmasked or nobly renounced in the last reel. For the rest, the East was neither the emergent Asia we know nor the Yellow Peril of William Randolph Hearst's imagining, but simply a stamping ground for vice —opium dens, gambling hells, white slavery, torture cells, and the like. On the whole it was a not inaccurate portrayal of colonial Asia of three generations ago, a place where the representatives of two colliding cultures corrupted each other. And when all these excitations could be brought to America in films about the Chinatowns of New York and San Francisco, the thrill was greater than ever.

The continuing popularity of such films brought fame to several Oriental actors. The great Sessue Hayakawa was the first. Anna May Wong rose from the extra ranks to leading roles and an international career on stage and acreen. For twenty years she was indispensable to any film dealing even remotely with Asia. The Japanese actor Sojin was imported by Douglas Fairbanks to play a Mongol khan in *The Thief of Bagdad* and remained to act Chinese villains (at this period Chinese were preferred to Japanese as villains) until the coming of the talkies. But for the most part, Asiatics were played by white men in yellowface.

Sojin and Anna May Wong unveil an American beauty to a visiting mandarin in the Chinatown sequence of *In Old San Francisco*, 1927.

WICKED PARIS

According to a Library of Congress catalogue, the word *Paris* occurs in more film titles than any other word except *love*. As soon as experienced audiences of the silent days saw the obligatory opening shot of the Eiffel Tower, they were prepared to expect: a) Montparnasse, Apache dances, the sewers of Paris, Le Rat Mort; b) Montparnasse, ateliers, artists and models, Le Moulin Rouge; c) a wealthy American woman, overwhelmed by Continental finesse and good table manners, abandoning her husband until it is (almost) too late (alternatively, when the wife found the husband straying after Parisian cuties, she just disguised herself, went to the Moulin Rouge, and captivated the fugitive anew). Many pictures combined all four motifs with exhilarating effects. What a loss it is to science that no one in the Teens and Twenties thought to survey the opinions of Parisians themselves as to what they saw on the screen in the Hollywood version of Paris.

The caption: "Having lost all her recollection of her convent-like life, Blanche de Montford (Gladys Brockwell) goes to the other extreme and becomes 'the Wildcat' of the Apaches." *The Devil's Wheel*, 1918.

SOUTH OF PAGO PAGO

South of Pago Pago! What a wonderland Polynesia opened to the studios! Dusky beauties! Beachcombers and remittance men! Drunken doctors forgetting it all! Volcanoes erupting and earthquakes quaking! Tidal waves swamping! Wild beasts menacing! There was simply no end to it all. Nor should an important variant be forgotten— the white-man-and-woman-shipwrecked-*alone*-on-a-desert-isle gambit. This was likely to be better in idea than in performance, since most of the time hero and heroine just pondered (and pondered) whether they had the right in the eyes of God and man to consummate their love—resolved, eventually, by an al fresco service, with the hero's key ring doing duty as the wedding band. After which, sad to relate, The End was likely to arrive before more than a token consummation had taken place.

But it was and is the white man and the dusky beauty who remain the central characters in dramas south of Pago Pago. Needless to say, the girls' duskiness is a matter of make-up, since they all have been played by white women, with the sole exception of the lovely Reri of *Tabu* (1931). Gilda Gray, the shimmy girl imported from Broadway for *Aloma of the South Seas* (1926), doubtless never heard of a sarong, but she started a stereotype that never fades. The particular male daydream involved here has survived the reports of returning GIs that neither Pago Pago nor the territory south of it is all it's been cracked up to be.

Dolores del Rio and Walter Pidgeon in *The Gateway of the Moon*, 1928.

Clara Bow in *Hula*, 1927.

109

RUSTIC DRAMA

Before 1917, more than half of American film dramas were played in rustic settings. Centering around the home and the church, they hymned the virtues of the simple life and, by contrast, the evils and the perils of the Big City. The heroes and heroines of these dramas were inarticulate country youths and gingham girls, the villains "city slickers." But while it was depicting this Puritanism and provincialism, the movie itself was destroying the isolation which kept them alive. Even at its most circumspect the movie urbanizes, introducing a relativist gray into the blacks and whites of traditional morality and belief. What happened is well illustrated by two versions of the same film, *State Fair*. The state fair, in the 1933 version still the symbol of agricultural pursuits and simple pleasures, had become in the 1945 remake an affair of automobile shows, "name" bands, and radio comedians. Today, it is doubtful if 5 per cent of the annual screen product has anything to do with life on the farm.

The Girl Who Ran Wild, 1921. Gladys Walton seems to rely more on her fetching smile than on her gun for protection from the whip.

Hail the Woman, 1922. The delicate caroling of Florence Vidor, right, would undoubtedly have been drowned out by the lusty hymn-singing of the rest of the choir, if that sort of thing had mattered in silent pictures.

Some Punkins, 1925. Charles Ray and Duane Thompson. Typed as the epitome of rustic shyness, Ray had to play bumbling youths into his late thirties, though in real life he ordered his shoes from London and his ties from Charvet.

Backstage

The Devil's Circus, 1926. Only a cloak stands between Norma Shearer and the fate thought to be worse than death but sometimes considered better than starving. John Miljan is the devil's advocate here.

Down to the Sea

Old Ironsides, 1926. The last of the sailing ships found their final haven in Hollywood, where they were used for sea fights of astounding realism. Wilson Mizner commented, "The public doesn't want to know what goes on behind the scenes. It prefers to believe that a cameraman hung in the clouds, mid-Pacific, the day Barrymore fought the whale."

The Fall of a Nation

The Fall of a Nation, 1916. The Hon. Plato Barker, a thinly veiled caricature of William Jennings Bryan, presides over a meeting which opposes preparedness for war.

Defenseless, America is overcome and invaded. Blindfolded are two Civil War veterans condemned to die by the commander of the European confederation's invading army.

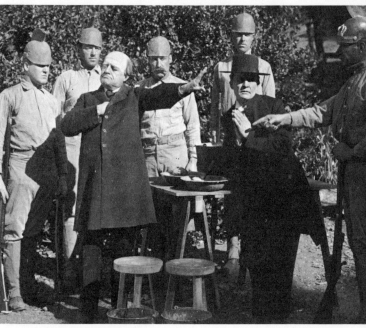

Hon. Plato Barker and the Rev. A. Cuthbert Pike, Peace Commissioners, repel with scorn the order that they must serve the Imperial General as potato parers in the camp kitchen.

The Peace Commissioners, who came out to welcome the invading army with flowers, are forced to the ignoble task of peeling potatoes for the Imperial General's soup.

WORLD WAR I

HOW TO SELL A WAR

The outbreak of the First World War in 1914 found the movies too much engrossed with their own burgeoning growth to recognize the opportunities it provided. But the arrival from Europe of films partisan to both sides of the conflict and the growing division of the American public into "preparedness" and "pacifist" camps soon opened new boxoffice possibilities. Then *The Birth of a Nation* demonstrated conclusively that the screen was an unrivaled medium for propaganda and polemics. In the autumn of 1915, J. Stuart Blackton, partly at the instigation of Theodore Roosevelt, filmed Hudson Maxim's book *Defenseless America* as *The Battle Cry of Peace*. It attacked the Germans as "Huns" and contended that only by arming to the teeth could America keep out of war. The film created an unprecedented controversy. No less a personage than Henry Ford took full-page newspaper advertisements to denounce the author of both book and film as a "merchant of death" whose real purpose was to increase the sale of his munitions stocks.

More extraordinary still was *The Fall of a Nation*, product of the unlikely collaboration of Victor Herbert and the Rev. Thomas A. Dixon. In it a leading pacifist, a thinly disguised William Jennings Bryan, persuades the country that all that is needed to defeat aggression is sweet reasonableness, with national catastrophe as the result. But such films, while appealing to the preparedness-minded, alienated pacifists and isolationists, and Thomas Ince's *Civilization* shrewdly straddled the

situation by being at once antiwar and anti-German. It featured a secret army of women pledged to stop the slaughter by refusing to bear any more cannon fodder. A similar theme animated Nazimova's *War Brides,* which was abruptly withdrawn in April 1917 because "the philosophy of this picture is so easily misunderstood by unthinking people that it has been found necessary to withdraw it from circulation for the duration of the war."

The fact that *any* motion picture had to be withdrawn for reasons of national morale was startling in 1917. Movie-makers suddenly found themselves the wielders of a formidable weapon. The Democratic National Committee had credited *Civilization* with helping elect Wilson in 1916 on the "he kept us out of war" platform. *Now* the movies were to be used for exactly the opposite purpose. The Committee on Public Information created a Division of Films "to sell the war to America."

War Brides, 1916, with Alla Nazimova.

American sympathies were exploited through the plight of the children of conquered Europe. The studio caption says: "Belgian children at school under a Prussian tutor" in Cecil B. De Mille's *Till I Come Back to You*, 1918.

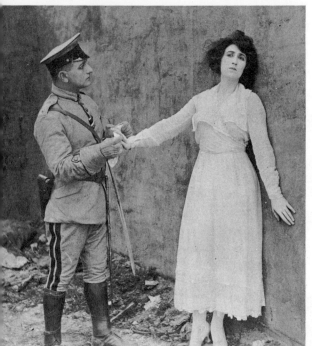

Rita Jolivet heroically refuses to have her eyes bandaged before she is shot as an American spy in *Lest We Forget*, 1918.

"Damn your insolence." Henry B. Walthal as a noble French peasant, or possibly intellectual, is threatened by Lon Chaney in *False Faces*, 1919 (below).

The very aspect of the hideous Hun. Walter Long as a Prussian officer in Mary Pickford's *The Little American*, 1917.

Mary Pickford in *The Little American*, 1917.

SCHRECKLICHKEIT

Pleasurably aghast at French and British reports of German brutality and vandalism, American film-makers concocted a cinematic frightfulness which even outdistanced its supposed model. The composite portrait of the hideous Hun, usually embodied by Erich von Stroheim, George Siegman, or Walter Long, showed him a fiendish torturer and sadist who thought no more of raping a ten-year-old girl than of sweeping a priceless piece of Sèvres from the table in order to make room for his feet, in the aristocratic French château which he invariably commandeered as his headquarters. He was not quite shown bayonetting babies but the screen did not stop short of much else. Over and over—almost routinely—audiences were treated to the spectacle of the honor of innocent American womanhood saved from despoil at the very last split second. Seldom, if ever, had so much venom been channeled through the medium of the screen. But the overdose brought its reaction. After November 11, 1918, films about the war, especially those aimed at stirring up hate, became totally unsalable.

Death before dishonor. Robert Harron prepares to shoot his sweetheart, Lillian Gish, rather than allow her to fall into the hands of the Huns, in D. W. Griffith's *Hearts of the World*, 1918.

Huit chevaux, quarante hommes. America's Answer, 1918, one of the first and
most pedestrian of the war documentaries sent home from the front.

DOCUMENTARIES

America's Answer. A mud-spattered YMCA canteen in a French monastery.

The war documentaries and newsreel compilations which began to
reach the United States toward the
end of 1917 disappointed a public
steeped in the synthetic horrors of
Hollywood. They caught very little
of the front-line fighting and
seemed chiefly to feature the minis-
trations of the YMCA. "Viewed as
drama," said D. W. Griffith of the
living death of trench warfare, "the
war is disappointing." Despite visits
to the front, Griffith concentrated
his own war film, *Hearts of the
World,* 1918, on the horrors of
Prussian militarism rather than on
the simple horror of war itself. The
great films of the war were made
after the war by men who had survived the guns and the mud.

WAR HUMOR

Chaplin, disguised as a German general,
clowns with Edna Purviance just before
winning the war singlehanded.

Meanwhile, in reaction to the violent melodrama of *schrecklichkeit*
and to the dullness of the films of
actual combat, the wartime public
increasingly turned to humor as
escape from monotony and anxiety.
Charlie Chaplin feared that his
great *Shoulder Arms* would offend
people, but it became his greatest
hit. In it, Charlie, by luck, pluck,
and devilish ingenuity wins the war
singlehanded and brings a captive
Kaiser in triumph to London. The
chief difference between this hilarious burlesque and some of the serious war dramas was that in
Charlie's case it all turned out to
be a dream.

Charlie Chaplin in his biggest hit, and one of the biggest of all time, *Shoulder Arms*, 1918.

Douglas Fairbanks kayoes the Kaiser with Liberty Bonds while the Devil looks on in glee. The Kaiser was acted by the actor Gustav von Seyffertitz, who changed his professional name to C. Butler Clonebaugh for the duration.

The Evil Eye, 1918. Heinric von Lertz, head of the German spy ring, with his henchmen, prepares to blow up a munitions wharf.

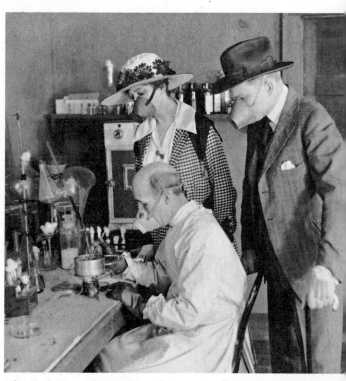

The Evil Eye. The studio caption says: "Heinric von Lertz and Baroness Verbecht watch Dr. Wolf prepare a paste culture of infantile paralysis germs to infect thousands of house flies by permitting them to walk through the paste."

Mae Murray and Robert Z. Leonard as "England" in one of the tableaux of a war relief rally in Los Angeles. Wallace Reid, who portrayed "America," at extreme right.

The war films accustomed audiences to the use of the screen for topical and propagandist purposes. Lewis J. Selznick, producer of *Bolshevism on Trial*, cabled the ex-Czar, Nicholas II, after the February revolution: WHEN I WAS BOY IN RUSSIA YOUR POLICE TREATED MY PEOPLE VERY BADLY HOWEVER NO HARD FEELINGS HEAR YOU ARE NOW OUT OF WORK GLAD TO OFFER YOU JOB WITH ME REGARDS.

THE HOME FRONT

By mid-1918, every branch of the movie industry was deeply involved in the war effort. Movie theaters were used as community centers for fund-raising rallies, producers distributed hundreds of "picturettes" urging the purchase of Liberty Bonds, and leading movie stars participated frenziedly in bond rallies, in partial atonement for the riches and freedom they were enjoying while most of American manhood was in uniform. Movies themselves were full of Red Cross nurses (including Marie Dressler in a film entitled *The Cross Red Nurse*, 1918), Gold Star mothers, heroic infantrymen, spies, and saboteurs—especially spies and saboteurs. The movies contributed more than their share to the 1918 wave of hysteria which saw sabotage in every accident and a sinister plot in any unusual occurrence. Small children fled from strangers in mustaches, since they knew from the silver screen that a stranger with a mustache was a German spy.

The Service Star, 1918, with Madge Kennedy.

An "artist's conception" of the Cathedral of the Motion Picture. The Roxy Theater, which opened in 1927, climaxed a decade and a half that saw the building of ever more sumptuous movie palaces. Named after the greatest of motion-picture showmen, S. L. "Roxy" Rothafel, the Roxy was the ultimate in opulence if not in taste.

THE GOLDEN TWENTIES

ENTER THE MIDDLE CLASS

During the course of the First World War, the middle class, by imperceptible degrees, became a part of the movie audience. The wartime need for escape and for news gradually overcame the old prejudices of the nickelodeon days. The nickelodeons themselves were fast disappearing. They were replaced not only by the Bijou Dreams but also, beginning with the opening of the Mark Strand Theatre on Broadway in 1914, by more and more lavish movie palaces. Ornamentation grew so lush that the eye was bewildered. Carpets grew so deep that they became a menace to navigation. Regiments of ushers were organized and drilled under the tutelage of West Point graduates. The more adult among the new audience professed much amusement at all this commercial splendor, but most of them secretly enjoyed it as much as the humbler movie patrons. A routine trip to a motion-picture palace now provided a pleasure equivalent to a tour of Versailles, with the added satisfaction that audiences felt *this* palace really belonged to them.

Not only in their surroundings but in their screen fare as well, the tastes of the new audience had to be reckoned with. They were changing tastes. The middle class, long the stern guardian of morality and respectability, entered the postwar decade with a gleam in its eye.

THE GREATEST SHOWMAN ON EARTH

CECIL B. DE MILLE

Cecil (pronounced to rhyme with *wrestle*) Blount De Mille owed to Mary Pickford his opportunity to become the most influential of all movie directors. Miss Pickford had just been offered $675,000 a year to leave Paramount for First National. If she left, Paramount would lose and First National would gain the most powerful boxoffice attraction in the industry with the possible exception of Charles Chaplin. To persuade her to stay, Paramount would have to pay her a yearly emolument likely to denude the company of all but nominal profits. Moreover, other Paramount stars would demand equivalent raises in salary. In this dilemma, De Mille convinced the heads of the company, Adolph Zukor and Jesse L. Lasky that he could make successful pictures without stars. He pointed out that it was the habit of D. W. Griffith, then the greatest name in the industry, to cast virtually unknown players, build them up toward stardom in successive films, and then, when they had attained national popularity, let them go to other companies which would have to pay them stellar salaries while Griffith repeated the whole process. Zukor and Lasky were persuaded by this argument. Miss Pickford was allowed to go, and De Mille began the production of a long series of "all-star" pictures—meaning, pictures without any stars at all.

It seemed a foolhardy step. Griffith was a "genius," and outside his portion of the motion picture realm the star system had reigned supreme since 1912. But De Mille had something with which to replace the plus that a star name gave to a film. He had and has a form of extrasensory perception that makes him aware of an approaching tidal wave of public taste long before anyone else, least of all the public itself, has detected the faintest ripple—or perhaps he just knows how to take a ripple and magnify it into a tidal wave. In the prewar screen world, people were heroes, heroines, villains, and vamps, and anyone who was not in one of these categories need not apply. But in a picture De Mille had made in 1916, *The Cheat*, a "good" woman was forced by the exigencies of the plot to behave for part of the time like a vamp. The favorable response to this brew convinced him that a new public was coming to the movies: one which preferred such qualities as courage and weakness, evil and good, which had hitherto been offered neat, all mixed up together in a potent cocktail of human fallibility.

Not yet was the Jazz Age, not yet the controversy over the younger generation, the eager emulation by their elders, or the open violation of the Noble Experiment. De Mille prepared the way for all three in a series of films in which he created a world peopled by charming people who did dangerous, reckless, even foolish but always exciting things against a background of luxury. His formula might have worked at any period; people have always been attracted by such daydreams. Morality, however, forbade. It was De Mille's peculiar insight that the strait-laced Puritanism of prewar days was weakening and needed only to be given lip service to be placated. He dedicated his pictures to showing people, at length and in intimate detail, what they ought *not* to do. His titles left no doubt at all of where his sympathies lay—*Don't Change Your Husband, Why Change Your Wife?, Forbidden Fruit.*

Cecil B. De Mille directing *The Call of the North*, 1921. The actor with the snow-rimed beard is Wallace Reid.

An advertisement of the Crane Corporation, 1930.

The caption: "When Cecil B. De Mille thinks of bathtubs he thinks hard! In addition to a glass bathtub in his new Metro-Goldwyn-Mayer picture, *Dynamite*, he presents also a 'bath-salts fountain.' Kay Johnson is illustrating the method of pouring salts into their holder."

DE MILLE DISCOVERS THE BATHROOM

Having decided to demote the gods and goddesses of the screen to ordinary human beings, De Mille began to analyze ordinary everyday life and probe it for situations which could be made more than ordinarily attractive. His first discovery was the bathroom. To a generation brought up never to mention personal sanitation, he introduced bathing as an art and disrobing as a prolonged rapture. In the shrine of cleanliness, deshabille and even partial nudity were so obvious a necessity that the most godly could not object to their display on the

screen. Whatever the story of a De Mille film of the Twenties, there came an obligatory point when the plot halted to allow for a lingering scene in which the heroine, or sometimes the hero, washed away grime and anointed herself in preparation for a gay masquerade ball or perhaps for some less public pleasure.

De Mille and his bathtubs became a national joke, like Ford stories—but a profitable one. The sophisticated used them as Exhibit A of movie absurdity. The less sophisticated may have laughed too, but they were also impressed. After generations of Puritanism, it was thrilling to be told that bodily beauties were not a shame and a weakness. American bathrooms, previously severely utilitarian, took on the gleam of marble, tile, and chromium, and the tactile luxury of great fuzzy towels and rugs. By the end of the golden decade plumbing corporations which had never dared mention their wares in public were taking full-page advertisements to display bathrooms frankly modeled on the De Mille splendors.

Cleanliness Is Next to Godliness

Phases of Gloria Swanson's ablutions in *Male and Female*. First, her maids fill a receptacle above her shower with Rose Water. Next, the ceremonial disrobing. Finally, the immersion. The bath water has been artfully colored for the sake of modesty.

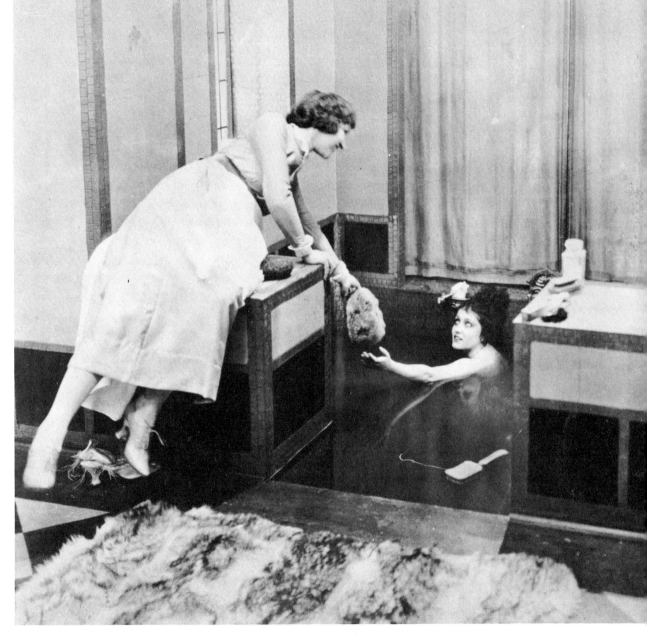

DREAM BEDROOMS

After the bathroom, the bedroom was the chamber that interested De Mille most. Here, too, disrobing and enrobing could be carried on at length and in full view of the camera. De Mille's beds were things to dream about, although they were constructed for more practical purposes than dreaming. They symbolized many things—art, culture, style, even sleep.

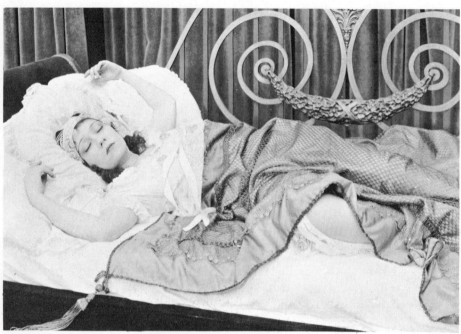

Male and Female, 1919. In her troubled slumbers, Gloria Swanson has inadvertently exposed one of her nether limbs.

Leatrice Joy in *Saturday Night*, 1922.

Lillian Rich in *The Golden Bed*, 1925, is the impoverished daughter of aristocratic forebears who marries beneath her to recoup her fortunes. The bed was "a gift of Louis XV" to one of her high-born ancestors.

127

Gloria Swanson in *Why Change Your Wife?*, 1920.

THE CLOTHES HORSE

While disrobing remained De Mille's most absorbing interest, he recognized that clothes must be worn on some occasions and he insisted that they be worth wearing. His brother William wrote of his interest in them: "Before this, Paris fashion shows had been accessible only to the chosen few. C. B. revealed them to the whole country, the costumes his heroines wore being copied by women and girls throughout the land, especially by those whose contacts with centers of fashion were limited or nonexistent. He achieved this, of course, not by accident but by engaging the best artists of dress he could find; his gowns, lingerie, shoes, hats, and hairdressing were all done by the best Parisian and New York style experts. This was, and still is, no simple problem, as the clothing and coiffures must be designed and in use in the studio at least six months before they become publicly fashionable."

But Mr. De Mille was not really concerned so much with being fashionable as with being sensational. He knew that Paris creations existed for the movie public only in imagination and that their imagining was lurid indeed. So although he used the best designers, he instructed them to exaggerate the mode and told them that the sky was the limit. His heroines smothered in ostrich plumes, staggered

The studio caption says: "Perfume, shoe, and hat cabinet used by Lillian Rich in *The Golden Bed*."

under the weight of their jewels, their coiffures, their extravagant gowns like sheets of metal tubing. The bizarre beauty of Gloria Swanson especially inspired him to go to extremes. She was soon stamped as a "clothes horse" in the public mind, and her gowns, and especially her headdresses, were often singled out as the great example of movie bad taste. But Mr. De Mille did not care that her satin swathings and the elaborate convolutions of her hair were copied only by rustic maidens and hash-house waitresses. The films he starred her in attracted women to movie theaters as no other films ever had.

Gloria Swanson, *The Affairs of Anatol*, 1921, *For Better, for Worse*, 1919.

Ecstasy at its height: The Candy Ball, from *The Golden Bed*, 1925.

Detail of the Candy Ball. The studio caption says: "The Marshmallow Girl—a novelty of Flora Peake Holtz's Candy Ball, given on the eve of her husband's financial disaster."

The Swimming Pool Masked Ball from *Saturday Night,* 1922.

ROUTS AND REVELS

Once bathed and adorned, the De Mille heros and heroines usually proceeded to balls of a magnitude and splendor unknown to Newport at its height, and featuring some titillating novelty picked up from current fads or invented for the occasion. In the subtitles De Mille deplored the extravagance and immorality of these routs, especially in *The Golden Bed,* where a ball given by his wife is the cause of her husband's financial downfall. But of course they had to be shown in order to be deplored.

WHY/WHY NOT CHANGE YOUR WIFE/HUSBAND

What action took place against the background of the elegant De Mille world? Boy meets girl, of course, but they were considerably older boys and girls than the adolescent screen was used to. In fact, they were married couples tempted to stray from their connubial vows. Of all the innovations De Mille introduced to the screen of the postwar era, this was the most revolutionary. Before Cecil, "love" was the exclusive prerogative of the young and unmated; such married couples as were to be seen were drab, gray figures in the background. Should a prewar wife or husband seek happiness outside the home, their action stamped them automatically as minor and malevolent characters, their only function being to highlight the goodness of the principals or temporarily delay their arrival in each other's arms. De Mille suddenly presented the movie audience with husbands and wives who were human, all too human, and he began his pictures where his predecessors left off, with the honeymoon over and the man and woman sitting down to

Gloria Swanson and Theodore Kosloff in *Why Change Your Wife?*, 1920.

dinner together night after night, pondering their bargain. Presently appeared the serpents in their shaky Eden. Villains or vamps they would have been earlier, on calculated malice bent, but De Mille showed them as unable to control their actions, sincerely and fatally attracted to the married hero or heroine. Who, then, was to blame for what followed?

As always, De Mille's titles rebuked his plots. *We Can't Have Everything*, 1918, and the like, upheld the sanctity of marriage and insured a last-reel return to the fold. But a wide territory had been explored in the meantime. And the explorers seemed to be saying marriage had better turn out as advertised because there are, after all, second and third and even fourth choices. Watching these films, audiences knew that somewhere the life of the emotions was organized on a more attractive scheme and that that somewhere might be the future. In 1920, the De Mille world seemed the world of tomorrow.

Gloria Swanson and Elliott Dexter in *Something to Think About*, 1920.

133

Gloria Swanson, Wallace Reid, in *The Affairs of Anatol*, 1921.

Gloria Swanson and Thomas Meighan, in *Why Change Your Wife?*, 1920.

Wallace Reid and Dorothy Cumming, in *Don't Tell Everything*, 1921.

Lillian Rich, Warner Baxter, in *The Golden Bed*, 1925.

Lillian Rich meets her fate.

DE MILLE AND THE MATRIMONIAL STATE

A trade paper of 1922, in an exultant review of *Forbidden Fruit* which praised the film's elegance, strong dramatic situations, and "human" characterizations, added primly, "There is no giddy and blatant sex appeal to prompt maidens of fifteen to ask their mothers embarrassing questions." To the extent that this was true of *Forbidden Fruit* or any De Mille film, it was true because De Mille showed sex where it "belonged." His preoccupation with the bathroom, the conjugal chamber, and the marriage bed provided opportunities for intimate glimpses of forbidden things, but since his lovers were so often married to each other it was hard for the censors to object. So maidens of fifteen saw in his films only what they might presumably see around the house. If what he chose to show of domestic felicity was over their heads, it was clear enough to their elders. Husbands and wives of the early 1920s found themselves watching on the screen experiences which they had shared but

which neither had ever dared mention to the other.

Not all De Mille heroines stayed within the bounds of licensed sex. Flora Peake Holtz (Lillian Rich) of *The Golden Bed*, whose "extravagant Candy Ball" we saw a few pages back, realizes on the night of the ball itself that she has bankrupted her husband (Rod La Rocque), and allows herself to be swept off her feet by a rich playboy (Warner Baxter) with whom she "goes away." A few months later the playboy tires of her and decamps, leaving her huddled amidst the pretties he has tossed out of bureau drawers as he packed his things. Miss Rich drew this harsh fate because of the taint of materialism in her amatory behavior. Other De Mille wives—and husbands—who "went away" with lover or mistress out of sincere emotion, simply returned to their proper mates when they realized their mistake. The interlude was presumably forgotten by both, though it was likely to leave a lasting impression on the spectator.

The Fall of Rome sequence from *Manslaughter*, 1922; the entrance of Venus.

REPENT! REFORM!

Nearly all of the De Mille moralities contained long flashbacks in which the modern characters were seen as people of ancient Rome, ancient Babylon, or even of Paleolithic times. In these flashbacks, the heroes and heroines faced much the same emotional problems as confronted their contemporary counterparts, and their solutions pointed the way of righteousness to these latter when the "vision" ended. The function of these vision sequences, besides correcting the errors of the characters' ways, was to depict Sin in some period when it was reported to have been unbridled. But in *Manslaughter*, 1922, De Mille struck a new note. The wealthy heroine in her craving for speed and excitement runs down and kills a motorcycle policeman. Her follies and those of her fellow sensation-seekers are compared in the inevitable flashback to the weakness of dissolute Rome just before its fall. This popular film sounded the first of the forebodings on the consequences of putting the nation on wheels. For De Mille it marked a turning point. He here emphatically says that the pleasures, freedom, and

Male and Female, 1919. In De Mille's version of *The Admirable Crichton,* Thomas Meighan reads Henley's "When I Was a King in Babylon" to Gloria Swanson. Follows a vision sequence in which they see themselves in ancient Babylon.

The Fall ot Rome sequence from *Manslaughter;* the Goths are coming!

excitements which his films had so relentlessly cele-brated might constitute a decadence that would bring upon the Republic the fate of Rome. He con-tinued the theme from here on in. Convictions fortunately coincided with commercial success.

De Mille's all-star-no-star policy had paid off for Paramount. In four years he directed 11 pictures which cost $1,416,365 and grossed $9,719,666 for the company. He had led toward stardom Gloria Swanson, Bebe Daniels, Rod La Rocque, Ricardo Cortez, Leatrice Joy—but as soon as they became actual stars he turned them over to lesser directors and sought new unknowns. As legends grew about him, his breeched and putteed form superimposed itself in the public imagination on the old-fashioned figure of D. W. Griffith as the apotheosis of movie directors. De Mille stood for the new age, the more abundant life that, everybody was convinced, the Twenties were about to usher in. "I believe that my pictures have had an obvious effect upon American life," he said in 1924. "I have brought a certain sense of beauty and luxury into everyday existence,

all jokes about ornate bathrooms and de luxe bou-doirs aside. I have done my bit toward lifting the level of daily life."

That this form of uplift had been highly profita-ble was not altogether beside the point for De Mille. But even as he spoke, he was preparing to turn a new page. *Don't Change Your Husband,* first of the bathtub-and-boudoir films, had cost $73,922 to make and grossed $292,394; *Adam's Rib,* the last, cost $408,432 and grossed $880,585. The less costly picture made proportionally the far greater profit, but De Mille realized that though he could avoid using expensive stars he couldn't get around the general rise in production costs. He had spent his time, according to his brother William, "in figur-ing how to make hit pictures without spending any money." He now decided to reverse himself and spend more extravagantly than anybody had dreamed was possible. The form his extravagance took showed that as usual his ear was applied very firmly to the ground. He was going to reform the nation his critics said he had corrupted.

Rodolpho Alfonzo Rafaelo Pierre Filibert Guglielmi di Valentina d'Antonguolla in *A Sainted Devil*, 1924.

LATIN LOVERS

SOUTH OF THE BOUDOIR

After November 11, 1918, war films overnight became a drug on the market. Those already made were unreleasable, those in work were abandoned. People were fed to the teeth, or so it seemed to the producers, with patriotism and sacrifice. But over at Metro, the brilliant scenarist June Mathis wondered if an *anti*war film might not appeal to this new mood of exhausted cynicism about wars to make the world safe for democracy. She could not get it out of her head that Blasco Ibañez' anti-German but also antiwar novel *The Four Horsemen of the Apocalypse* had run into more than one hundred editions in the United States since its publication in 1919. Although Richard A. Rowland, boss of Metro, had never read the book, she converted him to her way of thinking and preparations to film the novel began. What was more difficult, she induced Rowland and director Rex Ingram to cast in the leading role a young man about Hollywood variously known as Rodolpho di Valentina and Rodolph Valentino (both severe abridgments of his baptismal name). (See opposite.)

Valentino had been playing minor roles in pictures for about four years without attracting much attention. The popular leading man Milton Sills tried to help by taking him daily to the Goldwyn commissary in the hope that he would be seen by the mighty. Geraldine Farrar was one of the few whom he impressed. After meeting him on the Goldwyn lot, she said to a friend, "Wouldn't you think somebody'd be interested in trying out that young man, to see what he could do, what he had?" No one was, and his casting in *The Four Horsemen* was thought to jeopardize an already risky venture.

There is some disagreement as to the cinematic merits of *The Four Horsemen*, but none as to its boxoffice potency. As Ingram directed it, it was more than a "war"—or antiwar—film: it introduced American audiences and especially American women to a glamorous international money aristocracy shuttling between Buenos Aires and Paris, between dives and *thé-dansants*, studios and salons. Such milieus had been presented on the screen before—but always with frowning disapproval. Nor was the Latin Lover a novelty. Probably half the villains of the prewar screen were Latin—but they were sneering, greasy, black-hearted cads. Now the same character reappeared as a romantic Apollo who treated women with courtesy and deference but whose eyes promised (what the villains had threatened) that behind the deference, and behind the bedroom door, other, more exciting qualities would emerge—skill and experience. The strong, silent, he-man, Arrow-collar heroes of the American screen were designedly awkward in their movie romancing; it was their badge of self-respect, or perhaps of virginity. The magnetic pull Valentino exerted on millions of women signaled that they were tired of awkward love-making, on screen *and* off.

This scene made history. The moment Valentino first appeared in *The Four Horsemen of the Apocalypse*, the greatest screen idol was born and a new era begun.

The tango sequence from *The Four Horsemen*, 1921. Valentino and Helena Domingues.

THE SHEIK

Soon after the release of *The Four Horsemen*, and before Metro had had time to realize the gold mine that Valentino was to become, Paramount signed him for what was intended to be a minor film based on *The Sheik*, a British bestseller by E. M. Hull. Sheiks had been seen on the screen before this, but none so revolutionized the technique of love-making from Portland, Maine, to Portland, Oregon, as did this ex-gardener, dish washer, and gigolo. For reasons difficult for mere man to diagnose, he represented the ultimate in masculine appeal. Call it the mystery of the burning sands, the magic lure of the tropics, the titillating uncertainty of the unfamiliar, the reputed animal magnetism of the Arab aristocrat—these are mere words which leave the cult of this particular sheik unexplained. Give Valentino a burnoose, a bejeweled dirk and fancy belt,

a pair of riding boots, a luxurious tent with intimations of a harem in the background and a well-cushioned couch in the foreground, and he became irresistible. To be borne in his arms on a white Arabian steed, struggling virtuously but not too violently, was apparently the goal of nearly every woman's ambition.

Two years after its release, *The Sheik* had earned a million dollars for Paramount, and probably no one knows the exact amount it finally earned. In 1938, deep into the talkie period, Paramount reissued it with a musical accompaniment and it did surprising business. Valentino's leading woman, Agnes Ayres, then a long-time has-been, was exhumed from obscurity and sent on a vaudeville tour to capitalize on the resuscitated fame of a film seventeen years old.

The Valentino Attack

Much of the action of *The Sheik* consisted of a menacing Valentino staring at a pleading Agnes Ayres while they warily circled each other in preparation for the clinch that was a long time coming. This famous film was largely a tease, an art at which Valentino was adept. His employer, Adolph Zukor, wrote that Valentino's acting "was largely confined to protruding his large, almost occult, eyes until the vast areas of white were visible, drawing back the lips of his wide, sensuous mouth to bare his gleaming teeth, and flaring his nostrils."

SECOND STRING SHEIKS

The strong, specific appeal of Valentino for American womanhood obviously called for immediate imitation; it was clear that Latin Lovers were to be the order of the day and producers were quick to swing into action. In the first five years of the Twenties, any man with a Latin name or a Latin look could get a screen test. But though the looks were not hard to find and the names could always be fabricated, the essential Valentino quality was harder to come by. Jim Tully was probably the first to call it sex menace, and it was far from an exclusively Latin property, as Clark Gable and Jimmy Cagney proved a few years later.

In 1923, Valentino struck for more money and more control over stories, and walked out of Paramount. The studio got an injunction prohibiting him from appearing on the screen for any other company and set about finding a rival Latin Lover. The discovery that Jake Stein had "bedroom eyes" led to his rechristening as Ricardo Cortez and an elaborate campaign to build him up as an ersatz Valentino. Cortez did not escape this stereotype until the talkies revealed him as a plain American.

Ricardo Cortez.

The fading career of Antonio Moreno, who entered films in 1913, received a shot in the arm when his Spanish birth and name gave him a place beside Valentino's throne.

← Ramon Novarro was built up by Rex Ingram as Metro's Latin threat. His horde of feminine fans liked to see him as nearly in the nude as the censors allowed, as here in *Ben Hur,* 1926. The studio caption says: "This picture proves rather conclusively that he has no intention of entering a monastery or taking up the profession of concert pianist."

142

When Novarro was not in the altogether, he was likely to be found in Sheik costume. Above, in *The Arab,* 1924, with Alice Terry. Right, Novarro attempted a comeback in *The Sheik Steps Out,* 1937, with Lola Lane billed as a "madcapped American heiress." But fans of the new generation didn't know what a Sheik was, nor much about heiresses either.

John Gilbert in *Arabian Love,* 1922.

Norma Talmadge as "Rose of All the World," and Arthur Edmund Carewe in *Song of Love,* 1924.

The most rewarding of the Valentino imitators was Ben Turpin, seen here with Kathryn McGuire and the Sphinx in Mack Sennett's burlesque, *The Shriek of Araby,* 1923.

Innocent lust. Rudolph Valentino and Nita Naldi in *Blood and Sand*, 1922.

Filial.

Brutal.

Pursued.

Courtly.

Transfigured.

BUT VALENTINO TOPPED THEM ALL

If none of the substitute Valentinos quite managed to make the image of the Latin Lover real, Valentino himself always could. The answer perhaps was that he believed it all. A certain animal grace gave magic to all his movements, but beyond that, the crude situations of his movies rang true to him and he gave them everything he had. Adolph Zukor records an off-screen incident: "He was arguing with an assistant director—about what I did not know and did not inquire. His face grew pale with fury, his eyes protruded in a wilder stare than any he had managed on the screen, and his whole body commenced to quiver." Clearly, life was indistinguishable from the movies to him. But life, even in Hollywood, refused to measure up to the standards of dreamland, and the private loves of the greatest romantic idol of all time were anticlimactic and sometimes almost ludicrous.

THE LEGEND AND THE MAN

In addition to his beauty and grace, Valentino had the capacity to convey to any woman by a glance or gesture that between them there existed some rare and mystic bond. But this male, so irresistible on the screen and in the fan magazines, in real life sought women stronger than himself and was something of a pushover for any woman who was really determined. He married Winifred Shaugnessy De Wolf Hudnut, who preferred to call herself Natacha Rambova, before his divorce decree from his first wife, Jean Acker, was final, thus bringing about his arrest for bigamy. Natacha, like Valentino, believed implicitly in a special occult power with which she was in close communion, but the conjunction of their astral bodies was not entirely propitious. Along with her supernatural gifts, Miss Rambova was convinced that she possessed an almost equally abnormal infallibility in matters of film production. She had been a costume designer for Nazimova, and a successful one, but she also wished to supervise the writing, direction, and acting of her husband's productions. Her interference became so persistent that the Paramount executives were almost relieved when Valentino, at his wife's command, left the company for independent production. *The Hooded Falcon*, which Natacha wrote for Valentino, proved unproduceable after some $80,000 had been invested in it, and it would have been fortunate if *What Price Beauty?*, of which Natacha was sole author and producer, had also been left in limbo. Together this pair wrote a book of verses entitled *Daydreams*, of which the following is typical:

> *Your kiss*
> *A Flame*
> *Of Passion's fire*
> *The sensitive seal*
> *Of love*
> *In the desire*
> *The fragrance*
> *Of your caress*
>
> *Alas*
> *At times*
> *I find*
> *Exquisite bitterness*
> *In*
> *Your kiss*

Natacha presented Valentino with a slave bracelet without which he was never seen in public and which aroused considerable derision among envious males. So did his Beverly Hills home, Falcon's Lair.

Every Valentino film had to have a dressing or, preferably, an undressing scene. These two are from *Blood and Sand*, 1922, above, and *Monsieur Beaucaire*, 1924.

Indeed, Valentino's publicity, once he left Paramount, was consistently bad, reaching its culmination in an editorial in the Chicago *Tribune* called "Pink Powder Puff" which urged the desirability of drowning Rudy, "the beautiful gardener's boy," before "the younger generation of American males replaced razors with depilatories and the ancient caveman virtues of their forefathers were replaced by cosmetics, flopping pants, and slave bracelets."

Although his popularity was already on the wane, Valentino's early death in 1926 evoked a worldwide hysteria. Women who had never laid eyes on him except on the screen were reported to have committed suicide. Pola Negri, who had replaced Natacha in his affections, rushed to his bier accompanied by a nurse and a publicity man. Scenes reminiscent of the draft riots of Civil War days took place in the New York streets, only the demonstrators were exclusively females, who displayed more than male fortitude as they charged the police lines surrounding the funeral chapel where their hero's body lay in state. On the day of his funeral, over one hundred thousand women lined the streets to pay homage to his funeral cortege, and his grave in Los Angeles has become the mecca of loyal if aging members of the ageless cult of the Sheik.

Turbaned Natacha Rambova leaves Los Angeles for New York to arrange for the making of her production *What Price Beauty?*, 1925, while Valentino remains behind to continue acting in a film which had to get along as best it could without his wife's bossing.

After her divorce from Valentino, Natacha Rambova starred for the first and last time in a film bluntly named *When Love Grows Cold*, 1925.

The studio caption says: "Mme. Elinor Glyn in the act of composing her immortal masterpiece, *Three Weeks*."

The studio caption: "This valuable sphinx, with the body of pearl, is worn constantly by Elinor Glyn as a reminder of her creed. 'Live in the present—do not retrospect.'"

In 1928, Madame Glyn appeared in an early talking short, *What Is "IT"?*, in which she expounded the meaning of her famous discovery.

RURITANIA

ELINOR GLYN

Until the advent in Hollywood of "Madame" Elinor Glyn, writers had played only a small part in picture production. Stars and directors dominated the scene, while producers pulled strings behind it. True, Samuel Goldwyn had imported his "Eminent Authors," popular writers like Mary Roberts Rinehart and Rex Beach, and turned them loose to make pictures according to their liking, but the results were neither literature nor film but something less than either. Their downfall was their attempt to elevate the screen. Madame Glyn, as she liked to be called, knew better than that. Her biggest best-sellers had been written before 1914, and reflected a prewar world of stratospheric aristocracy as seen through the eyes of a servant girl. This world had been officially abolished in the democratic triumphs of 1918, but Madame Glyn, like other British authors before and since, was smart enough to see that the citizens of the United States of America were still secretly awed by titles and loved to picture the lives led by European nobility as a combination of luxury and depravity. For an industry invariably described as still in its infancy, she was just what the doctor ordered.

No sooner had Madame Glyn arrived in Hollywood than she proceeded to take charge of both its professional and social activities. She instituted the strange custom of afternoon tea as a badge of gentility, intimidated movie hostesses by her criticisms of their manners, and gave innumerable interviews to the fan magazines on the ever-popular topic, "What's Wrong with Hollywood?" Magnanimously she offered lessons in deportment to the local belles, and actually coached Gloria Swanson in the proper thing to do, something that took Miss Swanson many a year to live down. For her second protégée, Clara Bow, Madame Glyn invented the mysterious term IT, and dubbed Clara the IT Girl supreme. Stripped of her verbiage, IT proved to be our old friend sex-appeal, sieved of its concomitants, love and affection, and offered neat. Even so, IT took a good deal of explaining, and Madame Glyn was ceaselessly willing to oblige.

The authoress also insisted on supervising every detail of the films made from her books, each of which was offered as "An Elinor Glyn Production." Her dictatorship grew so irksome that the studios were forced in self-defense into a tacit conspiracy. If Metro and Paramount both contemplated productions of her works, they were likely to begin filming them simultaneously, forcing Madame to distribute her time between them.

Her vogue lasted through the Twenties, but by the time the full force of the depression struck, Madame Glyn found herself expounding IT to an unheeding audience. She returned to England where she supervised a few pictures on the strength of her Hollywood reputation. But in the atmosphere of the Thirties, Ruritania seemed long ago and far away, and no one appeared to care with Madame Glyn whether Lady Alyce had or had not dishonored the family name by marrying a common gamekeeper. It was not only that *Lady Chatterley's Lover* had put a new evaluation on gamekeepers, with or without marriage. It was also that, now, Lady Alyce, the gamekeeper, and those who had once thought no price too high for true love were exclusively concerned with the price of bread.

Madame Glyn poses to show her resemblance to Aileen Pringle, whom she chose to play the heroine of *Three Weeks*. The studio caption says: "Except for the difference of some thirty years in their ages, the two might be doubles."

Aileen Pringle and Conrad Nagel in *Three Weeks*, 1924.

THREE WEEKS

Three Weeks, Madame Glyn's official masterpiece, told of a beautiful queen of a Ruritanian kingdom who forsakes her loveless existence for three flaming weeks on a bed of roses in the company of a youthful British aristocrat. Then she sorrowfully renounces him and returns to her duty. That was all there was to it, but it was enough. Every hour of those three forbidden weeks was fully accounted for in Madame Glyn's pages and just as extensively (though more prudently) dealt with in the movie version. *Three Weeks* definitely proved the superiority of the movies to literature. It was delicious to read about tiger skins and beds of roses. Actually to see them was rapture hardly to be borne.

To play her queen, Madame Glyn chose the then unknown Aileen Pringle. Miss Pringle spent most of the rest of her starring career prone on tiger skins, chin cupped in hand, staring at the camera with eyes that promised nameless pleasures. No more ironic example of movie typing is known. Miss Pringle, daughter of a British governor of Jamaica, was as genuine an aristocrat as Madame Glyn's were phony. She was also urbane, witty, and caustic in her comments on Hollywood, her associates, and especially her roles. She became the darling of literary lights like H. L. Mencken and George Jean Nathan, and Hollywood, quick to seize an advantage, made her a sort of official greeter. "Whenever M-G-M signed a new author," she says, "they sent me down to the station to meet him."

When the bed of roses palled, there were tiger skins (below).

The Deaf and Dumb Society reproved Aileen Pringle for this tender scene. Her lips were actually saying to Conrad Nagel, "If you drop me, you ———, I'll break your neck."

Three and a Half Weeks

Soon after the release of her masterpiece, Mack Sennett generously presented Madame Glyn with *Three and a Half Weeks*, 1924, with a touch of Erich von Stroheim thrown in. Ben Turpin and Madeline Hurlock (Mrs. Robert E. Sherwood) are the impassioned pair.

151

The Prisoner of Zenda, 1922. Alice Terry (with Stuart Holmes) wears Hollywood's uniform for all European princesses. Any woman of noble birth could be spotted by her stand-up collar and beaded gown, both obligatory for Ruritanian heroines.

William Powell discreetly disentangles his spur from Virginia Valli's dress in *Paid to Love*, 1927.

Hauteur at its height. The studio caption says: "Lord St. Austel (Antonio Moreno) tell his bride (Pauline Starke) that she has discredited the family name, in a scene from *Love's Blindness*, 1926, an Elinor Glyn production for Metro-Goldwyn-Mayer.

The ultimate moment in *His Hour,* 1924, by Elinor Glyn, with Aileen Pringle, John Gilbert.

POMP
AND PASSION

Ruritanian romance remained a dominant screen cycle till the end of the silent era, sometimes under Madame Glyn's auspices, sometimes drawn from such outmoded turn-of-the-century favorites as Anthony Hope and George Barr McCutcheon. Already, at the beginning of the era of democracy that World War I was supposed to have ushered in, audiences displayed a hankering for pomps and glories, the stately behavior and volcanic emotions of the prewar world. Hollywood satisfied this longing with a will: American actors and actresses loved to play it haughty and dressed up.

Antonio Moreno discovers Marion Davies' true sex, in *Beverly of Graustark,* the 1926 screen version of George Barr McCutcheon's romance.

153

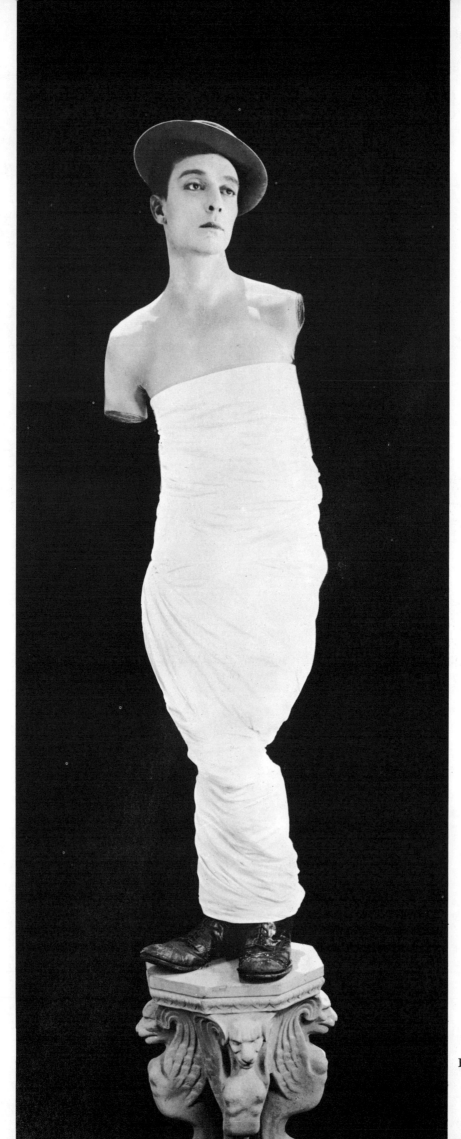

Buster Keaton.

154

COMEDY
IN THE TWENTIES

LLOYD, KEATON, CHAPLIN

To Europeans, comedy is the most aesthetically satisfying achievement of the American film. In this field the sentimentalities, reticences and evasions which the national morality or its self-appointed custodians impose on the dramatic film do not operate. The irreverence of the movie comedians spared neither social and political institutions, class pretensions, nor popular beliefs. Only the flag and the pulpit remained safe from their ridicule. These licensed jesters could analyze and criticize the fabric of contemporary life on a far deeper level than was ever permitted to "serious" films. After all, it was all in fun—wasn't it?

While Mack Sennett remained king of the comedy short, a series of comedy stars, following in Chaplin's footsteps, graduated into feature films in the Twenties. Of these, Harold Lloyd, whose films are said to have earned a total of $30,000,000, was by far the most popular. His "glass character," pitifully ill-equipped to get along in the world, tackled and overcame obstacles that made strong men quail. His was the welcome message: Get hold of those bootstraps and pull!

Buster Keaton, a greater artist, had profounder things to say about the terms of modern life. His natural state is a sort of permanent incredulity. Keaton moves in the mechanized world of today like the inhabitant of another planet. He gazes with frozen bewilderment at a nightmare reality. Inventions and contrivances like deck chairs and railroad engines seem insuperably animate to him, in the same measure that human beings become impersonal. Without friends or relatives, he is generally incapable of associating with his fellow-beings on a "human" basis, but mechanical devices, though often inimical to him, are, on the other hand, the only "beings" who can "understand" him. They are the real co-stars of his films. "He always wins in the end," says Iris Barry, "not, like Chaplin, by romantically escaping from the world of machinery into a realm of human freedom, but, on the contrary, by fatalistically throwing his humanity into the whirlpool of mechanical forces. He is a

hero by the grace of Un-reason and Un-feelingness, and in this respect is a very modern hero indeed." Man into machine is another way of putting it.

Through the Twenties Charles Chaplin made fewer and fewer films. The greatest artist and by far the most beloved personality motion pictures had brought forward, he seemed increasingly to withdraw from the movie industry, from the Hollywood scene, and from his adoring audience. He seemed to want to say things in his films that that audience, supremely content with his clowning, might not like. What they might be was not yet clear in *The Pilgrim* or *The Gold Rush*, but it is significant that he spent more time and care on directing *A Woman of Paris* than on any of his starring films. In this "drama of fate" he played the small part of a railway porter. It was a near-failure.

Harold Lloyd in *Speedy*, 1928.

"... A warm-hearted understanding of the secret ambitions of ordinary people."
In *The Freshman*, 1925, Harold's tuxedo, held together only by basting, comes apart.

HAROLD LLOYD

Safety Last, 1923. Lloyd's famous, spine-chilling "human fly" stunt was done without doubles or trick photography, and with only a net between him and the street below.

Why Worry?, 1923. In giant's shoes, and with his "slave of the lamp," Harold Lloyd breezes through a Central American revolution.

Girl Shy, 1924. In real life, Harold is too timid to attend the Saturday night dance.

But in Harold's dreams, the Flapper, the Old-Fashioned Girl, and here, the Vamp, vainly compete for his affections.

The Three Ages. A De Mille flashback to the Stone Age.

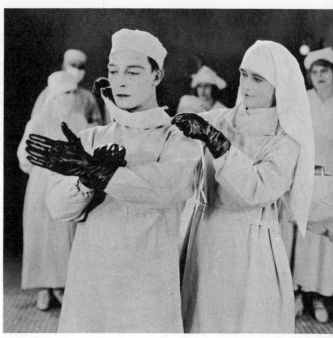
Day Dreams, 1922. In a forerunner of *The Secret Life of Walter Mitty,* Buster phantasies himself as a famous surgeon.

The Frozen North, 1922. The sheriff of Yonkers.

BUSTER KEATON

Day Dreams again. Keaton as Hamlet.

The Three Ages, 1923. Buster, in his parody on Cecil B. De Mille, as a Christian martyr thrown to an exceedingly indifferent lion.

The Gold Rush, 1925. The haunted, haunting face of the Lone Prospector.

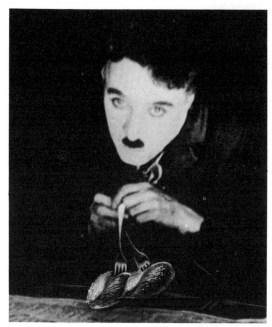

The dance of the Oceana rolls.

CHAPLIN

The Gold Rush. Treating the laces as spaghetti and the sole as meat, the starving prospector eats his shoe.

The party, with favors, to which nobody came.

Atta Boy, 1926, with Monty Banks, Fred Kelcey, Stan Laurel, assisted by a bootlegger's liquor belt.

The Cohens and the Kellys, 1926. Vera Gordon, George Sidney, Charlie Murray, and Kate Price in the obligatory scene from the first of their long series.

TYPICAL COMEDY MATERIAL

The foibles of the Twenties provided an endless supply of material for Hollywood's satirists, from the mysteries of the "beauty parlor" to the humors of the speakeasies, not forgetting the movies themselves, where every successful film was followed immediately by its burlesque—*Rob 'Em Good, One Week, Mud and Sand,* and Will Rogers' memorable *Two Wagons — Both Covered.*

Mud and Sand, 1922. The comics enjoyed poking fun at the undressing scenes in Rudolph Valentino's vehicles. Valentino's disrobing in *Blood and Sand* took place in a series of coy close-ups of those parts of him which extended from behind a screen. Stan Laurel was quick to see that a single long shot that should include all those close-ups would reveal an anatomical impossibility.

162

Leave 'Em Laughing, 1928. Stan Laurel and Oliver Hardy as usual surrender themselves to laughter prematurely, while Edgar Kennedy goes into the slow burn which never bodes him good and which made him famous.

The Girl in the Pullman, 1927. Harrison Ford, Marie Prevost, Franklyn Pangborn in a typical situation from one of many films modeled on *Getting Gertie's Garter*.

Hold Your Breath, 1924. The mishaps of pioneering days of the artificial hairwave provided unending fun in the Twenties.

His First Flame, 1927. Harry Langdon carries the primping Natalie Kingston to what may or may not be safety. For a few years Langdon challenged Chaplin, Keaton, and Lloyd, but his adult infantilism eventually wearied the public. A brilliant craftsman, he seemed unable to vary his technique.

Jubilo, Jr., 1924. The original Our Gang—Mary Kornman, Mickey Daniels, Joe Cobb, Farina, and Jackie Condon—all now grown up and some of them gathered to their fathers, but again entertaining youngsters through their rebirth on television.

163

The Open Trail, 1925, with Jack Hoxie.

The Pioneer Scout, 1928.

WESTERNS

THE BOY FROM MIX RUN

William S. Hart's films began to earn less money after 1920. Hart himself remained personally popular but exhibitors complained that his pictures were old-fashioned. Finally, Paramount asked Hart to relinquish control over the story and direction of his films and to appear as a star in vehicles supervised by others. Hart would not agree. What they were asking him to give up was just what he had worked hard to put into his films, old-fashioned or not. He was well aware of the difference between the romantic and melodramatic conception of the Old West and his own version of it; he rejected *The Covered Wagon* on the ground that corralling a wagon train in a blind box canyon in Indian country, or swimming oxen across a river with their neck yokes on were "errors that would make a Western man refuse to speak to his own brother." Paramount, however, was firm in its insistence on a new policy and, rather than give in, Hart let his contract with them lapse. Two years later, in his own production for United Artists release, he tried

a comeback. A "one-half life size" bronze statue (opposite page) of William S. Hart was donated by the star to the best bronco buster at the 1926 Cheyenne rodeo, as a half-hearted publicity gesture for *Tumbleweeds*. It didn't help. Nothing helped. The limp reception of the film proved conclusively that the new audiences of the 1920s were no longer interested in the actualities of the old West.

The Western star who succeeded Hart in popularity was a man whose background was very much like Hart's. Tom Mix was born at Mix Run in Clearfield County, Pennsylvania, January 6, 1880, and went west at an early age. Before he was twenty-five he had been Sheriff of Montgomery County, Kansas, and Washington County, Oklahoma; a Deputy U. S. Marshal in Oklahoma; and had spent three years as a Texas Ranger. He knew his section of the West as intimately as Hart had known the Sioux country. Yet it was Mix who created the male dream world, which Hollywood sold to the world as the American West.

The Bearcat, 1922, with Hoot Gibson.

The Pioneer Scout.

The Deadline, 1926, with Bob Custer and Nita Cavaleri.

The Covered Wagon, 1923. The wagon train encamps by the trading post.

WESTERN EPICS

The success of *The Covered Wagon* in the early Twenties brought a vogue of "epic" Westerns which momentarily eclipsed the standard Western star vehicle. Perhaps for once in the history of the movies the word *epic* should not be put in quotes in reference to these productions. In the simplicity and poetry of their images, they truly reflected the national saga of the winning of the West. In them, the pioneers crossed the plains, the daring Pony Express riders established communication with the distant East, the tarriers built the Union Pacific railroad and united the shores of the continent. In Europe as well as America they had deep appeal. Their events mirrored the strong impulse which had drawn the millions to cross the ocean in search of a new life in the New World.

The Covered Wagon. Ethel Wales as the mother crumbles the rich black loam of Oregon between her fingers. Jesse Lasky is credited with inserting this scene after the picture was completed, to provide emotional discharge and the feeling of triumph over the long hardships of the pioneers.

"Drill, ye tarriers, drill." *The Iron Horse,* 1924, John Ford's epic of the building of the Union Pacific.

The Pony Express, 1925. Ricardo Cortez brings the mail through during an Indian attack on a frontier town.

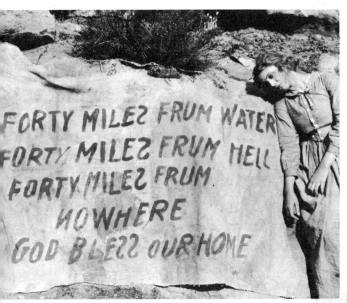

Tigerman, 1918. Jane Novak, lost, finds a discouraging sign.

The Pioneer Scout, 1928. Indians attack the wagon train.

167

Tom Mix in the white hat and suit he made the uniform of the Hollywood cowboy of the Twenties.

Tom Mix about the time he joined the U. S. Army to fight in the Spanish-American War in the Philippines.

TOM MIX

Tom Mix's life of adventure began when, at the age of eighteen, he joined the Army. He saw service in the Philippines during the Spanish-American War, in China during the Boxer Rebellion, and drifted to South Africa to get in on the fun of the Boer War. It was natural when he returned to this country that he should gravitate to the wildest remaining part of the West, the Oklahoma territory. In 1910, the Selig Company came to Oklahoma to make Westerns and hired him to supply locations and cowboy extras. Soon he was acting for them. Thus three years before William S. Hart made his first film, Tom Mix was already a Western star, although a minor one.

It was not long before he became very major indeed. In 1918 he signed a contract with William Fox which, a decade later, was netting him $20,000 a week. On this salary Mix lived like a rajah of old. His vast estate eclipsed even Pickfair. He loaded his wife with jewels and showered gifts on his small daughter Thomasina in full view of the publicity cameras. His collection of fancy boots and fancier costumes reflected the tastes of a cowboy on a spree. Even at formal dinners, he wore his familiar white suit and cowboy boots. As the Twenties wore on, the off-screen personality of this "King of the Cowboys" began to merge with his professional self. The frontier community life that Hart had labored to re-create on the screen was gradually stylized into a never-never land featuring the exploits of a cowpuncher who never punched any cows and who might as well have been called Robin Hood as Tom Mix.

As the country moved further in time from its memories of the real West, and as Hollywood's West became familiar and standardized, Mix became a curious figure on the national scene. Yet publicity stills of the country's leading exponent of virile action—and spotless honor—drinking in Hollywood night clubs, hobnobbing with nobility in Europe, and dancing with debutantes did not disillusion his admirers.

When talkies came in, Westerns were prematurely pronounced dead, and Mix retired to enjoy his large fortune. Two years later Universal enticed him back to the screen, but in 1932, after a series of falls from his horse, the 52-year-old star left the screen for good. Mostly for his own amusement, he toured the country intermittently during the Thirties with "Tom Mix's Circus." In 1940 he was killed in an automobile smash-up. Thanks to an interminable comic strip which uses his name, Tom Mix continues today to thrill small fry born long after the end of his career.

Tom Mix, a Lochinvar of the Plains, snatches Billie Dove from her wedding in *The Lucky Horseshoe*, 1925.

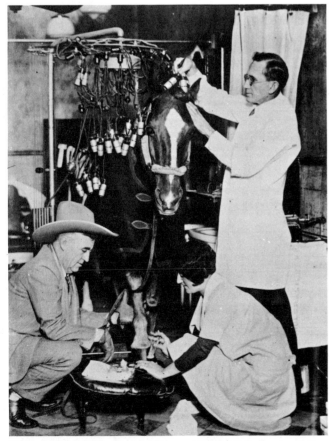

The studio caption says: "Tony, Tom Mix's horse, got a manicure and permanent wave in preparation for his appearance at the Paramount Theater, New York."

Tom Mix about 1919, with Victoria Forde, his leading woman and second wife.

The Law Forbids, 1924. Baby Peggy reunited Robert Ellis and Elin[o

Three Sinners, 1928. Even Pola Negri had to yearn over children occasionally to keep audience "sympathy."

Happiness Ahead, 1928. The power of a good woman: Colleen Moore teaches gangster Edmund Lowe to pray on their wedding night.

Standing in the rain, bedraggled Belle Bennett watches the weddin[g of her daughter, Lois Moran, to wealthy Douglas Fairbanks, Jr., i[n Samuel Goldwyn's supreme epic of mother love, *Stella Dallas*, 192[5

air at the very verge of divorce. The chief function of screen moppets.

GOODNESS

The Puritan tradition dies hard. Even in the Jazz Age, the screen continued to pay the wages of virtue, though the theme became a minor one. But kiddies from six to sixty are always with us, and for them producers continued occasionally to purvey invincible morality and ineffable domestic bliss much as they had a decade earlier.

The Man Who Had Everything, 1921. Kindly old Alec B. Francis, who, in spite of blindness, poverty, or other handicaps, was happier than anybody and solved all problems through love and faith.

The Man Who Fights Alone, 1924. The caption says: "The Miracle of Love when John Marble (William Farnum) can walk again in the woods with his wife (Lois Wilson) and their baby (Dawn O'Day)." This incredibly named tyke grew up to be the lovely Anne Shirley.

171

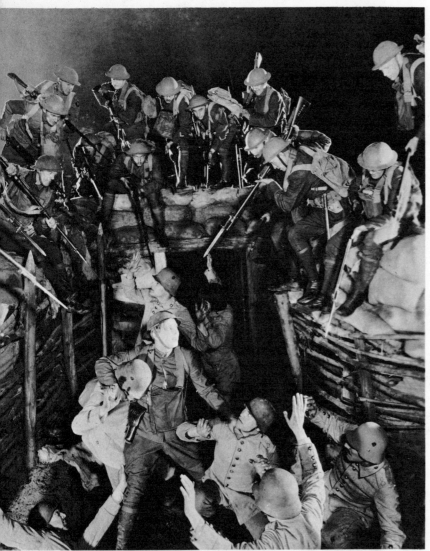

Shootin' for Love, 1923. Fighting Duke Travis (Hoot Gibson), pride of the A.E.F., subdues a trenchful of the Boche singlehanded, though with considerable moral support.

The Standard Ingredients

To classify as a legitimate war picture, each film had to have behind-the-lines humor and during-the-battle heroism, even when the most poignant tragedy climaxed the story; and if you could find a way to insert some grim Prussians or beautiful spies, so much the better.

Three Faces East, 1926. The Kaiser rewards a beautiful double agent, Jetta Goudal, in the most famous of spy dramas. William II was as usual portrayed by Rupert Julian, who took time off from his directorial work whenever someone was needed to impersonate the monarch.

Rookies, 1927, with Karl Dane and George K. Arthur. Behind-the-front humor was a staple in routine war films.

WAR
IN RETROSPECT

The war films of 1917-18 had been filmed far from the front by men who knew little of modern war, and their routine heroics and humor were continued in formula films through the early Twenties. Only when actual veterans like Laurence Stallings, John Monk Saunders, William Wellman, and Dick Grace got into film-making did Hollywood movies begin to render the real flavor of what was to a whole generation of Americans the most overwhelming experience of their lives. Of all the films they originated, *The Big Parade* was and remains the outstanding achievement. King Vidor's filming of the battle scenes in Laurence Stallings' story so excited the producer, Irving Thalberg, that he suggested that they be lengthened and featured in the film above its romance and comedy. Vidor was deliberately trying to introduce a new view of modern war and especially of infantry fighting. From much screening of wartime newsreels and Signal Corps records, he had observed that the pace of men moving into combat has a characteristic rhythm, which he imitated for the camera, and he cut his battle sequences at the same measured pace. The result was an illusion of experience and close participation in the action still unique in fictional war films.

The Big Parade did not, like plays and novels written by intellectuals, debunk war or deplore its causes. Both its artistic strength and its immense popular appeal stemmed from a certain neutral outlook, the viewpoint of the ordinary soldier to whom war may be hell but who is not concerned with whether it is morally or socially wrong. Vidor himself has described the picture he tried to paint: "A man walks through the war and looks at it, neither a pacifist nor a soldier, he simply goes through and has a look and is pulled into these experiences."

In addition to the authenticity of its battle scenes, *The Big Parade* portrayed with acute realism the affection amounting to love which grows up between men under combat conditions, and the frenzy of women parted from their lovers in the shadow of death. No one who has seen it will ever forget the scene in which Renee Adoree clings first to John Gilbert's boot and then to the truck which is carrying him away, in a compulsive attempt to prevent the inevitable.

"... In making contact with the enemy, the activity seems—to the soldiers engaged in it—brisk at the start, and then slows down as the tension grows. King Vidor has managed to suggest, with startling success, the second stage or slowing down. The long march through the woods succeeds in imitating the communal pace as it declines and intensifies into what has been called 'the ultimate loneliness of contact.' This loneliness is not actual, but grows from a state of depression intense enough to obliterate the sense of time. Most infantrymen will insist, however, that it is an absolute experience, for although friends are only a helping hand away, that hand may never be raised, since the line must keep its broken order and unbroken pace."

—ALISTAIR COOKE

173

In a famous scene, Gilbert, the American dough-boy, teaches the French girl, Renee Adoree, the technique of chewing gum.

John Gilbert starred in minor films for William Fox before *The Big Parade* brought out the dynamic magnetism which made him the top male star until the end of the silent era.

Tom O'Brien, John Gilbert, and Karl Dane, the three famous buddies of *The Big Parade*.

**THE
BIG
PARADE**

"What price glory now?" cries Leslie Fenton in the famous dugout scene, while McLaglen and Lowe bind their wounded and count their dead.

WHAT
PRICE
GLORY

In the Twenties two sweet old ladies attended a performance of the Broadway version of *What Price Glory*. At the final curtain, one said, "Shall we get the hell out of here?" and the other replied, "As soon as I find my goddamn glasses." This sulphurous aspect of the original was eliminated from the film version, which also often seemed less an antiwar picture than a portrayal of the amorous antics of Captain Flagg and Sergeant Quirt. In this it was so successful that audiences were given more of their adventures in subsequent films, including one of the biggest hits of all time, *The Cockeyed World*, 1929. But there's no mistaking the meaning of the famous scene in which the dying Mother's Boy, Barry Norton, cries out, "Stop the blood! Stop the blood!"

Lilac Time, 1928. Colleen Moore tries to extricate her lover, Gary Cooper, from his crashed plane.

The Dawn Patrol, 1930.

"IT'S SHEER MURDER..."

"It's sheer murder to send a mere boy up in a crate like that" was one of countless clichés familiar to movie fans once Hollywood discovered the spectacular possibilities of airplane combat. If trench fighting was dull to look at in the hands of lesser directors than King Vidor, almost anybody could put on a big show with plenty of airplanes, money, and stunt men, many of whom had been wartime pilots, whose philosophy was that in Hollywood at least they were risking their necks for good pay.

Lilac Time. "Dogfights" between camouflaged planes added pictorial excitement to the airplane films, especially when assisted by the "optical effects" men. *The Dawn Patrol* (left). Ground strafing provided thrills aplenty, particularly for the stunt men.

The Lone Eagle, 1927, with Barbara Kent and Raymond Keane. The studio caption says: "Should she let him sleep peacefully on or awaken and send him perhaps to his death?"

The Dawn Patrol, 1930. Begrimed Commander Richard Barthelmess erases the name of a shot-down pilot from the company roster.

ARMY LIFE, LAFAYETTE ESCADRILLE VERSION

Most of the airplane films were written by John Monk Saunders and directed by William Wellman, with assists from directors Clarence Brown and Howard Hawks, both air enthusiasts. For all five, stunt man Dick Grace risked his neck repeatedly— and broke it once. To routine ground crashes he added crashes in mid-air, crashes in treetops, on rooftops, in water. That he survived is a miracle.

Saunders, Grace and Wellman had all been wartime fliers, and from their romanticized experiences on the screen the movie public learned that the War I flyboys expected imminent death in their canvas-covered crates, that they drowned their anxieties in drink and French babes, and kept a stiff upper lip when the names of their fallen comrades were erased from the squadron roster by the Commander who was always on the verge of nervous breakdown from sending youths to their death.

The line between art and life began to blur when Saunders and Grace cannibalized their experiences in such films as *The Lost Squadron*, 1932, and *Lucky Devils*, 1933. In them, war aces bored with the monotony of peacetime seek excitement in Hollywood as airplane stunt men, and then repeat the escadrille pattern complete with erasure from the blackboard of the names of the fallen.

John Monk Saunders, author, Dick Grace, stunt man, and William Wellman, director, beside a plane which Grace has just crashed for their picture *Wings*, 1927.

The Legion of the Condemned, 1928. The Legion (left) drinks to missing comrades. Francis McDonald, third from left, Gary Cooper, third from right, Barry Norton, extreme right.

Lucky Devils, 1933. The Lucky Devils are ex-army pilots who go to Hollywood after the war to become stunt men. Here Creighton Chaney, William Boyd, William Gargan, and Bob Rose gloomily drink to departed friends.

179

Mary Miles Minter.

Virginia Rappe, star of two-reel comedies, attended a drinking party given by Roscoe "Fatty" Arbuckle and, while there, died of a "chronic pelvic illness." Arbuckle, a former plumber's helper who had risen to great popularity as a comedian, was acquitted by three juries of any responsibility for Miss Rappe's death, but the circumstances surrounding it threw a strange light on the way the movie people spent their enormous earnings.

THE BIG CLEAN-UP

PRESS FIELD DAY

The movie craze drew to Los Angeles not only thousands of girls bent on acting careers, and a host of doubtful characters looking for easy money, but also and in considerable numbers free-lance journalists who smelled sensation. Strange stories involving sex, narcotics, and riotous living began to seep into the national press. Many in the new middle-class screen audiences felt a twinge of righteous resentment at the huge sums being earned by former plumbers and shopgirls turned movie stars. Their feelings crystallized when a sudden series of unrelated events turned vague rumor into startling fact. The never-solved murder of the director William Desmond Taylor revealed unsavory facts about his past life and his associations with two reigning favorites, Mabel Normand and Mary Miles Minter. Miss Minter's indiscreet love letters to the director shattered the public image of her as a girl of spotless purity. Mabel Normand's producer, Mack Sennett, stood by her and she was cleared of any connection with Taylor's death. But shortly thereafter her chauffeur, whom she had invited to join a drinking party at the home of Edna Purviance, Chaplin's leading woman, shot another male guest. That was too much, and the screen's greatest comedienne found herself banned from her profession. Even as the industry reeled from these revelations, the sordid death of Virginia Rappe brought into the limelight Roscoe Arbuckle's custom of holding continuous drinking parties, some said orgies, at the St. Francis Hotel in San Francisco. Arbuckle, like Miss Minter and Miss Normand, was forcibly retired from the screen, and the current films of all three, representing an investment of millions, were banned or withdrawn entirely.

The press had a field day. The Taylor murder case was said at the time to have sold more newspapers, everywhere in the United States, than any previous event. Clubwomen, reformers, and busybodies seized upon the sins of some members of the movie colony as an unlooked-for bonanza, and even the average lay citizen came to regard Hollywood as a cesspool of iniquity.

Be A Movie Player!
Fame, Fortune and Joy of Succeeding Are United in This Newest Avocation

The Unknown and Untried Have Won Laurls With the Experienced Actor-Folk—Fame Has Come on the Wings of a Week's Passing — the Demand Grows —but the Pioneer Days Will Not Tarry!—NOW Is the Golden Time!

Be a movie actor or actress! Join the silent army of favorites of the films! Let millions learn to applaud your appearance on the screen! Be loved and lauded by the mighty public! Be known in the palaces of the great and wealthy and in the cottages of the lowly!

Can you succeed?

Read this interesting, absorbing story— and then look for the answer in your own heart!

Advertisements like this for "Schools of Photoplay Acting" and tales of the quick success before the camera of untrained nonprofessionals lured thousands of young girls to Hollywood. Unable to find work even as shopgirls or waitresses, many of them drifted into prostitution. To avoid the California vagrancy laws they habitually gave their occupation as "movie extra," enabling the newspapers to announce when they got into trouble: "Three Beautiful Film Stars Arrested in Bawdy House."

Will H. Hays (center), first president of the Motion Picture Producers and Distributors of America, with the founding fathers of the organization, set up by the major studios to impose a "dictatorship of virtue" upon the screen.

WILL HAYS

The roar of disapproval over the Arbuckle-Taylor-Minter-Normand sensations had hardly died down when fresh scandal arose in Hollywood. Wallace Reid's untimely death at the age of thirty revealed him to have been a drug addict. That this could have been true of an actor who symbolized healthy normality deeply shocked the nation. Not only zealots but nearly everyone agreed that something would have to be done about Hollywood before it became a national disgrace. The movie magnates were worried and duly penitent. Engrossed in cut-throat competition with one another, they had ignored the intensity of American moral standards.

Recognizing now their own inexperience, they turned to the citadels of righteousness. Acting on the analogy with baseball, they appointed Presbyterian elder Will Hays, then Postmaster-General in Harding's cabinet, as a "czar" with absolute authority to police the morals of the industry and to reform, or rather establish, its public relations.

Hays cleaned house swiftly. The studios inserted "morality clauses" in their contracts which permitted cancellation if players were so much as accused of immorality, while those whose behavior was beyond reform were promptly exiled from the screen. Hays established the Central Casting Agency, through which alone extras can find employment at the studios, and where applicants for registration must pass the scrutiny of a staff of professional sociologists. At the same time that he inaugurated a campaign to induce the press to report Hollywood news without exaggeration, he made it clear to everyone in pictures that their lives must be able to withstand public scrutiny.

In his effort to rehabilitate the industry, Hays then turned to his most powerful weapon, the screen itself. At his suggestion, James Cruze directed for Paramount a fascinating picture called simply *Hollywood,* a Cinderella story in reverse in which the beautiful girl comes to the picture capital and does *not* become a star. Mrs. Wallace Reid's attack on the dope habit, *Human Wreckage,* doubtless also owed something to Hays's inspiration. His most influential ally, however, proved to be none other than Cecil B. De Mille, who had introduced sex to the screen, and who now sought to use pictures as a pulpit. "Having attended to the underclothes, bathrooms, and matrimonial irregularities of his fellow-citizens," said his brother William, "he now began to consider their salvation."

LEFT TO RIGHT:
E. W. Hammons
J. D. Williams
Winfield Sheehan
Cortland Smith
Carl Laemmle
Rufus Cole
William E. Atkinson
Will H. Hays
Robert H. Cochrane
Samuel Goldwyn
Marcus Loew
Adolph Zukor
William Fox
Lewis Selznick
Myron Selznick

Human Wreckage, 1923. With the covert assistance of Will Hays, Mrs. Wallace Reid set out to avenge her husband's death by producing and starring in this anti-narcotics film. Encouraged by its boxoffice success, Mrs. Reid sought further sores on the body politic which required melodramatic disinfection. She pictured the horrors of modern youth in *Broken Laws,* ripped concealing veils from prostitution in *The Red Kimono,* then unaccountably left us to get along as best we could with the evils that remained.

THE TEN COMMANDMENTS

De Mille was the ideal director to rescue the screen from contamination. As a tract for the times, *The Ten Commandments* could not have served the industry's public relations needs better if the script had been written by Will Hays himself. In it, De Mille used his tried-and-true technique of the sermonizing flashback with a new twist. The picture began with an awesomely spectacular retelling of

1. *The Ten Commandments*, 1923. Moses (Theodore Roberts) tells Pharaoh (Charles de Roche) that all the first-born of Egypt will die if Israel is not permitted to depart.

2. Later, Pharaoh wanders through his palace with the body of his son.

3. Miriam (Estelle Taylor) adores the Golden Calf.

184

the flight of the Israelites from Egypt and the engulfing of Pharaoh's pursuing army. This was followed by a modern story which wagged a stern finger at contemporary Americans who had forsaken the Mosaic tenets for the fleshpots of industrial civilization. De Mille's 1956 *Ten Commandments* tells only the Biblical story, leaving contemporary movie-goers to tease out the moral as best they may.

4. The giving of the Law.

5. Moses denounces Miriam for sacrilege and announces the Commandments of God to Israel.

6. De Mille's ancient Egypt was bigger, if not more awe-inspiring, than Griffith's Babylon in *Intolerance*.

THE TEN COMMANDMENTS

7. John MacTavish (Richard Dix), Mother MacTavish (Edythe Chapman), Dan MacTavish (Rod La Rocque), and a waif of the streets (Leatrice Joy) whom the MacTavishes have taken in. Dix, a carpenter, is much under the influence of his Bible-reading mother, but La Rocque, who worships the golden calf of quick millions, decides to leave the religious atmosphere of her house, taking Miss Joy with him as his wife.

8. Sally Lung (Nita Naldi), a "Eurasian adventuress," wheedles a costly bauble from La Rocque, who has grown rich and neglectful of his wife, Miss Joy. Only the audience knows that Miss Naldi has escaped from the leper colony at Molokai.

12. Temporarily hidden from the police in his wife's bed, La Rocque is later killed in a speedboat accident as he races for the Mexican border.

11. Meanwhile, La Rocque, who has contracted leprosy from Miss Naldi, shoots her and flees.

9. Dix tells La Rocque that the sustaining fibers he intends to use in constructing a new cathedral are shoddy, but the latter scoffs.

10. When Mother MacTavish visits the new cathedral, it collapses upon her and kills her. Leatrice Joy, Edythe Chapman, Richard Dix, and Rod La Rocque behold the warning of the Lord's vengeance.

13. The repentant Miss Joy is lectured to by Dix on the folly of breaking the Commandments and worshiping the Golden Calf.

14. Miss Joy and Dix clinch atop a building which Dix is constructing, in a fade-out curiously anticipatory of the final scene of Ayn Rand's and King Vidor's *The Fountainhead*, 1949.

THE
KING OF KINGS

Cecil B. De Mille's first attempt to top his *The Ten Commandments* (the last was to remake it) was to film the life of Christ, *The King of Kings*, 1927. Here he was on dangerous ground, and he took all possible precautions. He kept H. B. Warner, who played Christ, secluded in his dressing room when not actually before the cameras, and with the other players he went much further than did the morality clauses of Mr. Hays. "It would never do," said William de Mille, "to have the Virgin Mary getting a divorce or Saint John cutting up in a night club. Therefore they all signed legal documents which underwrote their behavior and their chastity, it being clearly understood that, although breaking solemn vows taken at the altar was only human, breaking a contract with the Company was really important."

William Boyd as Simon the Cyrenian, takes the cross from the Christus, H. B. War

BEN HUR

Ben Hur, 1926, was filmed for purely commercial reasons, but its religious motif accorded well with Will Hays's campaign. Production was begun in Italy under the old Goldwyn company, but when Louis B. Mayer took charge of the merged Metro-Goldwyn-Mayer corporation, he scrapped most of what there was and reshot it at the M-G-M studio. It cost five million dollars and was generally regarded in the United States as the summit of screen art.

The virtuous Ben Hur maddened by the lure of the siren. Carmel Myers and Ramon Novarro.

188   Carmel Myers as Iras, Francis X. Bushman as Messala.

De Mille was unable to resist the temptation to elevate St. Mary Magdalene (Jacqueline Logan) from streetwalker to elegant courtesan.

The chariot race—Novarro vs. Bushman.

Clara Bow, the IT Girl, epitome of razz-ma-tazz, everybody's dreamboat from 1925 to 1930. Alice White (below) was Clara's closest rival.

Alice White.

Louise Brooks.

Sally O'Neil.

BUT FLAMING YOUTH FLAMED ON

SHEIKS AND SHEBAS

Hollywood's housecleaning did not extend to the movies themselves. Though Will Hays might impose a code of decorum on the (public) conduct of the public's idols, only the boxoffice's message was on-screen behavior, and the boxoffice's message was unmistakable: anything goes. The movies had made themselves a fast transmission belt for Jazz Age ideas, and nothing could arrest the process. In spite of censorial and ministerial protests, the young knew what they wanted to see on the screen, and many of their elders, despite their protestations, wanted to see the same. In a review of the film version of Scott Fitzgerald's *The Beautiful and the Damned, Photoplay* editorialized: "If he depicts life as a series of petting parties, cocktails, mad dancing and liquor on the hip, it is because he sees our youthful generation in those terms . . . it is our youthful fascisti possessing its measure of money and knowledge, fighting against the swing of the pendulum which has brought us the you-must-not era." In short, the said youthful fascisti no longer

cared whether their idols were damned as long as they were also beautiful.

As Valentino's twentieth-century *The Sheik* incarnated the desirable male for American boys, so Betty Blythe's *The Queen of Sheba* captured the imagination of their girl-friends. In an impressive example of the process of popular myth-making, American youth equated these two figures in time —though they were actually separated by two thousand years—on the simple score that both were Oriental and, therefore, ardent and unashamed in their sexuality. After 1921, the former "drugstore cowboy" (the phrase was coined during the earlier vogue of the Western hero) was metamorphosed into a Sheik, and his date became a Sheba. As parents watched their young cultivate sideburns and spit curls, the more reflective among them came to a startled realization that the old molding influences —home, church, school—had been superseded by the silver screen. The rest wished they were young enough to be Sheiks and Shebas themselves.

Donald Keith.

Malcolm McGregor.

Lawrence Gray.

The Stacomb Boys

The hallmark of a home-grown Sheik of the Twenties was hair that was hard and shiny with Brilliantine.

Publicity for *Prodigal Daughters*, 1923. Gloria Swanson proclaims the new creed of youth to her father, Theodore Roberts.

"THE MODERN GENERATION"

The chasm which opened between parents and children during the Twenties was without precedent in American culture. Men and women reared by prewar tenets of morality simply could not understand "the modern generation" which regarded the pursuit of pleasure as life's major purpose and challenged the values of chastity and self-restraint. The parents were not only bewildered but weaponless—authority had departed. The heavy father of tradition might still order his wanton daughter out, out into the storm, but he was more apt to receive a wisecracking comeback than the tear-dimmed repentance in which Lillian Gish had once specialized. All this the movies zealously highlighted in dozens of pictures depicting the conflict of the generations, with ample spicing of the unholy orgies into which Daughter wandered in her search for "freedom from conventions."

Generally she "went too far," and had to be saved and forgiven by Papa in the last reel, but it was a cinch she wasn't going to resume the Victorian shackles Papa held out to her.

Prodigal Daughters. The studio caption says: "J. D. catches his daughters in the act of returning from a ball *after midnight.*"

Prodigal Daughters. "After she has been saved from a shameful fate, Mrs. Forbes clasps a repentant Elinor in her arms while J. D. says, 'Praise God from whom all blessings flow.'" Theodore Roberts, Gloria Swanson, Louise Dresser.

Clara Bow, second from left, and Donald Keith, next, look on at a fraternity initiation in *The Plastic Age*, 1925.

A ukulele was a more indispensable part of a collegian's equipment than a fountain pen in the Golden Twenties. Eddie Phillips in *The Collegians*, 1929.

"YES, WE ARE COLLEGIATE"

If going to Hollywood was the beau ideal of American youth as the booming Twenties boomed on, going to college was a more immediately attainable goal—college conceived not as an institution of learning but as a playground, night club, or as Woodrow Wilson said of Princeton, the best country club in America. Certainly that was the way it looked on the screens of America, and the image received eager acceptance. After all, practically anybody could go to college if he could get the cash or played a good game of football. If not he could always work his way through selling subscrip-

tions or waiting on table as did the hero of *The Collegians*. This remarkable series of two-reel shorts ran uninterruptedly on the screen every week for four years, 1926-1930, to the delight of the Jazz Age adolescents. To their unspoken question—What do you go to college for?—*The Collegians* gave a highly acceptable answer: You go there to learn things—how to drink, how to pet, how to win the big game, and above all, how to meet people who will be useful to you when at last the four years of hedonistic freedom are over and you have to put your nose to the grindstone and make your pile.

The studio caption says: "Reckless youth runs a race with death on their way to a party with Joan Crawford being chauffeured by Douglas Fairbanks, Jr., in her first starring picture, *Our Modern Maidens,* 1929."

SPEED-CRAZY

Of the three principal ingredients of the Jazz Age cocktail—gin, jazz, and gasoline—gasoline was the most novel. The inventors of the horseless carriage thought they were simply improving transportation, but American youth, aided by the screen, soon discovered that the automobile could be turned into a mobile party, petting or otherwise, where illicit activities would be safe from the prying eyes of elders, and where the thrill of speed would heighten those of liquor and sex. "Thanks for the buggy ride" became a typical feminine sneer, and "walking back" and "mad money," realities not to be scoffed at. To-day's hot-rodders are the sinister, yet rather pallid, descendants of these reckless, feckless, possibly witless speedsters, tearing around bound for nowhere. And just as films about hot-rodders today stir doubts of their social value, so pictures about speeding drew feeble censure in the Twenties. But youth wanted to see speed on the screen, and youth was served, not only because it more and more constituted the main body of the movie audience, but, also more and more, because nearly everybody wanted to be young. Apparently the best way to be young was to be foolish.

The wildness of this wild party in *The Mad Whirl*, 1925, is balanced by the sedateness of the bridge-playing matron, center.

WILD PARTIES

"Wild parties" on the screen were distinguishable from "orgies," that other institution of the Twenties, by the fact that they were attended by healthy American youth rather than decadent aristocrats in Wicked Paris or Imperial Russia. They featured a great deal of drinking, dancing, petting, and what must have been an immense amount of noise; it is a mercy that their popularity on the screen did not outlast the silent era. Their structure never varied. As ecstasy reached its height, the screen dissolved into a montage of dancing legs, moaning saxophones, popping corks, and groping hands, followed by a second montage of dead cigarette butts, spilled wine, and guttering candles. The participants were invariably depicted as nursing horrendous hangovers the following day, but quite ready to attend another party scheduled for that very evening, if not afternoon. One thing must be said for the screen's wild parties: nothing staged in real life ever approached them in wildness, as moviegoing youths must have discovered to their disappointment.

Sally O'Neil takes a casual swig from her hip flask as Alice White looks on in a roadhouse scene from *Mad Hour*, 1928.

196

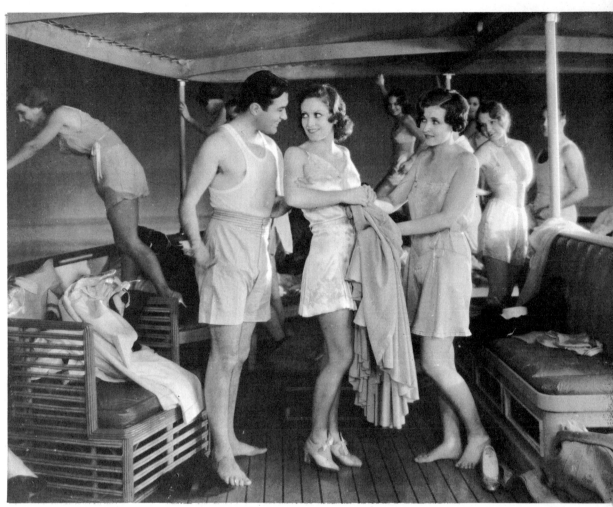

Joan Crawford holds a "lingerie party" on her yacht in *Dance, Fools, Dance,* 1931.

William Haines assists Mae Murray in whatever she is doing with the punch bowl in *Circe the Enchantress,* 1924.

Malcolm McGregor and Jacqueline Logan make a razz-ma-tazz entrance in *The House of Youth,* 1924.

197

Florence Vidor and Lew Cody struggle with that amazing innovation, the radio, in *Husbands and Lovers,* 1924.

Phyllis Haver takes a mud bath. *The Perfect Flapper,* 1924.

"Roll 'em, girls, roll 'em," was the "message" of a popular song of 1926, and of *Rolled Stockings,* 1927, with James Hall and Louise Brooks.

Dorothy Mackaill's "bee-stung" lips, in *The Next Corner,* 1924, exceeded even those of Mae Murray, who claimed exclusive copyright.

FADS AND FASHIONS

The changes which the industrial revolution made possible in American morals and manners were speeded up more by the screen than by any other agency except possibly the automobile. Especially did the movies accelerate the emancipation of women. Cigarette smoking by females was, until about 1900, confined to loose ladies and divorcées. At the end of World War I it was no longer a certain stigma of the sinful life, but was still rigidly confined to the fast and flighty. By 1928 it was a commonplace among flappers even in small-town America; the movies had licensed it. Bobbed hair and short skirts, a moral issue in 1920, were five years later close to compulsory. As women reached out for freedom and power, as the sense spread through the United States that everyone was on the threshold of a richer, freer, and much more exciting life, the movies fed these unformed expectations from a cornucopia of novelties which, trivial in themselves, nevertheless symbolized luxury, adventure, all the values loosely grouped around the word "modern." As soon as one fad lost its freshness another was provided, until at last the only thing distinctive about these ephemeral crazes was their similarity. But the appetite for them did not noticeably diminish during the Twenties. The abundant life was still too new and too shiny.

The airplane wedding was a movie commonplace by the time of *High Flying George*, 1927.

Joan Crawford does her famous Charleston in *Our Dancing Daughters*, 1928.

Moral:

He who would change the face of th
world must build first the little circl
of his own home; who does this in perfec
love has then the whole world at his feet

The final "art" subtitle in *The Face of the World, c.* 1921.

SCREEN ART

"WHY DO THEY DO IT?"

"In her last picture, Leatrice Joy got thrown from her horse and dragged about a mile. When she got up she wasn't even dusty." Such was a typical contribution to the "Why Do They Do It?" department, which ran in *Photoplay*, a leading fan magazine. Audiences of the Teens and early Twenties were constantly confronted with heroes who emerged immaculate from fist fights, heroines rescued from drowning with dry clothing and beautifully marcelled hair, characters who entered the drawing room in evening clothes and left it in golf costumes. Such errors were understandable in this early day, when it was usually necessary to shoot pictures out of sequence. The complicated marvel of "matching" scenes had barely begun.

But what roused the ridicule of the more sophisticated was not the upstart movie's innocent mistakes but its still more naïve pretensions to pictorial artistry and significance. "Bad taste" was the hallmark of the movies in the eyes of many urbanites whose own taste was perhaps of recent acquisition. "Symbolic" scenes and flashbacks, beloved of Mr. De Mille, impressed the hinterland but moved the highbrows to laughter, as did subtitles, which Hollywood, in an effort to mitigate a necessary evil, decked out with moralizing and "art" backgrounds. The seemingly rigid rule that all characters who were ill must wear head bandages regardless of the nature of their malady paid the rent for many a professional jokester. To an objective observer it would have been apparent that these crudities were inevitably part of the growing pains of a new art. But American intellectuals have never been distinguished for kindliness or critical restraint. It was the fashion to despise everything popular and profitable, and the movies were joyously seized upon as Exhibit A of American materialism and ingenuousness. Till the middle of the Twenties, to identify oneself as connected with the motion picture industry was to invoke pained reserve or open ribbing.

A symbolic scene depicting the sacrifice of Mae Murray on the Altar of Dollars in an unidentified film.

The composition and design of this scene from *Flesh and the Devil,* 1927, reveal the influence of German taste and studio craftsmanship on American films of the Twenties.

THE GERMAN INVASION

In 1919, defeated Germany's first bid to regain her export market was with films. Hungry Berliners furnished cheap extras for mob scenes and ambitious young directors were given free rein to create films designed to lead the world in artistry and at the same time to out-Hollywood Hollywood in all that was *kolossal.* So great was the distaste for all things German that the first of these films to be imported into the United States were labeled "Scandinavian" by their distributors, but the advanced techniques and bold sensationalism of the German productions found their intended marks. For most of the Twenties, German films were the vogue with such of the American intelligentsia as did not despise the movies in toto, as well as, for a time, with general audiences.

There arrived first a series of "historical" spectacles—*Passion, Gypsy Blood, One Arabian Night*—directed by Ernst Lubitsch and usually starring Pola Negri and Emil Jannings. In them, the cynical Lubitsch used history merely as a backdrop for boudoir intrigue. But in an era when history was being debunked by everyone from Lytton Strachey to Henry Ford, these films were thought to "humanize" delightfully the stiff and wooden figures of

historical personalities. The second wave of German films was much less to popular taste. Somber, unrelieved, they reflected the pessimism of a disintegrating society. But their use of arresting camera angles and of a mobile camera as a leading stylistic motif worried Hollywood. By their side, the best American product looked standardized and rigid.

Studio heads, smarting under the criticisms of the eggheads of the Twenties and the invidious comparisons between Hollywood vulgarity and German taste and skill, decided that if you can't lick 'em, jine 'em, or better still get them to jine you. Lured by what appeared to them incredible salaries, German artists and artisans crossed the Atlantic in a steady stream. Pola Negri led the van, quickly followed by Ernst Lubitsch, Dmitri Buchowetzsky, F. W. Murnau, Carl Mayer, Emil Jannings, Lya de Putti, Conrad Veidt, Erich Pommer, Michael Curtiz, and many others. Besides enriching the American roster of talent, this had the beneficial side-effect of weakening the German studios, sole effective rivals of U. S. films in the world market. The German "invasion" of Hollywood was really more like an elegant kidnaping.

Meanwhile, Hollywood absorbed and surpassed

"Expressionismus"—The Cabinet of Dr. Caligari, 1919. Hailed as the first truly "artistic" film, it owed its artistry more to stage expressionism than to the cinema.

Typically bad camera angle. *The Thirteenth Chair,* 1929.

the German technical advance by osmosis. The chief features of the Teutonic style were a continuously moving camera and unusual camera angles. Both devices were designed to make the audience identify with the protagonist, to share his point of view on the screen. American film-makers at first copied both indiscriminately and without regard to their dramatic purpose. The camera would follow an actor as he got up, shaved, dressed, breakfasted, and walked out the front door, though the only significant part of the action was his leaving the house; cameras peeked at actors from lampshades, bookcases, chests of drawers, and especially from the floor, leading Robert E. Sherwood to say of one film, "The camera angles throughout afford an excellent and uninterrupted view of the heroine's nostrils." But the eager artisans of California learned fast. They soon relegated camera movement and camera angles to their proper place in the repertory of film devices, and as rapidly absorbed the German lessons in design and lighting. Sets remained luxurious but became less "busy" with ornament, costumes achieved an expensive simplicity, light and shade were used for dramatic purposes. From about 1927, few technical boners appeared in American films.

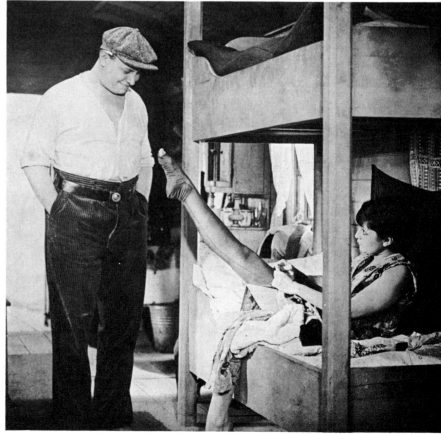

The censors passed this charming domestic scene from *Variety,* 1926, only on condition that Lya de Putti be transformed into Emil Jannings' wife, rather than his mistress.

The scent of her furs conjures up a vision of Thomas Meighan's inamorata, Bebe Daniels, while his lawful wife, Gloria Swanson, desponds, in Cecil B. De Mille's *Why Change Your Wife?*, 1920.

William S. Hart plays his own twin brother in a not entirely successful example of double exposure.

Her husband's aristocratic ancestors look sneeringly at the humbly born heroine in this "vision scene" from *Saturday Night,* 1922.

MOVIE MAGIC

The discovery, in early movie days, that the exposure of the same strip of film twice would result in the second image being superimposed on the first opened a hitherto closed door to the world of fantasy and the supernatural. Directors went hog-wild. Not only "straight" fantasies but perfectly ordinary dramas and comedies were filled with instances of this kind of movie magic which obliterated the boundaries of time and space. Cecil B. De Mille especially delighted in inserting highly symbolic and moralistic "vision scenes" in his gorgeous photoplays. Any girl in any picture about to take her first false step was likely to be visited by the shadowy image of her mother, hands clasped in prayer. Any boy about to succumb to the lure of a woman of ill repute was apt to find the outlines of his childhood sweetheart superimposing themselves over those of the seductress. Anybody at all whose furrowed brow denoted deep thought might fade from view beneath the acting-out of his thoughts.

The public gradually led Hollywood away from this tricky use of the powers of the medium. In silent films, double exposure was useful, often indispensable, in conveying ideas which only dialogue could have transmitted otherwise. But even in silent films, full-scale fantasies were rarely successful, and they were completely incompatible with the hundred-per-cent realism introduced by sound. The reaction went so far that even horror films of the Thirties continued to avoid double exposure. Its last conspicuous use was in Robert Montgomery's *Here Comes Mr. Jordan,* 1941 (one of the few genuinely popular fantasies) where, after long disuse, it pleased through novelty and skillful application.

MOVIE
MAGIC

In the early Twenties cameras were taken to any and every location, no matter how distant or dangerous, for the sake of an effective scene. Later, as the German influence grew, it became more customary and often less costly to re-create exterior scenes in the studios.

A train wreck is re-created in the studio for *The Crash*, 1928.

George Fitzmaurice directing Colleen Moore and Gary Cooper in a love scene from *Lilac Time*, 1928, while musicians play "mood music."

First National achieved the seeming ultimate in movie magic with *The Lost World*, 1925 (right). Clay miniatures of prehistoric animals appeared larger than humans.

Shooting a horse race for *Silks and Saddles*, 1928.

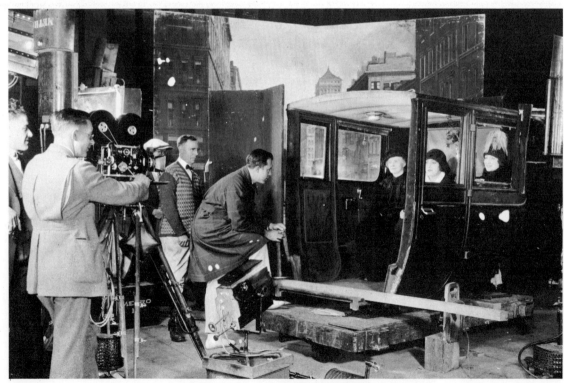

King Vidor directing Edith Yorke, Laurette Taylor and Hedda Hopper in *Happiness*, 1924.

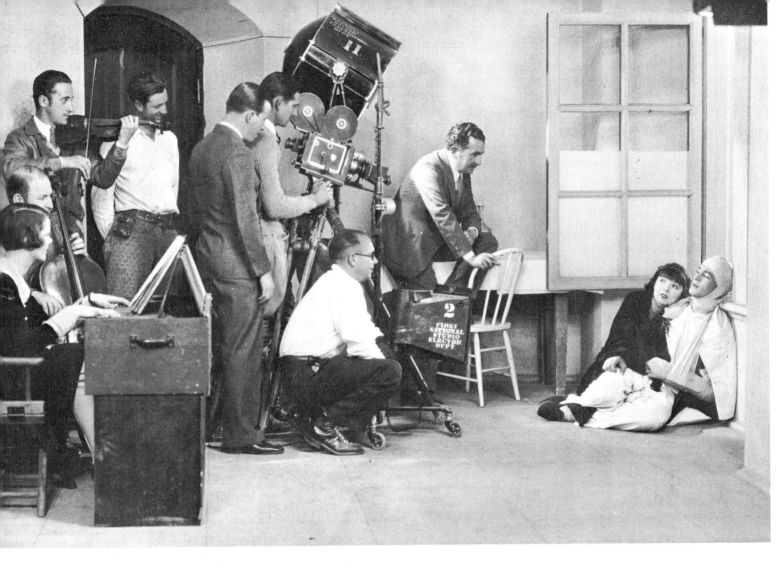

DECLINE OF D. W. GRIFFITH

As the mechanics of film-making progressed throughout the Twenties, they seemed to pass by a lone figure which once had dominated the entire screen. D. W. Griffith began the decade with great expectations. Freed of past obligations, a partner in United Artists, he sold stock to the public in his own company, D. W. Griffith, Inc., built an elaborate studio at Mamaroneck, and set out to surpass his own unbeaten record. He wanted to make films of weight and substance, films which would realize the instructional and propagandist possibilities which he had been the first to divine in the medium. Through motion pictures, history would come to life—he would film the French Revolution, the American War for Independence, and watching these films the millions would learn the origins and sacredness of their liberties. Master of the craft, he determined to consecrate it to its highest function.

But to finance all this, it would be necessary to make a few potboilers first. He began by buying the rights to the antique stage melodrama, *Way Down East*, for $175,000. For this he was ridiculed; people said that filming it would be "like trying to make a grand opera out of 'The Old Oaken Bucket.'" But the Old Master turned out to be right after all. *Way Down East* swept the country. In it he again at-

tained the vitality, pace, and structural magnificence of *The Birth of a Nation* and *Intolerance*. *Way Down East* proved, or seemed to prove, that it did not matter how leaden the subject matter, the Griffith touch would transmute it to pure gold.

Among the films of weight and importance, *Isn't Life Wonderful?*, 1924, was a remarkable topical picture about current inflation and unemployment in Germany, filmed on the spot. Forcibly it conjured up the tragedies of defeat and hunger in Central Europe after the First World War, but its financial failure ended Griffith's independence. Before it, he had made a series of films, including his saga of the French Revolution, *Orphans of the Storm*, 1922, and his tribute to our own Revolution, *America*, 1924, into which he had injected successively stronger doses of melodrama, violence, and a rather unpalatable kind of sex.

Was history, after all, not enough? If not, what was giving this increasingly unfashionable and even distasteful shape to the Griffith films of the Twenties? James R. Quirk of *Photoplay* magazine thought the cause was Griffith's isolation from Hollywood and from contemporary film-makers and film-making. In 1924 he boldly addressed Griffith in an editorial: "You have made yourself an anchorite at

"Out, out, into the storm!"

This classic group from *Way Down East*, 1920, includes, left to right, Burr McIntosh, Kate Bruce, Lowell Sherman, Lillian Gish, Mary Hay, Creighton Hale, Edgar Nelson, Richard Barthelmess, and Porter Strong.

Mamaroneck . . . your pictures shape themselves toward a certain brutality because of this austerity . . . your refusal to face the world is making you more and more a sentimentalist. You see passion in terms of cooing doves or the falling of a rose petal . . . your lack of contact with life makes you deficient in humor. In other words, your splendid unsophistication is a menace to you—and to pictures."

But Griffith's "splendid unsophistication" was nothing new. It had always been a leading characteristic of his style and was largely responsible for his early success. It was audiences that were changing. Even the DAR, the American Legion, and other representatives of the upper middle class on whose support he had counted, seemed more interested in films called *Dancing Mothers* than in films called *America*. The end was nearing. A casting up of accounts in 1924 revealed that D. W. Griffith, Inc., was living on the great profits of *Way Down East*. All subsequent films had incurred losses—losses due in part to the proud but uneconomic practice of maintaining a costly studio for the production of one picture a year, with the overhead rolling merrily along when no pictures at all were in progress.

Bank loans for further productions were no longer forthcoming. Griffith shook himself, abandoned Ma-

maroneck, signed with Paramount, and set out to regain his receding prestige. If "jazz" pictures were what "they" wanted now jazz pictures he would give them. The result was films which looked like slick copies of the work of his juniors and inferiors.

Further humiliation was in store for the Master. In 1927 he returned to United Artists, no longer as a producer but as a glorified wage-slave working for his former partners. In 1930 he turned to history again for his first sound film, *Abraham Lincoln,* and his talent flared up one last time. This sober film, remarkable in this transition period, earned him selection as the best director of 1930, an honor he had been without for many a year. But *Lincoln* did not appeal to audiences of the first year of the depression, and United Artists refused to finance further pictures. In desperation, Griffith rounded up what money he could and produced *The Struggle,* 1931. A contemporary reviewer wrote: "It's a struggle to have to report that D. W. Griffith, who directed some of the greatest pictures, now presents one of the worst."

To save what could be saved of Griffith's reputation, United Artists withdrew *The Struggle.* But it was too late. The sound era was in full swing. D. W. Griffith—who's he? Oh yes, of course . . .

Nanook of the North, 1922.

210

Moana, 1926.

ROBERT FLAHERTY

In 1921, a blond young giant from the north descended upon the New York offices of the film companies. Robert Flaherty, an explorer for mineral deposits, had spent twelve years with the Eskimos of the Hudson Bay country, and at the end of that period had made a film of their life. Travelogues had already been relegated to a minor place on the screen bill of fare, and nobody listened when Flaherty insisted that his picture of Nanook the Eskimo would open a new world to movie audiences. More by accident than by design, the redoubtable Roxy booked *Nanook of the North* into the Capitol Theater as the lower half of a double bill which featured Harold Lloyd's *Grandma's Boy*. He was stunned by the reviews. Nanook not only opened a new world, it was a new kind of film. Previous travelogues had sketched random aspects of the lives of primitive people. *Nanook* went to the heart of Eskimo life simply by chronicling the day-to-day struggle for existence of one man and his family. The timeless, classic flavor of this unique picture is most fully suggested by Flaherty's explanation of it to the people of the island of Sava'ii, when Jesse Lasky sent him to Samoa to make a film of Polynesian life like the one he had made of Eskimo life. To explain his purpose to the Samoans, Flaherty wrote a booklet about *Nanook* which was translated into the native tongue. Retranslated from the Samoan, his words were:

"This picture tells the story of the conduct and daily lives of the Eskimo people who live in a country where the water is frozen and covered with snow, near to the North Pole, as our own country is near to the equator. That country has no trees, no fruits or eatable plants. The animals which creep on the frozen sea, these the people kill every day to keep them alive.

"This chief, Mr. Flaherty, lived with Eskimos and imitated their customs and their conduct and dressed in their kind of clothes, made of the skin of the great white quadruped known as the bear of the North Pole. He made this picture because love overflowed in his heart for the people of this country, on account of their kindliness and their bravery, and also on account of their receiving him well, and because they look very happy every day of their lives, in a life most difficult to live in the whole world.

"The high chiefs in New York, the big village in America, they saw that Mr. Flaherty had made a very useful thing; so they gathered together in council and expressed themselves like this: 'Such pictures as this will create love and friendship among all the people of the world. Then misunderstanding and quarrels will end.'

"Then the council of high chiefs in New York prepared a great feast for Mr. Flaherty and told him to make a picture like the picture of the story of Nanook. And so Mr. Flaherty has come here to Samoa to find the genuine descendants of the pure Polynesian race of ancient times, and also their good customs, as they were in the days before the missionaries and traders came to spread their customs in Samoa."

Such an elevated view of the mission of motion pictures was not shared by everyone. The aforesaid high chiefs were daunted by *Moana*, the picture which Flaherty brought back from Samoa. The drama of Nanook's struggle to live had been as clear and strong as the contrasting blacks and whites of the old orthochromatic stock on which it was made. The structure of the new picture, instead of "another *Nanook*," was as delicate as the range of tones in its panchromatic photography. *Moana* failed to find an audience comparable to the one which had responded so warmly to *Nanook*. Still impressed with that first picture's record, Hollywood gave Flaherty several chances to adapt himself to the boxoffice but he was both unwilling and unable to compromise. He wanted to film the life of the peoples of the earth and that was all he wanted. Soon there were no more jobs for him in the United States.

But in England, the Scotch educator John Grierson, infatuated with the possibilities Flaherty had opened up, coined the term "documentary film" to describe the new kind of picture which the former explorer had created. Invited abroad by Grierson, Flaherty found the chance to make his great *Man of Aran* and *Elephant Boy*. Returning to America, he made *The Land* under New Deal auspices and *Louisiana Story* under those of Standard Oil, before his death in 1951. Meanwhile, under Grierson's leadership, a world-wide "documentary film movement" had grown up. Scores of young men dedicated themselves to the use of the Flaherty method for purposes of social enlightenment, and Flaherty found himself, considerably to his amusement, "the father of the documentary film."

Documentary films came into their own in World War II, but on the record to date no other maker of them has yet approached Flaherty's success in exploring and disclosing the basic patterns of human existence. He has left behind him not only the grand gallery of his films and the romance of a life led with proud distinction, but also an insistent sense that he and he alone has used the motion picture camera to its fullest capacity.

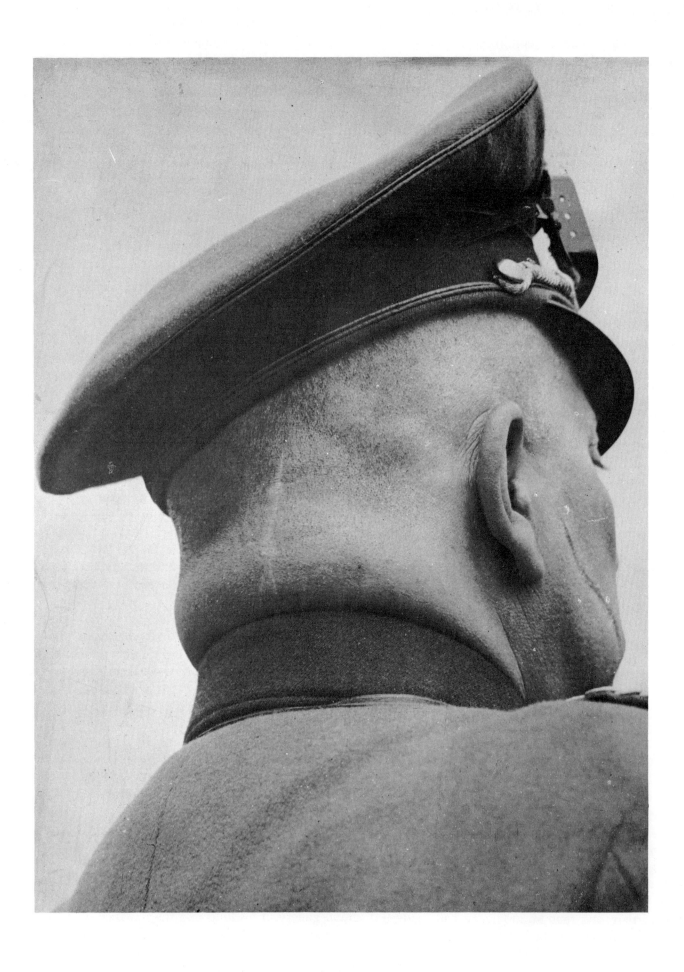

ERICH VON STROHEIM

Erich von Stroheim's origins are not clear (he claimed to have been a member of Franz Joseph's Imperial Guard). It is a fact that, for reasons best known to himself, he emigrated to the United States about 1913 and earned a precarious living as dishwasher, trackwalker and package-wrapper while he learned English. He turned up in Hollywood in the middle Teens, where Griffith gave him work as an extra and technical adviser. World War I was a bonanza to him because, though Austrian to the core, he could play Prussian officers to the life. To millions of Americans he became "the man you love to hate," the very image of the hideous Hun.

When the war ended there seemed little future for him. Somehow he persuaded Carl Laemmle to permit him to star in and direct his own story, *Blind Husbands,* 1919. It was at once apparent that an important talent had arrived. Stroheim's handling of his actors, his camera placement and cutting derived from Griffith, but here was an insistence and intensity which bespoke an individual vision of the world. That vision was certainly a novelty to movie audiences. They were familiar enough with the wickedness of Paris, the desperations of Monte Carlo, and the infidelities of *Alt Wien* as routinely portrayed by Hollywood, but Stroheim's versions of these worlds had a detailed, firsthand intimacy which carried new conviction. This was, obviously, the straight dope on European decadence. His films portrayed successively the prewar world dancing heedlessly on the volcano; the blindness and confusion of wartime society; and finally, pleasure-mad postwar Europe in full disintegration.

Stroheim's first two pictures were profitable. They also cost a good deal. When Stroheim began *Merry Go Round,* 1923, Irving Thalberg, then rising to power at Universal, decided to keep a sharp eye on proceedings. He found Stroheim insisting that, when a bell-pull was required for a scene, the pull be wired to a real bell which actually rang for the silent camera. He discovered that the director had ordered silk underdrawers with the monogram of the Imperial Guard for the Guardsmen in his picture, even though they would never be shown in less than full uniform. When Thalberg heard that Stroheim had (reputedly) spent three days teaching the Hollywood extras who played these Guardsmen how to salute in the correct Austrian manner, for a shot that would last a few seconds on the screen, Thalberg halted production, fired Stroheim, and turned over the direction to Rupert Julian, who finished *Merry Go Round.* In the released version, it was possible to tell accurately which scenes were Stroheim's and which Julian's.

As actor, Stroheim created an image of the lascivious, cruel, elegant German officer which both repelled and attracted postwar audiences.

As director, Stroheim would spend days teaching Hollywood extras like these how to salute in the correct Austrian manner for a minor scene.

"THERE'S A MADMAN IN CHARGE"

For reasons wrapped in obscurity, the Goldwyn Company next hired Stroheim and, even more incomprehensibly, gave him carte blanche to realize his old dream of filming Frank Norris' novel, *McTeague*. Stroheim was determined to film the novel exactly as written, page by page. He took his company to the actual location, San Francisco, where he bought a lodginghouse to use as his principal set, tearing off the outside walls of the rooms in order to shoot by natural daylight.

This amazing experiment emerged from the cameras in some fifty reels. Stroheim reduced it to twenty-four reels—about four hours' running time —and announced that it was finished. His employers were stunned. While production was under way, the old Goldwyn Company had merged with the Metro and Mayer picture companies, and Louis B. Mayer was in effective control of the studio. He had hired Stroheim's old nemesis, Irving Thalberg, as his second in command and Thalberg once more took the director's picture away from him. He reduced it to a neat ten-reel feature called *Greed*. Stroheim never saw *Greed*.

This ten-reel released version is an abrupt and fractured film. Continuity gaps are bridged by long subtitles, and the characters of Trina and Mac develop jerkily. But they are Trina and Mac, two living people, to everyone who saw the film. It quivered with vitality, with love and hate for the human condition. Though only a fragment of what Stroheim intended and realized, *Greed* is numbered among the screen's few masterpieces.

With the possible exception of *Intolerance*, it was also the screen's greatest flop d'estime. Audiences were not indifferent to it or bored by it—they actively hated it. People felt strangely threatened by it. As Paul Rotha wrote, "Americans frankly disliked it; its moral that money was worthless either roused their consciences uncomfortably or was passed over unseen."

Irving Thalberg showed his caliber when, after jettisoning *McTeague*, he continued to employ Stroheim. He proposed that he direct *The Merry Widow*, with Mae Murray and John Gilbert. Stroheim loaded every rift with Stroheim ore. Much that he shot had to be excised from the finished version of *The Merry Widow*. He protested, and Thalberg again fired him. *The Merry Widow* was a great success, but Stroheim was jobless.

P. A. Powers then picked him up and let him film his own script, *The Wedding March*. *The Wedding March* probably came closer to realizing Stroheim's ideal of what he wanted to put on the screen than any of his other films. Intended to be the last

word on the degeneracy and resulting collapse of Austria-Hungary, it was just that. But, again, he shot it in thirty reels, before production was halted by his alarmed backers. And, again, the picture was taken out of his hands and edited down to less than half its proposed length before release.

Things grew grim. Nobody was quite willing to chance it again. Then Gloria Swanson hired him to direct his own script, *Queen Kelly*, starring herself. For years they told conflicting stories of what happened. Stroheim says that all went swimmingly until one day, at the end of a scene, Miss Swanson said, "Excuse me, I have to make a phone call," left the set, and never came back. The star says that she was so eager to be directed by a man who apparently could get a great performance out of anybody that she bought the story unfinished and began production with the end not yet in sight. It concerned a pretty girl in prewar Germany who was seduced by an army officer destined to be the consort of the queen of a petty principality. Their amour discovered, the queen drives Miss Swanson from the palace in her nightgown. This much had been shot when the star inquired of her director-author what came next.

He explained. It seems that Kitty Kelly was next to learn that her dear old aunt in German East Africa had died and left all her worldly goods to her forsaken niece. When Kitty goes to Dar-Es-Salaam to collect, she discovers that her inheritance is a chain of brothels. The star-producer says that when she learned this she realized that even if the picture was completed it could not be shown in the United States, and phoned her backers that she must stop production because "There's a madman in charge."

That was about the end. Once more, in the early talkie years, Fox entrusted Stroheim with the direction of a film, *Walking Down Broadway*. It was finished in 1932, in thirty-some reels. *Walking Down Broadway* was largely reshot by another director and released in 1933 as *Hello Sister*, without directorial credits.

For several years thereafter Stroheim existed precariously in Hollywood, selling a few ideas, acting a few parts. It was hand to mouth. In 1935, he cabled desperately to Sergei Eisenstein, CAN YOU GET ME A JOB IN MOSCOW? Shortly thereafter, Jean Renoir brought him to France to play the prison commandant in the brilliant *La Grande Illusion*. He made Paris his headquarters, starring in French films and occasionally returning to Hollywood. Stroheim received the French Legion of Honor shortly before his death in 1957.

Death in the desert. In the final scenes of *Greed*, Jean Hersholt and Gibson Gowland find themselves without water, their packhorse dead, in the middle of Death Valley.

A corseted Stroheim bites the hand of one of his partners in crime in *Foolish Wives,* while she attempts to remove his ear. She is none other than "the ever-popular Mae Busch."

The Wedding March, 1928. While Erich von Stroheim makes love to a cafe entertainer in a rose garden, his father, the Archduke, meets with Vienna's corn-plaster king in a brothel to arrange a marriage between the Archduke's son and the magnate's lame daughter, Zasu Pitts. The two scenes are intercut throughout this sequence. Too drunk to stand, the Archduke and the magnate crawl to a corner with a champagne bottle. The Archduke complains that his toe hurts. The corn-plaster king takes out a box of his wares and proceeds to apply one. Between swigs from the bottle, the two old men haggle over the amount of the dowry the magnate must deliver to buy his daughter's way into the aristocracy. As their bargaining goes on, the director brings his camera closer and closer to reveal the sweaty cheeks, broken veins, and bloodshot eyes of these two members of the wedding.

The details of Stroheim's *ancien régime* were realistic to absurdity. Everybody wore corsets, chin reducers, and mustache pressers; most women smoked cigars.

Georgia Hale, George K. Arthur, Baby Bruce Guerin. The motionless movie, *The Salvation Hunters*.

REALISM

As the commercial pattern of the movies developed, it proved, or was thought to prove, that the surest path to success lay in pictured daydreams, and most directors strove to identify themselves with this kind of wish-fulfillment. The development of screen art, considered apart from mechanical progress, lay chiefly in the hands of comedians like Chaplin, Keaton and Langdon, whose laugh-provoking abilities were boxoffice insurance even when they turned their comedy toward "dangerous" themes, such as satire or social criticism. But a few brave spirits persisted in the belief that the raw material of American life as it was actually lived by movie audiences themselves was fit subject matter for a popular art.

The most conspicuous attempt to turn the movie camera on everyday life was a true experiment, conducted outside the industry. Josef von Sternberg, a film editor, produced with little capital and unknown actors *The Salvation Hunters*, 1925, which Fairbanks bought for United Artists release and which Chaplin proclaimed a masterpiece. But it did little to endear the idea of screen realism to audiences. It was the dreariest picture on record. Silent pictures were usually full of ceaseless activity: things had to be kept moving at all costs. Sternberg decided to explore the contrasting effect of complete immobility. *The Salvation Hunters* consisted of a series of scenes in which groups of characters stood or sat around without moving a muscle, looking extremely depressed and not even blinking their eyes. From time to time Sternberg cut in a shot of

the real star of the picture, a symbolic dredger which dipped into a harbor and brought up a load of slime. All this to express the idea that nothing ever happens in the lives of ordinary people. Audience reaction was, in substance: even *our* lives are not so drab as this, and if they are we don't want to know about it. Asked to comment on the failure of a film he had praised so highly, Chaplin said, "Well, you know, I was only kidding. They all take everything I say so seriously I thought I'd praise a bad picture and see what happened."

The fate of Sternberg was ironic. This devotee of the lower depths spent most of the rest of his career directing "glamour" vehicles for his profitable discovery, Marlene Dietrich.

Aside from this offbeat film, most attempts at realism were the occasional ventures of directors of standing who could not seem to get it out of their heads that an instrument like the camera, which could reproduce reality with such wonderful fidelity, should sometimes be used for this purpose. In striking contrast to his younger brother Cecil, William C. de Mille was continually poking into the seamier side with such dramas as Zona Gale's *Miss Lulu Bett*, and Owen Davis' *Icebound*. His most daring break with convention was in casting Lois Wilson in a picture called *Only 38*, which defied the law that all movie heroines should be no more than twenty years old and behave as if they were much younger. The elder de Mille had a theory that in concentrating exclusively on youth and youth's interests, the movies were losing their hold on older

The ant-heap. King Vidor probed the drabness of metropolitan life in his isolated masterpiece, *The Crowd*.

people, and he sought to recapture this vanishing audience. He was right oftener than his employers were willing to admit. His wife, Clara Beranger, records: "When the executives saw *Miss Lulu Bett* in the projection room they were not enthusiastic, but the picture went on to make a great deal of money, leading William to remark, 'Nobody likes this picture but the public.'"

King Vidor's autobiography, *A Tree Is a Tree*, reveals a drive to explore and disclose the patterns of life in the United States and the typical experiences of its people. He deliberately set out to build a reputation as a top boxoffice director in order occasionally to get his way. Sometimes he could combine doing what he liked with doing what the studio wanted. *The Big Parade*, 1925, was a boxoffice hit, and it was also the first realistic drama of World War I. Vidor's *The Crowd*, 1928, attempted to dissect the unconscious regimentation of metropolitan life; his hero was a digit in the incalculable total of city office workers. For years Vidor tried to persuade M-G-M to let him make a film about the American Negro with an all-Negro cast. When sound arrived, he insisted that this was the moment to act, since Negro music would greatly enhance the appeal of the film. To Nicholas M. Schenck, president of M-G-M, he offered to work without salary if the studio would let him make the picture. The offer appealed to Mr. Schenck's gambling instinct. "If that's your spirit," he replied, "I'd let you make a picture about whores." Vidor's *Hallelujah*, 1929, was a memorable screen achievement.

Gloria Swanson's *Manhandled*, 1924, depicted a day in the life of a salesgirl in Macy's basement with terrifying accuracy.

Richard Barthelmess brings the mail through in *Tol'able David,* 1921, the most brilliant of the regional dramas.

Gloria Swanson

Pola Negri

GLORIA AND POLA

While Mary Pickford at one end of the spectrum and Greta Garbo at the other have known greater popularity, it is Gloria Swanson who embodies most completely the genus Movie Star. Her camera-proof face, which can be photographed successfully from any angle, conforms to no known specifications of beauty, but the prognathous jaw, dished nose, and abnormally large eyes somehow blend into a bizarre loveliness which made her for years the idol and model of millions of women in the flapper era. But it was not her strange beauty alone that made Miss Swanson the dominant star of the Twenties. To women, she was a symbol of growth, of what a woman can make of herself. Allene Talmey described the process in 1927: "Her dignity is paralyzing. It is that dignity which makes her so magnificent and for which Hollywood can never quite forgive her. There in Hollywood hover the ghosts, always remembering that the cool Marquise de la Falaise de Coudray came as an extra, as a flat-figured girl in a Mack Sennett bathing suit of black and white checks. Hollywood, with its disturbing memory, can still see the haughty Swanson of the days of the De Mille society pictures, a funny impossible girl in her crazy clothes, an overdressed Chicago kid whose hair was black and hard and shiny with Brilliantine. She did not care that the elaborate fashionings of her hair were only copied by hash-house waitresses; she did not care that her satin swathings, clinging to her as sharply as a lobster shell clings to its white meat, were just further evidences of the impossibility of that Swanson girl. With her bad posture, her Illinois twang, her gamin toughness, the movie magazines posed her as the smartest dressed woman in Hollywood; and she loved it.

"But Gloria Swanson is acquisitive. She began to discard the crudities which had made her the great example of movie bad taste. She reserved those satin swathings, which she still loves and wears, for only those moments in her own bedroom when the eyes of Hollywood cannot peep in. Lessons taught her how to carry herself, how to enunciate properly. Her time came at a dinner at the Park Lane Hotel, given her by officials of Paramount when she returned from Europe several years ago, bringing with

STARS
OF THE TWENTIES

her the film *Madame Sans Gêne* and her new husband, a docile nobleman with a reckless taste in spats. After the usual publicity spasms of superlatives, the daughter of Capt. Joseph Swanson, U.S.A., and the former wife of actor Wallace Beery and businessman Herbert Somborn stood up in front of those paunchy, bald-headed men who remembered a hard-faced Sennett bathing girl and a spit-curled De Mille vamp. They saw a formal, cool woman, the Marquise de la Falaise de Coudray, magnificent in her re-creation of Gloria Swanson."

When this was written, her success was so great that she had become an independent star-producer at United Artists, the Everest of movie fame. *Photoplay* bubbled: "Ten years ago she was an extra girl waiting outside the casting office. Today, she is a Marchioness whose salary is $20,000 a week." *The New Yorker* said, "Gloria Swanson's greatest achievement is her own face in repose." But from her pinnacle, the greatest star of them all had some insight into the future. At a studio party given in her honor, she was heard to say faintly amidst the hubbub, "All this is very nice. But it's over at thirty-five And that's not a hundred years off."

Miss Swanson reached thirty-five in the year 1933, two years after the release of her last successful vehicle, *Tonight Or Never*. But it was not age that dimmed her popularity. The by then ex-Marquise de la Falaise had stopped growing. To a depression-struck audience, she still symbolized the lost and discredited Era of Wonderful Nonsense.

Imported by Paramount because of her success in German films, Pola Negri automatically challenged Gloria Swanson's supremacy at their studio, and the Swanson-Negri feud was on. It perhaps consisted of little more than mutual snubs, but it was troublesome enough to cause Adolph Zukor to put a continent between the warring divas, the Swanson productions being transferred to Paramount's Astoria studios while Miss Negri (or, as she preferred to be called, Madame Negri) held forth in Hollywood.

Pola lost the feud, not through any lack of ingenuity in pursuing it but because that infallible umpire, the boxoffice, decided against her. This was in part the fault of her studio. The fiery Pola had an enormous following when she arrived in the United States, but it was gradually dissipated by mishandling. The better she was photographed, the more lavishly she was coiffed and gowned and sleeked and groomed, the more standardized she became, until in the studied attitudes of stylized acting in her last films nothing was discernible of the highly individual heroine of *Passion* and *Gypsy Blood*. Paramount, in dismay, hired expensive writers like Carl Van Vechten, Joseph Hergesheimer, and Michael Arlen to try to provide her with "suitable" vehicles that would restore her popularity, but to no avail. "We try and try," said a Paramount executive, "but everything we do is wrong." By 1928, exhibitors were refusing to feature Miss Negri's name in advertising her pictures.

In part this extraordinary personality alienated her public by her off-screen behavior. Miss Negri made no effort to conceal her opinion that her German films were superior to her American productions, or that the cultural climate was not such as she had been accustomed to in Berlin. Worse, her efforts to sell herself were more appropriate to the era of Gaby Deslys than to the wisecracking Twenties. When she interrupted the filming of *Hotel Imperial* to rush to the funeral of Rudolph Valentino, a cynical press decided that it was just a publicity gag, and photographs of the black-swathed Pola fainting at Valentino's bier provoked laughter instead of the sympathy they were intended to arouse. A certain humorlessness was apparent in her behavior pattern. Vicki Baum has speculated that her affair with Valentino was based less on mutual attraction than on the following line of reasoning: I am Pola Negri, therefore I deserve the best man in the world. The best man in the world is generally conceded to be Rudolph Valentino. *Q.E.D.* The same lack of contact with reality is evidenced in an interview she gave in 1936 when she was once more starring in German films, rumored at the instance of Hitler himself. Reporters asked if this were true. She replied, "Why not; after all there have been many important men in my life—Valentino for example." Hitler did not say whether he was flattered by the comparison.

Mary Pickford and Douglas Fairbanks "dedicate" a new link of the Pacific Highway. The crowned heads of Hollywood, always called out to officiate at cornerstone layings, their popularity toward the end of the Twenties was perhaps more official than real, but none challenged their royal status as long as silence lasted.

Corinne Griffith was famed as "the orchid lady of the screen" and as its most beautiful woman, but her uncharacteristic appearance here in *Moral Fibre*, 1921, suggests opposite qualities. Today she is a Boadicea of big business.

Of the veteran stars, Norma Talmadge kept the steadiest hold on her legion of fans. Miss Talmadge was given to roles in which she aged a great deal and wept even more. She is seen here as Donald Keith's mother in *Secrets*, 1924.

THE GREAT CELEBRITIES

Nearly all movie star contracts of the silent days were written to last for five years. This was based on the universal belief that the life of the "average" star's career was five years, after which time the public presumably had had enough. By and large this theory held, at least for silent days. Such once raging favorites as Theda Bara, Clara Kimball Young, Carlyle Blackwell, and Maurice Costello had faded out by the early Twenties. But certain of the great celebrities of the pioneer days held their reputations and their fans down to the coming of sound and even beyond.

Mae Murray in *The French Doll,* 1923, at the time when she was building the reputation for eccentricity of behavior, pose, and costume which eventually was fatal to her career.

Pedro de Cordoba and Marion Davies in *Young Diana,* 1922. Miss Davies' popularity as a romantic heroine was long a figment of William Randolph Hearst's imagination, but she eventually won a following as a comedienne.

Lillian Gish with Ronald Colman in *The White Sister,* 1923, her biggest hit after she left Griffith.

Rex, "The King of Wild Horses," was an admirably trained tame one.

"Mortgage-lifter" Rin-Tin-Tin in *Rinty of the Desert*, 1928.

ANIMAL STARS

Probably the first nonhuman movie star was the Mack Sennett dog, Ben. By the Twenties, everything that ran, hopped, crept, or crawled had found a place in films. The winning spontaneity of animal players saved many an otherwise anemic film. The simple device of cross-cutting, added to superb training, gave to movie dogs supercanine and even superhuman intelligence. The first great dog star was Strongheart, owned and trained by Jane Murfin, the author of *Lilac Time*. He was succeeded in popularity by Rin-Tin-Tin, known to exhibitors as "the mortgage-lifter" because of his infallible boxoffice draw. He was the screen property of the Warner Brothers and their chief solace in the years before sound when most of their time and energy were spent in staving off creditors. "Rinty" had two successors on the screen and today has a lineal descendant on television.

Effective as animals are on the screen, all is not smooth sailing in getting them there. The late William C. de Mille once complained: "Probably every director in the world has noticed the ghoulish glee with which writers introduce dogs, flies, monkeys, mice, bees, ants, fish and babies into their plots.

They are so easy to write; so humorous on paper. A bee buzzes into the scene at exactly the right moment; an ant crawls upon a table exactly on his cue; a mouse dashes across the bed just as the lady is about to retire; these are incidents which no writer will pass up if he sees his chance to work them in. What does he care how long it takes to make the fly drunk enough to crawl in the right direction and not take to the air? He doesn't have to direct the mouse or make the baby stop crying and begin to smile. No; a simple sentence and it is done—as far as the writer is concerned. This is one great advantage which the author accepts as his special privilege. He gets away with it because the public loves animals on the screen and the director knows it. It is usually a good picture, but it is one reason why directors frequently look a bit driven."

Mr. de Mille had further cause to complain of animal stars. When his stage success *Strongheart* (the name of an Indian youth) was adapted to the screen, its title had to be changed to *Braveheart* to avoid confusion with the reigning dog star. Mr. de Mille commented, "The public liked the dog better than my play. *Cave Canem.*"

Jackie Coogan, greatest of the child stars, in *Daddy*, 1923.

Freckle-faced Wesley Barry as a Penrod of the early Twenties.

CHILD STARS

It was Douglas Fairbanks who first observed that children and animals make the best movie actors. From the beginning children played a more important part in pictures than they ever had in the theater, and many became stars in their own right. Of these by far the most beloved was Jackie Coogan, around whom Chaplin centered his peerless *The Kid,* 1920. Coogan's parents, small-time vaudevillians, were sharp enough to realize at once the immensely valuable property they had in their son, and bargained for his services with a rapacity which astounded even Hollywood. After his discovery, the five-year-old Jackie was signed to a starring contract which netted him a fortune of $4,000,000, and he remained a top favorite until he outgrew little-boy roles.

The fate of this infant gold mine was not uncharacteristic of show business. His performances of adolescent roles, especially in *Tom Sawyer,* 1930, demonstrated that young Coogan was a genuine artist, not just a cute bundle of mischief and pathos. But in maturity he could find no place on the screen. Nor did he enjoy a penny of his vast childhood earnings. When he turned twenty-one and asked for his money, his mother, who had remarried after the death of Jack Coogan, Sr., found a California law which held that the earnings of a minor are the absolute property of his parents, and refused her son any part of the fortune which had supported her in luxury for years.

The long-forgotten Baby Peggy was a prototype of Shirley Temple.

223

Daughter of the pioneer movie star, Maurice Costello, Dolores Costello had a madonnalike beauty that caused John Barrymore to demand her as his leading woman and later as his wife.

Billie Dove and Ben Lyon in *An Affair of the Follies,* 1927. Miss Dove's beauty and her

THE YOUNGER

From the founding of the star system on, the search for new stars has been constant and intense. Every girl of striking beauty, in any walk of life, anywhere in the world, soon became familiar with the "You ought to be in pictures" routine. Fallen aristocrats, society beauties down on their luck, athletes, and beauty contest winners all made the trek to Hollywood to face a screen test. Though few survived, everyone was welcome. No one could

Fresh from the chorus of *Innocent Eyes,* Joan Crawford played her first role in Jackie Coogan's *Old Clothes,* 1925. Born Billie Cassin, known on the stage as Lucille LeSueur, Miss Crawford has had the longest career of any woman star, including Mary Pickford.

Constance Bennett was rapidly climbing to favor as an ingenue when, in 1926, she married the wealthy Philip Plant and retired. Four years later, with a divorce and a million-dollar marriage settlement, she returned to Hollywood to become one of the most sensational stars of the Thirties.

figure made her a prime favorite with men in the latter part of the Twenties.

GENERATION

tell where the lightning would strike.

In the middle Twenties, the quest for star material intensified. The movies had hit one of their periodic slumps. From 1925 to 1927, a large new crop of "discoveries" appeared. In keeping with the spirit of the times, their common denominator was youth. Producers pushed them fast, little dreaming that within two years they would face a test for which youth did not equip them—sound.

The studio caption says: "Dolores del Rio, Mexico's heiress-social leader, who recently arrived in Hollywood with $50,000 in shawls and combs, is . . . said to be the richest girl in Mexico." (The money was her husband's.)

Myrna Loy's career was mostly confined to Oriental enchantresses until the talkies made her a star. Here she is seen in blackface with Tom Wilson in *Ham and Eggs at the Front*, 1927.

Norma Shearer, far from 100 per cent photogenic, fought her way to the top through executive ability as well as talent. She is seen here with Jack Holt in *Empty Hands*, 1924.

225

Greta Garbo as a Spanish peasant in her first American film, *The Torrent*, 1926.

Wild Orchids, 1929. Her dream-haunted eyes fixed on some unknown, Garbo mystified while she fascinated.

The invitation direct.
Flesh and the Devil, 1927.

"Well . . . ?" Greta Garbo with Conrad Nagel in *The Mysterious Lady*, 1928.

226

Garbo in 1928.

GARBO

Though Theda Bara spelled Arab Death, though Jetta Goudal let it be believed that she was the daughter of Mata Hari, the greatest screen siren of them all made no attempt to cloak in glamour the simplicity of her origins. Greta Garbo was born in Stockholm (1906), the daughter of a poor laborer. In her early teens she worked as a lather-girl in a barber shop, played extra in a few Swedish films, was discovered by the director Mauritz Stiller, and came to Hollywood in his entourage at the age of nineteen. That was about all that her early interviewers could pry out of this impassive, faintly scornful girl who held the public of 1926-30 in a vise of fascination. For the old, bold movie vamp, Miss Garbo substituted a more complicated and credible charmer—doomed, neurotic, torn by inner conflicts. She was poison to men and to herself, yet held in her eyes the promise of Cleopatra.

After Mauritz Stiller returned to Sweden, a failure in Hollywood, Miss Garbo shut herself off from society. Displeased by the inaccuracies of reporters, especially by the distortion of her one-sided romance with John Gilbert, she refused all interviews. Her relations with her co-workers at M-G-M were and remained rigidly formal, and she earned the lasting respect of Louis B. Mayer by conducting their business affairs with an icy candor which concealed no stratagem. Was she a sphinx without a secret? Yes, said her legion of detractors, who scoffed at her "pose" of mystery, her (supposed) big feet and thick accent, and her threats to go home to Sweden unless she got her way; while her legion of fanatical adorers, rightly called "Garbomaniacs," insisted that she dwelt apart because she was a woman apart, and found in her most trivial films, indeed in her slightest gestures, intimation of an acting talent greater than any the screen had yet produced. The battle between them was good for business, and there was no doubt where the victory lay when, by 1929, even the chubbiest American girl was wearing the shoulder-length bob and slouch hat which Miss Garbo had made synonymous with legendary beauty.

Vilma Banky and Ronald Colman in *Two Lovers*, 1928—roles they played under various names through five films.

Janet Gaynor and Charles Farrell were the sensations of 1927 in *Seventh Heaven;* they co-starred for over seven years.

Greta Garbo and John Gilbert in their first film together, *Flesh and the Devil*, 1927.

LOVE TEAMS

The first movie "love team" was Francis X. Bushman and Beverly Bayne, whose off-screen marriage was concealed from the public lest it take the edge off their movie love scenes. After their success, producers were ever on the alert for players who struck sparks from each other and who could be featured in a series of dramas which centered around Love and nothing else but. The most ravishing of all these teams consisted of the glamorous John Gilbert and the mysterious Greta Garbo—the most sensationally successful of all the younger generation. By their time, lip service to personal privacy (at least for screen stars) had been abandoned: their studio saw to it that the public was well aware of the fact that Gilbert was wooing Garbo in real life, that he had got as far as taking out a marriage license, that she had balked at the altar but continued to waver. After all this, seeing a Gilbert-Garbo film was like eavesdropping on their private life.

Reviewing *Love*, the 1927 version of *Anna Karenina*, *Photoplay* said: "It isn't Tolstoy, but it is John Gilbert and Greta Garbo, which, after *Flesh and the Devil*, is what the fans are crying for. And if you think there is even a hint in the picture of the romance of Kitty and Kostia Levin, you are nothing but a silly. The movies have separated the wheat of sex from the chaff of preachment." Though Gilbert and Miss Garbo made only three films together, the intensity of their screen love-making plus the rumors of their romance identified them in the public mind as the supreme symbols of screen sex. Nothing mattered in their pictures but numerous, prolonged, close-up embraces. Not everyone was swept away by this make-believe lechery. One heretic called their behavior "Gilbo-Garbage," a sobriquet that pleased the disgruntled. He added that their acting in the clinches was less suggestive of uncontrolled passion than of acute indigestion.

229

The first subtitle from *The Last Command,* 1928.

Polly Moran, Dorothy Sebastian, Louella O. Parsons, Estelle Taylor, Claire Windsor, Aileen Pringle, Karl Dane, George K. Arthur, Leatrice Jo

Seventeen stars assembled in the M-G-M

"HOLLYWOOD IS A STATE OF MIND"

Hollywood, the tiny suburb of Los Angeles where the movie pioneers established themselves, was soon outgrown by the giant film factories and the burgeoning movie colony. Stars and magnates built their homes in Beverly Hills and Malibu Beach, and by the middle Twenties the mansions and bungalows of the film people were creeping up the canyons which fan out from Los Angeles. Yet all these widely scattered localities and their denizens were and are known to the public by the generic name Hollywood. "Hollywood's not a place, it's a state of mind," said Wilson Mizner, the wit, promoter, and gambler who had come there to end his roistering days selling script ideas. The Hollywood of the Twenties was just that.

Its heterogeneous, rootless population had nothing in common except the fact that they were all in pictures, or wanted to be. They had come from everywhere, selling their specialties—writers, ac-

tors, painters, contortionists, cowboys, bankrupt aristocrats, bunco artists, promoters, "idea men"— and they hoped never to leave. Success had come by accident, it might leave just as accidentally, so why not live for today? Moreover, they lived under the world's most powerful spotlight, and in its unreal glare it was hard for them to distinguish their own drives and emotions from those staged by their press agents for the fan magazines and the gossip columns.

With six-figure salaries to back their whims, they staged the most spectacular display of libido on the loose since ancient Rome faded into the darkness. In this their instincts served them well. Hollywood in the Twenties was garish, extravagant, ludicrous, acquisitive, ambitious, ruthless, beautiful— which was just what its world public wanted it to be. Its very unreality was protective of the illusion. Dream worlds are not supposed to be lifelike.

ee Adoree, Rod La Rocque, Mae Murray, John Gilbert, Norma Talmadge, Douglas Fairbanks, Marion Davies, William S. Hart

missary for a single scene in *Show People*, 1928

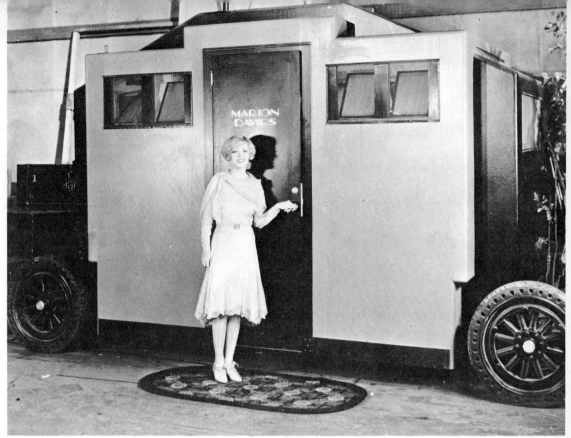

Marion Davies was one of the first to achieve a portable dressing room which could be wheeled to any corner of the M-G-M studio where she happened to be working. She seems also to have a special alighting-mat.

Every studio was compelled by law to maintain special schools where child actors could continue their studies while appearing in pictures. Here Olive Borden hovers over the juvenile cast of *The Auctioneer*, 1927.

STUDIO "LIFE"

Twenty-six fan magazines and "special correspondents" from all over the world, aided by an army of press agents, reflected and amplified the universal interest in Hollywood's doings. The smallest details of studio routine became fodder for the insatiable publicity maw, and when they did not

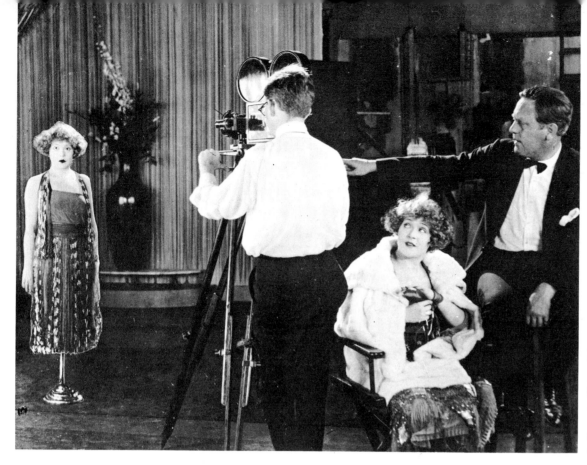

An ancestress of the stand-in. This dummy substituted for Mae Murray during camera rehearsals for double-exposure scenes in *Peacock Alley*, 1921. Miss Murray's husband and director, Robert Z. Leonard is seated beside the star.

Louis B. Mayer turns over to Lon Chaney the flag presented to M-G-M by the Marine Corps. Chaney raised it in the picture *Tell It to the Marines*, 1927. Left to right: Mr. Mayer, Hunt Stromberg, Harry Rapf, director George Hill, and Chaney.

exist, it was necessary to invent them. Audiences became as familiar with what was purported to go on behind the scenes as with what they saw in their theaters. Nor did this disillusion them. The portrait they received of the picture-making colony was even more fascinating than on-screen romance.

HOME LIFE
OF THE GODS

As publicity departments increasingly halved the public and private lives of the stars, a sort of double-image of the darlings of the screen was gradually built up for audience edification. All were the quintessence of remote glamour, yet all were homebodies too, plain as an old shoe, just like your next-door neighbor. At the same time, their cultural attainments were bounded only by the limits of their press agents' imaginations. Ramon Novarro's interest in philosophy was as well known to his fans as Douglas Fairbanks, Jr.'s painting and Jetta Goudal's genius at costume design. To feed the needs of the rapacious publicity machine, these gorgeous, homey, cultured creatures were continually photographed in fantastic poses which often made them seem to belong to some other species.

The caption says: "Dolores del Rio has placed the photos of her screen idols on her comb but has left the center space for the Great Unknown." Curiously Ben Lyon, Lloyd Hughes, Lewis Stone, Milton Sills, Ronald Colman, and Richard Barthelmess all belonged to her own studio.

A Day with Pola Negri

It was axiomatic that anyone gifted enough to be a movie star was gifted in more than one way, nor was it considered odd that the stars' creative aspirations seemed always to be on display in full view of the publicity department. Pola

Publicity for *The Taxi Dancer*, 1927, with Joan Crawford.

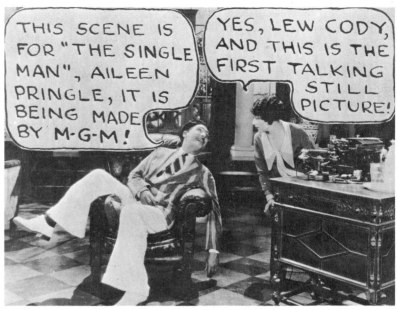

Publicity for *The Single Man*, 1929.

Negri's cultural pretensions made her particularly good copy as an exponent of the arts. Here we see her blue-penciling a new script, playing the organ, playing the violin, and modeling in clay.

The Marquise de la Falaise de Coudray (Gloria Swanson) and her husband greet Sir Henry and Lady Wood as Sir Henry arrives to guest-conduct at the Hollywood bowl.

THE BATTLE OF THE TITLES

When Pola Negri arrived in Hollywood, she had already married and divorced a Polish count. This enabled her to be referred to as the Countess Dombski, when she was not calling herself "Madame" Negri. That she was the only Hollywood star with any claim to a title was a sore point in the Swanson-Negri feud at Paramount, and Miss Swanson, an expert in one-upmanship, soon married the Marquis Henri de la Falaise de Coudray, thus putting herself far out in front in the Almanach de Gotha sweepstakes. She installed footmen in powdered wigs and knee-breeches in her home and issued invitations in the name of "Madame la Marquise."

This was intolerable to her fellow-divas. Something had to be done and Mae Murray did it; she became the first to corral one of the "marrying Mdivanis," thereby becoming a princess. Whether a genuine marquise was ranked by a doubtful princess (the status of the Mdivanis in their native Georgia has never been well defined) was a question which agitated Hollywood. In any case, however, Pola Negri, a mere ex-countess, was bested, and she

was too entangled in her romance with Valentino to do much about it. But less than a year after Valentino's death she rectified matters by marrying the remaining Mdivani, Prince Serge, thus becoming (though not for long) both an ex-countess and a dubious princess. A few years later a fan magazine wrote: "Pola Negri sailed for Europe with a prince and a contract. Now she has neither."

As Leo Rosten has pointed out, the behavior pattern of the stars of Hollywood follows that of Eastern plutocracy, but with a time-lag of about a quarter of a century. The Misses Swanson, Negri, and Murray had begun their pursuit of European titles a bit too long after the Henry James era for comfort. Miss Swanson read the danger signals when she found herself referred to as "la Marquise de la Etcetera," or sometimes as simply "the Marquise de Gloria," and parried by referring to her husband as "Hank."

Vital statistic: The Marquis de la Falaise married Constance Bennett when the latter succeeded Miss Swanson as queen of the boxoffice.

Mae Murray's marriage in 1926 to Prince David Mdivani. Among the group in the wedding party are, left to right: Pola Negri, Rudolph Valentino, Kathlyn Williams, Miss Murray, Prince Mdivani, Manuel Reachi, and Agnes Ayres. Miss Negri and Valentino were matron of honor and best man, and were then at the height of their romance.

Super-Wedding

A wedding of indigenous Hollywood aristocracy was that of Vilma Banky and Rod La Rocque, staged by Miss Banky's producer, Samuel Goldwyn, in a style so spectacular that no one has ever dared try to surpass it. But Mr. Goldwyn's fluent showmanship backfired when a reporter at the wedding feast bit into a papier-mâché turkey and discovered that many of the elegant comestibles were props.

THE END OF THE SILENT ERA

Queen Elizabeth, 1912. Sarah Bernhardt saw the film versions of her famous vehicles as "my one chance for immortality," but insisted on filming them as they were on the stage, "speaking my lines as usual."

Cenere, 1916, with Eleonora Duse. "Something quite different is needed."

The spoken word has been the actor's principal vehicle for expressing emotion since the days of Greek drama, when the actors' faces were hidden behind huge masks. The effect of its absence can be studied in a cruel light in the several film versions of Sarah Bernhardt's standard vehicles—*Camille, Queen Elizabeth,* and others. Bernhardt thought of the screen as a visual equivalent of a phonograph record of her stage performances and made no effort to adapt her technique to it, but without the "golden voice" to give them point, her stagy gestures seemed labored and meaningless. Eleonora Duse, on the other hand, thoroughly understood the difference between the old medium of which she was mistress and the unknown new one. She had hoped for much from her first film but when she saw it she said, "I made the same mistake that nearly everyone has made. But something quite different is needed. I am too old for it, isn't it a pity?"

Few shared her insight. Griffith had early discovered that under the merciless eye of the camera it is better not to act but to *respond,* but even before his time the directors and actors of workaday film-making had already arrived at the compromise which in the main ruled as long as the silent film lasted. They adopted the repertoire of conventional stage gestures and exaggerated it to compensate for the absence of speech. The majority of movie actors "registered" their emotions rather than felt them.

"Registering" was a curious business, seen from this distance. Specific gestures and grimaces were thought to convey equally specific meanings and it was not overwhelmingly difficult to get them all by heart and thus become a movie actor. Many of these devices did double duty. A widening of the eyes and parting of the lips expressed terror, but with slight modification also indicated passion. A certain yearning look, suggesting deep intestinal distress, was known as "soulful." Grief or anguish generally led in close-up to a thrown-back head and hand pressed to forehead, clutched to throat, or raised despairingly to Heaven. A pointing finger accompanied by tightly compressed lips represented the mood accusatory, while kneeling or groveling on the floor signified a wide range of feelings, from remorse to appeal. Ingenues were wide-eyed, while vamps and villainesses invariably betrayed their character by narrowing their eyes to slits.

The movie public rapidly learned this dictionary of the passions and the majority were convinced and even moved by it. But the fact that they never encountered such behavior in their own lives led Americans to revive the archaic word *emote* to suggest the difference between people on the screen and the people in front of it.

Gloria Swanson.

Barbara La Marr, Lionel Barrymore.

Alan Hale, Jacqueline Logan.

EMOTE
"v.i. To exhibit emotion"

Pola Negri, Conrad Nagel.

Pola Negri.

Unknown players.

Mae Murray.

Ronald Colman, Vilma Banky.

Bebe Daniels.

The first words spoken from the screen were uttered in the flat, Midwestern voice of Will H. Hays, who introduced the first Vitaphone program on August 6, 1926 with a timid prediction that sound would usher in a new era in "pictures and music."

THE WARNER BROTHERS

In the middle Twenties, the movie boxoffice sagged. Something seemed to have gone wrong; except for the big pictures, the audience was staying home in increasing numbers. In furious quest of novelty, exhibitors added vaudeville acts, "prologues," condensed operas, and musical comedies to their programs until the nominal feature, the movie itself, seemed in danger of getting lost in a huge variety show. Among the novelties available was a device called the Vitaphone, which the engineers and technicians of the Bell Telephone system had been working on since the days of Edison's early experiments with sound films. But when the Vitaphone was offered to the screen's major companies, they rejected it.

There were those who were not so cautious, perhaps because they were not so comfortable. The Warner brothers, Harry, Jack, Sam, and Albert, had fought their way up from the nickelodeons to the ownership of exchanges and, after World War I, had graduated into production itself. Their capital and everything they could borrow was all invested in their studio program, and as the battle for theater ownership developed, they found themselves unable on the one hand to secure access to the first-run theaters of their competitors or on the other to obtain sufficient backing to buy theaters of their own. No matter how good their pictures, slow death was the only prospect before them under this setup. Then the owners of the Vitaphone patents finally came to see them. With an enthusiasm born of desperation, the Warners contracted for the exclusive use of the Vitaphone device, rounded up their remaining capital, and began a grim race with time. The issue was simply whether they would be able to complete and market enough sound pictures before their silent pictures had disappeared from first-run screens and their ledgers turned from black to red. The industry stared aghast at this foredoomed gamble. How could these minor producers, sunk in debt, back a project which their mighty competitors had rejected? The strain must have

THE TALKIE REVOLUTION

been tremendous. Sam Warner died under it.

The first public performance of the Vitaphone was held August 6, 1926, at the Manhattan Opera House in New York. The program consisted of shorts featuring musical celebrities like Mischa Elman and Giovanni Martinelli, and a silent film, John Barrymore's *Don Juan*, with recorded musical accompaniment. To the opening night audience, the principal novelty seemed to be that the music came from behind the screen rather than from musicians in the orchestra pit, and it was a "canned" substitute for orchestral accompaniment that Harry Warner tried to sell to economy-minded exhibitors. Few of them were inclined to install his expensive equipment, and for a year after *Don Juan*, sound languished as an unproved gimmick in isolated theaters which showed only those "Vitaphone shorts."

But attendance at these few theaters was so consistently good that the Warners were encouraged to pursue their experiment. Trying to hang on to what little cash they had, they sought to induce Al Jolson to accept stock in their company in lieu of salary for his appearance in *The Jazz Singer*. Jolson demanded cash, and thereby turned down a fortune. *The Jazz Singer* was a mediocre silent picture with a shopworn theme, and mostly told its story with titles, but it contained three Jolson songs and a snatch of dialogue. That was enough. Once it was released, in October 1927, the revolution was under way. Exhibitors, watching the long lines before the Warner Theater in New York, decided to get in on the bonanza and ordered sound equipment, only to find that the manufacturers were already swamped with orders.

A tremor of uneasiness went through the industry when this fact became known. Most producers and exhibitors were watching the fortunes of the Warners but had not made up their own minds whether they would invest in the "novelty." Might they not wait too long? More and more Warner sound films were reaching the market; William Fox (whose Movietone sound-on-film device eventually supplanted the Vitaphone sound-on-disk method) had added sound to his newsreels and some of his short subjects. By the end of 1927 even the industry skeptics could no longer deny that any sound film, by whatever process made, was attracting large crowds to any theater that showed it.

By the spring of 1928, in any given community, the worst sound film would outdraw the best silent picture. This was genuinely alarming to the movie community. If talkies were not merely to exist side by side with silent films, but entirely replace them, a great many vested interests would be imperiled. Many of the mighty, among them D. W. Griffith, suggested a sort of conspiracy to suppress talking films, at least until they were perfected. But they reckoned without the public. Audiences took the bit in their teeth and demanded sound films—and there were the hungry Warners ready to supply them. Gradually the sober fact dawned that the 32-year-old silent motion picture medium was doomed.

Al Jolson in *The Jazz Singer*, 1927.

Captain Elmo Armstrong, forest ranger of Mad Mountains, while aiding Lucille Gray in her efforts to clear her father of a charge of murder fastened on him by his foes, is captured by Lucille's enemies and lashed to a rock which the surf is rapidly engulfing.

Universal

ELMO LINCOLN

THE VANISHING SUBTITLE

Whatever headaches lay in store for the veterans of silent pictures, there was one adjunct of silence which none of them regretted losing—the caption or subtitle. This necessary evil consisted of "voice of God" editorial comments on the action, supplemented when expedient by "spoken titles"—lines of dialogue printed on the screen. By the end of the silent era everything possible had been done to reduce them to a minimum. Dialogue scenes were carefully photographed to enable the editor to cut away from the actor to his "spoken title" at the moment he opened his mouth to speak, cutting back to his image just as he finished. Good editors could often obtain the illusion of actual speech by this device. But in spite of such skill, the subtitle was an irritating reminder that, because of its silence, this primarily visual medium had to rely on the crutch of words at crucial moments in the narrative. Moreover, the subtitle was a weapon in the hands of the producer against the director, if the former decided the latter had done his work poorly or had overstepped the bounds of decorum. He then merely hired a good cutter and a clever title-writer to tighten up the film or alter it completely. Actors were astonished to find that lines they had mouthed as "Get that harlot out of my house" emerged on the screen as "I think the lady had better leave," or that the mistress of the villain had been transformed by the title-writer into his maiden aunt. One of these professional title-doctors advertised his calling in the trade magazines with the slogan: "All bad little films when they die go to RALPH SPENCE."

Steve Blighton, with all the fear of the actual crook in his heart, is determined to procure the papers for himself—to destroy them and so fasten for all time the guilt on John Gray, one of his employees.

UNIVERSAL

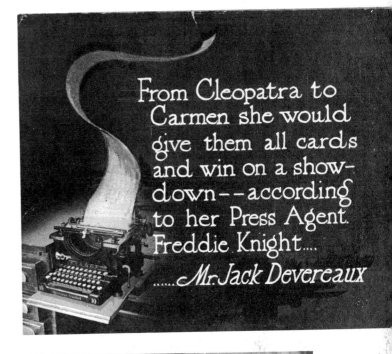

From Cleopatra to Carmen she would give them all cards and win on a showdown—according to her Press Agent. Freddie Knight....
......Mr. Jack Devereaux

Lucille 'dolls up' in the outfit provided by Blighton, hoping thereby to lull his suspicions and outwit him.

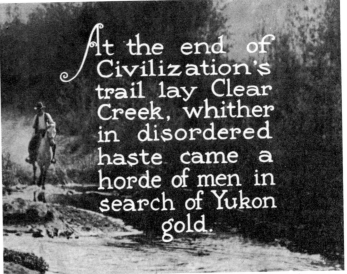

At the end of Civilization's trail lay Clear Creek, whither in disordered haste came a horde of men in search of Yukon gold.

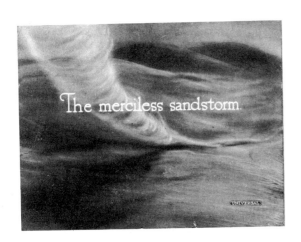

The merciless sandstorm.

UNIVERSAL

The Vitaphone camera which photographed *The Jazz Singer* had to be enclosed in a soundproof booth so that the whirring of the camera would not be recorded. Since air-conditioning was unknown then, the cameraman could remain in his prison only a few minutes at a time and usually emerged dripping wet.

KING MIKE

By mid-1928, all the great studios faced three stark realities. To survive, they had to re-equip their studios for sound without a moment's delay; they had somehow to salvage their stock of silent films which were rapidly becoming unmarketable; and they had either to retread or jettison their expensive contract players who had proved their worth in silent pictures but whose future was now an unknown quantity.

Chaos and panic swept Hollywood as the companies moved to convert to sound. Recording problems obsessed producers and directors whose whole efforts had for years been focused on doing without sound. The free-flowing action and continuity of silent films was abruptly displaced by a static, stage-like technique, both because the microphone was at first immovable and all action and "business" had to be geared to its location, and because the cameras, immured in soundproof booths, could no longer move about freely. Concealing the microphone so that it would not be photographed presented a daily problem. Directors tore their hair in frenzy when their most cherished dramatic effects were vetoed by the sound engineers—laboratory men trained by the telephone industry whose chief concern was that voices be distinct and that all conversation be conducted at one voice level. Gradually these mechanical difficulties were overcome and the fluidity of screen technique restored, but for more than three years the microphone was king, and an overbearing monarch at that.

Meanwhile there was the problem of the com-

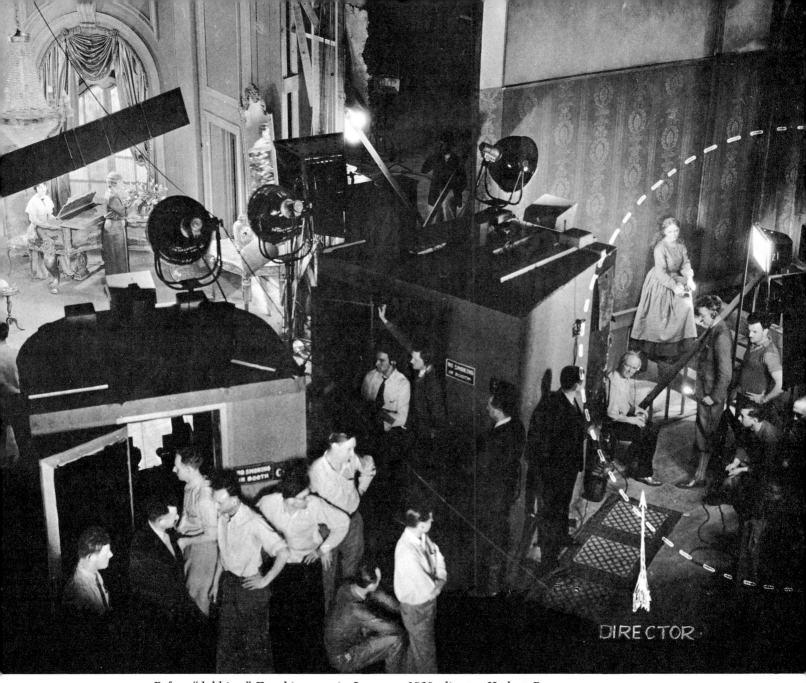

Before "dubbing." For this scene in *Lummox*, 1930, director Herbert Brenon, seated, right, wanted heroine Winifred Westover, right, to listen to her daughter singing in another room. Since sound tracks could not yet be "mixed," the two scenes had to be photographed and recorded simultaneously.

pleted silent films which still awaited release—millions of dollars worth of merchandise which, in the eyes of the talkie-conscious public, had suddenly become as antique as *The Great Train Robbery*. Producers solved the problem as best they could by introducing sound in some form into their remaining silents so that exhibitors could advertise that their pictures made noises. Fans quickly became adept at deducing from the ads the degree to which silent films had been made into audible ones. "Sound effects and music" meant a recorded orchestral accompaniment plus various bell-ringings and door-knockings introduced into the otherwise silent action. "With sound and dialogue" usually meant that the players remained silent for five reels, became briefly but excessively loquacious in the sixth, and

relapsed into silence in the seventh. There were extraordinary variants: *After* the final clinch in Cecil B. De Mille's *The Godless Girl*, 1929, the hero and heroine sat down on the curbstone and talked about the weather for ten minutes in order that the picture might be billed as "part-talking." The public was remarkably patient with these weird "goat-glands," as they were called in the trade, tolerating and even welcoming them until the time—about the middle of 1929—when the legend "all-talking" could be applied to all pictures.

"King Mike's" reign was toughest on the players. Even experienced stage stars suffered from the crudities of early talkie recording. As for the legendary favorites of the silent screen, many of them had not spoken in public since first-grade assembly.

245

Too Rich to Be Bothered

Some stars, the ones who had spent it as they made it, had no choice but to struggle on, whether or not they were equipped for sound. But those who had taken advantage of their huge salaries and low taxes to invest their earnings had to decide whether they would risk the possibility of failure in the talkies or take the sensible course of retiring while their laurels were still green. Since death is ordinarily the only retirement an actor will accept, most of them merely wavered.

A fan magazine used this publicity still of Norma Talmadge on its cover in 1929, but painted out the number 5 on the mike and substituted 13. A veteran of twenty years of the movies, Miss Talmadge had grown a little bored with stardom, but the talkies seemed to challenge her and after more than a year of voice instruction she made a successful sound debut in *New York Nights*, 1930. But her second talkie, based on Belasco's *Madame Dubarry*, evoked from a critic: "She speaks the Belascoan rodomontades in a Vitagraph accent." Her sister Constance, already retired, wired her, "Leave them while you're looking good and thank God for the trust funds Momma set up." A few years later a fan asked Miss Talmadge for her autograph. "Get away, dear," the ex-star replied, "I don't need you any more."

Colleen Moore was making $12,500 a week in 1929. She had appeared in two successful talking pictures, but with the vogue of the flapper waning, her employers let her contract lapse. She then financed and starred in a Broadway play. When no movie offers resulted, she returned to Hollywood in some alarm and signed for $2,500 a week, commenting, "I'm just getting a button compared to my old salary, but I'd work for nothing, it's so good to be back." Miss Moore showed her skill and versatility in the offbeat role of a timid schoolteacher in *The Power and the Glory*, 1933, but the picture failed to re-establish her. She could have cemented her comeback in any of four opportunities Hollywood gave her. She had the looks, the talent, the intelligence. She was too rich really to care.

"So she took the $250,000" was *Photoplay's* epitaph on the fourteen-year career of Corinne Griffith. Of her *Lilies of the Field*, 1930, *Time* had said: "Pretty Corinne Griffith talks through her nose in her first sound film." Miss Griffith released her studio from their contract with her on condition that she receive her full salary, and said, "Why should I go on until I am playing mother roles? I have plenty of money. I want to improve my mind. Most of the time you'll find me bobbing around in Europe." Miss Griffith not only improved her mind but changed it: she made one picture in England and several times fruitlessly attempted comebacks on the American stage and screen. Today she is one of the wealthiest of ex-stars, active in politics, the author of two books.

KAPUT

Secure in their long-term contracts, their incredible salaries, and their still more incredible fan mail (20,000 letters a week for Clara Bow), the silent-picture stars were at first unable to take sound seriously. But as the Jolson films swept the nation, as even the worst silent films garnered big box-office through the addition of a few talking sequences, the big stars had to face the facts. It was hard to start all over after they had reigned so long. How did you learn to "talk"? And without sacrificing what had made you talked about?

Some of them suffered cruelly. Even Dorothy Parker was compassionate about the fate of May McAvoy, one of whose lines in *The Terror* emerged as "I am thick of thutth thilly antickth." Miss McAvoy decided not to study with a voice coach on the ground that "the public would rather hear me speak in my natural voice." The public quickly decided it would rather not hear her speak at all.

Others whose voices did not fit their visual personalities were temporarily more fortunate. Marie Prevost's years of stardom as a romantic come-

No Spik

A favorite device of imported European stars who were dissatisfied with their roles, their salaries, or their studio prestige was suddenly to "forget" how to speak English, with resulting suspension of production until they could be bribed to remember. In 1928 they discovered that production could be suspended indefinitely for all their bosses cared.

Though most of the public thought that the talkies put an end to the American career of Pola Negri, actually she had already exhausted her once great popularity. In the early Thirties RKO reimported her, hoping to duplicate the success of Marlene Dietrich as a husky-voiced, German-accented singer of sexy songs. Miss Negri went her rival one better, since her singing voice recorded as basso profundo, but her comeback picture, *A Woman Commands*, 1932, was so badly made as to end her hopes. From 1935 to 1939 she starred in German talkies but left Hitler's Germany at the outbreak of war and arrived in America, penniless, after the fall of France. Today she lives in Hollywood, working on her interminable memoirs and going to the movies.

Even as he received the Academy Award for the best performance by an actor for 1928, the great Emil Jannings knew he was finished as an American movie star. His studio had decided that his English was too Teutonic to be acceptable in the talkies, and as soon as he had attended the Academy dinner and got his Oscar he left for Germany. He made one attempt to recapture his American audiences with a poorly made English version of *The Blue Angel*, filmed in Berlin, but even the presence of Marlene Dietrich couldn't put it across in the United States. He remained the reigning star of the German screen until his death in 1951.

Vilma Banky had just been elevated to stardom by Samuel Goldwyn when the talkies arrived. Mr. Goldwyn, with high hopes for his beautiful star, set voice coach Jane Manner to work on smoothing out her guttural Hungarian accent. But her coaching took more than a year and the results were not impressive. Rumor had it that Miss Banky was too lazy to work at her voice chores, although they took place in full view of the publicity department. M-G-M gave her one chance at the talkies, in a screen version of *They Knew What They Wanted* called *A Lady to Love*, 1930. Her accent was in keeping with the immigrant girl she played, but still at odds with her romantic appearance. She made a few subsequent pictures in Europe with her husband, Rod La Rocque.

dienne ended when her voice recorded like Judy Holliday's in *Born Yesterday*, but there was still demand for her services as a gum-chewing soubrette in supporting roles. Miss Prevost took her demotion hard. She sought to drown her disappointments in Scotch, and died in 1934.

There were of course the hopeless ones, the silent favorites who could not even remember their lines or delivered them as "The govment is gonna do some very ineressin things in Febewary." Some few had the sense to cut their losses, like the blonde who invoked the Act of God clause to obtain release from her contract. When her producer objected, she said, "A New York millionaire wants to marry me, and if that ain't an act of God, you tell me what is." The rest were the really damned. F. Scott Fitzgerald accurately described their fate in *The Last Tycoon*, with his portrait of the woman who saw her five years of silent stardom as a God-given birthright and the rest of her life as a dim and unjust limbo. "I had a beautiful place in 1928," she laments. "All spring I was up to my ass in daisies."

John Gilbert's first talkie was *His Glorious Night*, 1929, based on Molnar's *Olympia*. In torrid love scenes with Catherine Dale Owen he spoke the flowery dialogue in an actory tenor that brought snickers from audiences which a year earlier had hailed him as the greatest lover of the screen.

Gilbert's studio made a desperate effort to save him by switching him from romantic to he-man roles. After a year's preparation, he made *Way for a Sailor*, 1930. But what the public thought of the "new" Gilbert is shown by this poster in which the star is billed below a supporting player.

"WHITE VOICE"

The case of John Gilbert was classic. Inheriting the mantle of Valentino, Gilbert had been the screen's top male star for four years when, early in 1929, M-G-M renewed his contract for four years at a total fee of a million dollars. The huge sum was a reward to Gilbert for staying with the studio at a time when it needed his boxoffice power. Three months later his first talkie was released. It was the star's professional death warrant. Audiences which had idolized him in his silent days refused to accept his florid yet inexpert delivery of romantic dialogue. Gay and charming, a veteran of many years in the movies, he was popular in Hollywood and both his friends and his employers tried hard to help him. He was said to be suffering from a malady christened "white voice" which time, coaching, and improvements in sound recording would eventually cure.

The world outside the barricade thought otherwise. Of his third talkie, a critic wrote: "It is getting so that reviewing a John Gilbert picture is embarrassing. One wants to be considerate of him and fair to one's readers. Also a certain reportorial instinct must be served. Amidst three fires, it is nevertheless true that *Way for a Sailor* is an indifferent picture and Mr. Gilbert is the same, more interesting as a reminder of the past than a present joy. Why this is so is just another proof of the microphone's capriciousness. It isn't that Mr. Gilbert's voice is insufficient; it's that his use of it robs him of magnetism, individuality, and strangest of all, skill. He becomes an uninteresting and inexpert performer whose work could be bettered by hundreds of lesser-known players. True, he hasn't

much of a picture to improve, but it often happens that a star is better than his vehicle. Mr. Gilbert isn't."

After the release of *Way for a Sailor*, it was clear that Gilbert had no future and the studio tried to buy up his expensive contract at its full value. Like Corinne Griffith, he could have had a fortune with no further effort, but he grimly insisted that M-G-M fulfill the contract to the letter. Through a ghastly three years the movie world was treated to the extraordinary spectacle of the production and distribution of five not inexpensive films which no audience wanted to see. At the end of this long ordeal, Gilbert was ready to capitulate, but his former co-star Garbo insisted that M-G-M re-engage him to play opposite her in *Queen Christina*, 1933. For a moment hope flared. But as before, audiences found a glaring contrast between the way Gilbert looked and spoke. His fate seemed doubly sealed.

Then Columbia, which was at that time the refuge for fallen stars, cast him for a featured role in *The Captain Hates the Sea*, 1934. He gave a brilliant performance as a drunken Hollywood script writer, and his dialogue, the common speech of his everyday life, came from his lips with total conviction. The thin voice that could not carry "I love you, darling, I love you" was eloquently ironic in delivering "If you believe it, it isn't so." Gilbert died before his future could be determined, but his performance in this picture established a paradox. The talkies were for those who could create a new personality-image in keeping with their voices—but this was apt to involve professional demotion rather than progress.

SOME STARS SURVIVED, OTHERS EMERGED

Some of the silent players made the most of their native vocal equipment. Gloria Swanson and Bebe Daniels, neither of whom had had stage experience, triumphantly emerged with singing as well as speaking voices, and Gary Cooper's monosyllabic Montana speech matched his screen image perfectly. There was universal suspense about Greta Garbo, who was said to be handicapped by a thick Swedish accent and a low, husky, almost masculine voice. M-G-M, in spite of the total victory of the talkies, continued to star her in silent pictures the success of which was a startling exception to the public's verdict in favor of sound. Meanwhile Miss Garbo worked hard on her accent. Finally she took the plunge as Eugene O'Neill's Swedish-American heroine, Anna Christie. Her fans first sighed with relief,

Once a Broadway favorite, Ruth Chatterton was idling in Hollywood in 1928, where her husband, Ralph Forbes, was climbing to silent stardom. The talkies reduced Forbes to supporting roles, but swept the supposedly passé Miss Chatterton into the position of "First Lady of the Cinema" at half a million a year. She is seen here in *The Laughing Lady*, 1930, with Clive Brook, whose fortunes were also advanced by sound.

GARBO TALKS was the simple slogan with which *Anna Christie* was advertised when it was finally released in 1930, two years after the coming of sound. The first words the star spoke from the screen were, "Gif me a viskey, ginger ale on the side—and don't be stingy, baby."

Jeanne Eagels, the sensational star of *Rain*, made an equally sensational talkie debut in *The Letter*, 1929, followed quickly by *Jealousy*, 1929 (left, with the youthful Fredric March). Miss Eagels promised to become one of the screen's leading personalities, but she was already near death from drugs, as the painful thinness of her forearm reveals.

then swooned with delight. For her voice fitted her strange personality, and she used it with an eloquence beyond skill. In fact, speech humanized the "woman of veiled thought and unpredictable mood" which had been her silent image.

"Humanness" indeed turned out to be the touchstone of success in talking pictures. Ruth Chatterton used the same la-de-da "stage English" accent which caused the public to turn thumbs down on many stage imports, but the warmth of her characterizations won over audiences in spite of it. In mysterious contrast, the famed Ina Claire struggled in vain to become a favorite, perhaps because she was cast in sophisticated comedies, while Miss Chatterton established herself with time-tested tear-jerkers like *Madame X*, 1929.

ALL TALKING, ALL SINGING, ALL DANCING

No sooner had the "all-talking" picture been universally accepted than it was superseded by the "all-talking, all-singing, all-dancing" extravaganza which was likely to be in color too. Hollywood went music-crazy in 1929. Stars of stage musical comedy, vaudeville hoofers, ukulele artists, ballerinas, and low comedians descended on California by the trainload, and the only Hollywood stars who did

not take singing or dancing lessons were Garbo and Rin-Tin-Tin. The song-writing industry established new headquarters in the film capital, and "voice coaches" were a special colony. Antique operettas were dusted off for the cameras, wheezy gags got new laughs from hinterland audiences. Every studio made pictures offering its entire roster of stars in "novelty" numbers, which meant that every actor

The "Pageant of Lovers" scene from *Glorifying the American Girl*, 1929.

was featured in some specialty he wasn't good at.

As suddenly as it had begun, the craze for musicals died, for the simple reason that they had been done to death. In the somber autumn of 1930, audiences found that not even musicals could take their minds off the depression, especially when they were dated operettas featuring unknowns from the stage whose vocal qualifications failed to make up for

their visual inadequacies. By 1931, a reviewer was saying of *Safe in Hell:* "Here is a reminder of the dear dead days that we thought beyond recall. For this is a musical extravaganza, replete with prancing chorines, low comics, and 'backstage' stuff. The picture must have been long delayed in release, for all its much-touted principals have by now gone back to the obscurity from whence they came."

Paul Whiteman's "Melting Pot" number in *The King of Jazz*, 1930.

Dixie Lee in the "Crazy Feet" number from *Happy Days*, 1930.

ALL TALKING, ALL SINGING, ALL DANCING

Marie Dressler as Venus rising from the sea in a burlesque ballet from *The Hollywood Review of 1929*. A minor comedienne in silent films, Miss Dressler became one of the greatest stars of the talkies.

Composer Nacio Herb Brown played his perennial hit, "Singin' in the Rain" for the first time in *The Hollywood Review of 1929*.

Even Mary Pickford succumbed to the craze for all-talking, singing and dancing films, in *Kiki*, 1931.

TEACUP DRAMA

Many, in Hollywood as well as Broadway, assumed that once the screen had found a voice, picture production would consist largely of canning stage hits on celluloid, using the original players with little or no adaptation of the plays to movie terms. Many producers acted on this assumption, and a wave of drawing-room comedies and dramas swamped the screen, monopolizing it along with the musicals. But the new stage plays and their performers, despite their much-heralded "sophistication," were rejected by movie audiences in little over a year. Nicknaming the photographed plays "teacup drama," movie fans complained that nothing ever happened in them, that they left their characters where they found them, and that what passed for action in them consisted exclusively of hand-kissing, cigarette-lighting, and an eternal pouring and serving of tea. The fact that many of these plays took place in Mayfair did not help them. Mayfair in terms of sweet Elinor Glyn was one thing, but the real article bored movie-goers who found British repression less than amusing. By 1931 it was clear that a movie still had to move, and that the major job in filming a play was translating talk into action.

Norma Shearer and Robert Montgomery in *Private Lives*. 1934.

Ina Claire and Robert Ames in *Rebound*, 19

A typical stage grouping in the screen version of *The Last of Mrs. Cheyney*, 1929. Left to right: Cyril Chadwick, Madeline Seymour, Moon Carroll, Maude Turner Gordon, Herbert Bunston, Hedda Hopper, George Barraud, Norma Shearer, and Basil Rathbone.

Clive Brook's manner as the hero of *The Laughing Lady*, 1930, with Ruth Chatterton, was so stiffly formal that one critic pretended to mistake him for the butler.

SOUND TECHNIQUE MASTERED

The Cockeyed World, 1929. Edmund Lowe, Lili Damita. This sequel to *What Price Glory?* was a boxoffice smash not only because of its racy situations but also because its actors under Raoul Walsh's direction achieved a free-and-easy speech and manner in marked contrast to the stilted behavior which had characterized "teacup drama."

Hallelujah!, 1929. King Vidor waited five years for the chance to realize his cherished dream of a drama of Negro life with an all-Negro cast before the talkies finally gave him his chance.

All Quiet on the Western Front, 1930. Lew Ayres in his finest role, Raymond Griffith as the dying French soldier. Griffith, a stellar comedian of silent films, retired at the advent of the talkies because of a vocal affliction which made him unable to speak above a whisper, but returned for this last role in which he did not have to utter a word.

Morocco, 1930. In this extraordinary mixture of sophistication and naïveté, Josef von Sternberg told his story in pictures, with sound and dialogue merely a supplement to the visual rather than the major vehicle of the narrative. Here are Marlene Dietrich and Gary Cooper.

Lon Chaney's deformed cripple, seen here with Betty Compson in *The Miracle Man*, 1920, made his reputation.

THE GRIM THIRTIES

HORROR

Instead of true horror, what chiefly substituted for it on the screen of the optimistic Twenties was a species of mystery-comedy borrowed from the contemporary stage—*The Bat, The Cat and the Canary,* and *The Gorilla* were typical of both the stage and screen manifestations of this vogue. In them mysterious events were conjured up as much to amuse as to terrify, and all the apparently supernatural occurrences—clutching hands, ghostly apparitions, flashing lights, ringing bells—invariably turned out to be the elaborately engineered work of an archcriminal bent on concealing his nefarious designs. Incredible though it may seem from this distance, it more often than not *did* turn out to be the Butler whodunit.

The supernatural explained away is only momentarily frightening. The genuine supernatural produces a deeper tremor. In true horror films, the archcriminal becomes the archfiend, the first and greatest of whom was undoubtedly Lon Chaney.

No screen pantomime has been more eloquent than Chaney's, and it is conceivable that he might have become the finest actor in the motion picture medium. It turned out otherwise. Chaney's first important role was that of the cripple in the great hit, *The Miracle Man,* and his success in it convinced producers and the actor himself that his future lay in the creation with make-up of a succession of horrendously monstrous or mutilated characters designed to frighten the public out of its wits. To support his studio-coined title "The Man of a Thousand Faces," Chaney shunned publicity as much as possible, keeping his own personality concealed behind the series of grotesque masks he concocted for his professional roles. Make-up was not his only resource. He twisted his body into agonizing positions to simulate deformity or mutilation, playing a legless man in *The Penalty,* 1920; the title role in *The Hunchback of Notre Dame,* 1923; an "armless wonder" in *The Unknown;* a one-eyed man in *The Road to Mandalay,* 1926; and a paralytic in *West of Zanzibar,* 1929.

As his career progressed, it became obvious that Chaney's popularity was not dependent on his virtuosity at the make-up table. The most terrifying of all his disguises was the simple white wig, spectacles and shawl in which he impersonated an old lady in *The Unholy Three,* 1925, and his straight roles as top sergeant in *Tell It to the Marines,* 1927, tough detective in *While the City Sleeps,* 1928, and aging railroad engineer in *Thunder,* 1929, were liked by the public as much as his grotesques. But the actor (or his studio) seemed driven to conceal his sensitive and somewhat tragic features behind a series of sinister and ever more inhuman masks. He joined forces with a director, Tod Browning, who shared his taste for the outré, and together they packed their films with as many horrid details as they could concoct. In spite of their fascination with the ghostly, however, they seemed to fear audience skepticism and their pictures, like the orthodox "mysteries" of the day, always in the end explained apparently supernatural phenomena as the product of some human agency.

Mr. Wu

The Octave of Claudius

Road to Mandalay

The Hunchback of Notre Dame

The Phantom of the Opera

West of Zanzibar

In his only talkie, the 1930 remake of *The Unholy Three* (far right), Chaney, disguised as an old woman, gives him-

THOUSAND FACES

West of Zanzibar

Laugh, Clown, Laugh

Mockery

Where East Is East

West of Zanzibar

London after Midnight

Tell It to the Marines

self away in the witness box when his voice inadvertently drops to his natural deep tones. With John Miljan.

Count Dracula's three sisters, also vampires, sleep in coffins in the dungeons of Castle Dracula.

The year Lon Chaney died, his director, Tod Browning, filmed *Dracula* and therewith launched the full vogue of horror films. What made *Dracula* a turning-point was that it did not attempt to explain away its tale of vampirism and supernatural horrors. Something in the air of the early Thirties made audiences believe and enjoy believing what they would have scoffed at ten years earlier. *Dracula's* success led to a wild rummage through Edgar Allan Poe, Robert Louis Stevenson, medieval demonology, pseudo-science, and classic horror tales like Mary Shelley's *Frankenstein*, which, filmed with great skill and taste by James Whale, created an even greater sensation than had *Dracula*. These two films made stars of Bela Lugosi and Boris Karloff, and figures of popular mythology out of the characters they played. Eventually one enterprising exhibitor conceived the repulsive idea of double-featuring these two horror attractions, and they were rebooked everywhere with doctors, nurses and ambulances available for stricken patrons.

Dracula, 1931. Bela Lugosi as the vampire is not a figure in masquerade but a fiend who actually sucks the blood of humans, in this case Helen Chandler's.

264

This terrifying yet pathetic scene was cut by the censors of several states. Through the child who does not fear him, the monster discovers his own humanity. Yet he kills her.

FRANKENSTEIN

Frankenstein, 1931. The synthetic monster is raised to the top of Frankenstein's tower, where the play of lightning will infuse him with "electrical life."

Baron Frankenstein's sadistic assistant torments the monster with fire, the only thing he fears. Eventually it destroys him.

THE SONS AND DAUGHTERS OF FRANKENSTEIN AND DRACULA

Dracula, Frankenstein, and the other assorted creatures of the horror cycle, achieved a curious kind of commercial if not artistic immortality. There is a limit to human invention (though there seems to be none to human credulity), and it was necessary to resurrect these monsters, no matter how thoroughly they had been killed off in the preceding film. They "returned" either as themselves or as their "sons" or "daughters" or "ghosts." By the 1940s the public had supped full on horrors, and it became necessary to double the charge: wolf-men, vampires, and zombies were co-starred in the later chiller-dillers. Finally the cycle expired in self-burlesque, with such films as *Abbott and Costello Meet Frankenstein*.

Ironically, the star of many of these latter-day minor horror films was the son of the great Lon Chaney of the Twenties. Known as Creighton Chaney, he had set out to make his own name by serious acting, but the studios could not resist the temptation to trade on his father's fame, and he was billed first as Lon Chaney, Jr., and then simply as Lon Chaney—becoming, to a new generation born after his father's death, the only Lon Chaney there was. That an important talent was thus wasted by Hollywood is evidenced by his work in *High Noon* and *Of Mice and Men*.

The Mummy's Ghost, 1944. The studio caption says: "Determining by her weird birthmark that she is the reincarnation of the Egyptian Princess Ananka, 3000 years dead, Kharis (Lon Chaney) carries Amina (Ramsay Ames) off to the deserted mine shack where Youssef Bey awaits."

In *Bride of Frankenstein*, 1935, the pathos of the monster's distorted humanity was emphasized. His obliging creator makes him a woman of his own who takes one look at her prospective mate and screams in horror. Elsa Lanchester is the synthetic woman.

Ghost of Frankenstein, 1942. Boris Karloff having graduated to less strenuous parts, Lon Chaney, Jr. assumed the role of the monster in the fourth Frankenstein film. Evelyn Ankers, Sir Cedric Hardwicke, and Janet Ann Gallow are seen with him.

The Return of the Vampire, 1944. The Wolf-Man, Matt Willis, tenderly opens the coffin bed of the vampire, Bela Lugosi, apparently for the purpose of delivering a package.

THE
GANGSTER FILM

RAW MEAT

In 1930, Darryl F. Zanuck, newly appointed production head of Warner Brothers, let it be known that his production policy henceforth would be planned around headline news. By that decision he brought the gangster film, a minor cycle since the success of *Underworld* in 1927, to stage center. For gang warfare, and the impunity with which gangsters flouted the laws, especially the Prohibition laws, were hot news in the early Thirties. In focusing the camera on this "shame of the nation," Zanuck correctly sensed that the Great Depression audiences were in no mood for the unreal glamorous worlds Hollywood had been showing them. They wanted the raw meat of reality, and he was prepared to give it to them. It is startling, in this day of cautious disclaimers, to recall that the gangster films usually bore a prefatory note: "Every event shown in this film is based on an actual occurrence. All characters are portraits of actual persons, living or dead."

The aesthetic and sociological importance of gangster films in the history of motion pictures is frequently overlooked. They rescued the movies from the dialogue doldrums of the photographed play, and they themselves made a truly functional use of sound. The terrifying chatter of machine guns, the squealing of tires, and the grinding of brakes—all acted as physical stimulants on audiences. Newspapermen like Ben Hecht, John Bright, and Kubec Glasmon, steeped in the notorieties of Chicago, were brought to the Coast to write the gangster movies, and they enriched the dialogue of the screen with the argot of the streets. Such expressions as "So what?" and "So you can dish it out but you can't take it" became part of the language. A corps of knowing players, mostly from Broadway— Edward G. Robinson, Spencer Tracy, James Cagney, Joan Blondell, Warren Hymer, Warren William, Ruth Donnelly, Glenda Farrell and many others—furnished out the portrait of the underworld. To the gangster himself they added the

racketeering night-club proprietor, the gold-digging moll, the strong-arm henchman, the moronic hanger-on. These films showed "a certain section of America to itself against a background of poolrooms, stale beer, cigarette smoke, alleys, bare electric-light bulbs, cities at night. There was never any doubt that the setting was an American city of the Prohibition period."

In 1931 the gangster film dominated the movies. By the middle of the next year it had entirely vanished from the screen, though not because of any lessened popularity. It was suppressed. That sensitive litmus paper, Will Hays, turned blue with alarm at the torrent of protest which the gangster pictures evoked from the Daughters of the American Revolution, the American Legion, and that greater legion of women's and business clubs which run the machinery of community life in the United States. It was useless for Mr. Hays to reply that the gangster films moralized against crime and were grim object lessons that it did not pay. The small-town civic leaders knew, what indeed everybody knew, that Edward G. Robinson in the title role of *Little Caesar*, 1930, had become an ideal for emulation by hordes of young hero-worshipers. Nor did it help to argue that one of the purposes of the gangster films was to arouse the public to a consciousness of the prevalence of wrongdoing. There was in these topical films entirely too much evidence that existing government agencies weren't acting at all, perhaps because they were being paid off. But what probably most alarmed the respectable were certain assumptions, critical not of the breakdown of American institutions but of the institutions themselves. Spencer Tracy, the hero of *Quick Millions*, 1931, says that he is too nervous to steal and too lazy to work, but that a man is a fool to go into legitimate business when he can clean up by applying business methods to organizing crime. These films implied that during the depression the American get-rich-quick instinct could only lead to crime.

Little Caesar
It was against everyday settings such as this that the gangster film was enacted, linking crime with the ordinary life of audiences. (Top) Little Caesar (Edward G. Robinson) is shot in the street. (Bottom) Little Caesar about to commit the first of his murders.

1. James Cagney and his pal, Edward Woods, sneer at Cagney's older brother, who was fool enough to fall for the flag-waving and enlist in World War I where he was permanently disabled.

2. As boys, Cagney and Wood fall in with Murray Kinnell, a small-time sharper, who wins their loyalty by teaching them dirty songs. Then he graduates them to his school for petty thieves.

5. A milestone on the way to the big time is the first tuxedo.

6. Rival gangsters ambush the boys, killing Woods.

CASE HISTORY
OF A
CRIMINAL

The Public Enemy, 1931. This "biography of a criminal," featuring the virile, magnetic, and sinister personality of James Cagney, illustrates the extraordinary factual objectivity which the journalist authors introduced into the writing of gangster films. Its screenplay is as clinical as a case history. Cagney plays a boy whose lower-middle-class environment and shabby-genteel family offer him no

3. When Kinnell double-crosses them, the boys track him down and shoot him in cold blood.

4. The boys induce a speakeasy owner to buy their brand of beer.

7. James Cagney helps Mae Clarke to some grapefruit.

Rough Stuff

The gangster films provided an innovation in courtship techniques for the emulation of young America. When Clark Gable slapped his leading ladies, and Jimmy Cagney pushed the historic grapefruit into Mae Clarke's face, girls longed for a brutal lover who would treat 'em rough and make 'em like it. Mae Clarke's career was probably one of the most strenuous any actress has ever had to endure. Heroine of countless gangster films, she was slapped, kicked, pushed, knocked down, and dragged by the hair for reel after reel.

future other than a threadbare respectability. Rebelling, he falls in with petty criminals. The ward-heelers, fixers, and saloon-keepers of his Chicago district watch his progress in crime with the benevolent approval of school superintendents handing out prizes for perseverance. His life as an adult is detailed with a realism new to the screen. In danger more from rival gangsters than from the police, he moves uneasily from apartment to apartment, his surroundings at once luxurious and sordid, his women women and nothing more. Toward the end of the film, Cagney indicates his boredom with his current mistress by pushing a grapefruit in her face. A few minutes later, his befouled corpse is delivered to his mother's doorstep as though it were the day's supply of meat.

Scarface, 1932. "This is an indictment against gang rule in America and the careless indifference of the government. . . . What are you going to do about it?"

These words prefaced this last and most brutal of the big gangster films. Modeled on the career of Al Capone, *Scarface* depicted the St. Valentine's Day massacre and the hospital murder of "Legs" Diamond. Vince Barnett, to the left of Paul Muni above, supplemented his income as an actor by hiring out at dinner parties as a fake waiter who insulted the guests and "accidentally" spilled food on them. This singular form of humor was much prized by Hollywood hostesses.

The Last Mile, 1932. George E. Stone takes the final walk. Since gangsters—even Prohibition ones—saw the inside of prisons, movies about them spent a good deal of time there, too.

THE UNDERWORLD ON TOP

G-Men, 1935. Barton MacLane and Russell Hopton torment a captured Fed, William Harrigan, while their molls look on. After 1935, the gangster cycle was cautiously revived. Its rehabilitation in the eyes of the respectable was predicated on the canonization of the G-man whose somewhat unorthodox methods of capturing criminals were shown to succeed where normal law enforcement and juridical procedures fail. The public horror over the Lindbergh kidnaping had by then created a mood which tolerated wire tapping, third degree and other violations of civil rights.

Tear-stained Helen Twelvetrees was "betrayed" by no fewer than five men in Donald Henderson Clarke's *Millie*, 1931, each step down in moral degradation being also a step up in her standard of living. But the floods of tears Miss Twelvetrees shed over her betrayals clearly proved that it was all right to have ill-gotten gowns and furs if you didn't *enjoy* them. Here she is weeping in *Panama Flo*, 1932.

THE CONFESSION FILM

THE WAGES OF SIN

The second talkie cycle to follow "teacup drama" was, like its predecessor, depression-inspired. At least as impressive as the violence of the gangster films was their implication that legal ethics and business honor were disintegrating, and now the "confession" film proclaimed that American moral institutions, under the stress of economic panic, were also falling apart. The collapsing institution here documented was female virtue.

The composite heroine of the confession films of the early Thirties was a woman who gave up her chastity in cold blood. Sometimes she did it for money, sometimes—very often—out of self-sacrifice, sometimes she was simply talked into it, but she rarely did it for the fun of it and she always got paid off in some fashion. True, she too paid, for even on the depression screen your sin must find you out. But her payments grew smaller and her gains greater as the cycle rolled on. In fact, making these films became an elaborate game in which the problem was to invent new ways for the heroine to eat her cake and have it too.

These stories were lineal descendants of the servant-girl tales which have been a constant factor in American and English popular literature since the days of Richardson, and today are a genre by themselves in the field known as "confession magazines." Wish-fulfillment for shopgirls and stenogs, they reached the screen sporadically through the Teens and Twenties. When the depression struck, they suddenly gained a much wider audience acceptance. They were an answer to the frustration of the middle-class woman to whom industrial civilization had given a taste for luxury and adventure and who could see no way of achieving either in the economic world of the Thirties except by trading on her sex. But she needed the sanction of morality too, and the movie version of the confession tales neatly resolved her conflict. Watching her favorites on the screen, she learned that you accepted money and a penthouse from a man because you "trusted" him to do right by you. Was it your fault if he turned out a cad, and you were forced into a life of idle sin through the loss of your "reputation"? Obviously not. Obviously someone else was to blame.

The Confession Girl at the crossroads—Norma Shearer pleads with Chester Morris not to leave her merely because she has had an affair with Robert Montgomery. This became the obligatory scene in all confession films, beginning with Miss Shearer's *The Divorcee*, 1930, based on Ursula Parrott's novel, *Ex-Wife*. At first glance it appeared to be a continuation of This Freedom theme of the Twenties: a wife detects her husband's affair, condones it, but goes off on her own with another man for a while. There, ten years earlier, the tit-for-tat situation would have ended. But now the wife has to learn, through loss of her husband and a series of affairs, that sexual freedom may be theoretically accepted but is in practice rejected by the male. This salutary lesson learned, the husband relents and all is hunky-dory.

BENNETT'S BOXOFFICE BULL'S-EYE

Norma Shearer's extra-marital adventures took place from start to finish in high life, while Helen Twelvetrees did most of her weeping in the underworld or in the "gutter." For the feminine audience which so readily responded to this kind of fiction, something of identification and therefore of wish-fulfillment was lacking in both milieus and their central figures. The formula which satisfied the lack was developed around the unlikely person of Constance Bennett. Miss Bennett had starred in two photographed plays, *Rich People*, 1930, and *This Thing*

Called Love, 1929, in which her glazed smartness was an asset. Then she appeared in a talkie version of Cleves Kinkead's old tear-jerker, *Common Clay*, 1930. Miss Bennett seemed miscast in this parlor-drama of a maid seduced by the scion of the house and abandoned by him. Audience response, however, demonstrated that the ladies believed in her and that feminine martyrdom was to be the essential ingredient in the developing pattern of the confession film.

Swiftly Miss Bennett was martyred in a series of

Some confession girls strayed because

. . . they liked nice things, like Constance Bennett (with Adolphe Menjou) in *The Easiest Way* (below) . . . or maybe they were tricked into becoming artists' models, with shocking results, like Constance Bennett in *The Common Law* (right).

Some were animated by the purest motives

. . . like Joan Crawford, who, in *Possessed*, 1931, is a factory heroine who achieves luxury as the mistress of wealthy Clark Gable. He is a candidate for the gubernatorial nomination, and when Miss Crawford learns that their affair may spoil his chances she pretends she has only been playing him for a sucker. When he discovers her noble deception he insists on taking her back, even though they still cannot be married. (It wasn't made clear whether he got the nomination under those circumstances, but what the heck.)

such films—*Sin Takes a Holiday*, November 1930; *The Easiest Way*, March 1931; *Born to Love*, April 1931; *The Common Law*, July 1931; and *Bought*, August 1931—five seductions in less than a year. The star used her ten-week vacation from RKO to farm herself out to Warner Brothers at $30,000 a week. (When informed that taxes on such a salary would be ruinous, she replied to Warner's, "Oh, then you will have to pay the tax for I must have thirty thousand clear.") This display of financial acumen underlined the quality which made her queen of the confession films. In most of her pictures Miss Bennett was seduced by a rich man and left to her fate. Far from weeping by the wayside, after the manner of Helen Twelvetrees, she fought for her man so resourcefully that she eventually won a wedding ring from him. Brittle, articulate, and ingenious, Miss Bennett was unbelievable as the victimized stenographers and artists' models she played, but this very superiority to type helped her audiences believe that she would get out of traps that would hold them fast.

The early confession girls lost their virtue for fun, for luxury, or for nobly self-sacrificial motives. But as the depression continued, films began to touch on a more basic motive for streetwalking: staying alive. In the first of these, *Faithless*, 1932, Tallulah Bankhead is an heiress so wealthy that she refuses marriage with an impoverished $20,000-a-year executive (Robert Montgomery) because he insists that they live on his salary alone. When both are wiped out by the depression, Miss Bankhead in order to go on living in the style to which she is accustomed, becomes the mistress of a rich boor (Hugh Herbert). When she can no longer stand his ill-treatment, she seeks out the penniless Montgomery and they agree to marry and start over. But Montgomery is badly injured in a labor riot and his desperate wife dashes out into the night and hails the first man she meets, as the only way of keeping them going. She is picked up for streetwalking, but the kindly Irish cop relents and sends her home instead of to jail.

Another martyr was Irene Dunne in *Back Street*, 1932. Miss Dunne falls in love with John Boles, who is married and has children. He proposes that she became his mistress, which she does, and so is condemned to live out her years on a side street which he visits secretly. Through the years Miss Dunne ages and ages and changes her clothes, and sentimentalizes over the children she can never have, but she remains faithful to the end.

Common Clay, 1930. Lew Ayres, Constance Bennett.   *Common Clay*. Constance Bennett and baby.

Born to Love, 1931. Constance Bennett, Joel McCrea.   *Born to Love*. Constance Bennett and baby.

Rockabye, 1932. Constance Bennett, Joel McCrea.   *Rockabye*. Constance Bennett and child.

The Blonde Venus, 1932. Cary Grant, Marlene Dietrich.   *The Blonde Venus.* Marlene Dietrich, Dickie Moore.

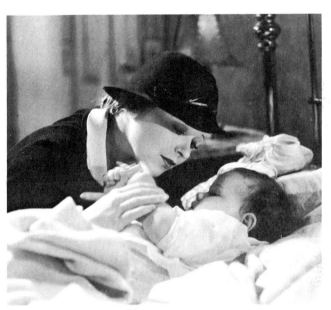

Call Her Savage, 1932. Clara Bow, Monroe Owsley.   *Call Her Savage.* Clara Bow and baby.

BABIES--JUST BABIES

As might have been anticipated, babies were all too frequently the by-products of the illicit love affairs which the confession film featured. Once a figure of shame, the unwed mother now asked for and presumably received the sympathy of her audiences. She always ended, of course, either in the arms of the father of her child or in those of some complaisant male willing to take his place. Constance Bennett had the most screen offspring (with Joel McCrea usually fathering them, so that it was no shock to the movie public when they beheld in 1933 a title credit which read: "Constance Bennett in *Bed of Roses,* with Joel McCrea"). Miss Bennett's children came in handy for many plot purposes, including breach-of-promise suits, marriages in name only, and the foreswearing of promising careers.

By the end of the confession period, babies were used to motivate just one thing—prostitution. Deserted by husbands and lovers, Marlene Dietrich and Clara Bow had to take to the streets in order to buy food for their young, thus ensuring them an even richer harvest of sympathy than Tallulah Bankhead reaped by sacrificing her honor for the sake of her sick husband. Miss Dietrich added a novel twist by taking her young son along when she went on the prowl for customers.

I Am a Fugitive from a Chain Gang, 1932. A jobless veteran, Paul Muni (top), tries to pawn the Congressional Medal of Honor he won in the A. E. F., but they're a drug on the market. He is framed for a robbery he didn't commit, and finds himself in a chain gang at four o'clock in the morning, headed for work on the roads. Edward Ellis is at his right.

TOPICAL FILMS

Though the gangster film temporarily disappeared from the screen in 1932, it left a permanent legacy. Audiences had become conditioned to seeing contemporary life dealt with from a critical point of view. This new attitude, along with speedy continuity, idiomatic dialogue, and naturalistic acting remained characteristic of films of the Thirties.

The policy of basing films on spot news, which had produced the gangster film, also resulted in the topical film, for many years the specialty of Warner Brothers although imitated by the other studios. Ostensibly these pictures did no more than capitalize on topics of current interest. But as the pattern emerged, as writers grew bolder and players more accurate in their reflection of character, the topical film, like the two cycles which preceded it, became a mirror of the subterranean discontent with the American social structure which slowly rose through the depression years.

Individual films in this genre usually attacked the special case and absolved the system as a whole. Frequently their critical tone was veiled by comedy. *The Dark Horse* displayed the naïve mechanisms of American electioneering in terms all too familiar to the citizen. The stupid candidate for governor, "Hicks, the Man from the Sticks," is a tool in the hands of his campaign manager, who has him photographed in fishing togs, newsreeled awarding blue ribbons to prize bulls, and made an honorary chief of an Indian tribe. The film was released during the 1932 presidential campaign, as was a similar satire, *The Phantom President*. Both pictures painted politics as a racket, public officials as hypocrites, and many voters as venal fools purchasable with flattery and government jobs. In like serio-comic vein *The Mouthpiece*, 1932, argued that lawyers were to be had for a price and were the bulwark of organized crime, while *Night Court*, 1932, chronicled the misdemeanors of a grafting judge. News reporters will commit almost any crime for the sake of a story, according to *Scandal Sheet*, 1931, *The Front Page*, 1931, and *Five Star Final*, 1931. *Is My Face Red*, 1932, *Okay, America*, 1932, and *Blessed Event*, 1932,

were films based on the career of Walter Winchell, depicting the rise of a newspaper columnist who grows rich by ruining reputations—and who is adored by the public. *American Madness*, 1932, informed disappointed speculators that banking was a confidence game in which the honest man was left holding the bag.

The majority of topical films were crude snapshots of American life. *I Am a Fugitive from a Chain Gang*, 1932, the apotheosis of the cycle, dealt directly with social abuse, but no picture could afford to be thus uncompromising unless it confined itself to so narrow a field as prison brutality. Nevertheless, the topical films succeeded in voicing a blanket indictment of depression America because their effect was cumulative. *It's Tough to Be Famous*, 1932, *Love Is a Racket*, 1932, *Beauty for Sale*, 1933—what wasn't a racket, what couldn't be bought, in the third year of the depression? Nothing, answered the topical films, which found a sordid story behind every newspaper headline. They were a reflexive and unconscious response to the despondency of a nation.

The giant Negro strikes off Muni's shackles.

The Front Page, 1931. Editor Adolphe Menjou and reporter Pat O'Brien conceal the escaped murderer, George E. Stone, in a rolltop desk while they scoop the rest of the nation's newspapers with his story.

Okay, America, 1932. A victim of famed gossip columnist Lew Ayres threatens to kill him for ruining her reputation, but he is unmoved.

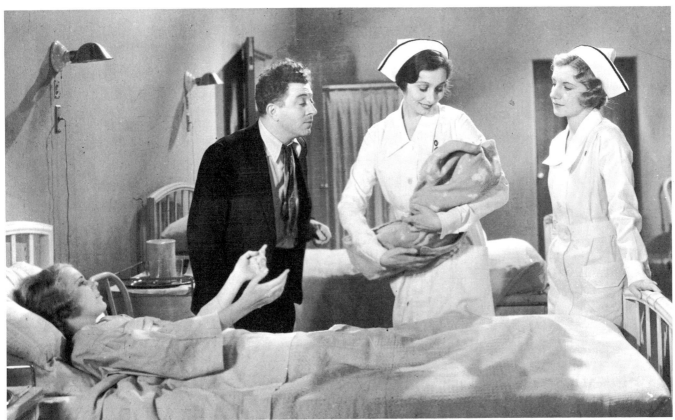

Life Begins, 1932. Nurse Aline MacMahon gives her baby to Gloria Shea while the father, Frank McHugh, looks on. This film, which took place entirely in a maternity ward, was typical of many hospital pictures of the early Thirties, in which audiences were familiarized to the point of burlesque with scalpels, anesthetics, and pulsating oxygen bags.

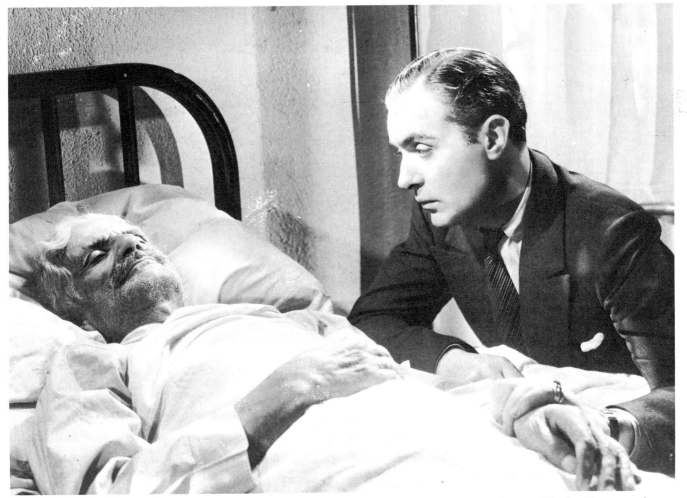

Private Worlds, 1935, was the first American film to dramatize mental illness. Here psychiatrist Charles Boyer comforts a dying Arab patient by speaking a few words to him in his own language.

THE DEPRESSION

The movies ignored the depression as long as they could. But by the end of 1931, prosperity just around the corner had become the grimmest of jokes, and the boxoffice was saying that films which faced the facts of life under the depression paid off. Some films, like *One More Spring*, tried to make light of conditions by picturing the joys of freedom from property and humdrum work, but the jest was

One More Spring, 1935. Jobless singer Walter Woolf King, and penniless producer Warner Baxter, delicately roast a partridge in their new home, Central Park.

Heroes for Sale, 1933, with Richard Barthelmess.

American Madness, 1932. Bank president Walter Huston tries to calm a panic-stricken mob that is making a run on his bank.

sour. Increasingly there appeared on the screen of the Thirties bonus marchers, Hooverville shacks, bank failures, governmental paralysis, embittered veterans. Few films dealt directly with the economic crisis, few placed direct blame for it or offered any precise solution. But in 1932 and 1933 the depression peered out from around the corners of even the brightest and shiniest romance.

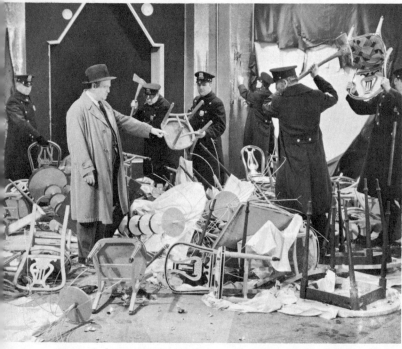

Framed, 1930. Robert Emmett O'Connor, the archetypal detective, supervises the wrecking of a speakeasy, essential to every cops-and-robbers film.

The Devil Is Driving, 1932. In opposition to the glorification of speed in the Twenties, some movies warned the public that gasoline and alcohol won't mix.

Lawyer Man, 1932. William Powell demonstrates to Joan Blondell his ideas about justice.

Hard to Handle, 1933. A survival of the wacky Twenties, marathon dancing was pictured as a racket in the Thirties.

Female, 1933. Surrounded by her executives, tycoon Ruth Chatterton firmly makes a world-shaking decision. As potent a day-dream figure for women as the confession gals, Miss Chatterton played the self-made president of a giant corporation who refuses to marry because she does not want to share her power. Instead, she asks her male subordinates to come up and see her some time, only she always sets the time.

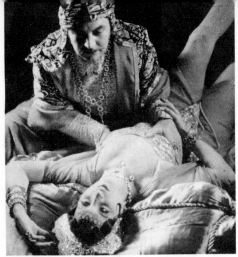

Kismet, 1930.
Sidney Blackmer and Mary Duncan.

Kept Husbands, 1931.
Joel McCrea and Dorothy Mackaill.

The Night Watch, 1928.
Billie Dove and Donald Reed.

Framed, 1927. The studio caption says: "Milton Sills and Natli Barr in a perfervid scene wherein she vamps the hero." The scene was removed from the film by the censors of several states.

DECENCY

THE GATHERING STORM

In theory Will Hays was czar of the movies, but his authority was by no means as absolute as that of the real czars who lay down the ground rules in the field of sports. He could, of course, have imposed his will by threatening resignation if the studios failed to obey his rulings—a resignation which would have signaled that the movies were not keeping their implicit bargain with the public. He chose not to exercise so autocratic a sway. Instead he used the arts of persuasion and cajolery, reasoning that gradual amelioration was preferable to brute dictatorship.

In truth his task was much thornier than those of his fellow-monarchs in baseball and elsewhere. Cleaning up Hollywood was one thing, but protecting the public by removing from pictures what most of the public paid to see was quite another. To simplify his task he caused to be gathered together a codification of all the regulations imposed by state and municipal censor boards upon motion pictures. Between 1927 and 1930 these were combined into a single instrument and promulgated as the Code of the Motion Picture Industry. This was designed as a guide for producers to enable them to anticipate the objections of local censor boards and thus avoid that variegated mutilation which hitherto had been the fate of a number of films. In the course of time the Code came to be regarded as a sort of gentleman's agreement between the Hays Office and the studios, binding the latter to good conduct in accordance with its provisions. But its principal targets were sex and violence, and sex and violence were just what most film-makers regarded as boxoffice insurance. Many an expensive but weak picture, approved in script form by the Code officials, emerged with scenes of undress or brutality added at the last moment to bolster its doubtful pulling power. How easily Mr. Hays's rulings could be evaded was shown in the case of the play *Rain*, which Gloria Swanson wanted to do but which had come under his ban. Miss Swanson simply purchased the original Maugham story and released her film, still substantially *Rain*, as *Sadie Thompson*.

Dante's Inferno, 1924.

Grand Slam, 1933.
Paul Lukas and Sally Blane.

When the depression struck Hollywood, evasions of the Code multiplied. Aside from the brutality and animalism of the gangster films, quite ordinary films increasingly featured "horizontal" love-making, risqué situations, and off-color dialogue, while the camera lingered more and more lovingly over the details of the heroine's preparations for retiring. Hollywood did not deliberately set out to scandalize the nation. Producers simply could not think of anything else as effective for the ailing boxoffice.

Breach of Promise, 1932.
Mary Doran and Eddie Borden.

Red Hair, 1928, with Clara Bow.

Beauty for Sale, 1933.
Charley Grapewin and Una Merkel.

Bachelor Apartment, 1931.
Irene Dunne, Mae Murray, and Lowell Sherman.

The Cockeyed World, 1929.
Edmund Lowe and Victor McLaglen.

A Royal Romance, 1930.
Pauline Starke and Buster Collier.

A Farewell to Arms, 1932. Gary Cooper and Helen Hayes in a scene excised from the film when it was reissued after the formation of the Legion of Decency.

Grand Hotel, 1932. Wallace Beery, Joan Crawford.

The Sins of the Fathers, 1929. Emil Jannings, Ruth Chatterton.

Sadie Thompson, 1928. Gloria Swanson, Raoul Walsh.

THE GATHERING STORM

The same constellation of civic-minded persons, reformers, and busybodies who had frowned on the gangster film watched the growing license of the movies of the Thirties with mounting alarm. They objected not only to leg art, lingerie, and love-making, but also, and even after Repeal, to what they considered excessive drinking in pictures, and to the purchase of novels and plays which by their frankness or realism were thought unsuited for the screen.

Perhaps most of all they disliked the irreverent, cynical, and increasingly critical tone of what was

292

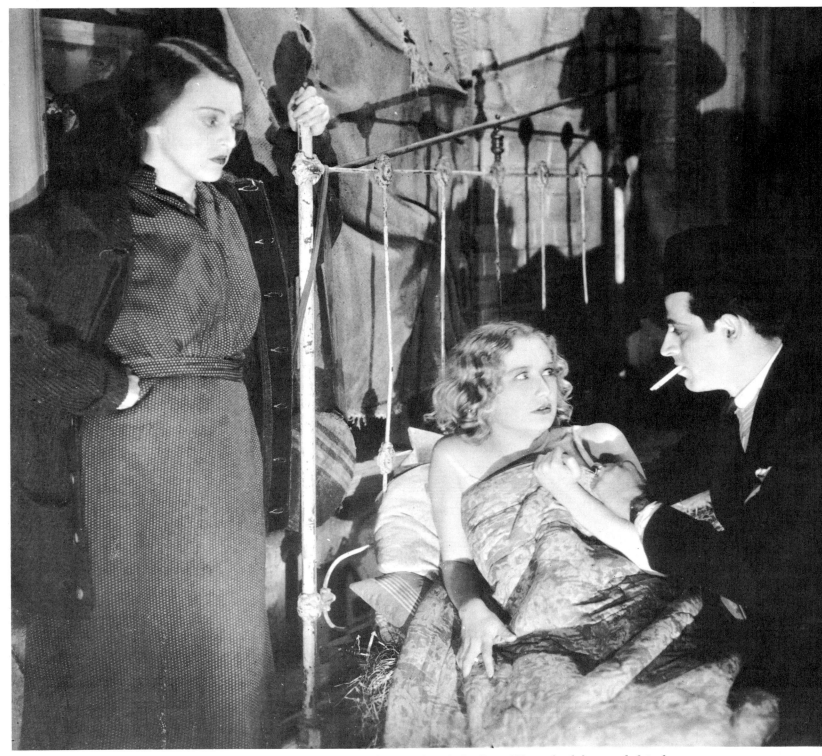

The Story of Temple Drake, 1933. Florence Eldridge, Miriam Hopkins, and Jack La Rue. Women's clubs recoiled in horror when Paramount bought William Faulkner's *Sanctuary*, even though the film was released under a disguising title. Sexual abnormalities were removed from the story, but reformers complained that it still condoned murder, though this one was as condonable a murder as ever was.

coming out of Hollywood. So long as the country lay prostrate under the depression, there was little they could do. They represented a "respectable" viewpoint which was then deeply discredited in the eyes of the country at large. But with the inauguration of the New Deal and the rebirth of hope, they

took courage. It needed only a single incident to set them in motion. Chance provided not one but two. The first was the publication of the results of the Payne Fund studies of the influence of motion pictures in a sensational book called *Our Movie-Made Children*. The second was Mae West.

She Done Him Wrong, 1933.

Mae West and production assistant Boris Petroff discuss "shooting script."

MAE WEST

How far the bars had been lowered is clear from the fact that Mae West was brought to the screen at all. Her stage play, *Sex*, was considered in the theater to be the next thing to straight pornography. Though she toned down her performances for the movies, she left little to the imagination with such bawdy-house songs as "I Wonder Where My Easy Rider's Gone" and "I Like a Man Who Takes His Time." But her success was phenomenal. The nation roared at "Come up and see me some time," "You can be had," "Beulah, peel me a grape," and "It's not the men in my life that counts—it's the life in my men." What delighted everyone, or nearly everyone, about Mae was her honesty. She didn't pretend, like the confession gals, that she had been tricked into turpitude, or that she hated the luxury that went with it. Nor did she atone or reform. She just had a royal good time, and picture's end found her wealthy, wicked, and well loved.

Mae was the last straw. Mary Pickford, apostle of virtue, who however had been around show business long enough not to be shocked at ordinary ribaldry, was quoted as saying: "I passed the door of my young niece's room—she's only about seventeen and has been raised, oh, so carefully—and I heard her singing bits from that song from *Diamond Lil*—I say 'that song' just because I'd blush to quote the title even here." Exactly six months after the release of Mae's first starring picture, *She Done Him Wrong*, the Episcopal Committee on Motion Pictures was formed in October 1933.

She Done Him Wrong, 1933. "I collect diamonds," says Mae West to Gilbert Roland, "it's m' hobby."

Goin' to Town, 1935, with Tito Coral and Mae West. "Mae West eyed a man from head to foot. All the time you knew she was evaluating him in terms of virility, as James Cagney eyed a woman."—LEWIS JACOBS.

Night after Night, 1932. Alison Skipworth with Mae West in Miss West's screen debut. When Miss Skipworth says, "Goodness, what lovely diamonds," Mae replies, "Goodness had nothing to do with it, honey."

THE LEGION OF DECENCY

The Episcopal Committee on Motion Pictures denounced the American motion picture of the Thirties as tending to promote immorality. Such denunciations had been heard before, but the Catholic bishops took action as well. In 1933 they formed the National Legion of Decency, the function of which was to review all new films before their release and classify them under the headings "Passed," "Objectionable in Part," and "Condemned." These findings were announced from pulpits. Communicants of the Catholic church were exhorted to stay away from "partly objectionable" films, and were told that attendance at those "condemned" by the Legion would constitute a venial sin. Jewish and Protestant organizations joined with the Legion in what was intended as a mass boycott aimed at forcing Hollywood to discontinue its ex-

posures and sensationalisms and make what were vaguely described as "good" films. In the big cities, especially those with a large Catholic population, the widely publicized campaign did cause decrease in theater attendance.

Appalled, Will Hays sought help. The old Production Code of 1927-30 was dusted off and rewritten by Father Daniel A. Lord working in close co-operation with Martin Quigley, prominent Catholic layman who also happened to be the publisher of the important trade journal, *Exhibitor's Herald-World*. A branch of the Hays office, the Production Code Administration, was set up in Hollywood under the supervision of a young Catholic newspaperman, Joseph I. Breen, to enforce the Code and, in effect, to police the production of every film from first screen treatment to finished product. All

A CODE

TO GOVERN THE MAKING

OF MOTION AND TALKING

PICTURES

the

Reasons Supporting It

And the

Resolution for Uniform

Interpretation

by

Motion Picture Producers and Distributors of America, Inc.

JUNE 13, 1934

The Motion Picture Code as amended in 1934, whose provisions govern the making of all films produced by the members of the Motion Picture Association.

producers, whether or not members of the Motion Picture Association, could submit their films for precensorship and all had to abide by the Code Administration's rulings, on pain of a fine of $25,000. Perhaps more painful than the fine was the knowledge that the leading theater circuits were at that time controlled by members of the Motion Picture Association, who were not likely to book films lacking Mr. Hays's seal of purity.

Thus was completed the dictatorship of virtue toward which Mr. Hays had been working for twelve years. Since then the Code has been evaded, strictly enforced, or more honored in the breach than the observance, depending on boxoffice fluctuations. Only now is it in the process of partial revision. Its more sympathetic critics urge its alteration in keeping with the changing times. Nothing

short of abolition will satisfy those who contend that, under cover of imposing decency on films, the Code prevents or makes difficult the frank treatment now allowed to books and plays of many phases of modern life. The abolition of the Code today would probably result in an increased demand for state or national censorship, or if that is declared unconstitutional, a sterner exercise of the municipal police power.

When the promulgation of the Code was announced in 1934, Mae West was about to embark on the production of her third film, *It Ain't No Sin*. Among other alterations made necessary by the new dispensation, the title was changed to *I'm No Angel*. Someone whispered at the time that all would have been well if she had simply called her picture *It Is A Sin*.

When the Production Code Administration was set up in Hollywood in 1934, a Jean Harlow picture called *Born to Be Kissed* was in the making at M-G-M. In a panic, the studio changed the title to *100% Pure*. Calm, if not logic, finally prevailed and the film was released as *The Girl from Missouri*, with Miss Harlow and Lionel Barrymore.

Little Women, 1933. Left to right: Jean Parker, Joan Bennett, Katharine Hepburn, Douglass Montgomery, Frances Dee. The success of this vibrant version of the Alcott classic, starring the new favorite Katharine Hepburn, helped the forces of Decency prove that the public really did want "good" films.

THE NEW DEAL

SWEETNESS AND LIGHT

Under the regime of Decency, Hollywood, with considerable grinding of gears, dragged its cameras away from their fixation on contemporary life and turned them on a sweeter and safer day. Charles Dickens, Louisa May Alcott, and Sir James Barrie were the spiritual, as they were often the actual, authors of the stories on which the screenplays of 1934, 1935, and 1936 were based. Victorian England and America, reconstructed with all the skill and care of which the makers of talking pictures were now capable, replaced the penthouse, the gangster, and the shady lady. The favorable audience response to these nostalgic memorabilia caused the trade to reflect that the public might possibly be glutted with sophistication. More likely is that the gradual return of confidence brought about by the early days of the New Deal made it possible for people to believe in goodness again.

David Copperfield, 1935. Frank Lawton as David; W. C. Fields and Jean Cadell as Mr. and Mrs. Micawber. With a bow to Decency, David O. Selznick brought this version of Dickens to the screen, and provided W. C. Fields with his best-loved role.

Little Lord Fauntleroy, 1936. Freddie Bartholomew, who had played the young Copperfield, as Fauntleroy, and C. Aubrey Smith as his grandfather, in another Selznick tribute to the new era.

"FAMILY"

Gangster and topical films had appealed to male audiences; the confession gals had supplied wish-fulfillment for women. Now producers initiated

Love Finds Andy Hardy, 1938, with Judy Garland and Mickey Rooney. Based on a play by Aurania Rouverol, the first film about Judge Hardy and his family was produced as an inexpensive "B" picture. Its success led to a series of immensely popular Hardy films featuring the adolescent antics of Mickey and Judy and the father-image of Lewis Stone.

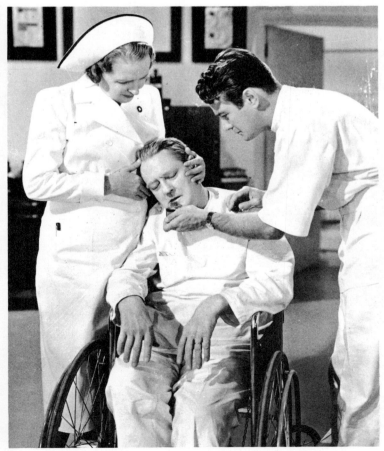

Blondie, 1938. The popular comic strip successfully transferred to the screen with Penny Singleton; Arthur Lake as Dagwood.

The "collapse sequence" from *The Secret of Dr. Kildare*, 1939, with Alma Kruger, Lionel Barrymore, and Lew Ayres. From his wheelchair, the all-wise Lionel Barrymore supervised the activities of Lew Ayres as Dr. Kildare—until it became known that Ayres was a conscientious objector, whereupon Dr. Kildare's shingle was replaced overnight by Dr. Gillespie's.

PICTURES

films designed for the whole family. Often they were *about* families as well, and were made in series—the screen equivalent of soap opera.

The endearing personality of Jackie Cooper and the calculated hominess of Chic Sale had begun to please audiences even before the dawn of the new era. *When a Feller Needs a Friend*, 1932.

Pepper, 1936. 20th Century-Fox teamed Irvin S. Cobb with Jane Withers in a vain effort to replace the late Will Rogers.

Little Miss Marker, 1934, with Shirley Temple and Adolphe Menjou. Displacing Janet Gaynor and Greta Garbo as top star of the Thirties, Shirley Temple achieved greater screen popularity than any child since Jackie Coogan.

Gold Diggers of 1933. Joan Blondell sings "Remember My Forgotten Man" to a chorus of the unemployed, while behind her in silhouette we see the same men when they were fighting in World War I for the country which neglects them now.

CONFIDENCE

"The only thing we have to fear is fear itself." The President's magic words made "Confidence" the slogan of the hour, and Hollywood hastened to do its bit toward restoring belief in the future. The musical film, a neglected corpse since it was done to death in the "all talking, all singing, all dancing" days, was now suddenly resuscitated. Besides providing licit escape from the importunities of landlords and grocers, it was a fitting setting for the fantastic view of New Deal economic panaceas which the movies offered. In *Stand Up and Cheer*, 1934, a Department of Amusement was added to the President's cabinet, its purpose to laugh the country out of the depression; and many musicals of the period featured Forgotten Men and choric hymns to the NRA. Little by little the strictly escapist began to dominate the sermonizing elements in these blithe films. In *Broadway Melodies, Big Broadcasts,* and *Gold Diggers,* Busby Berkeley disposed chorus girls in floral and geometric patterns photographed from above, while musical "fashion shows" exhibited fashions no woman would dare to be seen in. These pictures were merry and tuneful, provided vicarious luxury to the deprived, and were a nice way of "passing the time while waiting for the New Deal to get down your way."

"Hall of Human Harps" from *Fashions of 1934*. A critic observed, "The theme song of mothers of stage-struck daughters might well be, 'I Didn't Raise My Girl to Be a Human Harp,' but the chosen young ladies probably regard it as a royal road to stardom."

The Kid from Spain, 1932. The Goldwyn Girls.

ONE HUNDRED PIANOS, ONE HUNDRED

Dames, 1934. A Busby Berkeley production.

One hundred girls play one hundred pianos in *Gold Diggers of 1935.*

Rosalie, 1937. Nelson Eddy in the distance, back there up on the steps somewhere.

The Big Broadcast, 1932, with Bing Crosby, Stuart Erwin, Leila Hyams. Soon after the beginning of the talkies, radio started to cannibalize Hollywood talent. It offered stars huge sums for brief appearances on the air, to the great distress of movie exhibitors who claimed that people would rather stay home and hear their favorites than pay to see as well as hear them. Soon the screen returned the compliment, beginning with *The Big Broadcast,* which made a star of crooner Bing Crosby and also featured such radio personalities as Kate Smith, the Boswell Sisters, the Mills Brothers, Burns and Allen, and Arthur Tracy, the Street Singer.

Naughty Marietta, 1935. By 1931 operetta had been pronounced officially dead as a screen cycle. The camera emphasized the absurdity of its conventions too cruelly. But in 1935, Irving Thalberg and W. S. Van Dyke found a way to naturalize the marriage of song and plot. *Naughty Marietta* made singing co-stars of Nelson Eddy and Jeanette MacDonald through a decade's worth of mellifluous films.

One Hundred Men and a Girl, 1937. Fifteen-year-old Deanna Durbin's pure soprano enthralled the nation and helped bring "serious" music closer to public acceptance. She was aided by Leopold Stokowski and his musicians.

One Night of Love, 1934. Grace Moore sings the title song while pelting the populace with apples as she rides through the streets of Venice with Lyle Talbot. Miss Moore had made her screen debut in 1930 in *A Lady's Morals* and *The New Moon,* but fans decided that her prim dignity was better suited to the Metropolitan Opera. Determined to conquer the movies she returned in 1934, glamorized and jazzed up and in her first picture was a sensation. Thanks to the marvel of rerecording, she sang, or seemed to sing, better on the screen than she ever had at the Metropolitan. But the public soon found her acting limited and monotonous.

THE OPERATIC

I Dream Too Much, 1935. Lily Pons's coloratura soprano provoked the rude remark that her picture should have been called *I Scream Too Much.*

Here's to Romance, 1935. Nino Martini in a snippet of *Tosca*, Anita Louise in the wings. Operatic scenes on the screen were tolerated by the public only if they were brief, and the histrionic or physical inadequacies of the opera stars militated against their achieving popularity.

INVASION

Rose of the Rancho, 1936. The Metropolitan's Gladys Swarthout, here teamed with established movie singer John Boles, made four films in a doomed attempt to become a favorite.

Carefree, 1938. The dance-poems of Fred Astaire and Ginger Rogers are among the cherished memories of the screen, and their films are as brightly burnished when seen today as they were two decades ago. Astaire was the first to revolt against the Busby Berkeley tradition of photographing dancers from a variety of odd angles in order to exploit "cinematic" opportunities. Astaire insisted that his full figure be kept on camera throughout his dancing, and that it be presented from an audience-eye view, thus unconsciously following in the footsteps of Chaplin.

Second Fiddle, 1939. The movies' unending search for novelty led to the acquisition of Sonja Henie as a skating star of musical films. Miss Henie acquired something too—new millions to add to those she already had.

Born to Dance, 1936. Eleanor Powell in Cole Porter's brilliant musical. Miss Powell came from Broadway to take over as queen of dancing stars.

Thelma Todd, Jimmy Durante, Buster Keaton, and Hedda Hopper in *Speak Easily,* 1932. A reviewer wrote about it, "Buster Keaton's farewell to M-G-M gives major opportunities to Jimmy Durante, but we needn't inquire into that." There was indeed no need to. It had been obvious for two years that M-G-M was building up the Schnozzola at Keaton's expense.

COMEDY AND COMEDIANS

Of the great silent comedians, Lloyd and Keaton had voices well suited to their screen characters, but dialogue slowed their dizzy pace and blunted the fine edge of their miraculous timing. When they spoke, they ceased to be universal clowns and were automatically identified with the particular time and place which their words—often considerably less than inspired—conjured up. Lloyd, independently wealthy and his own producer, continued to make films as long as it pleased him, but Keaton was dispensed with as soon as his contract, signed in the silent days, expired.

No one took their place. There was no longer any nursery for new comic talent. In the first years of the talkies, Mack Sennett carried on in the grand tradition, "discovering" Bing Crosby and re-discovering W. C. Fields, but the growth of the depression-fostered double feature system hurt the short comedy, and the increasing popularity of Disney's cartoons finally killed it altogether. Sennett retired in 1933. Meanwhile screen comedy was in the hands of transients from the stage and vaudeville—stock comics using stock two-a-day material. By the middle Thirties, "slapstick" had become a dirty word. The talking screen had to evolve its own new comedy form.

Ginger Rogers and Joe E. Brown in *You Said a Mouthful,* 1932. Of the talkie newcomers, Brown was nearest the innocent clown of silent days.

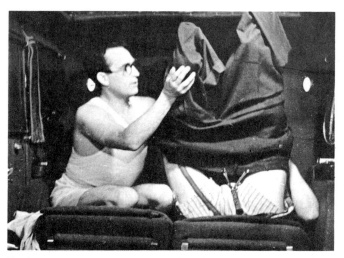

Professor, Beware, 1932. Harold Lloyd repeated his sight gags for the talking camera with fair success for some years, but his brilliant handling of dialogue was not revealed until Preston Sturges made *Mad Wednesday* in 1946.

Robert Woolsey, Bert Wheeler, and Raquel Torres in *So This Is Africa,* 1933. Among the hundreds of vaudevillians drawn to Hollywood by the talkies, Bert Wheeler and Robert Woolsey made an immediate hit and afflicted the screen for five years with wheezy vaudeville gags.

313

All show business predicted that the screen rights to George S. Kaufman's and Marc Connelly's hilarious *Once in a Lifetime* would never be sold. But Carl Laemmle of Universal bought the play, filmed it without change, and prefixed it with a subtitle congratulating himself on his own courage in doing so. The film, like the play, burlesqued the nondescript stage hangers-on who flooded Hollywood as "voice culturists" during the early days of the talkie panic. Mr. Glogauer, Gregory Ratoff, head of the studio, introduces his prize vamp and ingenue to the voice culturist, Aline MacMahon.

Veteran Ben Turpin instructs novice Stu Erwin in the art of pie-throwing, in *Make Me a Star*, 1932, the talkie version of *Merton of the Movies*.

314

Mack Sennett's parody of a Western star at the world premiere of one of his pictures in a small-town theater. Harry Gribbon as the star, Marjorie Beebe as his girl-friend, Andy Clyde as the theater owner in *A Hollywood Star*, 1929.

SATIRE

William de Mille once proposed the formation of a syndicate to purchase an island on which a new state should be erected, to be named Villainova. The inhabitants could be supported in luxury by a tax on Hollywood studios, which in return would receive the right to make the heavies in all their pictures Villainovans. In this fashion they could hope to avoid the protests of foreign governments and domestic pressure groups when one of their nationals or members, fictitious or real, was portrayed on the screen in a less than favorable light.

Lacking a Villainova, the picture industry has solved its problem by making Hollywood itself the major butt of cinematic satire. From *A Vitagraph*

Romance of 1912, to the projected *What Makes Sammy Run*, every facet of picture-making has taken a ribbing, the more acute because the ribbers knew their material at first hand.

Sound provided fresh material in the form of the crudities not only of the early talkies but also of the movies' most formidable competitor, the growing giant of radio. The rivalry of the two great industries had reached a standoff by the early Thirties, and their warfare was merciless. The movies had the advantage, since they could satirize the idiocies of sponsored entertainment visually as well as orally, while radio could only tell funny stories about the goings on in Southern California.

Six of a Kind, 1934. Fields and his famous crooked cue stick. He had an idea that it was funny if an object merely bent when it was expected to break. He was right.

Never Give a Sucker an Even Break, 1941. Fields's deep-rooted suspicion of children always turned out to be founded on fact.

Never Give a Sucker an Even Break. Mr. Fields absent-mindedly blows the head off an ice-cream soda.

The Old-Fashioned Way, 1934. Courtly love-making to an unlovely dame was a Fields specialty.

W. C. FIELDS

Micawber, Major Hoople, Monsieur Verdoux, Cagliostro—all have strong affinities to the character which, for lack of a single name, must be called after its creator, William Claude Fields. The character Fields portrayed was essentially the same in all his films, as were the characters created by Keaton and Lloyd. Originated on the stage in dialogue, Fields extended it by inspired pantomime on the screen into one of the inimitable figures of our time. Martini-drinking, child-hating, gifted with the strange ability to make even humdrum fact seem wildly implausible, the line between Fields's actual self and his screen creation was a blurred one. He became a popular idol as well as the center of a highbrow cult. At the time of his death he was working on a new screen play, *Grand Motel*.

Modern Times, 1936. Assembly-line Charlie: man into machine.

Modern Times. (Paulette Goddard's eye, lower left.)

Modern Times. Machine into satyr.

City Lights, 1931. Genteel tramp and symbol of labor.

Modern Times. Man-eating machine.

CHAPLIN

Charles Chaplin knew that his Charlie the Tramp could not survive speech, and he refused to put him into talkies. His films of the Thirties had musical and sound accompaniment but no synchronized talk. But though Charlie was not put to the test of speech, he was called upon by his creator to face the greater ordeal of survival in a world much more recognizably contemporaneous than the caricatured world of his early adventures.

City Lights, which when it was revived in 1950 *Time* called the greatest film of that or any year, began the process. Here for the first time Charlie was allowed a serious romantic attachment. It was right that his girl should be blind; right that she fall in love not with Charlie but with her imagining of him; not right, in the eyes of many of Chaplin's more critical admirers, that she should recognize him when she regains her sight. This nice question is still being argued.

Five years later, *Modern Times* was still more arguable. It begins with a shot of sheep going down a runway followed by a shot of workers entering a factory. Charlie is set down in the midst of industrial civilization, which is dominated by machinery and in which men are organized into mechanical units, Capital and Labor. Charlie's real enemies are no longer the Cop or the Boss, with whom he can always enter into some human relation, but a vast impersonality, invisible and invulnerable.

Modern Times offered a variety of minor attractions: it featured Chaplin's wife, Paulette Goddard; it had wonderful gags; it indulged in tricks of sound which came to the very brink of being dialogue. But what did the picture mean, what was it trying to say? Because Chaplin charged his usual enormous percentage for it, and because of foreign receipts, *Modern Times* made money, but exhibitors were not happy at the limited audience turnout. For the majority, the new Charlie was too serious; for the minority, not serious enough. Since the picture seemed to be about the dehumanizing effect of machinery, intellectuals called upon Chaplin to join them in reorganizing machine culture to some more human scale of things. Off the screen, Chaplin said nothing. On the screen, his anarchic enmity for any kind of machine culture expressed itself in scenes like that in which Charlie is fed by a machine and that in which, crazed by the assembly line, he runs into the street, his arms moving convulsively like two pistons. Charlie the rebel, Charlie the poet, Charlie the invincibly human, had been turned into a machine.

A Day at the Races, 1937. Chorus: "This woman is mine."

320

A Night at the Opera, 1935. Sig Rumann,. Margaret Dumont, Groucho.

THE MARX BROTHERS

Margaret Dumont recalls that on her first appearance with the Marx Brothers, in the stage version of *The Cocoanuts*, the moment arrived for her entrance but she received no cue. Peering out from the wings, she realized that the Brothers had long since abandoned the script and were improvising scene after scene. Since this could not go on all night, she entered without cue and stood apprehensively awaiting the Brothers' next move. Seeing her, Chico and Harpo made an unceremonious and unexplained exit. Clearly Groucho had no idea of what came next, but he met the situation characteristically. "Ah, Mrs. Rittenhouse!" he said. "Won't you—lie down?"

The reminiscences of other associates, such as S. J. Perelman, on the futility of writing scripts for Marx Brothers comedies, underline the fact that screen historians can contribute nothing to an understanding of the Brothers. The Brothers just exist—Harpo, mutely eloquent, poetic, musical, and fond of blondes; Chico, Greek chorus to the foibles of the others but blind to his own; lamented Zeppo, ineptest of straight men; and the great Groucho, whose conversation "sees to it that no idea gets anywhere, or, if anywhere, that its destination will be of maximum unimportance to the human race." Their pictures create the anarchy Chaplin yearned for. He would have been happier in their world than in that to which another Marx beckoned him.

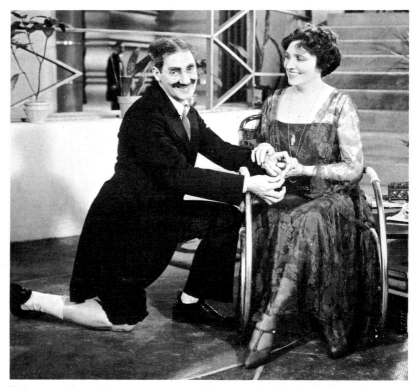

"There ought to be a statue erected," wrote Cecilia Ager, "or a Congressional Medal awarded, or a national holiday proclaimed, to honor that great woman, Margaret Dumont—a lady of epic ability to take it, a lady whose mighty love for Groucho is a saga of devotion, a lady who asks but little and gets it. Surrounded by brothers who are surely a little odd, she does not think so. To her, her world of Marx Brothers pictures is rational, comprehensible, secure. Calmly she surveys it, with infinite resource she fights to keep on her feet in it." *Animal Crackers*, 1930.

321

Horse Feathers, 1932. Professor Quincy Adams Wagstaff (Groucho Marx), President of Huxley College (its closest rival is called Darwin), confers with two of his colleagues in the higher learning, E. J. Le Saint and E. H. Calvert.

THE MARX BROTHERS

A Night at the Opera. Harpo temporarily substitutes a trombone for his usual musical weapon.

A Day at the Races. "Get your tootsie-frootsie ice cream" is Chico's siren song to gullible Groucho in search of a sure thing.

A Day at the Races. Groucho in "disguise" eludes Chico with tray and Harpo with seltzer.

It Happened One Night, 1934. The Walls of Jericho are trembling! Claudette Colbert and Clark Gable.

SCREWBALL COMEDY

Two seemingly routine films of 1934 revolutionized film comedy in the Thirties. The first was a purported murder mystery, the second, one of a short-lived cycle of pictures about bus travel. But both *The Thin Man* and *It Happened One Night* featured something new to the movies—the private fun a man and a woman could have in a private world of their own making. A new image of courtship and marriage began to appear, with man and wife no longer expecting ecstatic bliss, but treating the daily experience of living as a crazy adventure sufficient to itself. And if what went on in these private worlds was mostly nonsense, what sense could be found in the great world outside, where economic crisis and the threat of approaching war barred all the conventional roads to achievement and happi-

ness? It is hard to describe today what these films meant to a depression-bred generation, and it is not surprising that the "screwball comedies," as they came to be called, usually ended in slapstick or violence. They mirrored a world of frustration.

In this context William Powell's suave irony found ideal expression. So did Claudette Colbert's tongue-in-cheek manner and Carole Lombard's air of honest-to-goodness exasperation, while Myrna Loy's calm acceptance of the inevitable in her spouse made her suddenly, after ten years of playing "inscrutable" Oriental sirens, everybody's ideal wife. The brilliant dialogue and violent clowning of these Alice-in-Wonderland comedies held the screen until the onset of war, when the frustrations of the Thirties were replaced by an entirely new set.

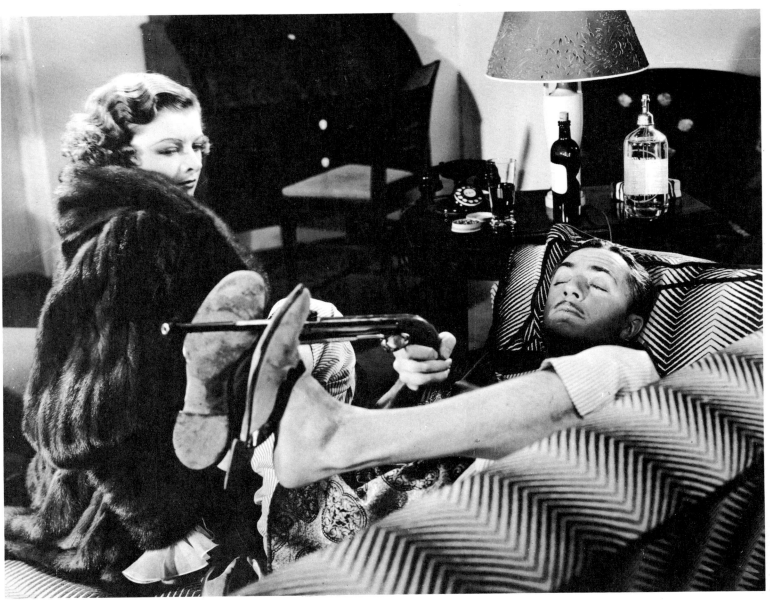

The Thin Man, 1934. "This is the best Christmas present you ever gave me," says Private Eye William Powell to Myrna Loy, as he casually picks off the Christmas-tree balls with his new air pistol.

My Man Godfrey, 1936. Dizzy matron Alice Brady proudly shows off her protegé, Mischa Auer, doing his monkey imitation, while her husband and daughter, Eugene Pallette and Carole Lombard, look on.

The Mad Miss Manton, 1938. Hattie McDaniel welcomes Henry Fonda as instructed by her mistress, Barbara Stanwyck.

Hired Wife, 1940. Rosalind Russell expresses her opinion of her employer-husband, Brian Aherne.

SCREWBALL

Nothing Sacred, 1937. Lombard vs. March: the battle of the century. March scores a kayo in Ben Hecht's and David Selznick's brilliant satire on publicity stunts.

After the Thin Man, 1936. William Powell and Myrna Loy give Asta his dental inspection. Next to Fala, Asta was the most famous dog of the Thirties.

Bringing Up Baby, 1938. Paleontologist Cary Grant tries to bring Katharine Hepburn up to his intellectual level.

Friends of Mr. Sweeney, 1934. Charles Ruggles helps Fred MacMurray cool off after one too many cocktails.

COMEDY

You Can't Take It with You, 1938. Left to right, Isobel Elsom, James Stewart, Jean Arthur, Samuel S. Hinds, Halliwell Hobbes, and Donald Meek hymn the joys of the simple life.

Joy of Living, 1938. Douglas Fairbanks, Jr. impersonates an Indian brave for Irene Dunne in a Tyrolean beer garden.

Topper, 1937. Roland Young stares aghast at the materializing Constance Bennett and Cary Grant. Trick photography gave a new twist to the screwball comedy. As ghosts, Grant and Miss Bennett could indulge in zany antics with even greater impunity than the fleshly screwball heroes and heroines.

The Invisible Man, 1933. Claude Rains orders the helpless William Harrigan to do his will. Rains made his picture debut in a film in which his face was never shown.

RETURN TO SPECTACLE

King Kong, 1933. Brains (plus brawn) vs. brawn. King Kong defeats a Tyrannosaurus while Fay Wray screams from the treetop.

WHITE MAGIC AGAIN

Temporarily suspended by the technical problems of the early talkies, both trick photography and spectacle began to return in the Thirties, with such films as Cecil De Mille's *The Sign of the Cross*, 1932, Cooper and Schoedsack's horrendous *King Kong*, and Universal's thriller, *The Invisible Man*. Gradually the two genres combined into the super-production, which joined camera wizardry to colossal sets and catastrophes of nature in the hope of recapturing the big grosses of an earlier day.

THE SUPER-PRODUCTION

A Midsummer Night's Dream, 1935. James Cagney as Bottom embraced by the enamored Titania, Anita Louise. Literature proved disappointing as a source for superfilms. Warner Brothers' production of Max Reinhardt's version of William Shakespeare's play, though staged with all the wizardry of the studios, did not find public favor.

Lost Horizon, 1937. With Shangri-La a household word, Frank Capra's version of the celebrated James Hilton novel could not miss at the boxoffice. But Capra's, or his set designers', Tibetan paradise was architecturally unconvincing and strangely unattractive. Jane Wyatt as the ageless girl, and Ronald Colman as the intrepid visitor.

THE SUPER-PRODUCTION

The Good Earth, 1937. O-Lan and Wang Lung find their food reserve exhausted. Four years in the making, with much background footage shot on Chinese locations, *The Good Earth's* spectacle and catastrophe impressed the public less than the strong and moving story of one Chinese family. Luise Rainer won an Academy Award for her touching O-Lan.

Mutiny on the Bounty, 1935, with Charles Laughton, Clark Gable, Donald Crisp. This sweeping sea story founded on fact had the bite of veracity in its handling of both ships and men. Laughton's Captain Bligh became one of the legendary villains of the twentieth century.

Romeo and Juliet, 1936. Far more successful than *A Midsummer Night's Dream*, M-G-M's *Romeo and Juliet* had the great advantage of performers like John Barrymore as Mercutio and Edna May Oliver as the Nurse. Norma Shearer and Leslie Howard seemed youthful when compared to the mature, sometimes venerable, players who traditionally have enacted the lovers on the stage, but the intimacy of the camera hardly helped the illusion of extreme youth.

San Francisco, 1936. The 1906 earthquake stunningly re-created by movie magic.

Disraeli, 1929, with George Arliss and Anthony Bushell.

Old English, 1930. George Arliss.

The Man of One Face

Brought back to the screen by the talkies, George Arliss was hailed as a distinguished actor by nice old ladies and other such judges. According to Arliss, Disraeli, Voltaire, Richelieu, and even Alexander Hamilton all looked exactly alike, except for details of costume, and all were crafty but benevolent old gentlemen who spent most of their time uniting unhappy young lovers.

MESSAGE PICTURES

BIOGRAPHY

Cardinal Richelieu, 1935. George Arliss pronounces the Curse of Rome.

Screen biography consisted chiefly of George Arliss tinkering with the course of history until the mid-Thirties, when Warner Brothers, who had adopted the slogan "Good films—good citizenship," began the production of a remarkable series of biographical films including *The Story of Louis Pasteur,* 1935; *The Life of Emile Zola,* 1937; *Juarez,* 1939; *Dr. Ehrlich's Magic Bullet,* 1940; and *A Dispatch from Reuter's,* 1941. Usually starring Paul Muni or Edward G. Robinson, these films shed the light of realism on the contributions to democratic life of healers, research scientists, newspapermen, and humble revolutionaries. Laid in the past, smelling a bit of the lamp, they nevertheless were forceful arguments for enlightenment and rational human progress such as the screen had not previously known. Their modest success encouraged the Warners to permit their writers and directors to take up similar themes in a contemporary setting.

The result was a startling and artistically as well as sociologically admirable series of films which came to grips with such national issues as strikes and strikebreaking, lynching, slums, sharecropping, vigilantism, and migratory workers. All that had been learned about the making of sound films was used to force audiences to recognize the scene as *their* scene and the problems as *their* problems. Vivid and direct, these films were the real social literature of their time. They remain among Hollywood's greatest achievements.

Such films, made by liberals who wanted to use the power of the screen for liberal causes, came to be known as "message" pictures and provoked considerable controversy and criticism within the industry. "When I send a message, I use Western Union," was a common wisecrack of the opposition, and Terry Ramsaye, the embattled editor of the *Motion Picture Herald,* wrote, "If they want to preach a sermon, let them hire a hall." Even Jack Warner said, "Voltaire, Voltaire, all these writers want to be Voltaire." But he continued as long as it remained profitable to encourage Voltaires on the Warner lot—at least.

Rasputin and the Empress, 1932. Lionel Barrymore as Rasputin, John Barrymore as Prince Paul Chegodieff, Diana Wynyard, center background, as Natasha. M-G-M assembled three Barrymores, Ethel, Lionel and John for this lavish, exciting, reasonably factual resumé of Rasputin's assassination and the downfall of the Russian Imperial family. But the widow of the leader of Rasputin's assassins successfully contended in British courts that this retelling of events which she did not deny as true caused her extreme anguish. She received an immense settlement and the film was withdrawn from circulation. The incident made the studios more cautious than ever about filming actual events and real persons in any but the most laudatory terms.

Viva Villa!, 1934. Stuart Erwin seen as an American newspaperman, with the dying Pancho Villa, Wallace Beery. This effective, realistic account of Villa's career revealed comedian Wallace Beery for the great actor he was.

The Story of Louis Pasteur, 1935. Paul Muni as Pasteur confronts the skepticism of Dr. Rossignol (Porter Hall). The Sheridan Gibney-Pierre Collings script concentrated on Pasteur's researches and discoveries and his controversies with his fellow-scientists, with practically no love interest.

AMERICAN OR UN-AMERICAN?

The press hailed Warner Brothers for bringing the art of the screen to maturity with these films in which the materials of the past were used to create a new affirmation of the democratic faith. A decade

MUNI

The Life of Emile Zola, 1937. "By all that I have done for France, by my works—by all that I have written, I swear to you that Dreyfus is innocent. May all that melt away—may my name be forgotten, if Dreyfus be not innocent. He *is* innocent." Paul Muni as Zola at the trial.

later, Jack Warner, appearing before the House Committee on Un-American Activities, heard the same films described as insidious, Communist-inspired propaganda.

Juarez, 1939. Paul Muni as the Indian president who liberated Mexico from the Austrian-born emperor Maximilian and Carlotta and their French supporters. For his work as Pasteur, as Zola, and as Juarez, Muni was acclaimed the screen's greatest actor, a new Jannings.

Mr. Smith Goes to Washington, 1939. James Stewart learns from telegrams that the public, far from supporting him in his dispute with the corrupt "Silver Knight," Senator Claude Rains, sides with Rains. Later, of course, it rallies to Stewart. Frank Capra's immensely popular message pictures argued that all would come right with the nation if we replaced politicians with idealists. His message was, Turn the rascals out, but he was somewhat vague about how to do it.

Black Legion, 1936. Humphrey Bogart takes the oath of fealty to the Legion, which he has joined because of resentment at the promotion of a fellow-worker who happens to be foreign-born. More than half of this extraordinary film was devoted to detailing the mentality, frustrations, and origin of the kind of man who would be attracted by a terroristic society.

MESSAGE PICTURES

Fury, 1936. The faces of ordinary citizens. Only here they are not ordinary citizens but a mob in front of a jail, bent on lynching an innocent man falsely accused on hearsay evidence. Behind his scenes of melodrama, of mobs and jail-burnings, director Fritz Lang brilliantly cross-sectioned the secret life of a small town, uncovering in gossip (left) the seeds of credulity, ignorance and hate which grew into the lynching.

SOCIAL REALISM

How Green Was My Valley, 1941. The crowd at the pithead receives news of the trapped miners, in John Ford's production based on Richard Llewellyn's novel of the Welsh depressed areas.

The Grapes of Wrath, 1940. The Joad family about to set out on their journey to distant California (right). Jane Darwell, Russell Simpson, Eddie Quillan and Henry Fonda say good-by to John Carradine, in John Ford's monumental epic of the Okie migrations. (Above) Russell Simpson, Henry Fonda, player.

Reaction:

Millionaire Walter Connolly looks inquiringly at his butler as his daughter holds a political meeting of her college friends in the living room in *Soak the Rich,* 1936. Most message pictures were frankly New Dealistic, but a few, such as this by Ben Hecht and Charles MacArthur, derided or deplored the rising tide of liberalism and radicalism. In an ad for this film which pained the more sobersides radicals, Hecht and MacArthur were depicted singing: "We're the boys who wrote the yarn/ And here's what it's about/ Class ideas don't mean a thing/ When love kicks 'em out."

Dead End, 1937. The great single set of Samuel Goldwyn's impressive version of Sidney Kingsley's drama of crime-breeding slums. The Messrs. Kingsley's and Goldwyn's humanitarian and reformist intentions in this film had a singular outcome. The famous Dead End Kids, seen in the foreground with Humphrey Bogart, won such popular favor that they were starred in a long series of cheap pictures the "message" of which, if any, was that it was a whale of a lot of fun to be a Dead End Kid.

Little Man, What Now?, 1934. Douglass Montgomery and Christian Rub in Frank Borzage's exposition of the roots of Nazism, one of the first such.

ANTI-FASCIS'

The only "ism" in which Hollywood believes, Dorothy Parker once remarked, is plagiarism. But as the Thirties advanced, as writers increasingly influenced Hollywood culture, as outside events like the depression and the approach of war began inevitably to impinge on the charmed city beside the Pacific, a change became apparent. Theatrical folk traditionally "do not want to be counted," but players, writers, and directors joined antifascist committees, sent ambulances to Spain, food to China, urged the boycott of Nazi and Japanese goods, and sought to persuade the conservative producers to enable them to use the entertainment screen to further these ends. The producers were reluctant. Many of them were as violently opposed to fascism as they were to communism or any but the mildest liberalism; their opposition to producing political pictures was not itself political

Blockade, 1938. Henry Fonda and Madeleine Carroll in the ruins of Madrid. With the outbreak of the Spanish Civil War, Hollywood liberals turned from their preoccupation with domestically oriented message pictures and sought to use the screen to warn of foreign dangers in store. Walter Wanger dared to film the Spanish conflict itself, but his cautious script made it difficult to decide who were the good guys and who the bad. Fearing that the picture would prove a flop, a zealous publicity man reported that it had been banned in Spain. Franco promptly took the hint and banned it.

Confessions of a Nazi Spy, 1939. Francis Lederer and player, Nazi spies, heil the Fuehrer with his secret representative, George Sanders.

ICTURES

but an outgrowth of their rooted belief that people came to the movies to forget just the things which the writers and directors wanted to remind them of. And there were also foreign markets to worry about. Still, yielding to a sense that the times were urgent and ordinary policies might temporarily be suspended, they cautiously permitted the making of pictures which attacked the Nazi, Japanese, and Fascist dictatorships. Although sufficient at a later date to cause them considerable tribulation with Congressional investigating committees, what actually reached the screen was mild indeed.

The one exception was *Confessions of a Nazi Spy,* which, founded almost wholly on fact, used a brilliant blend of documentary and fictional techniques to report to the nation in vivid terms an espionage plot of which few were aware.

Edward G. Robinson as an FBI man in *Confessions of a Nazi Spy* arrests a spy against the background of an actual munitions plant.

Gene Autry (with Smiley Burnette in *Sunset in Wyoming*, 1941) triumphed with vocal and equestrian prowess.

Cimarron, 1931, restored the epic sweep of the old-time Western. The land rush into the Oklahoma Territory was its high spot.

WESTERNS OF THE THIRTIES

In spite of the success of the two early talkies, *The Virginian*, 1929, and *In Old Arizona*, 1929, Hollywood believed that Westerns were washed up when sound came in. Sound-recording problems did initially make outdoor shooting difficult, but with the release of *Cimarron* it was clear that the old-time Western epic would hold the same important place in sound that it had in silence. What did decline to the vanishing point was the routine Western, once the mainstay of the cinema program. Stars like Ken Maynard, Hoot Gibson, and Tim McCoy continued their careers, but in cheaper and cheaper pictures for more and more obscure companies. Then the situation changed overnight with the screen debut of radio singer Gene Autry. Autry still dislikes riding a horse, but his singing of pseudo-hillbilly ballads brought back to the screen the rural audience it had lost to radio. Soon he was joined by singing stars Tex Ritter and Roy Rogers, also from radio and equally innocent of experience as cowboys. William S. Hart, Tom Mix, and other Western stars of the Twenties were actual Westerners, and what they put on the screen had real relation to the West of the nineteenth century; their dramas had the classic simplicity of myth. The world of the new singing cowboys was a strange never-never land where the social conditions of 1880 rubbed shoulders with the costumes and dialogue of 1935.

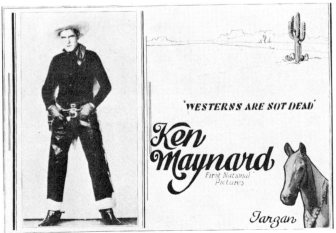

Ken Maynard belligerently proclaimed his faith in the future in an advertisement in the trade press.

Destry Rides Again, 1939. The off-type casting of James Stewart as a nonviolent sheriff and Marlene Dietrich as a very violent saloon songstress turned this old Tom Mix vehicle into a subtle burlesque on Westerns, and bailed out Miss Dietrich's floundering career.

Jesse James, 1939. Mr. Howard's victim. Tyrone Power as Jesse James is shot as he nails "God Bless Our Home" to the wall.

Stagecoach, 1939. The coach, followed by cavalry, winds through the desert. John Ford gave this film the shape and unity of *The Covered Wagon* by focusing on the adventures of a single stage and its occupants.

William Boyd, idolized as the rugged Hopalong Cassidy, began his career as a romantic and marcelled leading man in the costume dramas of Cecil B. De Mille and D. W. Griffith. Here he is in Griffith's *Lady of the Pavements*, 1929, with Jetta Goudal and Lupe Velez.

Anticipating standard television practice, advertisers of the Thirties used stalwart Western stars to induce small fry to buy their products. Here Buck Jones whoops it up for Moxie.

As Western stars increasingly became not only idols but models of conduct for their young audiences, they had to cast their private lives in the im-

After a long career in romantic roles, William Boyd was considered "through" when Harry Sherman cast him as Hopalong Cassidy in several cheaply made films. Since Boyd had detested playing the matinée idol, he gladly adapted not only his screen but his private personality to the new role of Hopalong.

WESTERN

age of rectitude, particularly in view of the publicity cameras. Here Roy Rogers reads grace from the Bible to his family.

While the Western heroes of the Thirties were only actors who got paid for doing a job, their fans expected them to be what they pretended to be, and the line between reality and fiction grew blurred. Here Charles Starrett in an off-screen moment is supposedly ribbed for using make-up by his colleagues, Allan Brook, Clem Horten, and Iris Meredith.

STARS
OF THE THIRTIES

GARBO

Greta Garbo's eagerly awaited talkie debut settled affirmatively the question of whether the spell she wove stemmed from some trick of personality or from great acting talent. But her immediate triumph in talking pictures hastened a serious crisis: the unfortunate effect of the maturation of her talent on her boxoffice draw.

Overshadowed by her later prestige as the screen's greatest actress, Garbo's potent sex appeal in the silents and early talkies has now largely been forgotten. There was in her eyes in those days a look that said to men that for her sex was beside

the point, that indeed she held it so unimportant that she didn't mind if she did. In that derisive gaze was invitation without responsibility, from a woman obviously much too proud to be beholden to a man or ever call him to account. Pride was perhaps indeed the sphinx's secret; the early Garbo was in the literal sense an adventuress of life and love. But Miss Garbo grew older, and something happened to that amused, self-sufficient look. Alistair Cooke has well described the change and its consequences:

"This is the spirit of tragedy, where all is already inevitable before the curtain goes up, and imper-

Grand Hotel, 1932. Greta Garbo and John Barrymore were the top stars of this famous all-star film. Barrymore considered Miss Garbo the screen's greatest artist.

Queen Christina, 1933. The Swedish queen seemed the ideal role for the great Swedish actress, but though the picture marked the exact peak of her popularity it was also the beginning of its decline.

ceptibly, without conscious intention on anyone's part, she moved toward tragic roles as the Thirties wore on, and in tragedy lost her original masculine audience. It was hard to feel the dominant male with this superior woman whose eyes saw and discounted everything in advance. The women remained faithful for a time to this woman who held men so lightly, and they even preferred her films to have tragic endings."

"Garbo was the only one we could kill off," J. Robert Rubin of M-G-M remembers. "The Shearer and Crawford pictures had to end with a clinch, but the women seemed to enjoy watching Garbo die." Even so, the artistic queen of the screen (so regarded by her fellow-players) was in boxoffice trouble by the time of her greatest prestige success, *Camille*, 1936. For one thing, her films were becoming more and more expensive, what with her salary of $250,000 per picture which had to be paid before a camera turned, and her insistence on the best in cast, sets, and especially camera-work. Only her supreme European popularity compensated for the poor domestic returns. Her successful comedy debut

under Ernst Lubitsch's direction in *Ninotchka* turned the tide for a while, but audiences of the late Thirties were slowly withdrawing from this increasingly remote and, to them, somewhat inhuman figure. When the war cut off the European market, Miss Garbo left the screen without officially retiring from it. She could have continued in cheaper films at a lesser salary. She chose the pinnacle or nothing.

Renewed offers have come her way since the war, both in Europe and America, but she has responded seriously to none. She is said to lack confidence in any producer or studio other than M-G-M. She is said to have refused to appear on the stage unless the first fifteen rows of the theater are kept clear of spectators, something no producer could afford. She is said to have rejected fabulous television offers on the ground that she doesn't like to watch television and therefore wouldn't want to appear on it. All this is hearsay and conjecture. Miss Garbo has revealed her mind to no one. Some years ago reporters asked her plans. In the most explicit reply she has ever made to any question, she said, "I don't know, really. I suppose I'm just drifting."

Ninotchka, 1939. Greta Garbo and Melvyn Douglas. By the late Thirties, Garbo had become too austere and remote for average audiences. *Ninotchka* cleverly exploited this by making her a humorless Communist drawn to laughter and love under the spell of Paris.

Camille, 1936. By now the legendary face had both hardened and softened into a mask of tragedy.

Spencer Tracy and Freddie Bartholomew in *Captains Courageous,* 1937.

Mae West and George Raft in *Night after Night,* 1932.

Ann Harding and Thelma Hardwick in *The Right to Romance,* 1933.

Phillips Holmes in *An American Tragedy,* 1931.

GLAMOUR VS. HOMESPUN

Glamour and sophistication were the watchwords of the early Thirties, in terms of screen personalities. But the femmes fatales who crowded the screen in feeble imitation of Garbo, Dietrich, and Mae West

Marlene Dietrich in *Morocco*, 1930.

Tarzan and His Mate, 1934, with Johnny Weismuller, Maureen O'Sullivan. Edgar Rice Burroughs' fantastic character made Olympic champion Weismuller a durable movie star of the depression days.

Gary Cooper and Jean Arthur in De Mille's *The Plainsman*, 1936.

Carole Lombard and James Stewart in *Made for Each Other*, 1939.

soon faded out. In sound as in silence, the audience preferred for daily diet stars who were not too goddess-like for personal identification. Carole Lombard, Jean Arthur, Claudette Colbert, Norma

Shearer among the women, like Clark Gable, Gary Cooper, Spencer Tracy, and James Stewart among the men, were earthy enough to provide lasting ego-images. Most of them lasted well into the Forties.

Grand Hotel, 1932. Joan Crawford, John Barrymore, Lionel Barrymore, Lewis Stone. Beginning with this famous film, M-G-M, with "more stars than there are in heaven," revived the all-star film, which flourished throughout the Thirties, climaxing in *The Women*.

Ruggles of Red Gap, 1935. Charles Laughton, Charlie Ruggles, Maud Eburne, Zasu Pitts.

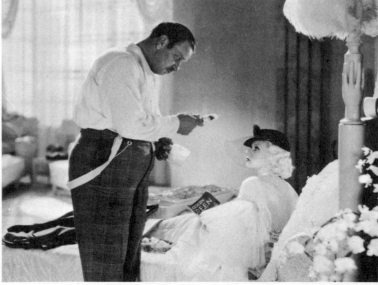

Dinner at Eight, 1933, with Wallace Beery and Jean Harlow.

Cavalcade, 1933. Clive Brook, Diana Wynyard, Irene Browne.

Shirley Temple and Gary Cooper in *Now and Forever*, 1934.

Lightnin', 1930. Until his untimely death, Will Rogers upheld the homely virtues against the tide of sophistication and sex.

The Women, 1939. Rosalind Russell, Joan Crawford.

Mary Pickford and Leslie Howard in *Secrets,* 1933. The last of Miss Pickford's literally hundreds of starring vehicles, after which she voluntarily retired from the screen and devoted herself to producing.

Marie Dressler and Wallace Beery in *Min and Bill*, 1930.

Katharine Hepburn made her sensational screen debut in *A Bill of Divorcement*, 1932, in which John Barrymore gave his finest screen performance.

After a slow start, Bette Davis struck her screen stride as Millie, the venal waitress in *Of Human Bondage*, 1934, seen here with Reginald Sheffield, Reginald Denny and Tempe Piggott.

Hold Your Man, 1933. Clark Gable and Jean Harlow attracted a huge public in a

OF THE THIRTIES

Henry Wilcoxon and Claudette Colbert in Cecil B. De Mille's *Cleopatra*, 1934.

Girls About Town, 1931. Lilyan Tashman and Kay Francis competed for the fashion crown of Hollywood until the former's death in 1934.

series of sexy comedies until Miss Harlow's death ended their association.

Janet Gaynor, Fredric March, and Adolphe Menjou in the first version of *A Star Is Born,* 1937.

HEDDA VS. LOLLY

After the fabulous and reckless Twenties, pressure was brought to bear on Hollywood's merrymakers to draw in their horns. The depression was no time to flaunt sudden wealth or unconventional behavior, especially as Will Hays sought to take over control of fan magazine publicity at the same time that his Production Code imposed its standards on the content of films. Outright scandal was now not available to the more than 200 newspaper correspondents centered in Hollywood, and innuendo perforce took its place. The successive news that Mr. X and Miss Y were "feeling the glow," "smoldering," and "on fire" chronicled their supposed progress toward bed.

Louella O. Parsons, veteran Hearst journalist, proved herself supreme at this form of oblique reporting, and many were the tall tales of her abil-

Playing herself in the movie *Hollywood Hotel*, 1937, the high priestess of movie gossip, Louella O. Parsons, comforts a star, Lola Lane, in a moment of stellar crisis.

The sudden advent late in the Thirties of the veteran player, Hedda Hopper, as gossip columnist and radio chatterer challenged the reign of Louella Parsons as arbitress of the rise and fall of movie careers. Miss Hopper's candid and sometimes acid wit came as no surprise to those familiar with the smartly knowing society women she had played in more than a hundred films.

HOLLYWOOD IN THE THIRTIES

ity to make or break careers, and even affect the destinies of studios. Her supremacy was suddenly challenged at the end of the Thirties by Hedda Hopper. The rivalry between the two produced a distillation described by S. J. Perelman as "sugar and strychnine," but which, however poisonous, became the favorite tipple of an army of fans, perhaps for want of better. For want of better, also, the stars were now seen and photographed exclusively on the set or in night clubs, more intimate glimpses being officially tabu. (The vogue of night-club photographs of stars was no doubt due to the advent of the candid camera, whose cruelties applied to everyone and therefore were tolerated by all.) The game of seeing and being seen in Hollywood hot spots eventually became as elaborate and as compulsory as a court minuet. Many a player

longing for bed because of a 7 A.M. shooting schedule had to make the weary round of the *boîtes;* many the stars who, with absolutely nothing in common, were seen and photographed together in public by studio decree for the sake of ephemeral mention in the columns.

The public, except the very youthful public, was not really deceived by all this. The pitiless glare which had beat on Hollywood so long had revealed every publicity device for what it was. But if people no longer dreamed of movie stars as gods and goddesses of legendary romance, they could still identify with them as successful Americans whose professional secrets they knew and whose private lives were a façade behind which they did as they pleased, which was pretty well understood to be what you and I would please, if we were they.

Nightly, lonely appearances in movieland cabarets were the almost-forgotten D. W. Griffith's last bid for the attention of Hollywood. He gained the attention of few besides veterans such as W. S. Van Dyke, director of *The Thin Man* and *San Francisco,* who had served his apprenticeship with the Master on *Intolerance,* and is shown here with Griffith.

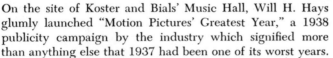

On the site of Koster and Bials' Music Hall, Will H. Hays glumly launched "Motion Pictures' Greatest Year," a 1938 publicity campaign by the industry which signified more than anything else that 1937 had been one of its worst years.

Jeanette MacDonald finger-blends her lipstick while Allan Jones looks on on the set of *The Firefly*, in full view of a disillusion-proof public.

Movie stars in person retained their fascination in the Thirties. Here Tyrone Power and Henry Fonda are ogled by a crowd in Pineville, Missouri, while on location for *Jesse James*, 1939.

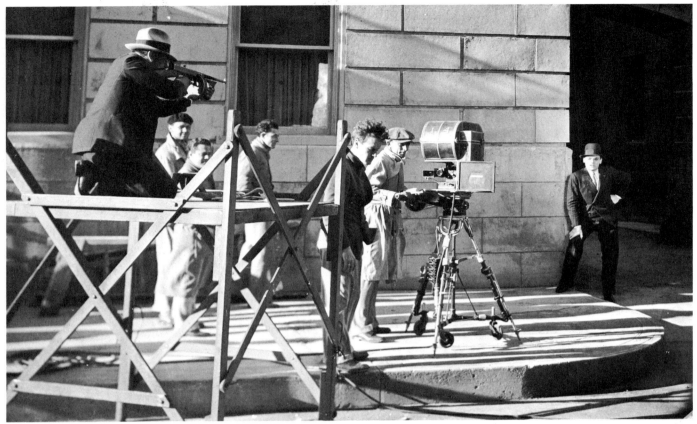

Movie magic reached its zenith in the 1930s. Here an expert marksman prepares to fire a sub-machine gun at a point a few inches from James Cagney's head so the camera can photograph the slugs hitting the building. For *The Public Enemy*, 1931.

Hollywood consolidated its influence over American everyday taste as the decade wore on. Sets like this from *Top Hat*, 1935, invariably furnished and decorated in white, were dubbed "Hollywood modern" by a contemporary decorator and set the national standard for modern elegance.

"Dish Night" and its concomitants, Screeno and Bingo, were doubtful boxoffice panaceas in the slumping Thirties.

In the teeth of the slumping boxoffice the courageous Samuel Goldwyn produced Ben Hecht's and Charles MacArthur's admirable screen version of *Wuthering Heights*, 1939, with Laurence Olivier and Merle Oberon. The Brontë classic did not earn back its cost until it had been reissued twice. Mr. Goldwyn's *The Little Foxes*, 1941, on the other hand, with Bette Davis as the tarantula played on stage by Tallulah Bankhead, earned profits commensurate with its intelligence and dramatic excitement.

INTERLUDE

THE SLUMP BEFORE THE STORM, 1939-1941

Movie tycoons on the eve of American participation in World War II believed that they were suffering all the pains flesh and the screen are heir to. Leading stars were demanding stratospheric salaries. Clark Gable's pay zoomed to $7,000 a week. Garbo received $250,000 per picture, Irene Dunne $100,000. Ann Sheridan, justly indignant at a beggarly $600 a week, fought and eventually won her one-woman war for $2,000 every Friday night. Educators complained that Hollywood treated the public as though it had a twelve-year-old mentality. Reformers bewailed the movie-makers' reluctance to depict the less agreeable aspects of American economic and social life, while Congress proceeded to investigate them as warmongers because of their occasional timid explorations of totalitarian tyranny and brutality. Double features were under attack by clubwomen, clergymen, and crackpots—indeed by everyone except picture patrons who continued to attend them in preference to single films. A Federal court decree banned block booking, the practice of selling at one time a studio's projected output for an entire year; no picture could be merchandised unless it was first displayed to theater owners. But the exhibitors, understandably reluctant to sit through what they would eventually have to play whether they liked it or not, stayed away from the ordained screenings in large numbers.

What was worse, the public stayed away from the subsequent theater showings. According to a Gallup poll, movie attendance, formerly estimated by the Hays office at 85,000,000, had shrunk by 1941 to 55,000,000, and even such tried-and-true boxoffice stimulants as Screeno, Bingo, and Bunko failed to revive the fabulous invalid. Indeed, *Fortune* reported that 79 per cent of the public preferred listening to the radio to movie-going. Incidentally, Mr. Gallup described the typical movie fan as being 27 years of age, earning $28 a week, and strongly averse to patronizing pictures which dealt with the causes or probable consequences of the war. His or her favorite actor was Mickey Rooney.

The highly successful M-G-M musical, *The Wizard of Oz,* 1939. Ray Bolger, Jack Haley, Judy Garland and Bert Lahr.

The only big new star to emerge at the end of the Thirties was Hedy Lamarr, introduced by Walter Wanger in *Algiers,* 1938, with Charles Boyer. The picture itself introduced the diehard catch-phrase, "Come with me to the Casbah."

The burning of Atlanta. Clark Gable as Rhett Butler rescues Belle Watling (Ona Munson) from the holocaust.

Vivien Leigh as Scarlett O'Hara in the famous traveling camera shot of the makeshift hospital in the railroad station, the biggest attempt to reproduce Civil War carnage since *The Birth of a Nation*. From the depths of his involuntary retirement, D. W. Griffith issued a parting shot: "Chaplin says I got the same effect with a close-up of a few corpses."

Louisa Robert, Susan Falligant, and Alicia Rhett, three of the more than a thousand Southern "belles" tested by David O. Selznick for the role of Scarlett O'Hara in *Gone with the Wind*. The book's hordes of fans agreed with Mr. Selznick that an unknown should be found to play Scarlett, but they unanimously decreed that Rhett Butler must be played by Clark Gable. In order to get him, Selznick had to agree to release the picture through his studio, M-G-M.

GONE WITH THE WIND

The faltering Thirties achieved a Gargantuan climax when David O. Selznick's *Gone with the Wind,* destined to gross over $33,000,000, opened in Atlanta late in December 1939. It had taken three years, thirteen scenario writers, three directors, and close to $4,000,000 to translate the 1,037-page colossus of a novel into an even more colossal picture. Four hundred and seventy-five thousand feet of film had been shot, but by dint of Herculean Selznickian efforts these had been cut to 25,000—three and three-quarter hours of epic entertainment. The world had been ransacked for a suitable Cinderella to play the brash and bitchy Scarlett O'Hara. At just the correct moment she was unearthed, not among the unknowns, but in the person of a minor though well-known British film actress, Vivien Leigh.

Even Sherman did not take Atlanta as overwhelmingly as did *Gone with the Wind.* Two thousand of its most eminent citizens were granted the privilege of purchasing expensive seats for the première. Even the critics had to pay and, possibly as a consequence, shouted tumultuous hosannahs. The Mayor declared a three-day festival and urged the city's manhood to raise sideburns or goatees and to wear tight-fitting pants and beaver hats, while its womanhood was admonished to appear minus rouge and abbreviated eyebrows, in hoop skirts and pantaloons. The less distinguished proletariat lined the streets for seven miles to welcome the movie aristocracy with cheers and confetti. As the band blared "Dixie," the delectable Miss Leigh is reputed to have remarked, "How sweet of them to be playing the theme song of our picture."

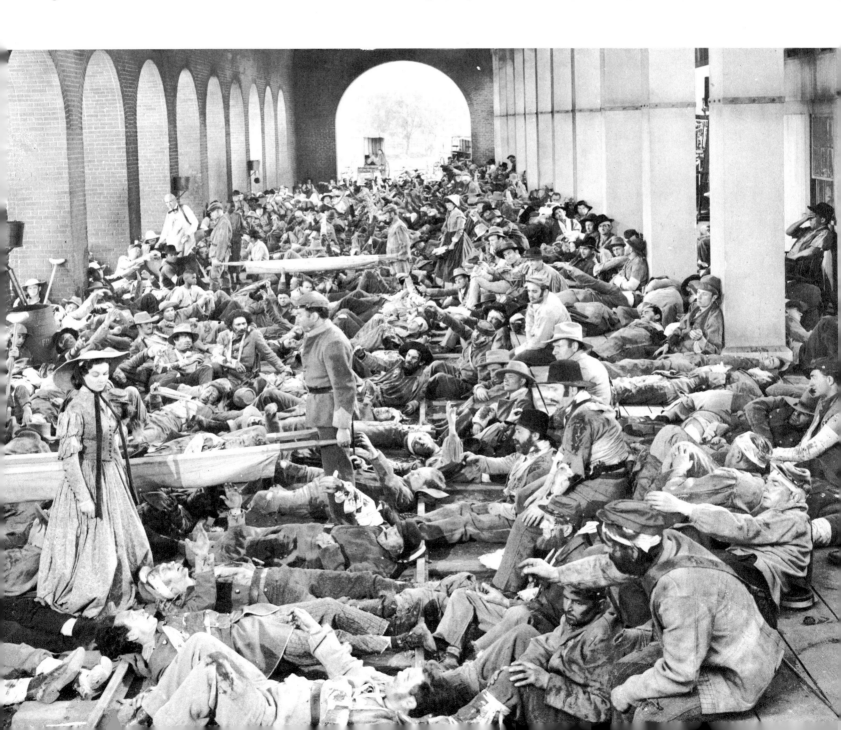

Citizen Kane, 1941. Orson Welles and Joseph Cotten. Welles's admirers took particular satisfaction from the fact that, contrary to usual practice, he put ceilings on his sets and shot scenes so that they were visible. What ceilings portend for the cinematic art has never been explained.

The Magnificent Ambersons, 1942. The great central set of the Amber-

ORSON WELLES

After he had unintentionally hoaxed the citizens of New Jersey half out of their wits with his documentary-style radio version of H. G. Wells's *The War of the Worlds,* it was inevitable that Orson Welles should be sought by Hollywood. RKO gave him an extraordinary contract as producer-writer-

Macbeth, 1948. Orson Welles, in the title role of this "archaeologically correct" rendering, wore the horns and furs of ninth-century Scotland.

director-actor, with control over his material and, apparently, *carte blanche* in the matter of expense.

His first film, *Citizen Kane,* was widely believed to be a thinly disguised treatment of the life of William Randolph Hearst, and as such was denounced sight unseen by Louella O. Parsons in the Hearst papers, which also refused to accept any advertising for the picture. The resulting notoriety aroused widespread expectations, and the reviews were for the most part ecstatic. "It's as though you'd never seen a movie before," said the veteran Cecelia Ager. Some commentators permitted themselves to observe that Welles's much-discussed camera virtuosity consisted largely of devices more experienced directors had learned to avoid because they drew attention to the film-making process. The picture was modestly profitable and Welles, declared an official success, embarked on the production of Booth Tarkington's once-famous, long-forgotten novel *The Magnificent Ambersons* and of Eric Ambler's thriller *Journey into Fear.* He played no part in the first but was Col. Haki in the second. Both pictures were in the cutting stage when a shake-up at RKO resulted in the abrupt cancellation of Welles's contract. Announcing that their future slogan would be "Showmanship in place of genius," the new studio managers released the two Welles films as cut by others. Whether their poor

son mansion. Tim Holt and Agnes Moorehead in vertical conversation.

"This is the biggest electric train any boy ever had to play with," said Orson Welles on being shown over the RKO studio for the first time. Here Welles lines up a scene with his director of photography, the late Gregg Toland.

showing at the boxoffice would have been bettered had Welles been permitted to put in the finishing touches remains conjectural.

A genius fired is more recognizably a genius than ever, and Welles stayed on in Hollywood, acting a few roles from time to time, notably a bravura Rochester in *Jane Eyre*, 1944. After the war he was permitted to direct two films, *The Stranger*, 1946, and *The Lady from Shanghai*, 1948—the latter starring his then wife, Rita Hayworth. Neither was particularly notable, financially or artistically, though both were earmarked with his outré—and nonfunctional—camera-work. Then Herbert Yates of Republic gave Welles the chance to film *Macbeth*. This extraordinary production ended his Hollywood career. Since Scots nobles of this period could not be expected to read or write. Welles had Macbeth dictate his highly incriminating letter to his wife to a priest (generously presented to Shakespeare), but Lady Macbeth was unaccountably able to read. Macbeth's hall, described by King Duncan as "This castle hath a pleasant seat . . . the air is delicate" was shown against Stygian skies as the castle of an ogre. Last authenticity of all, the characters spoke in a thick Scottish burr, and Lady Macbeth's famous lines emerged as "Wha', can thase haands ne'rr be clane." Mr. Yates sadly ordered a dubbed version in which the players spoke

ordinary English, but the picture was still a total debacle at the boxoffice.

Welles went into temporary exile in Europe, where he has been canonized by the intellectuals as a victim of American materialism and indifference to cultural values.

Citizen Kane. Kane, played by Welles, launches his unsuccessful campaign for the Presidency.

369

Mission to Moscow, 1943. Walter Huston as Ambassador Joseph E. Davies, Manart Kippen as Josef Stalin. Three pictures made in 1943 with the laudable intent of aiding the war effort eventually proved embarrassing to their producers: *Mission to Moscow, North Star* and *Song of Russia.* Later they appeared to many either subversive or naïve, or both.

Foreign Correspondent, 1940. Joel McCrea, player, Eduardo Cianelli. Walter Wanger had been preparing to film Vincent Sheean's *Personal History* for five years when the war enabled him to give a new, grim, and timely slant to the adventures of American newsmen in Europe. It seemed a cry for help from a submerged continent.

Casablanca, 1942. Conrad Veidt and Humphrey Bogart. Another lucky break for Hollywood: Warner's *Casablanca,* which was made without knowledge of the American landings in North Africa, was released just a week after the landings took place in Casablanca itself.

Mrs. Miniver, 1942. While Hollywood was deciding how the actual fighting should be treated, it rehearsed the events of the preceding three years, with the Continent succumbing to Hitler while Britain held fast. *Mrs. Miniver* gave eloquent expression to Americans' indignation over the terror-bombings of London. Here Greer Garson and Walter Pidgeon protect their children in the shelter.

WORLD WAR II

THE FIRST DAYS

Picture-making, like gestation, ordinarily requires nine months from conception to delivery. Europe was hit by the Second World War in the fall of 1939 but nothing tangible emerged from Hollywood until midsummer of 1940.

Hollywood's two most ambitious early war efforts were 20th Century-Fox's *Four Sons,* 1940, which attempted to depict the effect of Nazism on the individual members of a Sudeten family, and Metro's *Mortal Storm,* 1940, which far more effectively illustrated the grim realities of life in Nazi Germany. Both of them unfortunately proved boxoffice failures, discouraging further serious efforts of this nature. Much more popular were *Foreign Correspondent,* in which Hitchcock's capacity for creating suspense and excitement prevailed over fourteen script writers, and *Escape,* 1940, taken from a hair-raising suspense novel that cost M-G-M $60,000, a considerable sum at the time. The outstanding war picture of 1941, and also its major boxoffice attraction, was *Sergeant York,* the tender and touching biography of the number-one hero of World War I, a man who, in his simplicity, courage, and religious nature, typified the democratic virtues which we were arming to protect.

Although Hollywood was not particularly successful with its early war efforts and though its major wartime sacrifice, made with tight-lipped gallantry, was the abandonment of the Santa Anita racing meet, the war refused to overlook Hollywood. While the blitz of Britain was at its height the London *Mirror* instructed its California correspondent to cable full details of Ann Sheridan's feud with Warner Brothers, and as the Australian troops in North Africa marched across the desert sands of Libya they lifted their voices to sing a refrain from *The Wizard of Oz.*

The most popular picture of 1942 happened also —this occurs occasionally—to be one of its best. *Mrs. Miniver* dealt honestly with the impact of war upon the life of a middle-class English family, re-

flecting the inner significance of the great struggle rather than its outward trappings. It happily grossed over $6,000,000.

In all, eighty pictures of 1942's output, most of them of little merit, touched in some fashion or other on war if not The War. For a time, the demand for combat titles clogged the machinery of the Motion Picture Association. Six companies sought simultaneously to establish priority on "Remember Pearl Harbor" and three promptly registered "Send Us More Japs," when the Wake Island commander cabled this defiance. After a gallant flyer named Kelly sacrificed his life, one producer wanted to make "Kelly of the U.S.A.," another "Tribute to Kelly" and a third "Kelly the Third."

One of the great sleepers of movie history came out of Hollywood at this time. *Hitler's Children* was produced on the proverbial shoestring but was publicized with the first all-out radio campaign ever tried for a movie. It worked itself up into a high lather and even higher receipts by exposing such tidbits of Nazi brutality as the flogging of lovely damsels with well-developed (and uncovered) torsos for their refusal to cohabit with Prussian supermen.

Hitler's Children, 1943, with Bonita Granville and Tim Holt.

The Story of G. I. Joe, 1945. Robert Mitchum at the left.

Battleground, 1949. Player, Van Johnson and Richard Jaeckel. The Battle of the Bulge re-created four years after.

BLOOD, SWEAT, TEARS--AND PROFITS

War, like crime, may not pay, but it certainly helps the boxoffice. By 1942 everybody not in the army was working, making more money than ever before, and looking for an agreeable way to spend it. What with gas rationing, the automobile was worthless for speeding to roadhouses or necking on lonely lanes. Night baseball was out for the duration. TV was as yet only a faint disturbance on the distant air waves. Few new homes were available, and there were no refrigerators or washing machines to make the few that were available homelike. So that, though the bright lights of the theater marquees were browned out on Broadway and Main Street, the absence of illumination did not diminish the public's appetite for what was inside the theaters. Exhibitors gaily quipped, "You can open a can of sardines and there's a line waiting to get in."

But although the theater owners gloated, an ominous gloom permeated Hollywood. Rumor followed distressing rumor, most of the rumors bearing as little relation to reality as the pictures in production did: the government planned to set up under the OWI a dictatorship over all motion picture production; film raw stock was to be rationed; double features were to be banned. When a maximum of $5,000 was actually established for the

use of new materials in any single set, everybody agreed that this spelled finis to smash musicals and super spectacles, but in a brief time it was discovered that the skill and ingenuity of studio technicians made the regulation only a minor inconvenience. The proposed $25,000 ceiling on salaries, later raised to $67,000, set all movieland in a dither. What executive or star could be expected to labor for so beggarly a sum! Apparently, however, there was little cause for anxiety, for the Treasury tax report for 1942 indicated that Mr. L. B. Mayer of M-G-M had received a salary of $949,765.

By 1944 the movie producers had conspired, wisecracked Nunnally Johnson, that "no writer should get under $250,000 for a script." In the meantime most of the male performers, directors, and technicians had of their own accord taken themselves off the studio payrolls and transferred to Uncle Sam's less generous one. One hundred members of the Screen Writers' Guild alone were in the Signal Corps. The Army, Navy and Air Forces were bursting with cameramen. And the older the star, the more eager he was to join the armed forces and to demonstrate his patriotism, to say nothing of his youth and virility. Most of the big names—Gable, Power, Fonda, Montgomery, Stewart, etc.—man-

Sands of Iwo Jima, 1949. Amphibious landing craft, most important war engine of the Pacific conflict.

Action in the North Atlantic, 1943. Humphrey Bogart cries, "Abandon ship!" in Warners' fearsome account of the perils of the Merchant Marine.

As combat footage and firsthand accounts of the fighting filtered through to Hollywood, war movies took on a convincing toughness which sometimes made it hard to believe they were filmed in a studio. Just as happened after the First World War, several of the best were made by returning veterans who knew the smell of battle.

aged however to get a picture or two under their civilian belts before they replaced them with military ones.

New faces, not to mention new bodies, became an absolute necessity. With the shortage of other handsome young males Van Johnson, M-G-M's fair-haired boy, was the reigning favorite of Hollywood, particularly after his stellar performance in *Thirty Seconds Over Tokyo*, 1944. Lauren Bacall's sultry personality gave *To Have and Have Not*, 1944, something sexy well worth having. Twelve-year-old Elizabeth Taylor raised *National Velvet*, 1944, from a pleasant racing film to an earthy, tender story of a girl who loved and knew how to handle a horse (as well as a disreputable but lovable boy, Mickey Rooney). Esther Williams made her first film dive in *Bathing Beauty*, 1944, and remained on the crest of the wave of popularity for ten years. Jennifer Jones emerged from the *Bernadette* cloister in *Since You Went Away*, 1944, to prove that she was not only a devout girl but a very glamorous one. She played opposite her estranged husband, Robert Walker, whose premature death a few years later was to deprive Hollywood of one of its most promising young performers. June Allyson scored her first musical success in *Music for the Millions*, 1944,

with more than an assist from little Margaret O'Brien. Danny Kaye, fresh from his Broadway triumphs, exercised his fast feet and even faster tongue in Goldwyn's movie version of *Up in Arms*, 1944, and another eastern exile, Frank Sinatra, created a riot among the bobby-soxers upon his arrival in Los Angeles if not in his first important screen appearance in *Step Lively*, 1944. To all intents and purposes the deft and debonair Clifton Webb was also a newcomer when he returned to the screen in *Laura*, 1944, after an absence of twenty years.

When quality of story and performance became less than adequate, Hollywood turned hopefully to quantity. Never before had so large a percentage of pictures sought to atone for their limited merits by the length of their screen footage. *The Story of Dr. Wassell*, 1944, a tale told originally by F.D.R. to Cecil De Mille, and surely told more briefly and cogently, ran 136 minutes. *Dragon Seed*, 1944, dragged on for two and a half hours and *Thirty Seconds Over Tokyo* lasted 138 minutes. As for *An American Romance*, 1944, an epic of the steel industry, it proved that it was an epic by running over two and a half hours. One cynic remarked of *Mrs. Parkington*, 1944, which ran 121 minutes, that "it is two hours too long."

THE WAR DOCUMENTARIES

The American people watched World War II from a grandstand seat without parallel in history. Thanks to the bravery of combat cameramen and the increasing skill of the military film-makers, the war documentaries provided a panorama of the world conflict in a manner which suggested that the cinema was destined to become the history book and the pulpit of the future. The outlook for documentary films seemed unlimited in 1945. But its promise went unfulfilled. In sharp reaction to their widespread showing in wartime, the postwar public turned abruptly back to escapist films.

The True Glory, 1945. Garson Kanin's and Carol Reed's vast record of the liberation of the European continent.

The Life and Death of the U.S.S. Hornet, 1944. "Old Glory" still flies from the staff of the U.S.S. *Hornet,* after a Japanese dive bomber has crashed on the signal bridge of the carrier.

The Battle of the Beaches, 1943. American audiences grew accustomed to seeing their soldiers in scenes of exotic beauty and of unimaginable horror as the Army and Navy attacked and captured one Pacific island after another.

The Fighting Lady, 1944. Filmed in color by the renowned and venerable photographer, Edward Steichen, this saga of an aircraft carrier was one of the most beautiful and honest films of the war.

The Battle of San Pietro, 1944. The bodies of American soldiers (right). Major John Huston's commentary says, "These lives were valuable—valuable to their loved ones, to their country, and to the men themselves," a suggestion unprecedented in a culture which habitually evaluates war casualties in terms of their damage to the feelings of female relatives.

The Great Dictator, 1940. Charles Chaplin as Der Phooey, Adolf Hynkel, contemplates the object of his affections. Chaplin began this hilarious spoof of the Nazis in the Thirties, but by the time it reached the screen audiences found the subject of Hitler too grim for laughter.

Caught in the Draft, 1941. Bob Hope, Eddie Bracken, and Lynn Overman do perfunctory justice to the familiar humor of army life in a typical wartime comedy.

Pardon My Sarong, 1942. Marie McDonald, Bud Abbott, Nan Wynn, Lou Costello. The wartime need for primitive humor sparked the popularity of Abbott and Costello.

COMEDY
IN
WARTIME

Aside from combat documentaries and war dramas, the wartime screen afforded space for little other than comedies and musicals. A few of these, such as *The Great Dictator* and *The More the Merrier*, tried to

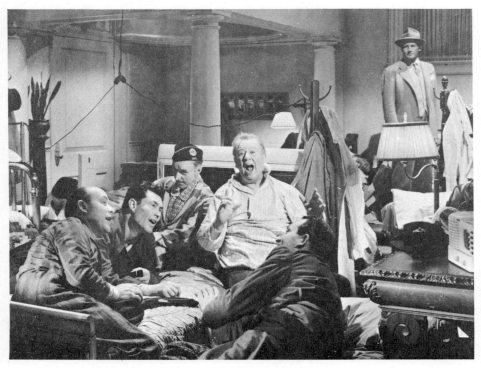

The More the Merrier, 1943. Charles Coburn, center, Joel McCrea, right. Garson Kanin's account of the hazards of housing in war-crowded Washington.

The Road to Morocco, 1942. Dorothy Lamour, Bing Crosby, and Bob Hope in one of the best of their successful "road" series.

find fun in the exigencies and ideologies of the war, but most of them ignored the struggle completely. Hollywood was performing its old function of providing an emotional refuge for the nation.

The Miracle of Morgan's Creek, 1944. William Demarest, Betty Hutton, Diana Lynn. Preston Sturges brilliantly revived the slapstick tradition.

Stage Door Canteen, 1943. Katharine Cornell and Aline MacMahon serve the soldiers.

Babes on Broadway, 1941. Judy Garland and Mickey Rooney in the Hoe Down.

Meet Me in St. Louis, 1944. Judy Garland and Margaret O'Brien.

Yankee Doodle Dandy, 1942. James Cagney and Joan Leslie.

WARTIME MUSICALS

In the years immediately preceding the war, the old-fashioned musical with its hackneyed backstage story serving merely as a pretext for introducing a series of interminable specialties ("clambake shows" in movie gobbledygook) was waning in popularity. A new era was ushered in by *Alexander's Ragtime Band*, 1938, which played a different and irresistible tune—or rather thirty tunes all culled from the six hundred compositions of Irving Berlin. The lyrics were as familiar to American audiences as the stilted story, but together they constituted a cavalcade of the preceding quarter of a century brimming over with sentiment, nostalgia, and patriotism.

The best musical of 1942 and one of the year's highest grossing pictures was *Yankee Doodle Dandy*. It was not only an affectionate, melodious biography of George M. Cohan but a nostalgic evocation of a colorful era in the American theater. *This Is the Army*, 1943's super-duper musical, was a melange of flag-waving, star-singing, fast-stepping hokum showmanship tied up into an unbeatable bundle of boxoffice allure with seventeen smash Berlin songs. By 1943, 40 per cent of the year's films were musicals, and this percentage was maintained for the remainder of the war. Musicals provided escape from war worries and at the same time they permitted the expression of vigorous and unabashed patriotic emotion.

This Is the Army, 1943.

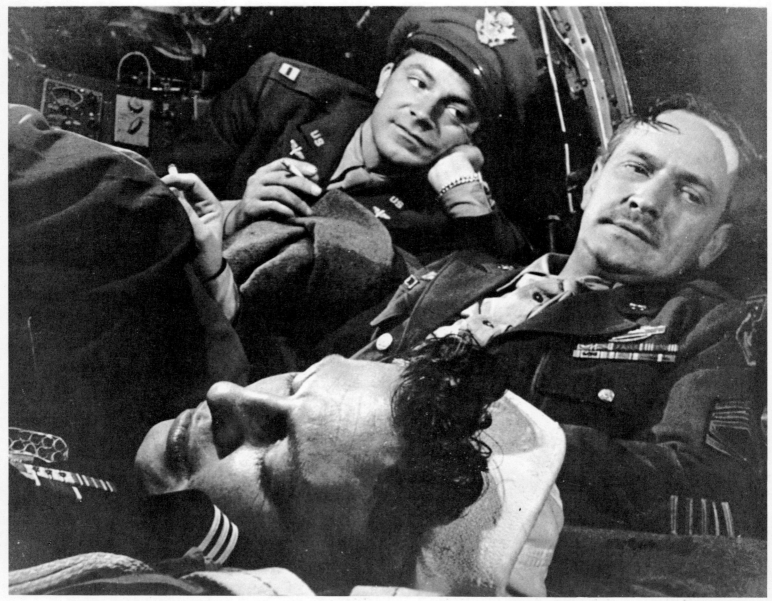

The Best Years of Our Lives, 1946. Three Americans. Captain Dana Andrews, Sergeant Fredric March, and 1st-Class Seaman Harold Russell in the nose of the bomber that is taking them back home.

THE POSTWAR DECADE

"MATURE" FILMS

Through the years the intelligentsia has bitterly criticized "Hollywood" for its failure or refusal to make "mature" films about social and economic problems of national importance. In vain did industry spokesmen reply down through the years that all the evidence showed that the movie audience consisted primarily of children and adolescents of all ages, and that the minority of grownups who said they wanted grown-up films were too casual in their movie attendance to make the production of such films anything but the riskiest of gambles. But the modest success of "message" pictures in the Thirties and the flood of wartime documentaries encouraged hopes that after the war the liveliest and most popular of the arts would assume the responsibilities its more serious-minded well-wishers wanted to confer on it. The men of Hollywood had seen service in all parts of the world and had once again rubbed shoulders with their fellow-Americans. They wanted—or said they did—to project what they had learned onto the screen. There was a general air of expectancy in 1946 that the future of the movies would be very different, and more mature, than their past.

The Best Years of Our Lives seemed to fufill all these hopes. This American masterpiece, the crowning achievement of Samuel Goldwyn's long career, came as near perfection as popular art contrives to be, from its beautifully equivocal and suggestive title to the magnificent performance elicited by William Wyler from the nonprofessional amputee Harold Russell. Goldwyn had enlisted the services of novelist McKinlay Kantor, playwright Robert

Sherwood, and director William Wyler, all of whom had been involved in the war effort. Their film epitomized both the dream and the reality of the postwar world. This intimate engagement with the psychological facts of American life gave it an almost universal audience. But, unlike contemporary and preceding "message" pictures, it was not a preachment. It showed Americans as they are, presented their problems as they themselves see them, and provided only such solutions—partial, temporary, personal—as they themselves would accept. The picture's values are the values of the people in it.

The Best Years of Our Lives. Ex-flyboy Fred Derry (Dana Andrews) in the airplane graveyard.

The Lost Weekend, 1945. Ray Milland in d.t.'s.

The Song of Bernadette, 1943.
The apotheosis of Jennifer Jones.

REST, REST, PERTURBED SPIRIT

The stresses of war gave rise to a generally heightened consciousness of the loneliness of the individual in the modern world, and of his search for anodyne. Three panaceas of the solitary spirit—alcohol, religion, and psychiatry—were examined, suddenly and intensively, by the movies just as war was turning to peace. Charles Brackett's and Billy Wilder's magnificent *The Lost Weekend* chilled and titillated the nation but distillers reported no notable reduction in their profits; in fact it was noted that audiences coming out of theaters where this appalling object lesson was being shown headed straight for the nearest bar. The short-lived spate of psychiatric films, of which the best was Anatole Litvak's *The Snake Pit*, were not particularly scientific in their approach to the growing national problems of neurosis and psychosis. In fact they treated psychiatry as a form of new sorcery, and while they were successful enough in depicting the nightmares of mental disease, all the hopes they held out for its speedy cure were completely unconvincing. Only the religious cycle, that began with *The Song of Bernadette* and reached its climax with *Going My Way*, 1944, and *The Bells of St. Mary's*, 1945, has continued fitfully into the Fifties.

The Snake Pit, 1948, Olivia de Haviland in the depths of her pit.

"SEMI-DOCU-MENTARIES"

The thousands of documentaries produced and shown during the war years were not entirely without influence on subsequent commercial motion picture production. Louis de Rochemont's *The House on 92nd Street* was the first tangible evidence of their impact on the entertainment film. Using many of the techniques he had already developed with "March of Time," and basing his story on FBI files, he told, at a time when the telling could still arouse surprise and consternation, of the operations of an enemy spy ring in our midst. Because it used actual locations and unknown or little-known actors, it escaped from the old-fashioned cloak-and-dagger fustian into the honest excitement of real places and real people.

Its success encouraged such films as de Rochemont's *13 Rue Madeleine*, 1946, *Boomerang*, and Henry Hathaway's memorable *Kiss of Death*, 1947. But these exciting semi-documentaries died in childhood. Their documentary approach had grown out of purposes more serious than plain film-making or money-making. Detached from the inspiration of those purposes, the task of teasing a dramatic pattern out of the materials of everyday life soon came to seem too hard. And, after all, the studios were still there.

Boomerang, 1947. The assassination of a priest.

The House on 92nd Street, 1945. The files of the FBI.

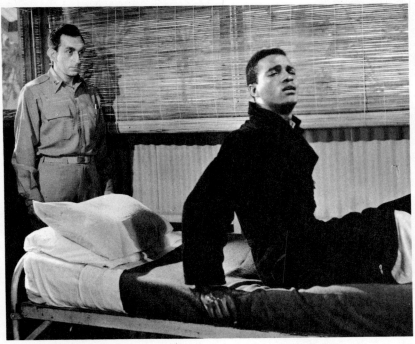

Pinky, 1949. Jeanne Crain, a Negro girl passing as a white, seeks the consolation of her grandmother, Ethel Waters, after she has fallen in love with a white doctor.

Home of the Brave, 1949. "Walk!" Army psychiatrist Jeff Corey tries to get Negro GI James Edwards to overcome his phobias and walk.

Intruder in the Dust, 1949. Claude Jarman, Jr. and Juano Hernandez in the last and best of the Negro dramas, Clarence Brown's version of William Faulkner's novel, which failed to attract a public surfeited with racial films.

HOLLYWOOD LOOKS AT THE MINORITIES

In the late Forties, a sudden spurt of films arguing for racial justice evidenced a considerably greater degree of courage in Hollywood than Hollywood's detractors are willing to grant it. Unfortunately these films also illustrated the almost insuperable obstacles which have to be hurdled by any film-maker who wants to make an honest social statement. In 1946, the literate Dore Schary bought Richard Brooks's wartime novel, *The Brick Foxhole,* for reasons nobody could understand since the book dealt with the tabu subject of homosexuality. Schary changed its theme to the almost equally tabu subject of anti-Semitism. The resulting excellent film, *Crossfire,* 1947, had considerable success. Shortly thereafter the youthful Stanley Kramer, a veteran of Signal Corps "nuts and bolts" films, bought the play *Home of the Brave,* which attacked anti-Semitism. Kramer substituted a Negro for the Jewish hero. *Home of the Brave,* quickly and cheaply made, earned a lot of money, elevated Kramer into the position of the fair-haired boy of the industry, and entirely failed to incite predicted race riots.

Schary and Kramer had realized that the tradi-
tional tabus against public discussion of racial and religious injustice had weakened, and they had had the courage to act on their belief. Then the inevitable happened. The studios attacked the newly freed theme with righteous frenzy. The resulting films, of which the most notable were *Gentleman's Agreement, Intruder in the Dust, Pinky, Lost Boundaries,* 1949, and *No Way Out,* 1950, varied widely in quality. Some hedged, some spoke out plainly against the unresolved dilemma of race and religions. But the flood of such films speedily exhausted public interest in what had been a fresh as well as a brave screen subject. The abrupt end of the cycle again indicated the precarious nature of "mature" films in an industry which had fashioned its mass appeal to a primarily immature audience. At that, the cycle achieved to some extent the social effect so desired by the champions of adult films. Intellectual Negroes boggled at the compromises and evasions in the race films, but no Negro can have been unaware that the fact of his second-class citizenship, so long concealed or denied, was at last being shown on the public screen for all to see.

Gentleman's Agreement, 1948. Gregory Peck, Celeste Holm, and John Garfield in the climactic scene.

Johnny Belinda, 1948. Doctor Lew Ayres introduces the deaf mute Jane Wyman to music.

From Here to Eternity, 1953. Monty Clift blasts it.

Come Back, Little Sheba, 1952. Burt Lancaster, Shirley Booth, Richard Jaeckel, and Terry Moore. Miss Booth's triumphant screen debut in Daniel Mann's admirable version of her stage vehicle.

HOLLYWOOD LOOKS AT BOOKS AND BROADWAY

Hollywood has never had much faith in its own procreative processes. It tends to rely on the seal of success achieved in kindred arts. In its postwar search for "mature" material, it turned, as it had so many times before, to popular current plays and books, and to Broadway for new faces such as Marlon Brando, Judy Holliday, Shirley Booth, Paul Douglas, Richard Widmark and Montgomery Clift.

A Place in the Sun, 1951. Elizabeth Taylor and Montgomery Clift. For the love scenes between this attractive pair, director George Stevens used huge close-ups which "sent" youthful intellectuals who knew not the days of Vilma Banky and Ronald Colman. Told about this, Stevens said, "They'll fall for anything."

All the King's Men, 1949. Broderick Crawford in Robert Rossen's much-praised version of Robert Penn Warren's novel based on the rise of Huey Long.

387

HOLLYWOOD SEES RED

The presidents of the major companies were thoroughly alarmed at the investigation of the "Hollywood Ten" script writers by the Committee on Un-American Activities of the House of Representatives. Believing that the best way to counter the charge that the movie colony was infected with communism was to make anti-communist films, the magnates turned to their writers and directors and said, in effect, "All right, you're so anxious to make message pictures, and to use the screen for serious purposes—be serious about this."

The craftsmen duly sought to be serious, but the

results were weak, routine cloak-and-dagger stuff or imitations of the old Nazi spy melodramas. It was as though the film-makers could not really believe in the menace of communist espionage. Their pictures had the unreality and languor of a command performance. The one obviously honest one, Leo McCarey's *My Son John*, proved the most distasteful. Its hatred of communism seemed mingled with a hatred of everything intellectual. It also implied, probably unconsciously, some curious things about the role of American motherhood and family life in creating future left-wingers.

My Son John, 1952. Robert Walker swears on the Bible to his mother, Helen Hayes, that he is not a Communist.

HOLLYWOOD LOOKS AT THE STARS

The public's enduring fascination with the private lives of actors is shared by actors themselves, and indeed by everyone with whom they are professionally concerned. As a result, every period of Hollywood's history has seen the recurrence of a cycle of films about show business. The latest spate of them produced two of the best pictures of the past decade, *Sunset Boulevard* and *All About Eve*, both released in the same year, 1950. *Sunset Boulevard,* Charles Brackett's and Billy Wilder's mordant study of the old and the new Hollywood, brought the great Gloria Swanson back to the screen, after many years of absence, in the role of a rich but forgotten star slowly moving toward madness as she broods over her vanished fame. The conviction Miss Swanson achieved in this role is the more remark-

All About Eve, 1950. Bette Davis in a prize display of temperament. Anne Baxter, Gary Merrill, Celeste Holm, Miss Davis, Hugh Marlow.

able in that she herself has never ceased to fight for her place in the sun, even after the end of her screen career.

All About Eve dealt with that older forcing-bed of animosities, the theater, where another aging star, Bette Davis, was threatened with the loss of both her career and her man to a scheming newcomer, Anne Baxter. A very funny picture, it had nothing in it quite so novel or quite so penetrating as the contrast in *Sunset Boulevard* between the barbaric grandeur of the silent days and the slick, sharp, safe playing of more recent days. The dialogue in *Sunset Boulevard* was really unforgettable. "You were a big star once," Joe Gillis says to Norma Desmond. She replies, "I'm still big. It's the pictures that got small."

Sunset Boulevard, 1950. Gloria Swanson recounts her past glories to an embarrassed William Holden.

Clara Bow, the IT girl of the Twenties.

Jean Harlow, reigning sex-queen of the Thirties.

Hot Sex

The Outlaw, 1943 (right). Jane Russell in all her glory and in the hay. Miss Russell's first picture, Howard Hughes's *The Outlaw,* was completed during the war but not released until 1946. Meanwhile publicity stills of the star-to-be were adopted as pin-ups in every theater of war and Miss Russell was world-famous before she ever appeared on the screen.

Public Enemy, 1931.

Violence

Detective Story, 1951 (right). William Bendix watches Kirk Douglas get it. This film's serious portrayal of police routine did not lessen its brutality. The public had acquired a taste for violence and even sadism from wartime films which could be satisfied only by a revival of the gangster film.

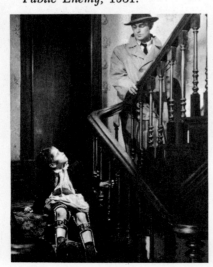

The Maltese Falcon, 1941.

Double Indemnity, 1944.

This Gun for Hire, 1942.

OLD RELIABLES

Despite their desire to bring the movies out of their infancy with mature films on new subjects, American film-makers had to consider the desires of their audience as the Forties wore on. The peacetime cornucopia was pouring forth new cars and new housing, television was racing across the nation, and, above all, Americans were suffering from a sort of "ideological fatigue" after so many years of sacrifice and dedication. Those who had predicted that the movies would never be the same after the war were amazed at how very much the same they were turning out to be. Major emphasis on sex and violence, those basic appeals, speedily reappeared. Tragic romance returned to the screen with *The Heiress,* 1949, and even Ruritanian romance reared its long-forgotten head in *Roman Holiday,* in which Audrey Hepburn presented as lovely and appealing

a princess as the movies had ever offered. Location trips to Italy and Africa were much in vogue, with luxury-loving stars enduring physical hardships to bring the public spectacular thrills. A particular sign of the times was the renewed cultivation of the small-town audience, generally ignored by the major studios in lush periods. *Ma and Pa Kettle,* 1949, was designed for what is insultingly known as the family trade. Costing less than $500,000 and exhibited in the less imposing theaters, it grossed an amazing $2,300,000 and ushered in an apparently endless series of Kettle adventures. Another successful Universal release in the low-bracket field, introducing an almost equally profitable series, was *Francis,* 1949, the comic adventures of a mule who talked and acted more intelligently than most two-legged performers.

Three Weeks, 1924, with Aileen Pringle.

Thirty Day Princess, 1934, with Sylvia Sidney.

Roman Holiday, 1953. Gregory Peck and Audrey Hepburn.

**RURITANIAN
ROMANCE**

The Swan, 1925, with Frances Howard Goldwyn.

The Swan, 1930, with Lillian Gish, O. P. Heggie, Marie Dressler.

The Swan, 1956. Sophisticates of the Thirties and Forties thought Ruritanian romance belonged to as remote a past as *Where Is My Wandering Boy Tonight* until Audrey Hepburn made *Roman Holiday* and Miss Grace Kelly, of Philadelphia and Hollywood, married the reigning Prince of Monaco, thus one-upping Pola, Gloria, Mae, and all the other title snatchers of the Golden Twenties. By stunning coincidence, M-G-M released Miss Kelly's new version of Molnar's old Ruritanian play, *The Swan*, just before the big wedding.

High Noon, 1952. The symbol of integrity. Though he has been in pictures thirty years, the lines which have settled in Gary Cooper's face seem imposed by the physical and emotional climate of his native Montana rather than of Hollywood. Made out of the most ordinary materials of the familiar Western formula, *High Noon* achieved the shape of a democratic allegory which reached people in much the same way and for the same reasons that *The Best Years of Our Lives* had done. Its cutting suspense was the hallmark of director Fred Zinneman's mastery of the movie medium.

High Noon. The sheriff fruitlessly asks the help of the towns-people whom he has stayed to protect.

The Treasure of Sierra Madre, 1948. The last moment. Humphrey Bogart surprised by the bandit chief who he knows will kill him.

WESTERNS

For forty years Hollywood has been sustained by the knowledge that, in good times or bad, a Western, any Western, will play in a minimum of 6,000 theaters and will be gratefully welcomed by a host of fans. But those 6,000 did not include the top-grossing first-run houses of the big cities. Essential to small-town exhibitors, Westerns were believed to be boxoffice poison in the big theaters. But when John Wayne became the nation's top male favorite, it was clear that Westerns were becoming as popular in the first-runs as they had always been everywhere else. This subtle revolution in audience tastes was further pointed up by *The Broken Arrow,* 1950, with its $3,500,000 gross, and *Shane,* 1953, with earnings of more than $8,000,000. The return to the oldest of movie genres meant not so much that films were rounding on their own past but that the country at large was hankering after a vanished America, where danger was the tangible menace of physical combat rather than the fear of losing a job or of an invisible death from the sky. The new vogue of Westerns has not only rolled up big grosses but has also permitted the making, within the Western formula, of two great films, *The Treasure of Sierra Madre* and *High Noon.*

Gary Cooper in a 1929 Western, *Wolf Song,* with Lupe Velez.

POSTWAR MUSICALS

On with the Show, 1929.

The presiding genius of the modern musical—dancer, singer, actor, chore-ographer, and film director—is Gene Kelly. Here he is in *An American in Paris,* 1951, and (center) in *Take Me Out to the Ball Game,* 1949, with Frank Sinatra.

Joan Blondell and chorus in *Gold Diggers of 1937*.

What slapstick comedy was to the silent screen, the Hollywood musical is to movie-goers and movie-makers today. Sometimes the story means something, sometimes it gets lost and stays lost; in any case, these blithe carnivals just keep rolling along. Because they are nearly always about show business show men love them. They love to bring back the old songs and corn of vanished theater and vaudeville days and polish them brightly for a new audience. They disarm even the sophisticates because they are fundamentally so innocent.

Easter Parade, 1948. Judy Garland and Fred Astaire dance to Irving Berlin's "When the Midnight Choo-Choo Leaves for Alabam'." Officially retired, the indestructible Astaire has let himself be lured back before the cameras time and again to show the Forties and Fifties what a really great dancer is like.

399

Sitting Pretty, 1948. Clifton Webb introduced a genuinely novel character with the omniscient Mr. Belvedere. He is shown here in a scene that would have delighted the late W. C. Fields.

The Chaser, 1928.

His Wedding Night, no date.

Born Yesterday, 1950. Broderick Crawford and Judy Holliday in the superb gin rummy scene. Miss Holliday's—and Garson Kanin's—dumb but all-wise blonde was another novel character creation.

POSTWAR COMEDY

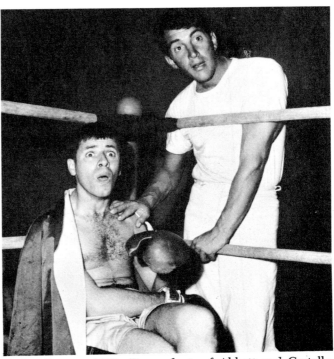

Sailor, Beware, 1951. Descendants of Abbott and Costello, and before that of Wheeler and Woolsey, Martin and Lewis have been the supreme boxoffice comedy team of the Fifties.

Destination Moon, 1950. The former puppet film producer, George Pal, initiated the recent vogue of science-fiction films with this modest descendant of Melies' *A Trip to the Moon* of 1902. Not really very different from the old "mad scientist" horror films, they were given a new look by the improved gadgetry and a wider appeal by the recent spread of technological knowledge. To the satisfaction of the industry, their success has relegated the cheaper science fiction to TV.

A Trip to the Moon, 1902.

Robby the Robot combs Anne Francis' hair. M-G-M's *Forbidden Planet,* 1956.

SCIENCE FICTION

When Worlds Collide, 1951. George Pal's staging of the inundation of New York.

Noah's Ark, 1929.

SPECTACLE

Samson and Delilah, 1949.

When business turns bad some industries economize, but Hollywood finds it pays to spend more —and the most expert of all more-spenders is Cecil B. De Mille. *Samson and Delilah* was his 1949 answer to all that was wrong at the boxoffice. Its huge popularity demonstrated once again that the Bible is the picture-maker's best friend, a never-failing source of spectacle, sex and sadism that no censor could dare to suppress and no movie-goer could afford to miss. It was the direct precursor of such incredibly costly and successful "epics" as *The Robe, Quo Vadis?* and De Mille's latest and greatest spectacle, *The Ten Commandments*, which is well on the way to becoming the biggest boxoffice blockbuster of all time.

Male and Female, 1919.

The Greatest Show on Earth, 1952. Only De Mille could top De Mille. His circus picture grossed over $12,000,000.

405

Ingrid Bergman was several times voted the nation's movie favorite, but withdrew into European exile after the fiasco of her *Joan of Arc* and her elopement with an ace Italian director, Roberto Rossellini. In 1956 she returned triumphantly in *Anastasia* (top). Blessed with bone structure which allowed their faces to age interestingly, Katharine Hepburn and Humphrey Bogart achieved top success together in *The African Queen*, 1951 (left). Miss Hepburn, having exhausted her popularity after five years as a youthful star, achieved a comeback with *The Philadelphia Story*, 1940, which she has maintained through an exacting choice of roles. The late Humphrey Bogart's private peccadilloes confirmed the popular image of him as a what-the-hell guy. He began his career as a stage juvenile said to have been the first to utter the immortal line, "Tennis, anyone?"

Asked how she saw her future a few years ago, Barbara Stanwyck answered, "I want to go on until they have to shoot me." Miss Stanwyck made her first picture, *The Locked Door*, in 1930, and has made more than fifty since. Here she is in *Sorry, Wrong Number*, 1948 (above).

Put out to pasture by M-G-M under its pension plan, "The King" no longer officially reigns on his old lot. But Clark Gable still makes pictures whenever he can be bothered. He made *Four Queens and a King* in 1956 (above left).

Cast as cryptic bums and toughs in the early Thirties, Spencer Tracy hit his stride as the Portuguese fisherman in *Captains Courageous*, 1937, and has been a firm but benign father-figure ever since. Here he is (right) in *The Old Man and the Sea*, 1957.

STARS
OF THE FORTIES
AND FIFTIES

THE INDESTRUCTIBLES

The traditional canon of five years as the life-span of a movie star's career has been shattered to smithereens by the amazing survival capacity of many favorites of the 1930s. It would almost seem that American audiences are beginning to develop the same kind of lifetime loyalty which enabled Bernhardt and Mistinguette to remain stars for half a century in Europe. Not all stars of the Thirties have withstood the ravages of time. Ann Harding, a contemporary of Barbara Stanwyck, is today playing character roles while Miss Stanwyck goes indefatigably on as a youthful heroine. Clark Gable's contemporary, Robert Montgomery, has risen (or fallen) from the screen to the political arena. Gary Cooper, as reliable a favorite as there is today, made his first hit in 1926 in *The Winning of Barbara Worth*. Ponce de Leon was looking in the wrong place: the Fountain of Youth is in Southern California.

The American career of Marlene Dietrich, which began in 1930, has been pronounced finished no less than three times by industry wiseacres, but nobody told Marlene. She is the permanent symbol of sex appeal. She is seen here in *A Foreign Affair*, 1948.

Cary Grant, Grace Kelly in *To Catch a Thief*, 1954. Cary has been the screen's most relaxed Dapper Dan for over twenty-five years.

THE

Barry Fitzgerald and John Wayne in *The Quiet Man*, 1952. An obscure star of Grade-Z Westerns throughout the Thirties, Wayne was molded into top-flight stardom by John Ford. "Ford taught me not to act for the camera but to react," says Wayne.

Bob Hope in *The Seven Little Foys,* 1954. Nobody can kid Bob but Bob, but his every move is a gesture of self-depreciation.

James Stewart as Charles A. Lindbergh in *The Spirit of St. Louis,* 1957. Like Gary Cooper, Stewart has long specialized in playing popular heroes.

INDESTRUCTIBLES

White Christmas, 1954, with Danny Kaye, Bing Crosby. Bing made his first screen appearance crooning in a Mack Sennett talking comedy of 1931.

Brandon De Wilde and Alan Ladd in *Shane*, 1953. The sharpest peak of Ladd's popularity was in the late Forties, but even today he is never idle.

Tyrone Power and Susan Hayward in *Rawhide*, 1951. Does anyone remember how long ago it was that Power had to be billed as Tyrone Power, Jr., to distinguish him from his stage-famous father? Answer: 1937.

Jennifer Jones and Gregory Peck in David O. Selznick's *Duel in the Sun,* 1946. As Mrs. Selznick, Miss Jones has had a steady, calm success reminiscent of Norma Talmadge's long reign in silent films.

MAYBE THEY'LL MAKE IT

None of these stars has been around long enough to prove himself a bona-fide Indestructible—most of them began in the late Thirties or early Forties—but their endurance record so far holds out hope that they too will join that pantheon of personalities whose hold on the public derives, as in the mythologies of old, from the fact that each strikingly exhibits some single attribute of fundamental human nature.

Stewart Granger and Deborah Kerr in the fourth *The Prisoner of Zenda,* 1952. Miss Kerr, refusing to be type-cast, cops the best parts in many of the best pictures.

Ava Gardner and Gregory Peck in *The Snows of Kilimanjaro,* 1952. Miss Gardner was tabbed "a miniature Gloria Swanson" at the beginning of her career, but she has established her own line of sex, magnetism, and off-screen publicity. Peck has been one of the most sought-after male stars of the past decade.

Monsieur Verdoux, 1947. Charles Chaplin in his penetrating "comedy of murders."

THE GREATEST STAR OF THEM ALL

Abandoning for the first time his character of Charlie the Tramp and creating the new and intriguing one of Monsieur Verdoux, Charles Chaplin subtitled his first film in seven years "a comedy of murders." This was meant to shock, as was the picture's attack on war and on capitalism as the source of war, not to mention its ironic sidelights on Christianity—but to shock us to our senses. *Monsieur Verdoux* managed to shock the American middle class, but not in the way its maker had intended. The public connected the distasteful message of this "crazy" film with vague memories of scandals in Chaplin's personal life and his supposed left-wing leanings. *Monsieur Verdoux* was a disaster at the American box-office and was promptly withdrawn from release.

The screen's greatest actor, its most important creative figure, the most famous man in its history, known to more of his contemporaries than even the central figures of the great religions, Chaplin for the first time tasted defeat and failure.

Limelight, which appeared five years later, was booked into only 3,000 theaters instead of the 12,000 which in earlier days had always been eager for any Chaplin film. This debacle had nothing to do with the quality of the picture but stemmed from the efforts of pressure groups which, incensed at Chaplin's defiance of accepted moral and economic standards, exerted all their power to persuade exhibitors not to show and the public not to attend it. Only its tremendous European success, as in the

Limelight, 1952. Chaplin and the beautiful Claire Bloom in what may prove the final appearance of the "Little Tramp" at least in films distributed in the United States.

case of *Monsieur Verdoux,* saved it from financial catastrophe.

But bigotry and hate were not the only reasons for the failures of these two highly personal confessions. They are the films of a man who has withdrawn to a distance to observe the human comedy, and it is from a distance that he sends us his messages. Their Sophoclean irony and detachment are matched by a latent savage anger and an infinite compassion. They deal in high style with our highest concerns. Above all they seek to speak the truth, not the acceptable truth, not necessarily the whole truth, but the truth as an aging man leaving illusions behind sees it. If they have a film counterpart, it is Von Stroheim's *Greed,* and, pressure groups or

no, they were bound to meet the fate of *Greed.*

When Chaplin sailed for Europe for the premiere of *Limelight,* the State Department effectually barred his re-entry to the country where he had made his fame and fortune and contributed so monumentally to the world supremacy of the American film. The Soviet Union invited him to make pictures in Moscow, but he has remained in Switzerland. At the end of one of his early films, *The Pilgrim,* Charlie finds himself between the United States and Mexico, unwanted and menaced in both countries, doomed to straddle the border forever. Perhaps that is where Chaplin stands today. Perhaps that is where he has always stood and has wanted to stand.

Paris, 1926.
Joan Crawford with Charles Ray.

Our Dancing Daughters, 1928.
Joan Crawford, John Mack Brown.

This Modern Age, 1931.
Joan Crawford with Pauline Frederick.

"The greatest star of them all," the phrase with which Erich von Stroheim appeased the crazed Gloria Swanson in *Sunset Boulevard,* has been applied by every female star's admirers to every female star. Professional longevity would seem to be the most objective test of this, and by that yardstick Joan Crawford wins hands down. Mary Pickford's screen career lasted twenty-four years; Miss Crawford began in 1925 and today makes at least a picture a year. As good an explanation as any of her amazing survival value has been her inventiveness and adaptability. Every year the "new" Joan Crawford has looked out from the pages of the fan magazines. Beginning as an ingénue, she made her mark as a jazz baby, became a leading exponent of the "God, the pain of it all" school, turned café society élégante, and ended (for the moment) in her present incarnation of tough-minded career woman fighting for success and love. She has the priceless knack of seeming to create fashions in heroines rather than to follow them.

Only three times in thirty-two years has Miss Crawford's foot slipped, the first when she made two pictures, *Rain,* 1932, and *Today We Live,* 1933, which were beyond her dramatic reach and outside the interests of her fans. She quickly turned the tide with a smash-hit musical, *Dancing Lady,* 1933. Four years later, after a string of undistinguished pictures, an exhibitors' poll listed her among other stars as "boxoffice poison." Such a statement by theater men could be damaging indeed to a studio with unreleased Crawford pictures on its hands, and M-G-M ostentatiously gave her a new contract to prove their faith in her future. But the new contract provided nothing new in the way of story material or handling, and in 1943 Miss Crawford announced that her eighteen-year tenure at M-G-M had been severed by mutual agreement and that she was mov-

Rain, 1932.

Dancing Lady, 1933.
Joan Crawford with Clark Gable.

ing to Warner's. There she remained idle for almost two years while the Warner storysmiths tinkered with possible vehicles for her, and rumors began to fly that she was being gently eased onto the skids. Advised of this, Miss Crawford replied with flashing eyes, "Let them try it!" Evidently "they" didn't dare, for Miss Crawford emerged triumphant in 1945 with one of her biggest hits, *Mildred Pierce*.

"Let them try it!" The bugaboos of Hollywood have no terrors for Lucille Le Sueur, née Billie Cassin, who fought her way up from an ugly and poverty-stricken childhood to the Broadway chorus line and to what then seemed an inauspicious screen debut. Her screen name was chosen for her by a Rochester housewife in a contest conducted by *Photoplay* magazine. Her screen manner, a sort of subdued gutsiness, was achieved after many and sometimes ludicrous experiments, amid the ridicule of the sophisticates. Blessed with bone structure which made her a perfect camera subject, she has continued to mold and remold the outlines of her face with the assiduity of a sculptor seeking unattainable perfection. Her first three marriages ended at the first sign of conflict with her career. She has achieved and enjoyed a sort of marginal motherhood by adopting four children. Miss Crawford's original fans of the dancing-daughter days are balding, graying nonmovie-goers now, and no one knows what segment of the audience supports her pictures. Perhaps the entire audience, and Hollywood itself, feels a sort of religious awe at the spectacle of a woman who has exemplified the American dream by fighting for success, holding onto it, and loving every minute of it. As Miss Crawford stood drinking in the applause after the premiere of *Mildred Pierce*, the ladylike Greer Garson said to her, "Well, none of us should be surprised. After all, my dear, you're a *tradition!*"

Autumn Leaves, 1956.
Joan Crawford with Cliff Robertson.

Sudden Fear, 1952.
Joan Crawford.

Mildred Pierce, 1945.
Joan Crawford with Zachary Scott.

Ice Follies of 1939.
Joan Crawford, James Stewart, Lew Ayres.

Sadie McKee, 1934.
With Edward Arnold and her husband, Franchot Tone.

415

PIN-UPS
AND
SWEATER GIRLS

Rita Hayworth. Although the public is not aware of it, Miss Hayworth's career has lasted about twice as long as that of most stars considered her contemporaries. Brought up in show business from childhood as a member of the troupe known as the Dancing Cansinos, little Rita Cansino began as a plump movie ingénue in Westerns of the early Thirties. Columbia changed her name, streamlined her figure, and launched her on a career in which she became, with Jane Russell and Betty Grable, one of the favorite pin-up girls of the armed services. Originally a favorite with men, Miss Hayworth endeared herself to feminine audiences too through a spectacular private life reminiscent of the glamour queens of the Twenties, and especially through her marriage to the Ali Khan, in which she beat Grace Kelly to the post in the revived title sweepstakes.

Lana Turner in her brunette days.

Jane Russell in *The French Line*, 1954.

A strong contender for first place among the pin-up sister-hood, Betty Grable was top star of the 20th Century-Fox musicals for more than a decade. She is seen here with her admirers in *Meet Me After the Show*, 1951.

At the premiere of *The Seven Year Itch*, 1954.

PIN-UP GIRL SUPREME

Marilyn Monroe hit the star-starved screen with the impact of a tidal wave. "It's Jean Harlow all over again," deliriously declaimed 20th Century-Fox's casting director, Ben Lyon, when he first laid eyes on her. What matter that her acting talent appeared limited to a capacity for manipulating her hips and eyelashes simultaneously, half-closing her eyes, opening her moist lips, and speaking in a high-pitched baby voice? Other less intuitive Fox executives disagreed. After they previewed *Scudda-Hoo, Scudda-Hay,* the first Fox film in which Marilyn appeared, she disappeared. Her role had consisted of one word, "Hello."

They acquired a clearer understanding of dramatic values when, two years later, M-G-M intro-

duced her in a minor part in *The Asphalt Jungle.* To those with their ears to the ground and their eyes on fan mail, it was immediately clear that America's favorite legend, the Cinderella story, was about to be re-enacted on the flamboyant scale that only Hollywood can achieve.

Born June 1, 1925, Norma Jean Martenson was an illegitimate child. Her mother, deserted by both husband and lover, suffered a nervous breakdown; a crazed neighbor tried to smother the baby; at six she was raped by a friend of the family. She was boarded out with no less than twelve indigent families; was sent to an orphanage where for her services scrubbing dishes and toilets she was paid five cents a month. She grew up without affection, education, or self-confidence; but nature had blessed her, in addition to her physical endowment, with a hard inner core of courage, common sense, and resiliency.

Twentieth Century-Fox also had resiliency. After *Asphalt Jungle*, they re-engaged her at six times her previous salary. Five pictures of less than world-shaking consequence in 1953 and 1954 promptly propelled her to the head of the boxoffice parade. Sixteen magazines simultaneously selected her as their cover girl. Psychiatrists wrote lengthy dissertations about the little waif who, deprived of a normal home life, turned to men for love and understanding. The Communists denounced her as capitalism's latest opiate for the masses. Gossip columnists came up with one juicy bit of gossip: Marilyn had posed in the nude for a calendar. Such exposure might have been fatal to anybody else, but Marilyn simply explained that she had needed the money and all was forgotten and forgiven while the sales of the calendar vaulted to six million copies. "Didn't you have *anything* on?" quizzed one sob sister. "Oh yes," answered Marilyn, "I had the radio on."

Other pertinent replies to impertinent questions might have conveyed to the observant that another popular folk myth was in the remaking—the dumb dizzy blonde who is far from being dumb or dizzy. "Is it true you wear falsies?" asked an interviewer. "Those who know me better know better," was Marilyn's succinct reply. "Is it true that you are having trouble with the Johnston Office?" she was queried. "Their trouble," she answered, "is that they worry whether a girl has cleavage. They ought to worry if she hasn't any." In *Gentlemen Prefer Blondes* she gave her first intimations of a gift for light comedy. One critic asked her to explain how she interpreted her role. "I cannot define Lorelei's character," she

replied. "I know what's in her mind." About a favorite subject of many of her admirers, she once said, "Sex is part of nature, and I go along with nature."

The studio executives recognized in Marilyn the perfect replacement for Betty Grable and were nonplused when they discovered that she aspired to study Stanislavsky. (When in a radio interview she discoursed for twelve minutes on the Stanislavsky method, her press agent was accused of ghosting the material for her. He replied, "What press agent knows that much about Stanislavsky?")

In 1955, after she had finished her part in *The Seven Year Itch* (as well as her marriage to baseball's Joe DiMaggio) she told the studio what it could do with her contract and flew east to study at the Actors Studio in New York, read the world's best books, be analyzed and mingle with the intelligentsia. Hollywod was convulsed with laughter—until Marilyn announced the formation of her own production company whose first film would be *The Prince and the Showgirl* with Laurence Olivier as co-star and director. Joshua Logan called it "the best combination since black and white."

Fifteen months after her departure, Marilyn staged a triumphal return to Hollywood accompanied by the accolades of egghead directors such as Kazan and Strasberg, and Pulitzer Prize-winner Arthur Miller as a husband, not to mention a handsome bonus from 20th Century-Fox and a voice in her future stories and directors. Her performance in *Bus Stop*, 1956, indicated that she was on her way to becoming a deft and skillful performer and that an acquaintance with Freud was not necessarily fatal to sex appeal. Marilyn may yet fall on her fabulous fanny, but if she does so it is safe to predict that she will get up and go on to almost as noteworthy ends.

Marilyn Monroe and Jane Russell put handprints in wet cement at Grauman's Chinese Theater, 1953.

Marilyn Monroe.

Marlon Brando and Jean Simmons in *Desirée*, 1954.

Kim Hunter and Marlon Brando in *A Streetcar Named Desire*, 1951.

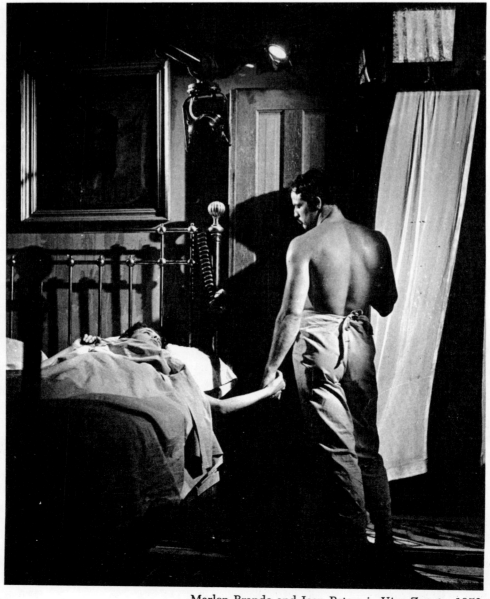

Marlon Brando and Jean Peters in *Viva Zapata*, 1952.

Marlon Brando in *On the Waterfront*, 1954.

Marlon Brando as Marc Antony in *Julius Caesar*, 1953.

Vivien Leigh and Marlon Brando in *A Streetcar Named Desire*.

MARLON BRANDO

Carefully type-cast by Elia Kazan and tailored to the role which he played in both stage and screen versions of *A Streetcar Named Desire*, Marlon Brando gave a portrayal of the brutish Stanley Kowalski which fascinated while it repelled. To his elders, Brando's performance was an accurate exposition of D. H. Lawrence's instinctual man, but carried no more significance than that. But the young man's combined savagery and inarticulateness struck flaring response in teen-agers, to whom they reflected their own frustration at a society they could not understand or participate in. Overnight a new Hollywood white hope was born. This accidental success happened to a young intellectual who, however reserved and withdrawn, took his profession seriously and was not minded to depart from his own aims in order to follow the standard routine of the climbing movie star. He refused interviews, or gave brief and rude ones; the middle-aged as well as the adolescents were inwardly delighted when his rebellion against the system took the form of turning up in sloppy clothes at Hollywood soirées. He was equally intransigent in professional matters. He allowed Stanley Kramer to cast him as a teen-age cut-up in *The Wild One*, but for the most part he has cut his teeth on roles as varied as Zapata, Antony, Napoleon, Sky Masterson in *Guys and Dolls* and Sakini in *Teahouse of the August Moon*. The depth and bite of his acting have suffered somewhat through these strenuous efforts at versatility, but it is evident he does not consider acting to consist of making over traditional characters into the image of Marlon Brando.

Grace Kelly

New feminine stars are usually impecunious small-town cuties with well-developed mammary accessories who are discovered by some alert Hollywood scout checking hats or serving sodas. They acquire public recognition as starlets by dint of assiduous press agentry, a readiness to submit to cheesecake photography, and a succession of minor roles. Grace Kelly's movie career bore no resemblance to this carefully molded Cinderella pattern. A reserved, well-bred girl from a wealthy Philadelphia family, she studied hard to become an actress, rejecting Hollywood bids until she was sure they would give her an adequate opportunity to develop her talents and to display her charms. In eighteen months, after she first attracted attention as Gary Cooper's wife in *High Noon*, she was paired in rapid succession with Gable, Milland, Stewart, Holden, Grant and Crosby in costly films directed by such masters as Ford and Hitchcock. With amazing speed she acquired international popularity, an Oscar as 1954's best actress, and a royal husband. Hollywood's hope, as well as that of millions of movie-goers, is that her Palace engagement in Monaco will not permanently end her cinematic career.

Grace Kelly did her most ambitious acting in her least glamorous role, in *The Country Girl*, 1954.

THEY CAME,
THEY SAW,
THEY CONQUERED

James Dean

Even more meteoric than Grace Kelly's career was that of James Dean. In his only year in Hollywood, this moody, intense, 24-year-old Indiana farm boy, reminiscent of Brando but with a sensitivity and capacity to express emotion distinctively his own, starred in three films, *East of Eden*, *Rebel Without a Cause*, and *Giant*. A week after the completion of *Giant* he was killed in an auto collision, a loss the commercial movie world he so despised could ill afford, but which enshrined him forever as the idol and symbol of a restless, confused, but fundamentally idealistic younger generation.

The mask of rebellion. James Dean in *Rebel Without a Cause*, 1955.

Tony Curtis cavorting à la Fairbanks on the Universal-International lot.

Tab Hunter (center) and friends.

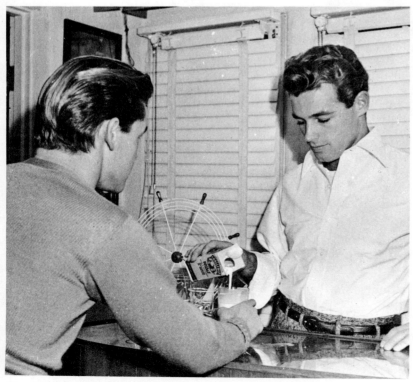

Guy Madison serves William Mosely at the milk bar of Guy's home.

TEEN-AGE FAVES

Tab Hunter and friend.

It has recently been established that the backbone of the steady movie-going audiences consists of adolescents (though some say it is "kiddies from six to sixty"). The tastes of teen-agers therefore play an important part not only in determining what is shown on the screen but also what is issued in publicity about Hollywood and its inhabitants. But since teen-agers are constantly becoming twenty-agers, and new teen-agers are emerging from puberty, the turnover in teen-age favorites is terrific. The white-hot favorite in the fan magazine popularity polls in April may be only a corny memory by December. Relatively few teen-age "faves" survive their brief vogue and go on to become favorites of the more mature. These happy few, for the duration of their popularity with the young, must live a life in front of the still camera which suggests nothing so much as the world of advertising. They eat and drink nice wholesome things like ice cream and milk, go to the beach a great deal, dash about in automobiles, indulge in horseplay at the studio "between takes." Nothing here to worry the most proper parent, everything to offer wish-fulfillment to impressionable youth. Is it believed? Maybe.

Deborah Kerr and Yul Brynner in *The King and I*, 1956. Brynner was considered so off-beat a type that his personal success in this film was thought to be a flash in the pan, but *Anastasia* and *The Ten Commandments* seem to have confirmed his success.

Carroll Baker had the good luck to have her first important role in a film which provoked threats of censorship, with accompanying floods of publicity. Here she is with Eli Wallach in the least believable scene of *Baby Doll*, 1956.

The authors' personal nomination for top-flight stardom: Kim Novak. She is already way up there with *The Man with the Golden Arm*, 1955, shown here, and *Picnic*, 1956.

WAITING IN THE WINGS

At what precise moment and by what imprecise means a starlet or her nameless male equivalent graduates to stardom no one can say. The nature of the films in which he or she is cast and the quality and quantity of the publicity extended them are largely responsible. Yet all Sam Goldwyn's wiles and willingness to spend money could not sell beautiful Anna Sten to the American public, while a steady stream of mediocre stories could not stay Garbo's rise to glory. The personal magnetism which makes girls like Marilyn Monroe and young men like Mar-

lon Brando world-wide favorites almost overnight is as unpredictable and indefinable as what makes some unheralded picture open to stand-out business while some highly publicized one does a Brodie from the opening night. Poised, as of this moment, on the edge of stardom are such talented people as Kim Novak, Eva Marie Saint, Carroll Baker, Susan Strasberg, Rod Steiger, Natalie Wood, Don Murray, Ben Gazzara, John Kerr, Paul Newman, Jean Seberg, and Anthony Perkins. Before the year is out they may be famous, forgotten—or still poised.

427

HOLLYWOOD TODAY

THE NEW PROCESSES

As television took hold of the country's imagination (and its roof tops) in the late Forties, the picture industry tried at first to ignore its menace. In the impending battle between entertainment at home free of charge and at theaters where it had to be paid for, the movies seemed hopelessly handicapped. Moreover the leadership of the industry appeared ill-qualified to cope with the emergency. Most of the company heads dated back to the early pioneer days. The years seemed to have undermined the energy and initiative which had enabled them to build their empires. Even worse, the fabulous stars who had helped them to survive previous crises were also aging. The cruel cameras showed wrinkles unbecoming to irresistible young lovers. It looked as though Hollywood's psychiatrists might well be replaced by gerontologists.

But the industry was not so superannuated as it appeared. The exhibitors, long dismissed as parasites on the body cinematic, came out fighting. They developed drive-in theaters which eliminated the parking problem and enabled the auto and the movie, the two most influential engines of the age, to join forces. But their major source of income (not to mention that of many of the old-fashioned enclosed theaters) came less from the recreation they afforded than the refreshments they supplied. For every dollar taken in at the drive-in gate, close to fifty cents' worth of concessions was sold.

Meanwhile the industry responded characteristically to the alarm. It came up with a few young and exciting stars—Brando and Dean, Monroe and Kelly had what it needed—to lure teen-agers, as well as a lot of their elders, from their TV sets. But more than new faces were required to meet the new emergency. The movie tycoons remembered how the coming of sound had once saved the movies from a similar threat and above all how the American public has always responded to the novel, the bigger, and perhaps the better. They dusted off half-forgotten three-dimensional and wide-screen processes to create giant theater screens which, they hoped, would dwarf the home screen into insignificance.

Cinerama, the first, and in some respects still—in spite of its obsession with travelogues—the most impressive of these new techniques, was actually being tested and perfected long before the living-room console became an active competitor to the theater screen. Its development, perhaps significantly, was carried on by scientific and financial interests unconnected with regular motion-picture production.

Bosley Crowther welcomed its arrival on the front page of *The New York Times*, an honor occasionally bestowed on such blue-ribbon entertainment events as the opening of the Metropolitan, or the arrival on Broadway of a foreign ballet troupe, but rarely, if ever, attained by even the most ambitious of picture premieres. "The distinguished gathering," wrote Mr. Crowther in his capacity of reporter rather than that of critic, "was thrilled by the spectacle as if it were seeing motion pictures for the first time. On the program the most spectacular and thrilling presentations were those which combined magnificence of scenic spectacle with movement of an intensely actionful sort. . . . Although no claim is made for the system actually projecting a third-dimensional image, the illusion of depth is variously achieved . . . through the use of a giant wide-angle screen, that sweeps in an arc of 146 degrees across the front of the theater auditorium, is taller than the ordinary screen and upon which is thrown from three projectors a tri-panel picture in color that has the appearance of a single panoramic display."

Much as audiences back in 1896 had ducked the onrushing Empire State Express, in 1952 they held their breath in pleasurable horror as they seemed to zoom down Coney Island shoot-the-chutes. Some of the original magic and mystery that had endeared it to millions had returned to the screen.

Nineteen fifty-three was sensationalized by the arrival of *Bwana Devil*, the first of the actual three-dimensional pictures. Produced inexpensively by an enterprising independent outfit, it was completely lacking in taste or talent. It created, however, a sense of depth through the use of polarized glasses, which blended the superimposed images produced by two studio cameras and two interlocking theater projectors. Like Cinerama, 3-D was no new invention dreamed up to meet the box-office emergency. It had been introduced as far back as 1936 in a series of shorts, and the industry vaguely thought of it as an ace in the hole which could be reintroduced, like sound, when the time was ripe. Because of the imperfections of the process, it had seemed that the time never would be ripe. The success of *Bwana Devil*, however, demonstrated that a jaded public would accept leaping lions and spears hurtling from the screen as a genuine novelty. It was followed in rapid succession by substantially improved, if still imperfect, specimens of three-dimensional craftsmanship. There was a steady stream of "firsts": the first 3-D picture from a major studio, the first with stereophonic sound, with a star name, with feminine appeal, the first by Technicolor, or on a wide screen, the first out-door thriller, Western, science fiction, the first of every type except one with intelligence and imagination. The most successful, Warner Brothers' *House of Wax,* grossed over $5,000,000 and was directed by Bryan Foy, who twenty-five years previously had produced the first all-talkie, Warner's *The Lights of New York.* For a brief, delirious moment, movie-makers as well as patrons looked at the world through rose-colored glasses by courtesy of the Polaroid Company. Jack Warner was so elated that he ventured to predict that in the future "audiences will wear such viewers as effortlessly as they wear wrist watches or carry fountain pens."

Whether because of basic mechanical defects, or a lack of sagacity on the part of its practitioners, the initial three-dimensional dementia dwindled almost as rapidly as it had arisen. Fists threatening the collective noses of audiences, Zombies stalking down the aisles, even the prospect of Marilyn Monroe fleeing from a snarling ape and landing in Papa's lap failed to hold movie-goers who wanted a gripping story rather than a startling gimmick.

Meanwhile the public was flooded with almost daily announcements of new technological processes, which claimed, with dubious veracity, to produce stereoscopic effects without the use of polarized glasses. So intense was the furor that, according to *Variety,* the marquee of the first-run theaters in Buffalo read one week as follows: the Century, "First Time in Buffalo, Giant Magic Mirror Panoramic Screen"; the Paramount, "First Time in America—Dynoptic 3-D"; the Lafayette, "Giant New Magniflow-Astrolite Screen"; and the Buffalo, "CinemaScope—Without Glasses." Only the Center was just showing pictures!

Among the new processes, Todd A-O, utilizing 70 mm. film, afforded the most dramatic sense of depth and clarity of definition, and Paramount's VistaVision, in which the film ran through the camera horizontally rather than vertically, thus substantially increasing the size of the negative, was the most agreeably proportioned and the most practical for the average theater.

Twentieth Century-Fox's CinemaScope was, however, the best publicized and the most boldly handled. Consequently it quickly outdistanced its competitors. Spyros Skouras, the dynamic head of the company, guaranteed skeptical exhibitors that although no feature had ever been made in Cinema-Scope it would be exclusively utilized for all of his future productions.

Actually, CinemaScope too was only an adaptation of an anamorphic process designed by Professor Henri Chrétien of France in the early Twenties. By means of distorted wide-angle lens, a compressed image is registered on the film and subsequently

A 3-D audience.

corrected by a compensatory lens on the theater projector in such a fashion as greatly to extend the range of vision and to suggest a sense of depth to a picture two and a half times as wide as it was high. CinemaScope was, so to speak, the poor man's Cinerama and was rapidly adopted by American exhibitors, rich as well as poor. It did not require three cameras or three projectors. It could be installed with stereophonic sound in practically any theater, with no loss of seats, for about $20,000. It made its initial bow with the opening of *The Robe* at the Roxy Theater and promptly proceeded to smash the house boxoffice record there and everywhere else it was shown. By early 1957 *The Robe* had grossed $30,000,000, putting it next to the all-time movie high of $33,500,000 established by *Gone with the Wind.* It made a contribution to show history as memorable as that of *The Jazz Singer* twenty-six years previously.

On the other hand it cannot be denied that the immense new screen militates against the intimacy and sense of personal involvement that marked the motion picture's happiest moments in the past. The big screens aim to make the spectator feel that he is actually present at the scene of action—but an observer so present may be so overwhelmed by the vastness of the forest that he cannot see the individual trees. The more that can be shown simultaneously on the screen, the more the eye of the observer must be guided by stage business. With longer scenes and less rhythmic cutting, the greater the emphasis on the technique of the theater rather than that of the cinema. The problem that still confronts all lovers of the movies is not how deep the dimensions of the screen but how deep its insights. It is of more than passing interest that three of the most highly praised films of the Fifties, *From Here to Eternity, High Noon,* and *Marty,* were all small-screen "flats" in black and white, and all followed the most ancient tradition of screen art, which is to select from the total field of vision the one detail which at the given moment is of prime narrative interest and concentrate all attention upon it.

This frame from *The Robe* shows how the anamorphic lens compresses the image on film. At right, the same scene from *The Robe* as projected on the screen.

THE NEW PROCESSES

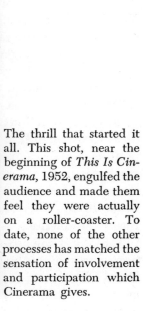

The thrill that started it all. This shot, near the beginning of *This Is Cinerama*, 1952, engulfed the audience and made them feel they were actually on a roller-coaster. To date, none of the other processes has matched the sensation of involvement and participation which Cinerama gives.

Giant, 1956. The enlarged screen invited directors to try new forms of pictorial composition.

THE SUN NEVER SETS
ON THE AMERICAN CAMERA

With the end of the war foreign lands, long deprived of Hollywood fare, went on a prolonged American movie spree. In a brief time close to 50 per cent of the major companies' grosses were being earned abroad. But though earned, they could not, with dollars at a premium, be remitted. These blocked funds, however, were available to adventurous picture-makers who quickly discovered that,

freed from big studio overheads and union requirements, they could make movies in Italy or Japan more cheaply and just as satisfactorily as in Hollywood. The overseas invasion fitted in nicely with the interests of American stars and directors who could (until hard-hearted legislators changed the law), by staying abroad for a year, avoid heavy income tax liabilities. To the surprise of all concerned,

War and Peace, 1956. King Vidor staged the Battle of Borodino in Italy.

Cantinflas and David Niven in *Around the World in 80 Days,* 1956.

The Pride and the Passion, 1957. The ancient earth of Spain.

most of these pictures were greeted with delight by New World audiences. As a consequence, out of 288 pictures distributed by the leading companies in 1956, 55 were made in Europe, Africa, and Asia. The phenomenal success of *Around the World in 80 Days* and *The Ten Commandments* showed in what direction the trade winds were, at least temporarily, blowing.

Gregory Peck in *Moby Dick,* 1956, filmed largely in Ireland.

EPILOGUE

Sixty years have passed since Mr. Edison said, "Let there be light" and, in less clarion tones, "Let there be pictures that move, or at least seem to move"—sixty years in which the plaything he regarded with so little paternal pride became an art and an industry, in which shabby, indomitable little men blossomed over night into financial giants, and photogenic boys and girls into world-wide idols. Mr. Edison's plaything helped to mold the manners and mores of our times. Above all it has brought joy to millions who had little interest in its commercial or aesthetic achievements.

The certainty of the late nineties that science would fertilize a brave new world devoid of disease, poverty and brutality has been transformed into the dread that it might annihilate our not too bad old world. White magic has turned to black and the vision of Mr. Edison bearing gifts to mankind has been replaced by the specter of Dr. Einstein speaking in equations and logarithms, incomprehensible but terrifying. The age of electricity which we welcomed so rapturously is about to be replaced by the era of atomic energy which may turn our earth into a paradise or into a wasteland.

But though man's faith has become man's fear, and his naïveté has been replaced by what he regards as sophistication, he is not greatly changed—not at least that aspect of him with which this book has been concerned. Theatrical entertainment, of which he formerly had so little, is now running out of his eyes and his ears. But what makes him laugh or cry, what he finds endearing, exciting or exalting remains substantially unaltered. The grandchildren of those adventurous souls who shuddered so pleasurably in their collapsible wooden chairs as the Empire State Express bore down upon them now shrink in their plush divan seats with similar delicious apprehension as Cinerama's shoot-the-shoots impel them downward at breakneck speed. It was as much fun to hold hands in a nickelodeon while the hero and heroine exchanged less chaste embraces as it is now in a picture palace. And recently it has been discovered that it is equally agreeable in the living room.

If there's a story to be told—and that's what movies are made for—it will grip you on the little old flat screen with the same compelling intensity as on CinemaScope, VistaVision, Todd A-O, or any other of the wide-screen processes which engulfed us in the early 1950s and which will in turn be engulfed by something equally novel and sensational in the 1960s. The more things change, the more they remain the same! Grandpa did not think

it ludicrous when Theda Bara hissed, by means of a printed caption, "Kiss me, my fool." Papa and Mama gave each other a fond reminiscent glance when boy whispered to girl, "Listen, darling, they're playing Our Song." It is inevitable that words and situations we today accept without misgiving will be the laughingstock of tomorrow. The pendulum of taste swings backward and forward, but the fundamentals of entertainment remain static.

Cinematic prophets, commentators and tycoons alike, have been wrong with a rare consistency. They discouraged films running longer than twenty minutes, they disparaged sound, they discounted television. One prediction, however, requires no clairvoyance. The fans of the future, like those of the past, will have and hold dear Westerns and comedies, melodrama and romance, spectacles and musicals. The Westerns may well be more psychological, the comedies less slapstick, the melodrama more credible, the romance less sentimental, the spectacles more spectacular, and the musicals less formalized. Our guess—and it is only a guess—is that tomorrow's movies will be more flexible and experimental in style and substance than the movies of the past. They will turn increasingly, as source material, to the great classics of fiction and drama. Occasionally they will flirt with fantasy, occasionally they will even dare to face the honest realities of daily life.

Regardless, however, of subject matter, moviegoers will continue to insist on glamorous personalities to identify with and to idolize—stars like Garbo and Monroe, Valentino and Brando. There will be sweethearts and vamps (though of course they will be called something smart and snappy), girls with curls or with impressive mammary developments, Latin lovers or taciturn he-men. Their impact on the dreams of young people—and plenty of old ones for that matter—will not differ greatly from one generation to another. If we cannot share the current teen-age passion for Elvis Presley, let us recall that our parents could not see what we saw about Frank Sinatra that was so wonderful. And also there will be the men who will make fans of the future laugh, the successors to Keaton, Langdon, Lloyd and Lewis. And if God is very, very kind, there may come another Chaplin to make them cry as they laugh.

But these gods and goddesses are not the sum or even the greatest part of the hold the movies have had, or will have, on us. Our true allegiance lies elsewhere. "Even little children," wrote Gilbert Seldes, "know that the thing which seems to be real

The Ten Commandments, 1956. De Mille's answer to television is the same old answer, and it still works.

Joe Mantell, Jerry Paris and Ernest Borgnine in *Marty*, 1955. With no assets but a moving story beautifully told, *Marty* found a mass audience, proving that the story still tells the story.

EPILOGUE (Continued)

on the screen is not real, and the riddle of appearance and reality enchants them, although not in the same degree as it enchanted Berkeley and Hegel and Kant. The appeal of the moving picture, to the subconscious, touches those regions in which we are still little children, puzzled by the question of where the light goes when it goes out." Our true allegiance, then, is as it has always been, to illusion —in the case of the movie, the most literal and therefore the most satisfying illusion ever devised. Now this illusion, in its familiar form, is being mortally challenged by a newer form of itself. Will television kill the movies? Of course not, for television is movies too. All that can happen is the death of a system of production and exhibition which we have identified so long with the movies that we cannot imagine them produced and distributed otherwise. But it is time to stretch our imaginations. Whether the movies of the future will come to us via the big screen, the small box, or some as yet unknown channel will depend on which of them best serves illusion.

We cannot guess now which of them that will be. We are living in days of heart-breaking uncertainty for picture-makers and delightful fluidity for picturegoers. Independent production is replacing the forty-year reign of the mass-producing factories. The major companies may well, in the coming years, become primarily bankers, landlords and distributors, rather than picture producers. They will merge and consolidate into vast entertainment empires, producing plays and television shows, making records, owning television stations and music-publishing concerns.

Meanwhile, many of the old hard-top film houses will disappear. But as they grow fewer in number they will grow more varied in character. There will be theaters specializing in long runs, in reserved seats, in unique types of projection such as Cinerama, Todd A-O, and their successful successors. There will be small art houses, drive-ins, and, for all we know, fly-ins. Above all there will be a theater in practically every American home. What was formerly man's castle will have become his picture palace. Even in the home, however, there will be diversity: movies on old-fashioned television but with larger screens, stereophonic sound, and—who knows—maybe 3-D minus polaroid glasses, toll TV so that first-run pictures can be shown to those prepared to pay for the privilege, films transmitted via closed-circuit wire relayed for a fixed annual fee from the local movie house.

One thing is certain: more Americans will see pictures every hour of the day than ever saw them before. Their importance in our daily life not only for purposes of entertainment but for education and propaganda will be greater than ever before achieved by any medium of communication. Will they be better, will they be worse than the movies of yesterday and today? It is a foolish question. To those of us who have lived through the wonders of the past sixty years there can be no misgivings about the glories of the future. The authors of this book are jealous of the men who will write its sequel in 2017!

Where once the stars' names shone; the former Stoddard Theater, New York, N. Y.

INDEX

438

439

440

ALCATRAZ

GOLDEN GATE
NATIONAL RECREATION AREA

10,000 YEARS
OF
LIFE ON THE ROCK
BY
NICKY LEACH

From-Frank & Linda
2006

SIERRA PRESS
MARIPOSA, CA

DEDICATION

To all whose lives have been touched by Alcatraz. May your stories always be remembered and your spirits set free. —N.L.

ACKNOWLEDGMENTS

For any author, researching the history of one of America's most famous icons is a daunting project. So much has been written. I was helped enormously by the enthusiastic support of the combined staff and volunteers of Golden Gate National Recreation Area Alcatraz Island and Golden Gate National Parks Association whose teamwork, creative vision, and passion for interpretation are truly inspiring. Thanks to Craig Glassner, Lori Brosnan, John Cantwell, Christian Hellwig, Sam Vasquez, Benny Batom, Rich Weiderman, Howard Levitt, Clover Earl, Nicki Phelps, and Susan Tasaki. Finally, special thanks to two fellow writers for creative inspiration: historian and ex-NPS ranger John Martini, for putting the word "story" back into history and brilliantly recreating life on Alcatraz—I enjoyed our free-form conversation; and Tara Ison whose moving and well-researched novel, *Child Out of Alcatraz*, suggests that fictionalized true-life stories can help us feel the truth instead of merely recording it.   —N.L.

FRONT COVER
Dock Guard Tower, sunrise.
PHOTO ©JEFF GNASS
INSIDE FRONT COVER
Alcatraz seen from the Presidio.
PHOTO ©FRANK S. BALTHIS
TITLE PAGE
Door and windows of the Model Industries Building.
PHOTO ©JEFF GNASS
PAGE 4/5
Cellhouse and water tower seen from Recreation Yard. PHOTO ©JEFF GNASS
PAGE 6/7
Alcatraz Island seen from San Francisco.
PHOTO ©FRANK S. BALTHIS
PAGE 7 (LOWER RIGHT)
Alcatraz warning sign along Agave Trail.
PHOTO ©JEFF GNASS

CONTENTS

WELCOME TO ALCATRAZ

"Free" masthead above Cellblock entrance.   PHOTO ©JEFF GNASS

On March 21, 1963, U.S. Penitentiary Alcatraz closed its doors for the last time. For 29 years, the three-story concrete cellhouse atop the windswept 22-acre island in San Francisco Bay had housed inmates who had worn out their welcome in other penitentiaries—from incorrigible gangsters like Al Capone to petty thieves, murderers, kidnappers, and political prisoners. There would be no last-minute reprieve. Attorney General Robert Kennedy's decision to retire the aging facility was final.

Like its predecessor, the U.S. Army, which had operated a fortress then a military prison on the island from 1853 to 1933, the Bureau of Prisons could not afford the millions of dollars necessary to repair the crumbling prison. It had always been expensive to run and had generated controversy from the beginning. Now, with the pendulum swing of public opinion favoring rehabilitation, not retribution, Alcatraz had gone from being a necessary "big stick prison" during the violent Depression years to a symbol of a dated penal system criticized for dishing out "cruel and inhuman punishment" to caged men.

As helicopters hovered, invited members of the press were ferried from the mainland early in the morning to witness the departure of the remaining prisoners to other penitentiaries. After a tour of the prison, the reporters were ushered into the large dining room, where just hours before, the inmates had enjoyed a final breakfast of "Assorted Dry Cereals, Steamed Whole Wheat, Scrambled Egg, Fresh milk, Stewed Fruit, Toast, Bread, Butter, and Coffee." Now, as the institution wound down, the visitors were offered coffee and donuts and use of telephones in the sealed Control Room to file their stories.

The dog-and-pony show reached its climax later that morning, when 27 convicts, neatly dressed in crisp new denim shirts and pants and pea coats, were escorted silently down Broadway, the 300-foot-long corridor between Blocks B and C, to the area outside the dining room known as Times Square. "It was like something from medieval times," wrote one reporter. "These men shuffling down the corridor in leg irons. The sound was what I remember the most, a silence, but a strange sound from the shackles. Strange

feeling."

What a long, strange journey it had been, indeed. A total of 1,545 federal inmates served sentences on what was dubbed "Uncle Sam's Devil's Island." But the oppressive atmosphere, the sheer weight of human misery, and palpable sense of hopelessness and isolation from civilization went back much farther than the Penitentiary years to the military era, when soldiers, traitors, conscientious objectors, even Native Americans, occupied the island that came to be called "the Rock."

The most popular unit in San Francisco's Golden Gate National Recreation Area, popularly known as Golden Gate Parks, Alcatraz has more than human stories to tell. It is an island ecosystem undergoing constant change as nature works to take down what people have put up. The island's principal resource is its fast-disappearing architectural district. Victorian, Mission Revival, Greek Revival, and Industrial style buildings sit by side in a fascinating disharmony, their future as uncertain as the San Francisco weather. A medieval-looking Sally Port, complete with dry moat, drawbridge, cannon and rifle slits, and the island's first guardhouse prison, protects the road above the dock. Civil War-era guns mounted in walls next to roadways. Inside the 1866 Bomb-proof Barracks that is now Building 64, a rabbit warren of storage areas, kitchens, and privies, known since Army times as "Chinatown," serve as park offices, exhibit rooms, a bookstore, and theater. Atop the never-used, painted-brick casemates are concrete apartments, home first to military guards, then Penitentiary correctional officers and their families.

Living things have all had to adapt to life on an island that, although surrounded by water, has no fresh water of its own, thin soil, and little vegetation. Cormorants, western gulls, pelicans, black-crowned night herons, and other nesting seabirds thrive on the island, but human beings have had to alter nature in order to live here. The U.S. Army completely reshaped the island for defensive fortifications in the mid-1800s, and transported fresh water to the island, where it was stored first in underground cisterns, then, during the years of the Penitentiary, in a water

OPPOSITE: Sweet alyssum blooming in the Recreation Yard. PHOTO ©JEFF GNASS

Afternoon light striking the cells of D-Block.

tower. Soil was brought in from neighboring Angel Island for earthworks and the flower gardens that now run riot across the island. Alcatraz is a superb example of a unique island ecology, combining both natural and human elements.

To most of the 1.5 million visitors making a pilgrimage to the island each year, what they know about Alcatraz and its most infamous inmates—Al Capone, the Birdman of Alcatraz, and famous escapees like Frank Morris and the Anglin Brothers—has been gleaned from sentimental films and books. But for all its fame, Alcatraz remains an enigma. The prison hides in plain sight in the middle of one of the busiest ports in the world. Its introspective, conservative appearance seems at odds with the expansive surrounding vistas of San Francisco, a city known for its liberalism

and extroversion. The island is a place of many moods, at the mercy of the fog, rain, and winds that funnel into the bay through the Golden Gate each day.

One outcome of a visit to Alcatraz is that we taste, however briefly, what it might mean to lose our freedom—an experience even more potent in the light of the September 11, 2001 terrorist attacks on New York City and Washington, D.C. Former prisoners commented that Alcatraz stripped men of their individuality, something Americans recognize as an essential right of citizenship. For writer John Dos Passos "Individuality is freedom lived." On Alcatraz Island today, we have the opportunity to imagine losing that most precious aspect of our humanity, then sail away. Free.

MODEL INDUSTRIES BUILDING
POWERHOUSE
WAREHOUSE
WATER TOWER
POST EXCHANGE/ OFFICER'S CLUB
ELECTRIC REPAIR SHOP
GUARDHOUSE & SALLY PORT
BARRACKS (BUILDING 64)
WARDEN'S HOUSE
CHAPEL
RESTROOMS
DOCK
LAUNDRY/ NEW INDUSTRIES BUILDING
GREENHOUSE (SITE)
RECREATION YARD
CELLHOUSE
WEST SIDE ROAD
LIGHTHOUSE
BARRACKS (RUBBLE)
PARADE GROUNDS (SEASONAL CLOSURES)
FOGHORN
AGAVE TRAIL (SEASONAL CLOSURES)

ALCATRAZ ISLAND
GOLDEN GATE NATIONAL RECREATION AREA

ILLUSTRATION ©LAWRENCE ORMSBY

Alcatraz Island is a designated National Historic Landmark and part of Golden Gate National Recreation Area. It is located in San Francisco Bay, 1.25 miles from the mainland, and preserves the West Coast's first lighthouse, Civil War-era military fortifications, remnants of the U.S. Federal Penitentiary cellhouse, signs of the 1969-1971 Native American occupation, and unique natural features, including endemic flora and fauna, naturalized flower gardens, tide pools, thriving bird colonies, and dramatic views.

The park is open daily from 9:30 a.m. until 6:30 p.m. in the summer; 4:30 p.m. in fall, winter, and spring. It is closed Christmas and New Year's Days and in foul weather. Access is via a 10-minute ferry ride from Pier 41 on Fisherman's Wharf. Ferries run every 30-40 minutes throughout the day, beginning at 9:30 a.m. Advance ticket purchase is strongly recommended and is available by calling Blue & Gold Fleet at (415) 705-5555,

logging onto www.blueandgoldfleet.com, or calling in person at their ticket booth at Pier 41.

Dock orientations are given on arrival. Visitors may tour the island at their own pace, using inexpensive, themed, multilingual, self-guided tour booklets sold through self-serve racks and in park bookstores on the dock, in Building 64, and in the cellhouse. A 14-minute video presentation of the island's 200-year history is offered in the park theater in Building 64. Exhibits behind the theater present the various periods of park history, including a video presentation about the 1969-1970 American Indian occupation, entitled *We Hold the Rock*. An award-winning 35-minute recorded multilingual audiotour of the cellhouse may be rented at the cellhouse door. Outdoor interpretive walks are offered throughout the day by National Park Service rangers and volunteers highlighting a variety of topics including military history, famous inmates, escapes, natural history,

and the Indian occupation. Special evening tours of the island are also available, offering a different perspective on the park.

The walk from the dock to the cellhouse is about 0.25 mile, with an elevation change of 130 feet. Visitors with disabilities may use SEAT (Sustainable Easy Access Transport), an electric shuttle that runs to and from the cellhouse once an hour. There is no food service on the island. Food, drinks, and smoking are only allowed on the dock. (An exception is bottled water, which is sold in the bookstore on the dock on Alcatraz.). Restrooms are available on the dock and next to the cellhouse.

Fog is common in the summer, rain in the winter; cold winds are a daily feature. Dress warmly and wear flat shoes. Some areas of the park are closed for safety reasons or seasonally to protect nesting birds.

DANCING ON THE BRINK OF THE WORLD

In ancient times, what is now San Francisco Bay was a broad delta, where rivers flowing west from uplands drained into the sea. Eventually, though, volcanic activity along the shifting Pacific and North American crustal plates pushed up the mountains of the Coast Range, blocking the route of the rivers except at the small gorge we know today as Golden Gate. In this spot, 16 tributary rivers flowing from the Sierra Nevada converged into one mighty river that emptied into the Pacific Ocean.

As the continents drifted, climatic conditions changed. During cooling periods, glaciers covered the mountaintops and valleys. When the climate warmed again, the valleys filled with glacial meltwater. An early version of San Francisco Bay came into existence 300,000 years ago, during one such warming period, but it wasn't until the end of the last ice age, 10,000 years ago, that modern San Francisco Bay appeared: a huge estuary with innumerable island and rocks of varying shapes and sizes, surrounded by tidal waters that ebbed and flowed, mixing salt and fresh water.

Closest to the Golden Gate, in the center of the bay, was Alcatraz, a sandstone peak covered with thin soil that was eventually washed away revealing the rock below. "The stone is full of seams in all directions which render it unfit for any building purposes and probably difficult to quarry," reported U.S. Army Topographical Engineer Lt. William Warner during the United States' first survey of the bay in 1847.

The first Spanish fleet to chart the bay had concluded the same thing: "I found it quite barren and rugged and with no shelter for a ship's boats," recorded Lt. Juan Manuel de Ayala, captain of the frigate San Carlos, who sailed into the bay on August 5, 1775, to follow up earlier reports by two other Spanish land expeditions. Ayala gave Alcatraz its curious name, calling it Isla de los Alcatraces, (a word variously translated as pelicans, gannets, cormorants, or simply "strange-looking birds"). Most researchers now concur, though, that Ayala was actually referring to present-day Yerba Buena. The names were switched on an 1828 map made by English Captain Frederick Beechey, whose misspelt "Alcatrasses" eventually became Alcatraz.

Birds were numerous throughout the bay, but Alcatraz was distinctive for the sheer numbers found there. By the mid-1800s, residents of new city of San Francisco were calling the humpbacked rock Bird Island or White Island because of its thick covering of guano. Hundreds of pairs of nesting western gulls, cormorants, and other sea birds congregated there seasonally, marking and defending small patches of ground. Whenever disturbed they flew into the air, screeching and whirring, "in a dense cloud like that of a noise of a hurricane," according to one observer. In later years, this "bird alarm" would prove useful to prison guards intercepting escapees from Alcatraz.

The first people arriving on the San Francisco Peninsula were transient paleo hunters from the north following big game herds. But by 5,000 years ago, the peninsula had a more permanent population of hunter-gatherer people. North of the Golden Gate were the Coastal Miwok. South of the Golden Gate and around the Bay were the Ohlone, or "western people." Spanish colonists, confused by the numerous tribes and subtle distinctions between them, dubbed all these Indians Costenos, or "coast people," a word anglicized to Costanoan.

Spanish diarists recorded 10,000 Costenos living between Point Sur and Monterey Bay in the late 1700s. Some 40 tribelets, made up of about 250 people, lived in extended clans in large village compounds of domed tule reed huts and wore clothing made of rabbit skins, bird feathers, and tule reeds. Though their territories adjoined, tribelets spoke different languages and lived separately, coming together only in highly ritualized ways to trade, marry, and occasionally go to war with each other.

The convergence of seven major life zones created an unimaginably rich natural environment. The bay and rivers teemed with trout, salmon, and other fish, and enormous quantities of whales, dolphins, sea otters, and other sea mammals. Estuaries were filled with abalone, mussels, oysters, and other shellfish. Wetlands and marshes supported reeds, rushes, seed-bearing grasses, and hundreds

GOLDEN GATE NATIONAL RECREATION AREA • PACIFIC • TIBURON • ANGEL ISLAND STATE PARK • SAUSALITO • BERKELEY • ALCATRAZ • TREASURE ISLAND (BUILT IN 1930S) • OAKLAND • N • SAN FRANCISCO (FORMERLY YERBA BUENA) • YERBA BUENA ISLAND (FORMERLY ISLA DE LOS ALCATRACES) • San Francisco Bay • SOUTH SAN FRANCISCO • Western Gull • OCEAN

of geese and ducks. Thick oak forests clad the foothills and yielded protein-rich acorns that were the mainstay of the native peoples' diet.

Coyotes hunted rabbits and were admired for their cleverness by these Native Americans, whose origin myths designated Coyote as their creator god. Wolves and mountain lions pursued elk and deer, also prized by hunters who prepared for deer hunts through an elaborate series of rituals. Enormous grizzly bears, the long extinct symbol on the modern California flag, roamed the shoreline. Though unrecorded, it's likely that every spring, the Ohlone and Miwok paddled out to Alcatraz and other islands to gather gull and cormorant eggs, then returned in June to collect newly hatched chicks.

Throughout the growing season, people managed the landscape through fire and other practices and moved around, collecting seeds, shoots, roots, berries, acorns, and other wild foods. Animals were respected as equals, honored for their powers and as allies that came to people in dreams that guided daily life. The relationship between man and animals was one of reciprocity, wherein the life of one might have to be sacrificed so that the other might live. Time for San Francisco Bay Indians ran together in one long continuum—the lives of the ancestors were their ways, too. A complicated code of etiquette governed daily life and ensured the survival of the group, sometimes at the expense of the individual. Spanish explorers like de Anza remarked on the happiness of the Indians they encountered, their love of singing and dancing, generosity, and bottomless hospitality.

This harmonious world disappeared forever almost as soon as native people made contact with Europeans. The Spanish Crown moved quickly to defend Alta California from English and Russian claims, sending soldiers to build forts, or presidios, and Franciscan missionaries to save the souls of these new heathen subjects. Though well-intentioned, the padres exhausted themselves trying to convert the natives, luring them to missions with trade goods, enthralling them with stories about Jesus, then after succeeding in baptizing key members of the tribe—usually chiefs and young children—locked them inside the missions, in an attempt to draw out the rest of the villagers.

For the once joyous native people of the bay, the missions became death camps, where imprisonment, overwork, and fatal diseases reduced their numbers catastrophically. In an eerie echo of the later prison on Alcatraz Island that would be accused of turning even hardened criminals into lifeless zombies, the Ohlone, Miwok, and other California tribes responded to the relentless regime of punishment, prayer, work, and cultural deprogramming by trying to meet these new "Men of the Mule God" on their own terms, then fighting back and trying to escape. When this did not work, the light inside them seems to have simply gone out. Visitors to the missions were shocked by what they saw. "All operations and functions both of body and mind appeared to be carried on with a mechanical, lifeless, careless indifference," noted British Captain Vancouver on a visit in the early 1790s.

Overcrowding at the missions proved disastrous. European diseases for which New World people had no immunity, such as measles, smallpox, and influenza, killed thousands. As California passed from Spanish to Mexican and finally into American hands, things went from bad to worse. Gold fever gripped the nation, and thousands of new settlers flooded into California. Natives found themselves on the receiving end of frontier justice with no legal rights and few defenders.

It wasn't until the late 1960s that native people regained a foothold in the Bay Area. The occupation of Alcatraz Island by Indians of All Tribes in 1969-1971, which sought to focus attention on the plight of dispossessed urban Indians, helped spark a renaissance of Indian culture. Today, the Ohlone are coming back from their "Museum Indian" status and are once more a presence in San Francisco, caring for a small wetland and pocket park known as Muwekma Ohlone Park, next to Pier 80. Though small, this community effort is a symbol of how things used to be when as an Ohlone song goes, "[we were] dancing on the brink of the world."

FORTRESS ON THE BAY (1859-65)

Original Alcatraz light, commissioned in 1854.

In 1847, a year before California was ceded to the United States, the U.S. Army had surveyed Alcatraz as a potential defensive site. At that time, explorer and U.S. Army officer John C. Fremont, who had briefly staged a small revolt against Mexico by seizing the abandoned San Francisco Presidio and Mexican barracks at Sonoma in 1846, claimed to have purchased the island with his own money. When the Mexican-American War ended, he demanded compensation.

In court, Fremont testified that he had bought "Alcatrasses" from a naturalized Mexican citizen called Francis Temple. Temple's father-in-law, Julian Workman, had received the island as a land grant with the stipulation that he build a lighthouse there. Since these conditions had obviously not been met, Fremont's claim was voided. Alcatraz was officially U.S. government property.

This decision proved fortuitous, for in 1848, gold was discovered on the American River. Within three years, the population of San Francisco swelled from 500 to 35,000 and its wealth made it vulnerable to attack. In 1850, a joint Army-Navy commission recommended two multistory, masonry forts—one at Fort Point and one at Lime Point—be built either side of the Golden Gate, with small backup batteries on Alcatraz and Angel Islands and Point San Jose (Fort Mason). In this way, any enemy ships managing to outrun the crossfire from the forts at Lime Point and Fort Point would find themselves under fire from all sides once inside the bay. On November 6, 1850, President Millard Fillmore signed an Executive Order reserving "for Public Purposes" selected lands around San Francisco Bay, and work began on Fort Point. The government, however, was never able to come to terms with the owner of Lime Point. Centrally located, a mile from the Golden Gate, Alcatraz then assumed strategic importance, and fortification began right away.

Work began on the island in 1853. Busted Gold Rush miners, attracted by high wages, cut a dock, roads, and gun emplacements around the island and tunneled into the cliffs to carve out water cisterns and storage rooms. In 1857, a guardhouse was built above the dock. It contained a defensive sallyport, a narrow passageway

with a drawbridge over a 15-foot-deep moat at one end and sets of double doors and rifle slits in the walls. At the top of the 130-foot-high island—next to the Cape Cod-style lighthouse that had begun operating in 1854—workers carved a level plateau for a defensive barracks, or Citadel, and a parade ground. The three-story brick building had two-foot-thick walls and its own dry moat and drawbridge. It could hold 100 men in peace time and double that under attack. With half a mile of defensive walls ringing the island, Alcatraz looked like a medieval fortress.

The first 11 cannons were old navy guns and horse-drawn field pieces, mounted in 1854. A few years later, smooth-bore Columbiad cannon provided long-range fire on the north, south, east, and west sides of the island. Deadly Howitzers, firing grape or cannister shot at short range, were emplaced in two defensive towers, or caponiers, on the north and south sides of the island, as well as in the guardhouse.

In 1859, 86 men of Company I, 3rd US Artillery took up their posts on Alcatraz. They joined Second Lt. James Birds-eye McPherson, an engineer supervising construction of the batteries who was decidedly unenamoured of his first assignment. "This beats all countries for wind I have ever inhabited," he complained. Some of the new soldiers had even more cause to be disgruntled. As soon as their boat landed, 11 of their number were locked up in the damp basement of the guardhouse for two days, probably for crimes committed before reaching the island. They were Alcatraz's first prisoners.

In 1860, rumor of Civil War put San Francisco on high alert. The Union considered the affluent city a prime target for Secessionists, a legitimate fear due to the presence of a group of Southerners calling themselves the Knights of the Golden Circle whose aim was to create a Confederate Republic of the Pacific. The Post on Alcatraces Island, as it was called, was the only permanent fort west of the Mississippi River. U.S. Army Col. Albert Sidney Johnston, a Union officer whose sympathies lay with the South, beefed up San Francisco's defenses, mounting more Columbiad and Howitzer cannons and transferring 10,000 muskets and

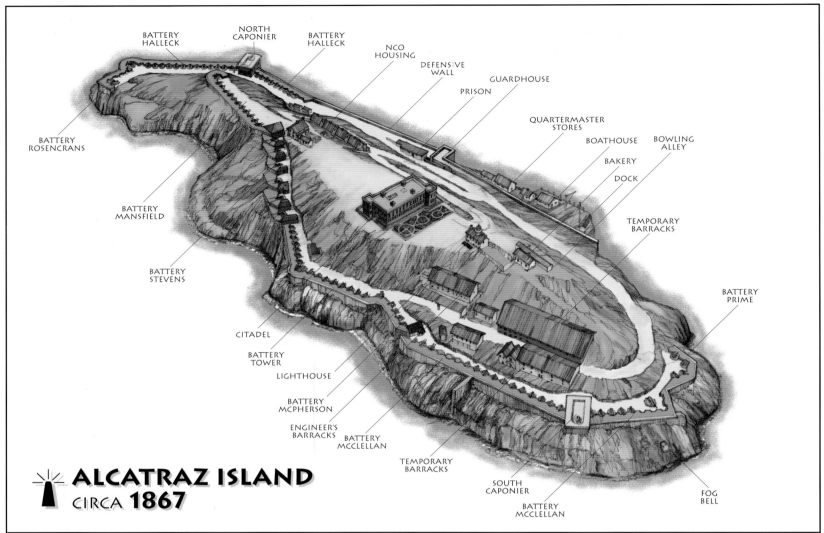

BATTERY HALLECK • NORTH CAPONIER • BATTERY HALLECK • NCO HOUSING • DEFENSIVE WALL • PRISON • GUARDHOUSE • QUARTERMASTER STORES • BOATHOUSE • BOWLING ALLEY • BAKERY • DOCK • BATTERY ROSENCRANS • BATTERY MANSFIELD • TEMPORARY BARRACKS • BATTERY STEVENS • BATTERY PRIME • CITADEL • BATTERY TOWER • LIGHTHOUSE • BATTERY MCPHERSON • ENGINEER'S BARRACKS • BATTERY MCCLELLAN • TEMPORARY BARRACKS • SOUTH CAPONIER • BATTERY MCCLELLAN • FOG BELL

ALCATRAZ ISLAND
CIRCA 1867

ILLUSTRATION ©LAWRENCE ORMSBY

150,000 cartridges to Alcatraz. An honorable soldier, whose loyalty had been questioned yet never found wanting, Johnston upheld his duties until relieved of command when war was declared in April 1861, then went to fight for the Confederates. He died at the Battle of Shiloh.

By 1864, 104 guns, including the first 15-inch caliber Rodman cannon, capable of firing 440-pound solid shot, ringed the island in nine batteries, all named for Civil War generals. A two-tiered "bomb-proof barracks" above the dock was begun a year later. Only one story was completed, containing supply rooms, kitchens, and gun casemates, before it was deemed out of date in 1866 and construction halted.

At the start of the Civil War, Alcatraz was officially designated Military Prison for the Department of the Pacific. Conditions in the 20-foot-by11-foot basement of the guardhouse were primitive. Up to 35 men slept head to foot on the floor with just a bucket for sanitation. The only light and air flow came from seven tall, narrow, rifle slit windows. Illness was rife. In 1862, the Army erected a temporary wooden structure, north of the guardhouse, to relieve overcrowding. It began filling up with deserters and disobedient, criminal, and insane soldiers. Civilians were also incarcerated for speaking against the Union. Thirty-nine men were

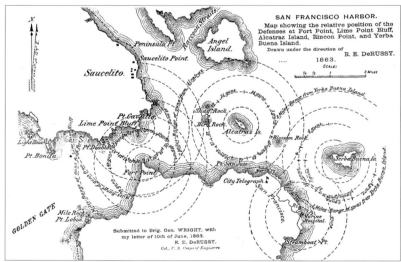

Military defense plan for San Francisco Bay, 1863.

GGNRA ARCHIVES ILLUSTRATION

sent to Alcatraz for rejoicing when President Abraham was assassinated in 1865. One newspaper reported that they were shackled with a ball and chain and were "having the treason sweated out of them," breaking rock for the new bombproof barracks. Those refusing to work were locked into a cramped "sweat box," the precursor to the dreaded "hole." But it was just the beginning of "hard time on the rock."

15" Rodman cannons, 1905.

Alcatraz received its first official Civil War prisoners March 1863, when the *J.M. Chapman*, a Confederate privateer ship, was seized in San Francisco harbor and its crew arrested for treason. The ship, a converted schooner that had been outfitted with cannon, was the focus of an elaborate plot by San Francisco Secessionists to capture an ocean-going steamship and sail it to Mexico. There it was to be armed as a Confederate warship and used to blockade San Francisco and perhaps raid shipping off the coast to fill the Confederate war chest.

But, as the saying goes, "loose lips sink ships." Many of the conspirators let slip details of their plans to others. Inevitably, word reached the military. The U.S. Navy intercepted the vessel and arrested the 15-man crew. Three leading San Francisco citizens—Asbury Harpending, Ridgeley Greathouse, and Alfred Rubery, former

Knights of the Golden Circle—were identified as the ringleaders. Harpending was carrying letters signed by Jefferson Davis granting him an officer's commission in the Confederate Navy. The men were immediately locked up in the new wooden prison on Alcatraz and convicted of treason. Fortunately for them, a pardon from President Lincoln spared them 10-year sentences.

Pro-Union San Francisco was still feeling nervous about this incident when the commander of Alcatraz, Capt. William Winder, nearly caused an international incident on October 1 of the same year. At noon that day, an armed warship was towed into the bay on an unusual course, headed for Racoon Straits on the north side of Angel Island and directly for the Benicia Arsenal and Navy yard at Mare Island.

Unable to make out the ship's flag on the still day, Winder ordered a blank charge fired from

North Battery signaling the ship to heave to. "Apparently not attracting her attention, I directed a gun to be loaded with an empty shell and to be fired 200-300 yards in front of her," Winder later reported. The shot across the ship's bows caused the vessel to halt, drop anchor, and begin firing a 21-gun salute, but not before Fort Point joined in on the firing.

Adm. John Kingcome of *HMS Sutlej*, commander of Her Majesty's Naval Forces in the Pacific, signaled his fury to Alcatraz, then reported the matter to Col. George Wright, commander of the Department of the Pacific. Wright expressed his regret but supported Winder, considering that his actions were justified during wartime. Many San Franciscans went further in their praise. Winder, they considered, was the hero of the day. He had saved San Francisco.

MILITARY PRISON YEARS (1870-1933)

Hopi men imprisoned on Alcatraz, 1895.

At the end of the Civil War, not a shot had been fired in anger, but new military technology had already outdated Alcatraz's defenses. In 1870, the U.S. Army initiated the Plan of 1870, which called for new earthwork batteries on top of the old scarp walls. Rodman cannons would now be mounted in pairs separated by earth hills called traverses and connected by brick-lined tunnels. Convicts began working on the most ambitious reshaping of the island yet.

Only five Rodman cannon had been installed when Congress cut off funding, and even these guns were obsolete before they were installed. Nevertheless, work continued on six batteries planned for Alcatraz under the guise of creating a new parade ground. By 1876, convict workers had sliced off the whole southern section of the island to 60 feet above sea level. Debris thrown over the cliffs inadvertently extended the shoreline and changed the shape of Alcatraz Island. It now looked less like a footprint than a huge battleship.

The profile of the prison population was changing, too. Recruiting officers, desperate to fill quotas during peacetime, gladly took allcomers. Murderers, thieves, rapists, and insane men soon found themselves in the island prison alongside petty criminals and deserters. A sprawling complex of temporary wooden buildings, dubbed Lower Prison, sprang up to contain the new arrivals. The wooden cells were "no bigger than horse stalls," according to writer Jolene Babyak, so it was just as well that most prisoners were put to work around the island quarrying rock each day. The free prison labor allowed the Army to add, what the *Daily Alta California* newspaper in 1885 reported were "a succession of charming gothic cottages, occupied by the commanding officers [sic] of the garrison and their families, each with a little garden plot, and the voices of merry children make the air musical."

The U.S. Army was now engaged in fighting guerilla Indian Wars on the rapidly expanding western frontier. Between 1873 and 1895, a succession of Paiutes, Modocs, Apaches, and others found themselves locked up on what was now called "the rock." One group stood out. In 1895, Chief Lomahongyoma and 18 other Hopi Indian "hostiles" from Oraibi, Arizona, served a seven-month

sentence for resisting efforts to set up a tribal farming system and refusing to send their children to government-run boarding schools. These unusual prisoners captured the attention of San Francisco media, who reported approvingly, that the Indians were visiting San Francisco schools "so that they can see the harmlessness of the multiplication table."

In 1898, the Spanish-American War and the ensuing Philippines Insurrection, brought the prison population up to an all-time high of nearly 500 prisoners by 1901. The overcrowded conditions led to the hasty construction of a new wooden Upper Prison on the parade ground, yet this did little to solve the problem of overcrowding, poor sanitation, and fire hazard. The commandant appealed to his superiors for help. The War Department responded by decommissioning Alcatraz as a fort and redesignating it "Pacific Branch, U.S. Military Prison, Alcatraz Island" in March 1907. Infantry officers were immediately replaced by military prison guards and the Citadel was torn down to make way for a new prison.

The new three-story prison building, completed in 1912, was a marvel of engineering—often cited as the largest reinforced concrete building in the world at the time. The interior was equally impressive. The Main Prison Building consisted of an administration building with offices and an auditorium; a cellhouse containing four cellblocks with a total of 600 cells equipped with individual toilets, sinks, and electricity; a kitchen; a dining hall; a hospital; and a high-walled recreation yard. A power plant, built atop the old North Battery, produced electricity and steam heat. The Post Exchange, or PX, which housed a canteen, gym, barbershop, bowling alleys, a lunch counter, and a post office, was added in 1910. In 1921, a 15-room Commandant's Residence, with a superb view of San Francisco, was completed. Both structures were built in the Spanish Mission Revival style. In 1909, a taller lighthouse replaced the 1854 structure—the first operating lighthouse on the West Coast—when engineers realized the new prison would block the old light.

Although it represented a vast improvement over previous

Upper Cellblock under construction, 1909 (note Victorian-style Officers Quarters to left).

prison buildings, the enormous prison building dominated San Francisco Bay, and its "hard labor" philosophy continued to incur criticism. In 1915, the military adopted a new approach to its prisons, emphasizing rehabilitation, and Alcatraz was renamed Pacific Branch, U.S. Disciplinary Barracks. Prisoners now attended military, educational, and vocational training, and some became white-uniformed "trustys" in officers' homes. Most prisoners were only locked into their cells at night. Rule breakers were placed in solitary confinement in the damp basement of the Citadel, the infamous (and misnamed) Spanish Dungeons, now directly below the cellhouse. In 1917, World War I conscientious objectors, nick-named "slackers," were taken to the island, put to work breaking rock, and if they refused, chained in converted storage areas in the pitch-black dungeons until public outrage condemned the practice.

As the affluent 1920s gave way to the Great Depression of the 1930s, louder voices among the military authorities called for the closure of the expensive and unpopular prison. As luck would have it, another branch of government expressed interest. Attorney General Homer Cummings and FBI director J. Edgar Hoover were conducting a very public nationwide search for a site for a new maximum-security prison that would act as a deterrent to orga-nized crime, bootleggers, kidnappers, and violent criminals then housed in the general prison populations of Federal penitentiaries

Powerhouse and Officer's Exchange seen from the Sallyport.

at McNeil Island, Leavenworth, and Atlanta. Surrounded by 53-degree waters and swift currents, Alcatraz was deemed escape-proof. On October 13, 1933, Secretary of War George Dern trans-ferred Alcatraz to the federal Bureau of Prisons, whereupon it became known as USP Alcatraz Island.

OPPOSITE: Circular stairway in A-Block. PHOTO ©JEFF GNASS

FEDERAL PRISON YEARS (1934-1963)

Barge with "Prisoner Train", 1934.   GGNRA ARCHIVES PHOTO

Frank Weatherman, the last prisoner to leave the Rock in 1963, famously said "Alcatraz was never no good for nobody." But Alcatraz was never intended to be good for anyone. From the beginning it was designed to punish not reform—to remove the rotten apples from the prison barrel and cast them adrift from mainstream society, where they would sink or swim, depending on their strength of character.

Alcatraz had echoes of Eastern State Penitentiary, built in Pennsylvania in 1829 as a new kind of jail that would deprive men of their freedom rather than physically punish them. Inmates at Eastern State occupied individual cells, each with its own walled exercise yard, so that they would have "only the light from heaven, the word of God (the Bible), and honest work as a road to penitence." Visitors like novelist Charles Dickens criticized "this slow and daily tampering with the mysteries of the brain" and thought it "immeasurably worse than any torture of the body."

The experiment at Eastern State was eventually dropped in favor of congregate prisons, but a century later, criminal activity had risen to such a degree, the government was willing to once again reconsider earlier methods of punishment. Attorney General Homer Cummings hired James A. Johnston, a veteran of Folsom and San Quentin prisons, as warden of Alcatraz and instructed him to create a model modern prison combining the best of the old and new. "We expect great things of Alcatraz," Cummings declared.

Johnston set to work remodeling the old prison. In B and C blocks, he replaced the soft flat cell bars of 336 cells with toolproof steel bars and converted them to an automatic locking system that allowed cells that could be either opened singly or in rows. Weapons and keys were banned from the cell floor. Armed guards would instead patrol from elevated gun galleries and lower keys on pulleys. Tear gas cannisters were installed in the ceiling of the dining room, earning it the nickname the Gas Chamber. Everyone had to pass through "Snitch boxes," or metal detectors, at the front and side of the cellhouse, where electric doors controlled access. The exterior of the prison took on a grim appearance. Imposing

guard towers linked by catwalks were built around the island for 24-hour surveillance and manned by guards with high-power rifles. Large signs were put up warning boats to keep at least 200 yards away. Barbed wire fences ensured minimal contact between prisoners and the families of guards living on the island. Military era tunnels were sealed to prevent escapes.

The prison's first occupants were 32 of the army's worst convicts, left behind from the military prison. Starting in August 1934, they were joined by the first transfers from other Pens. Afraid that accomplices might try to break out infamous criminals, authorities kept secret the actual arrival dates of convicts. The shackled prisoners were transported by train to San Francisco and taken by boat to the prison before nervous citizens of San Francisco knew what had happened.

Newly arrived inmates were issued a prison handbook of rules and regulations. Rule No. 5 was: "You are entitled to food, clothing, shelter, and medical attention. Anything else you get is a privilege." Every aspect of prison life was prescribed: prison uniform, hair length, cell furnishings, lineups, time allowed to eat meals, permitted activities in the recreation yard. Prisoners were locked up for 13 hours a night. Jobs in the cellhouse, kitchen, gardens, or New Industries building were an important way of relieving boredom. The prisoner-guard ratio of three to one was the highest ratio of any prison. Guards kept order through intimidation rather than brutality, counting prisoners 12 times a day and engaging in target practice from guard towers to dissuade any escape attempts.

Prisoners caught trying to escape or disobeying rules were at first locked in the pitch-black military dungeons below the cellhouse. After 1940, D block was converted to a separate isolation, or treatment, unit. The worst offenders were placed for up to 19 days in a new and diabolical version of the "hole"—one of six specially converted cells with a second door fitted with a pullup window that blocked light and airflow. The only good thing about D Block was that it was the only cellblock to face barred windows that let in some of the sights, sounds, and smells of San Francisco

Prisoners in Recreation Yard.

Bay. But for the inmates marooned on the island, the outside world was just a memory. Newspapers were prohibited, and books and magazines were heavily censored, along with letters to and from approved correspondents. Visits by relatives were no consolation. Convicts were given an hour and a half a month in the visiting area with an approved relative. Thick glass separated loved ones, and all visits had to be conducted by telephone.

During the prison's first three years, a Rule of Silence was strictly enforced. Locked in their cells for long periods and prohibited from speaking, inmates became psychologically unstable. Already unable to cope with life, many went "stir crazy" and had to be confined to "bug cages" in the hospital. A number tried to commit suicide or mutilated themselves by cutting Achilles tendons and veins with razors, nail clippers, and other contraband implements. Others simply gave in and submitted to the prison regime, hoping to earn time off their sentences and be paroled to another prison.

By 1938, it was already obvious to Attorney General Frank Murphy that Alcatraz was a place "conducive to a psychology that builds up a sinister and vicious attitude among prisoners." For most, the only hope was to break out or die in the attempt.

Solitary confinement cells in D-Block.

Warden James A. Johnston

The first warden of Alcatraz was an unusual choice. Educated in San Francisco, James "Saltwater" Johnston had served as warden of California's feared Folsom and San Quentin prisons, where he had earned a reputation for reform by abolishing striped prison uniforms and corporal punishment. Strict but fair, the 60-year-old former lawyer, banker, criminologist, and writer was a quiet, thoughtful man who said of his new job: "The way we left it was this: They would select their worst and I would take them and do my best."

Johnston applied a lifetime's understanding of prison psychology in preparing Alcatraz for its new role. The superprison was to be a model of efficiency—escapeproof, safe, clean, modern. Johnston solved the water problem by installing a 250,000-gallon water tower in place of the old underground water cisterns. Men showered with warm fresh water in the basement shower room and had their clothing and bedding laundered every few days. Knowing full well that little everyday dissatisfactions could lead to riots, Johnston made sure all the basics were covered. Above average meals in the mess hall were served in portions limited only by as much as a man could eat. A liberal amount of tobacco was issued weekly. A doctor visited from the mainland and performed minor surgery. If they toed the line, men could work in prison industries and earn a few cents an hour. These "privileges" were overseen by a large force of seasoned correctional officers handpicked from other prisons. They lived on the island and guarded the inmates in shifts, watching their every move and performing numerous counts and cells shakedowns.

Johnston's methods began to be criticized in the late 1930s, when paroled convicts wrote of their experiences on what train robber Roy Gardner dubbed "Hellcatraz." Complaints that a strict rule of silence pushed too many men over the edge led to its abandonment. A highly publicized court case by inmate Henri Young, who claimed inhumane treatment had led him to kill another inmate, also brought public scrutiny to the secret prison.

In a final disaster for Johnston, a takeover of the cellhouse by six convicts in May 1946 left three inmates and two guards dead, several badly injured, and led to the execution of two of the three surviving members of the conspiracy. Accused of responding too slowly, then inappropriately firing on D block, Johnston found himself defending his actions to his bosses and the media, who were given access to the prison for the first time since 1934. He retired two years later and published his memoir, *Alcatraz Island Prison and the Men Who Live There*, in 1949.

Anti-aircraft gun and crew on Alcatraz rooftop during World War II.   GGNRA ARCHIVES PHOTO

The U.S. Army returned once more to Alcatraz in 1942, following the Japanese bombing of Pearl Harbor and the United States' entry into World War II. Antiaircraft guns, the first new military guns on Alcatraz since 1907, were placed on the roof of the cellhouse, the Model Industries building, and the married guards apartment building. Soldiers of the 216th Coast Artillery, housed at the Presidio, were ferried daily from Fort Mason to man the defenses. In the fall of 1942, a full detachment from Battery D of the 259th Coast Artillery moved onto the island altogether.

Warden Johnston had got off to a rocky start with the army's Western Defense Command at the Presidio. He—and most of San Francisco—had refused to black out lights in the city during the army's first air raid drill on December 8, 1941, causing General John de Witt to fume, "I never saw such apathy. It was criminal . . . . It was shame-

ful." By the time the army showed up on the island, ruffled feathers had been smoothed and the warden was cooperating fully with the army. Johnston issued the soldiers a list of rules and regulations to prevent guns, knives, and other weapons getting in the hands of convicts. The men mingled freely with the 50 families on the island at the Officer's Club, the grocery store, and were invited to dances and parties in private homes, where a few forbidden romances blossomed with the daughters of guards.

The ban on relations between soldiers and convicts was widely ignored, according a memoir by inmate Alvin "Creepy" Karpis. Gunners atop the cellhouse roof took to throwing sandwiches and cigarettes to convicts in the recreation yard and exchanged stories. The ban on outside news on the island was partially lifted during World War II, and Warden Johnston issued regu-

lar bulletins about the war effort, largely to inspire patriotic pride in the men. Prison industries were expanded between 1942 and 1945 to include laundering military clothing, sewing military uniforms, making nets, and repairing damaged buoys used on the 2.5-mile-long antisubmarine net strung under Golden Gate Bridge. Convicts earned 5 to 12 cents an hour; many bought war bonds with their pay.

United in the war effort, everyone on the island felt a renewed sense of purpose. "Man for man," Johnston later wrote, "they compared favorably with the rank and file of citizens in producing goods for the Army, Navy, Marine Corps, Maritime and Transportation Service. Regardless of what they have done or may do, I like to record and remember them at their best—when they were working to win the war."

OPPOSITE: Inmate repairing buoy for submarine net during World War II. GGNRA ARCHIVES PHOTO

Late one stormy summer night in 1961, the prison launch "Warden Johnston" crosses the choppy waters of San Francisco Bay to Alcatraz Island. The 1912 cellhouse, guard towers, and rocky shoreline appear and disappear, illuminated every few seconds by the powerful beam of the lighthouse, as the boat's wipers flip back and forth in the driving rain.

Below deck, a tall, self-possessed man sits chained to a guard, staring without emotion at the island as it gets closer. At the dock, the prisoner is hustled from the launch onto shore. His arrival is monitored by an armed guard in the dock tower, who trains his spotlight on the prison van as it crawls through the sallyport tunnel and winds its way up to the cellhouse. The two guards and their prisoner enter the building through electronic gates controled by a guard in a sealed room, then hand over their charge and return to the boat. The prisoner is ordered to strip and given a cursory medical check before passing through a metal detector into the main cellhouse. Prison uniform in hand, the man walks naked to his cell in full view of other inmates. As one guard pulls the lever to automatically lock the cell, the other sneers: "Welcome to Alcatraz."

A flash of lightning illuminates the face of the man who will go on to become one of Alcatraz's most famous escapees—Frank Morris—here compellingly recreated by actor Clint Eastwood in the tense prison drama *Escape from Alcatraz*. The movie captures better than almost any other life in the aging prison. In the 1950s, Warden Paul Madigan, a former correctional officer, had loosened restrictions on cell décor, reading, writing, painting, and playing instruments, and allowed inmates to listen to selected radio shows using earphone jacks. But these small changes did little to relieve the tedium of the unbending daily routine at the prison. The

men were like drones in an enormous beehive, each cell filling with bitterness not honey.

The day began with the echoing scream of the cellhouse alarm at 6:30 a.m. Convicts had 20 minutes to brush their teeth, clean their cells, make their beds, get dressed, and stand at the front of their cells to be counted. Then, as though taking part in some carefully choreographed performance, the men stepped out onto the shiny cellhouse floor in unison and march to the dining room for breakfast, their every move monitored by armed guards in elevated gun galleries.

At 7:20 a.m., the whistle blew again, and the convicts fell in line to wait while utensils were counted, then proceeded to the recreation yard, where they were allowed to smoke but not socialize. At 7:25 a.m., guards and work details moved out to the laundry, the tailor shop, the cobblers, the model shop, and other workshops in the New Industries Building, passing through a long caged corridor and "snitch box." Those working on the dock, tending the gardens, and other labor duties followed next. Lunch, known as dinner, was at 11:30 a.m. At noon, the men returned to their cells for 20 minutes, then at 12:25 p.m. marched back to their jobs.

Work ended for the day at 4:15 p.m. and the inmates ate supper at 4:25 p.m. before final lockup at 4:50 p.m. Lights went out at 9:30 p.m. Prison counts took place 12 times a day. "Sometimes I think all this island is is one long count," complains the black inmate English in *Escape from Alcatraz*. "We count the hours. The bulls [guards] count us. And the king bulls count the counts." At Alcatraz, doing time took on new meaning.

A prisoner's only free time outside his cell was a few hours in the recreation yard on weekends. Inmates played handball and baseball, sat on steps and talked, or crouched at one end and played bridge, watched by an armed guard on the prison yard wall. If visibility was poor due to fog, the men were kept in. The haunting sound of the island foghorn, the sight of soaring birds, and passing boat traffic in the bay only served to remind inmates of what they were missing. "It

---

ABOVE: Kids playing on cannon above the Agave Trail, south end of island. GGNRA ARCHIVES PHOTO

was exquisite torture," said one.

The correctional officers, known in prison parlance as guards, bulls, hacks, or screws, were as regimented as their charges. In the beginning, few were prepared for their jobs at Alcatraz. They were given uniforms, lists of regulations, a week's training, and thrown in the deep end with only advice from their colleagues. Those who were easily intimidated never made it past the one-year probationary period. New or unpopular guards pulled guard tower duty, the most dreaded shift on the island. "They shoved you in the dock tower on the morning watch for eight hours," remembers one former guard. "Boy, that was rough! No one to talk to. You don't see a damn thing. And you got to keep your eyes open for the lieutenant."

The lieutenant was probably Philip Bergen, who worked on Alcatraz from 1939 to 1955 and served as captain of the guards from 1949 to 1955. "Tough, unassailable, and respected," according to writer Jolene Babyak, the daughter of assistant warden Art Dollison, Bergen was not always liked. But his support of Alcatraz remained strong even after the prison closed. Until his death in spring 2002, he frequently returned to the island to share stories of his life as a guard.

In the claustrophobic world of Alcatraz, relationships ebbed and flowed like the tides in the bay, but in the all-male atmosphere of the cellhouse, guards and inmates evolved a

grudging respect for one another. Compared with other "pens," the "hacks" on Alcatraz generally treated you square, if you played by the rules. Friendships between cons and guards could be dangerous to both, if observed by a third party, but little gestures meant a lot. Leon "Whitey" Thompson remembers receiving candy from one officer, an act of kindness that was one of his strongest Alcatraz memories. Like veterans on opposing sides of a long-running war, guards and inmates found their lives permanently changed by their experiences in the prison. Several guards have stayed in touch with former inmates over the years. Many ex-cons, former guards, and children who grew up on the island attend annual reunions and share "war stories." They remain a unique living history resource.

Some 50 families lived on Alcatraz, including about 60 children. While the warden lived next to the lighthouse in the elegant 1921 Mission Revival-style home built for the army commandant, new arrivals were housed in the dingy apartments in Building 64. Some families eventually moved into cot-

tages and apartment buildings on the parade ground, where the stunning panoramic views of San Francisco and cheap rent were major draws for correctional officers trying to survive on the $4,480 a year paid guards in 1959. The island was considered far safer than a home in San Francisco. Jolene Babyak remembers: "Islanders quickly saw advantages to their lives. Children were safely tucked away from busy streets, in a neighborhood where everyone knew everyone else."

Babyak and other youngsters played on the windy parade ground. A favorite game was "guard and con," using toy guns made from popsicle sticks that were confiscated if found. Children took the prison launch to school in San Francisco every day and were allowed to bring envious school friends for a visit. Christmas at the penitentiary was lonely for the inmates. They created mats and other homemade gifts for the guards and their families and looked forward to the exact same turkey dinner every year. But, for many, the most poignant part of Christmas was hearing the children sing Christmas carols below the cellhouse. "It was an island tradition," remembers Don Hurley, son of a guard. "We stopped and sang a couple of carols, then all the children would yell 'Merry Christmas' to the inmates. Within a few seconds, many shouts of similar nature would echo back . . . Each year I thought that our happiest night might have been their saddest."

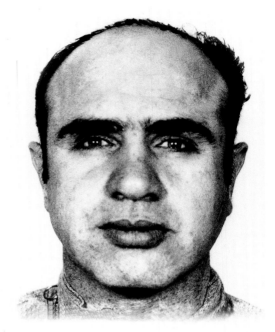

Alphonse "Al" Capone.

George "Machine Gun" Kelly.

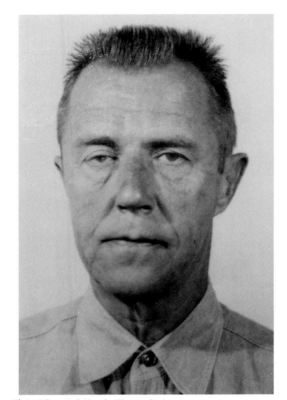

Alvin "Creepy" Karpis (Karpavicz).

Even before USP Alcatraz opened, its place as America's most infamous prison was assured when word got out that some of the country's most notorious criminals were to be sent there.

The name on everyone's lips was Alphonse "Al" Capone, a well-known Chicago bootlegger and gangster who would stop at nothing, including murder, to protect his interests. Arrested numerous times then freed for weapons offenses, fraud, murder, gambling, and traffic violations, Capone was finally jailed for 10 years for tax evasion. He was transferred to Alcatraz from USP Atlanta to stop him using family members and prison guards to continue his illegal activities.

Arriving with the first shipment of prisoners in August 1934, Capone served four and a half years on the island. His health was declining due to advanced syphilis, and he was forced to do menial cleanup jobs around the cellhouse, where he was often targeted by fellow inmates. His mother came to visit him only once. The metal stays in her corset set off the alarms in the snitch box and she was forced to strip to her underwear before being allowed to enter. Humiliated, the old lady never returned.

George "Machine Gun" Kelly arrived in September 1934. A bootlegger, bank robber, and kidnapper, Kelly was captured on September 26, 1933, whereupon he reportedly threw his hands in the air and cried "Don't shoot, G-men," coining the famous phrase. He was the first person to be sentenced under the new Lindbergh kidnapping law and received a life term. At USP Leavenworth, Kelly was considered a model prisoner, leading to speculation that J. Edgar Hoover had personally requested the transfer to Alcatraz.

Far more flamboyant was Alvin "Creepy" Karpis (Karpavicz) who had hooked up with Kate "Ma" Barker and her sons to form the Barker-Karpis gang, which laid waste to the Midwest between 1931 and 1936. Named Public Enemy Number One by Hoover, Karpis was captured in 1936 and sent to Alcatraz, where his "big man" status created friction with other prisoners. One of the longest serving convicts, he was transferred to USP McNeil Island in 1962, and deported to Canada shortly thereafter. In typical dramatic style, Karpis wrote a book about his experiences at Alcatraz, describing the prison as "the greatest fraud put on the American people. . . . It was a bad place."

Clarence Carnes, a well-liked Choctaw Indian, was one of the youngest prison inmates. Carnes progressed from petty thefts to bigger robberies and received a life sentence at the age of 15 after accidentally shooting a gas station attendant in a holdup in 1943. He avoided the gas chamber for his part in the botched escape attempt of 1946, probably because he spared the lives of captured officers. When Alcatraz closed, Carnes returned often to the newly opened visitor attraction and a TV movie was made about his life. Despite the acclaim, Carnes never got used to life on the outside and drifted back to jail at the end of his life.

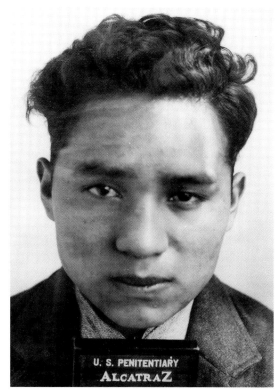

Clarence Carnes.

Robert "Birdman of Alcatraz" Stroud.

Morton Sobell.

Another man who spent most of his life in prison was Robert Stroud, the so-called Birdman of Alcatraz. Following a particularly troubled upbringing, the young Bob Stroud developed a lifelong taste for pederasty, manipulating older female mother substitutes and confronting masculine authority. At 19, he was sentenced to 12 years in USP MacNeil Island for the premeditated murder of the client of a female prostitute who had befriended him. Unable to get along with others, Stroud stabbed another inmate and had six months added to his sentence. Then, after transferring to USP Leavenworth, he killed a prison guard in full view of 2,000 other inmates. Stroud was sentenced to death for the killing, but with the help of his mother, who begged President Wilson to personally intervene, the sentence was commuted to life in prison. Incensed, the warden and attorney general illegally interpreted the judge's original sentencing language to place Stroud in solitary confinement for life.

In solitary, Stroud's reputation as a bird doctor grew after he successfully treated the sick canaries of fellow inmates and began publishing the results in bird magazines. With the help of a lonely widow he turned his hobby into a lucrative business, conducted from his prison cell. In 1942, forced to give up his birds under new Bureau of Prisons rules, he was transferred to Alcatraz, where, confined to D block, he began studying law. He was universally disliked by other prisoners for his devious behavior, which included inciting riots, and tried the patience of prison officials with his numerous real and imaginary self-diagnosed ailments. In 1948, new warden Edwin Swope moved Stroud to a solitary cell in the hospital. Confined to his room for 10 years, and not even allowed out to exercise, Stroud became suicidally depressed.

In the 1950s, a media blitz about Stroud's situation at Alcatraz caused a sentimental outpouring from the public. There were renewed calls for his release. Prison authorities repeatedly refused, citing Stroud's violent psychopathic tendencies. In 1959, an ailing Stroud was transferred to the Springfield Medical Center for Federal Prisoners in Illinois. His mental problems were confirmed, but he found fulfillment at last as a kingpin in the general population.

Coincidentally, he was found dead on November 21, 1963, by another former Alcatraz prisoner of some notoriety. Sentenced to 30 years imprisonment for espionage, Morton Sobell was one of the few inmates sent directly to Alcatraz after the Supreme court denied his appeal on personal order of J. Edgar Hoover. He got to know Stroud after both men were moved to Springfield. Stroud's narcissism didn't bother him, and the two men enjoyed each other's lively intelligence, humor, and honesty right to the end.

"Adolph Zukor presents "KING OF ALCATRAZ."

GAIL PATRICK · LLOYD NOLAN   J. CARROL NAISH · HARRY CAREY · ROBERT PRESTON · ANTHONY QUINN
Directed by Robert Florey · · Original Story and Screen Play by Irving Reis · · A Paramount Picture

Poster promoting "King of Alcatraz" from the late 1930s.

Both the products of myth making, Alcatraz and Hollywood are a match made in heaven. More than 26 movies about or using Alcatraz and numerous TV shows and documentaries have been made. The biggest production was the over-the-top blockbuster *The Rock*, starring Nicholas Cage and Sean Connery. It filmed on the island in 1995 and had a star-studded premiere there in 1996. Movie blood can still be seen on the hospital ceiling, despite a massive cleanup effort.

The prison has also yielded some famous movie sound effects. Remember the chilling sound of the Death Star doors slamming shut in *The Empire Strikes Back*? That was the cellhouse doors closing in a real "slammer": Alcatraz.

Before 1972, filmmakers were forced to use film set recreations and newsreel exterior footage of the prison. Plot driven movies of the 1930s and 1940s, such as *King of Alcatraz* (1938), undoubtedly found inspiration for their lurid tales of inmates' lives and escape attempts from newspaper accounts and books like Roy Gardner's *Hellcatraz,* written after Gardner was paroled from the prison in the late 1930s. The first film billing itself as a true story was made in 1962. *Birdman of Alcatraz*

remains THE classic Alcatraz film, more for its dramatic story telling and sympathetic acting than for its accuracy.

Based on the book of the same name by former parole officer Thomas E. Gaddis, both book and movie were the culmination of a decades-long struggle by Gaddis and others to secure Stroud's release. As played by Burt Lancaster, Stroud is a sweet, gentle, wronged man who only wishes to care for his birds and get out of prison. Left out are such unsavory details as the psychopath's predatory homosexuality, tendency toward cold-blooded violence, self-aggrandizement, and hypochondria.

Most of the movie is set in USP Leavenworth, where Stroud was known as the Bird Doctor of Leavenworth (he was not allowed to keep birds on Alcatraz). But the 1946 Battle of Alcatraz is powerfully recreated, as is Stroud's relationship with fictitious Alcatraz warden Harvey Shoemaker, dapperly played by Karl Malden and obviously based on Warden Johnston. The scenes between them are the heart of the movie. Johnston, a reformer, is convinced that men can be rehabilitated and is personally offended by Stroud's manuscript on the history of prisons critiquing Bureau of Prisons policy. Stroud denounces Johnston's notions of rehabilitation and tells him: "You rob prisoners of the most important thing in their lives: their individuality." Who wouldn't cheer?

By far the best and most accurate film about Alcatraz to date is *Escape from Alcatraz* (1979), a thriller about the 1962 Morris-Anglin based on the book by J. Campbell Bruce. Starring Clint Eastwood as Frank Morris, the movie benefits from having been filmed on location on Alcatraz. Much of the film is a buildup to the successful escape and captures the suspense well with vivid scenes of prison life accompanied by a dark, industrial-sounding film score and great dialogue. Before filming, Paramount repainted Broadway, the dining room, and D block. Fictitious, though, are the nonexistent yellow line along Broadway and the watchcaps the prisoners wear in the film; in real life, inmates wore peaked caps.

Alcatraz buffs will enjoy spotting where real life inmates and historic incidents have been worked into the movie. The black inmate "English" is based on Elsworth "Bumpy" Johnson, a gangster known as the "Black Capone," who did time on Alcatraz, worked in the prison library, and helped Morris escape. Another prisoner, "Doc," whose passion is painting but has his privileges revoked, is inspired by Rufus Persifal, a 1930s prisoner who tried to convince prison offi-

cials he was insane by cutting off his hand with a hatchet to obtain a transfer to the prison hospital at Springfield, MO.

On the other end of the extreme are films "inspired by" real life inmates and incidents that mix up fact and fiction so confusingly, officials feel they must put the record straight (ensuring the film will be a huge box-office success!). Such a film was *Murder in the First* (1995), a gripping, semi-fictitious account of Henri Young, an inmate serving time during Warden Johnston's era. As portrayed by actor Kevin Bacon, Young is an innocent among wolves who stole money to feed his orphaned sister and got sentenced to the "pen." After an escape attempt fails, he is put in the Hole for years—not the 19-day maximum stay prescribed by Bureau of Prisons regulations—and ends up murdering a fellow escapee after being let out. Essentially a courtroom drama, the action centers on Young's trial and his relationship with his rookie lawyer, played by Christian Slater, who eventually proves that Alcatraz was to blame and saves Young from the death penalty. In a Pyrrhic victory, Young is returned to Alcatraz and commits suicide, after scratching the word "Victory" on the wall.

In fact, Young was a bank robber and murderer who had been in and out of prison before being sent to Alcatraz (the innocent victim is really Joseph Bowers, an insane man who was shot trying to escape in 1936). The dungeon scenes were vastly overplayed for movie effect. According to contemporary accounts by Johnston, he sometimes used the old military cells below the cellhouse in the 1930s, before D block was remodeled in 1940, but certainly not for years at a time. Young did not die on Alcatraz but was transferred to Springfield, then Walla Walla, for a murder he committed in 1933, to which he confessed on Alcatraz. He was paroled in 1972, violated his parole in 1973, and is wanted by the State of Washington. He may still be alive.

Burt Lancaster as Robert Stroud in "Birdman of Alcatraz".

Movie poster for "Alcatraz Island".

Poster for "Escape from Alcatraz" starring Clint Eastwood.

"Doc" Barker.   NATIONAL ARCHIVES

Frank L. Morris.   NATIONAL ARCHIVES

Henri Young   NATIONAL ARCHIVES

According to the government, Alcatraz was selected as a maximum-security penitentiary because it was surrounded by "deep rushing waters and is 100 percent escape proof." But San Franciscans knew differently, having read newspaper reports about escapes—some successful—since 1861.

Military prisoners employed a variety of ingenious methods to escape. Some tried to paddle across the bay using homemade wooden rafts fashioned from butter churns, bread kneading troughs, even ladders; they were usually stymied by strong tides. Others walked away from labor crews on shore detail, forged release papers, or disguised themselves as officers. Nor was the bay unswimmable. In October 1933, on two separate days, three young women swam across the bay to the island (one even swam back) as a publicity stunt sponsored by women's clubs lobbying to stop the prison from opening.

To allay fears, Warden James Johnston gave a media a tour of the newly fortified prison in 1934 and lined up his large guard force for inspection. Once the prison opened, the numerous daily head counts, armed gun galleries and guard towers, barbed wire fences, and blocked tunnels made escape close to impossible. Even those who successfully made it into the water either drowned or were picked up, exhausted. The girl swimmers had been athletes acclimated to the cold water with access to tide tables. Isolated from society, living on prison food, out of shape, and not used to the frigid water, inmates had to be exceptionally lucky to make it to shore. Only one did: John Paul Scott, the last man to escape Alcatraz on December 4, 1962. He got as far as Fort Point, more dead than alive, and was found by two boys. Hours later he was back on the Rock.

In the 29 years that USP Alcatraz was open, there were just 14 escape attempts. The first, on April 27, 1936, may have been a tragic misunderstanding. Joseph Bowers, a mentally ill inmate, was on garbage detail on the west side of the island, when, according to one convict, he climbed atop some empty barrels next to a fence to feed the birds and was shot to death by a tower guard. The guard claimed that Bowers ignored commands to get down and a warning shot. There were four escape attempts between 1937 and 1943, all from the old Model Shop, which guards disliked because it was so dangerous. The first guard death occurred on May 23, 1938, when Rufus Franklin, Thomas Limerick, and James "Tex" Lucas broke out of the woodworking shop after clubbing Officer Royal Cline to death. They then made an assault on the nearby guard tower, but were overpowered by the tower guard, who killed Limerick and wounded Franklin. Lucas was recaptured.

The first cellblock breakout was on January 13, 1939. Arthur "Doc" Barker, William Martin, Rufus McCain, Dale Stamphill, and Henri Young escaped the old D Block by using contraband tools to cut the bars. Barker was mortally wounded; the others were recaptured. Young, who was sentenced to a long period in the Hole, later killed McCain but, in an infamous trial, successfully pleaded that long isolation had caused temporary insanity and avoided the death penalty.

Bloodiest of all escape attempts from the cellhouse was that made by Bernard Coy, Joseph Cretzer, Sam Shockley, Marvin Hubbard, Miran Thompson, and Clarence Carnes on May 2, 1946. In what came to be known as the Battle of Alcatraz, the men managed to enter the gun gallery, overpower guards, capture weapons, and take over the cellhouse. They found themselves trapped when they could not get the key to the exterior door and mangled the lock trying to pick it. By the end of a three-day siege, Coy, Cretzer, and Hubbard and guards William Miller and Harold Stites were dead (Stites of

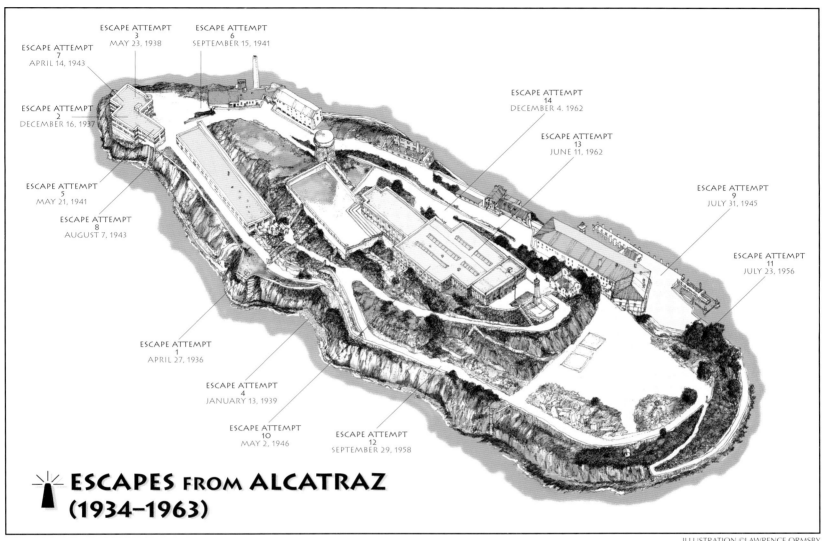

ESCAPE ATTEMPT
7
APRIL 14, 1943

ESCAPE ATTEMPT
3
MAY 23, 1938

ESCAPE ATTEMPT
6
SEPTEMBER 15, 1941

ESCAPE ATTEMPT
14
DECEMBER 4, 1962

ESCAPE ATTEMPT
2
DECEMBER 16, 1937

ESCAPE ATTEMPT
13
JUNE 11, 1962

ESCAPE ATTEMPT
5
MAY 21, 1941

ESCAPE ATTEMPT
9
JULY 31, 1945

ESCAPE ATTEMPT
8
AUGUST 7, 1943

ESCAPE ATTEMPT
11
JULY 23, 1956

ESCAPE ATTEMPT
1
APRIL 27, 1936

ESCAPE ATTEMPT
4
JANUARY 13, 1939

ESCAPE ATTEMPT
10
MAY 2, 1946

ESCAPE ATTEMPT
12
SEPTEMBER 29, 1958

ESCAPES FROM ALCATRAZ (1934–1963)

ILLUSTRATION ©LAWRENCE ORMSBY

vived shelling by the military by using mattresses to barricade their cells, considered the whole incident an overreaction. A ceasefire was finally called when "Birdman" Robert Stroud, acting as intermediary, surprised everyone by courageously climbed up to a window and shouted to Warden Johnson that the ringleaders were dead. Shockley and Thompson were executed for their roles. Clarence Carnes was given life imprisonment, probably because he spared the lives of several hostages.

By 1962, a decrease in the number of guards and an aging facility suffering from salt-air corrosion led to the escape attempt that inspired the book and Clint Eastwood movie, *Escape from Alcatraz*. Over many

months, Alan (Clayton) West, Frank Morris, and Clarence and John Anglin used homemade picks and drills made from cannibalized appliances to enlarge the air vents in the back of their cells. In workshops, the Anglins secretly created a homemade raft out of rubberized raincoats. The men fashioned dummy heads out of papier-mache and used art materials and barber shop hair to make them look realistic.

After lights out on June 11, 1962, the men placed the heads in their beds to deflect suspicion during night counts and shinnied through the air vents, up the utility corridor to the third floor and out the cellhouse ventilator shaft onto the roof. West could not fit through the hole he had made and was

forced to stay behind. Avoiding the spotlight, the escapees dropped down on the northeast side of the cellhouse and made their way past the water tower to the beach in front of the Powerhouse. Despite the Bay Area's largest manhunt, they were never seen again and are presumed drowned. An editorial in the *San Francisco Chronicle* on June 14, 1962, secretly spoke for many: "If Morris and the brothers Anglin have in fact gotten away with it and stultified all the art, science, and penological abracadabra that went into making Alcatraz 'escape proof,' we offer them a silent cheer for having at last destroyed the myth of its inviolability."

WE HOLD THE ROCK

Graffitti above Alcatraz dock.   PHOTO ©FRANK S. BALTHIS

It didn't start out as a 19-month occupation. It was originally intended as another symbolic gesture to draw attention to a people whose plight went unnoticed by Americans. But when their moment arrived, the self-proclaimed Indians of All Tribes who took over Alcatraz on November 20, 1969, seized the day. "This was body and spirit politics," remembers Indian leader John Trudell.

After the 1964 Civil Rights Act granted minorities new rights, American Indians felt left behind. In the late 1800s, Indian tribes had signed government treaties agreeing to give up self-sufficiency on native lands and move to reservations with the assurance that they would receive adequate education, housing, medical care, jobs, and maintain control over resources and mineral rights. Instead, treaties had been widely ignored and reservations neglected, and enforced boarding school education had disrupted cultural traditions and splintered families. These fractures became full breaks in the 1950s, when the twin policies of termination and relocation withdrew recognition of tribal status to 109 tribes. For many poor Indians, government programs promising vocational training, jobs, and housing in urban relocation centers were the only hope of survival. By 1968, 40,000 native people from 100 tribal groups lived in the Bay Area alone.

When jobs failed to materialize, Indians found themselves cut off from their tribes in frightening urban ghettos. Some spiraled downward into alcoholism, crime, violence, and despair. Others, though, began meeting at storefront urban Indian centers. Here they could receive services, socialize and reconnect with an emerging pan-Indian culture through powwows and other events. Some, like Adam Fortunate Eagle, a successful Ojibway business owner and chair of the United Bay Area Council of American Indians, capitalized on their political connections to begin bridging the gap between Indians and the larger culture.

The seed for the Alcatraz takeover was planted in March 8, 1964, when a group of 40 Sioux Indians traveled to the vacated island and claimed it as Indian land, using an obscure clause in the 1868 Black Hills Treaty that granted Sioux men ownership of surplus federal property. They were politely but firmly evicted. Five years later, when a fire burned down the San Francisco Indian Center, Fortunate Eagle suggested to the San Francisco City Council that his group take over Alcatraz as an Indian educational and cultural center.

Ignored by the City Council, Fortunate Eagle enlisted the help of local media and a handsome young Mohawk student leader named Richard Oakes and staged a publicity stunt on Pier 39 on November 9, 1969. He had Oakes read a tongue-in-cheek proclamation offering to buy the island from the government for $24 in trade goods—an echo of the white man's purchase of Manhattan Island. The ironic document reasoned that Alcatraz's many similarities to Indian reservations made it an appropriate choice: It was isolated and lacked transportation, running water, resources, jobs, productive soil, and game. Historically, it too had a population kept prisoner and dependent on others. A contingent then sailed out to Alcatraz and, eluding security guards, spent the night on the island. They agreed to leave the next morning, after handing their proclamation to T.E. Hannon, regional director of the Government Services Administration responsible for the island's upkeep.

Emboldened, Oakes and 78 others, many of them university students, returned to Alcatraz on November 20. Outrunning a Coast Guard blockade in the predawn hours, they took possession of the island. Large signs in bright red paint announced that this was Indian Land; Red Power graffiti appeared on walls. Families moved into the old warden's house and apartment buildings on the parade ground. The cellhouse dining room was opened for meals. Oakes and others formed an American Indian Government to run this unofficial Indian republic (with a Bureau of Caucasion Affairs) and began negotiating with the government about the cultural center. It had all the appearance of summer camp.

Sympathetizers donated food, money, and other supplies. A San Francisco restaurant sent over food for the occupiers' first "Un-Thanksgiving" on the Rock, a healing reversal of the first Pilgrim celebration. Mindful of public opinion and hoping to avoid violence, White House officials personally negotiated with the

---

OPPOSITE: The Warden's House destroyed by fire in 1970. PHOTO ©FRANK S. BALTHIS

Golden Gate Bridge and teepee on south side of island during 1969 occupation.

occupiers. Using a siege mentality, their strategy was to wait until the Indians got tired of the uncomfortable conditions and gave up the protest. Instead, the occupation served as a wakeup call for dispossessed Indians across the country. Hundreds arrived to support the cause, including Indian activists who later used the occupation as a springboard for other Indian protests, such as those at Wounded Knee. Some even tried a similar symbolic takeover of Ellis Island but the project never got off the ground.

Within six weeks, things on Alcatraz had begun to unravel. Richard Oakes's stepdaughter Yvonne fell to her death in an apartment house on January 3, 1970, and a griefstricken Oakes and his family left the island. Without the media-savvy Oakes, the fragile leadership alliance eroded. Problems escalated when drifters from outside the Bay Area showed up. Negative press reports about drinking and vandalism turned public opinion. On

June 1, 1970, suspicious fires broke out that destroyed the the warden's house, the prison doctor's home, the social hall, and the lighthouse keeper's quarters. The Alcatraz Lighthouse went dark for the first time since 1854.

With reports that occupiers were stripping copper and brass scrap from fixtures and selling it, the federal government had the excuse it needed to act. But by the time federal marshals landed and removed the last 15 protesters on June 11, 1971, the Alcatraz occupiers had lost the battle but won the war. In December 1970, President Nixon returned sacred Blue Lake to the Taos Indians and signed a bill paving the way for tribal self-determination. Today, Indians honor Alcatraz as the beginning of Indian political activism. Many make pilgrimages to the island or attend annual Un-Thanksgiving ceremonies, giving thanks for the incalculable ways the occupation of Alcatraz helped Indians remember who they are.

POSTER CHILD of A NEW ERA

Artist's rendition of "Baghdad-by-the-Bay", a proposed space playground, 1980.

The 1969-1971 Indian occupation helped crystallize Alcatraz's future. A 1964 government plan had suggested the island as a memorial to the United Nations, which had been founded in San Francisco following World War II. But State Department officials felt the infamous prison was a poor advertisement for American accomplishments. The plan quietly died.

When the GSA declared Alcatraz surplus federal property in 1968, the City of San Francisco immediately threw its hat into the ring. Given two months to come up with a proposal and funding, the city opened the debate to the public. Among the 500 suggestions were a casino, a gangsterland theme park, a bird sanctuary, an Indian university, a home for stray dogs and cats, and, logically enough, restoration of the prison complex for public tours. The city chose a proposal by Texas oil millionaire Lamar Hunt that called for demolition of the historic buildings for commercial development and a space museum, complete with Seattle-style

needle. Appalled San Franciscans immediately rallied around a "Save Alcatraz" campaign, and 8,000 people wrote to Secretary of the Interior Walter Hickel urging him to preserve the island as open space for public recreation. Columnist Herb Caen weighed in, lampooning the Hunt plan and describing the needle as a "phallus with a ten-gallon hat on top."

Serendipity intervened at this point. Hickel was a proponent of what he called "Parks to the People," an urban open space program in perfect harmony with the prevailing environmental ethos in San Francisco. Hinkel ordered the Bureau of Outdoor Recreation (a now defunct agency) to study Alcatraz Island's potential for public recreation. In November 1969, they recommended Alcatraz be immediately transferred to the National Park Service and opened to the public. A second report, published the following month, urged that Alcatraz and the other surplus federal properties around San Francisco be part of a new 34,000-acre

urban park: Golden Gate National Recreation Area.

It was at this time that American Indians added their voice to the mix, occupying Alcatraz to push the federal government to agree to an Indian university in the proposed national park. When the GSA bulldozed the vandalized apartment buildings used by occupiers for 19 months, concerned San Franciscans, led by the ranking Democrat on the House Interior Committee Phillip Burton, pushed Congress to fast-track legislation establishing Golden Gate National Recreation Area. On October 27, 1972, President Richard Nixon signed Public Law 92-589, creating the park. Newly hired park service rangers like native San Franciscan John Martini, who began a distinguished career as a ranger historian on Alcatraz, figured public curiosity about the island would taper off after five years. Few could conceive then that visitation would only grow each year, until Alcatraz emerged as northern California's top visitor attraction.

ALCATRAZ TODAY

Masks on display in Cellhouse.

From the top of 84-foot-high Alcatraz Lighthouse, the view of San Francisco Bay is stunning. I can see Fisherman's Wharf, Fort Mason, and cable cars ascending hills beyond. The Bay Bridge, connecting the city with the East Bay, stretches inland. The magnificent Golden Gate Bridge, with the Presidio, Crissy Field, and Fort Point to the south and the lusciously green, foggy Marin Headlands to the north, is bathed in sunset glow. A yacht with billowing sails, rises and yaws on the choppy glacial waters below, dwarfed by a passing tanker. The last Alcatraz ferry of the day maneuvers round into the dock and disgorges visitors onto the gangplank, where a ranger welcomes them with a familiar greeting: "Welcome to Alcatraz."

Ranger John Cantwell turns to the tiny group of ex-Alcatraz residents, new rangers, and visiting media on this rare behind-the-scenes tour of the lighthouse, courtesy of the U.S. Coastguard, and winks: "Ready?" he asks. We nod. "Let's go, then," he says. We step out onto the tiny platform surrounding the beacon and are flattened by freezing wind. Holding hands we inch round the tower. I steel myself, open my eyes, and look around.

The roof of the cellhouse is clearly visible, and I can see exactly where Clint Eastwood and his fellow escapees made a run for it in *Escape from Alcatraz*. The newly restored dock guard tower looms above the Sally Port like an alien from H.G. Wells's *War of the Worlds*. "Great, isn't it?" grins Cantwell. "This is my favorite place on Alcatraz." My stomach lurches with vertigo as I look down on the breeding sea gulls massed on the parade ground. In a rushing, screeching, whir of wings they fly up and attack a family of pelicans flying too close to nests. The juxtaposition of the glorious views with the Hitchcockian scene suddenly fills me with terror, and I realize that I've reached my limit. "Can we go now" I ask.

Walking inside the cellhouse, I remember ranger historian John Martini's childhood memory of Alcatraz as an island that seemed to be filled with factory buildings with no visible workers. It does indeed look like a factory—a factory farm, perhaps, for battery hens, not people. I can't imagine how human beings lived for years this way, in five-by-seven-by-nine-foot cells that have all the appearance of cages.

The cellhouse is packed with visitors taking a self-guided audio tour. Except for the sound of shuffling feet, there is almost complete silence as people examine the dummy heads in the Anglin and Morris cells, a recreated late-era cell with painting supplies and canvases, and swivel their heads up to see where Al Capone bunked. We all seem to be part of some strange waking dream, deeply reflective, listening to the voices of ex-cons Jim Quillen and Leon "Whitey" Thompson and guard Philip Bergen echoing inside our heads. I've never seen visitors at any national park so quiet, orderly, and reverent. This is not the park service's doing; rules are few here (no eating or drinking). No, this is self-imposed, self-regulated behavior. Warden Johnston would surely approve.

The air inside the "dark" cells of D block hangs heavy, weighted down with human suffering. In Tara Isom's haunting, meticulously researched novel, *Child Out of Alcatraz*, the warped, upside-down world of men guarding men "up top" while wives and children play out their own psychological dramas below in guard housing offers a rare female perspective on Alcatraz. After growing up on the island, Olivia, the troubled young daughter of a prison guard, returns when the prison closes and tours the cellhouse for the first time. Both fascinated and repelled by the Hole, she has her father shut her in. "I knew it would be like this," she reflects. "This extreme of how it's always been, if I could only, ever, get deep enough away, find this isolation, womblike, fluid around me, surrounding me like sea around an island."

Former inmates recalled that Alcatraz wasn't particularly brutal compared with other prisons, but it tortured men psychologically until real death seemed preferable to "burial in plain sight." Many went over the edge. One prisoner described "hell-nighting," when, at night, men driven mad by the voices in their heads started to destroy their cells, engage in animal behavior, and quietly try to kill themselves with anything they could lay their hands on. Despite a century of evidence that "Control Units" drove men insane, authorities refused to admit that Alcatraz's

Alcatraz Island seen from Fort Point, sunrise.

"death by regulation" was a failure. As with so much in the 1960s, public pressure ushered in a new era of prison reform—a debate still raging in today's overcrowded prisons.

In the old bandroom, next to the showers, where Capone and Karpis used to play, I break away from the crowd and sit down on a wooden bench painted with the words "Escape from Alcatraz: Paramount Pictures." Outside the thick walls, I can hear echoing footsteps, the screams of gulls, the mournful drone of the island foghorn, a child crying. Inside, the walls are covered with colorful life masks made by inner city high-schoolers, exploring the theme of freedom as part of the park's innovative educational program "Unlocking Alcatraz." Imagining themselves either as Native American occupiers or prison guards, they tour the prison, return to the classroom, and help each other make masks. Many are covered in red paint, feathers, or scrawled with graffiti such as "freedom." Some show duality by splitting the masks down the center using two paint colors—black and white, silver and gold. The frozen faces are filled with hopes, dreams, fears, questions. I feel the human stories behind each one. "What does Alcatraz mean to you?" reads the sign. I am inexpressibly moved. To me, this room is the heart and soul of visiting Alcatraz today.

What does Alcatraz mean to me? I'm a woman. I grew up on a former island in the drained fens of England, an island nation that expresses individuality in a quite different way to America—conforming on the outside but cherishing secret lives of wild eccentricity within. Here in the United States, I now understand duality as a minority, walking simultaneously in two worlds. My writing often deals with the jigsaw puzzle of solitude versus society and finding healing by being brave enough to confront experiences head on. On Alcatraz, I feel sad, surrounded by shadows, the disowned aspects of the human experience: pain, anger, violence, evil. A visit to Alcatraz forces a take-no-prisoners, face-to-face engagement with difficult questions. What are the limits of freedom and human rights in a democracy? How do we safeguard society without losing our humanity? How do we live in the world as individuals, members of society, and answerable to a higher morality?

This is heady stuff. Walking outside, I breathe the invigorating air of the bay deep into my lungs and my eyes rest on the simple beauty of the bay and the island. Red valerian, calla lilies, wild roses, and nasturtiums splay from cracks in ruins. Diving cormorants mass on an old concrete block on the shoreline. Speckled-breasted gull chicks run around ridiculously tiny territories, atop a roof, a stump, a brick wall. Yet it all seems perfect, somehow. Not ruined but very much alive—a constantly evolving story.

I'm struck by the sheer number of stories on Alcatraz, and the way everyone associated with the island tells them over and over. Therapists know that the telling and retelling of our human stories helps us heal, acting like a salve on a gaping wound. The beacon of Alcatraz winks on and off—a friendly, reassuring presence in a chaotic world. It's easy to see what Indian activist Richard Oakes meant when he said, "Alcatraz is not an island." Indeed not. The meaning of Alcatraz is waiting to be discovered, inside every one of us.

OPPOSITE: Lighthouse rising above rubble on Parade Grounds.

BIRDS, ANIMALS, AND SEALIFE

Egret in Rodeo Lagoon, Marin Headlands. ©GALEN ROWELL

California sea lions at Pier 39. ©FRANK S. BALTHIS

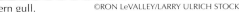

Western gull. ©RON LeVALLEY/LARRY ULRICH STOCK

The lush appearance of modern Alcatraz belies its history. It was once a barren rock beloved mainly by birds. In altering nature for their own purposes, humans have created an evolving ecosystem quite unlike the one that used to thrive here.

Insects seem to have hitched a ride over in soil imported from Angel Island, but Alcatraz supports just three land animals. Deer mice are believed to be the only mammals inhabiting Alcatraz. Varying from 3 to 4 inches long, with a tail 2.5 to 4.5 inches in length, these nocturnal animals feed on insects, berries, and fruit. They are particularly fond of human food scraps and have been known to get trapped in garbage cans. A 1994 study found that some of Alcatraz's deer mice are genetically different, with an unusual light tan coat that makes them more able to blend into the rocky landscape.

Yellow banana slugs can be found in the moister areas of Alcatraz. They reach 6 to 8 inches in length and feed on vegetation, fungi, and dead animals. Slugs produce slime that allows them to retain water, defend themselves, and move around. California slender salamanders also inhabit moist places. In size and color, salamanders resemble earthworms with tiny feet. The salamander breathes through its skin and, if caught by a predator, can snap off its tail and grow a new one. They prefer living underneath rotting woods. Studies indicate that the salamander population on Alcatraz is old and has a low reproductive rate.

Seals and sea lions used to visit Alcatraz but lost their favorite sunbathing spots when military construction buried beaches in rocks and other debris. One animal's loss is another's gain. The new rocky shoreline created an unusual feature—tidepools—exposed every time the tide receded (about every six hours). Anemones, mussels, crabs, sea snails, sea stars, nudibranches, and other tidepool denizens are a favorite meals of birds. Fishing was an enduring passion of many an off-duty guard on Alcatraz. Bass, sardines, and other fish live around the island. Of particular note are the huge rockfish. Tales of shark-infested waters made many potential prison escapees think twice, but the only sharks in San Francisco Bay are harmless tiger and sand sharks with beautiful striped coloring.

A total of 108 different bird species live on Alcatraz, including 18 species that breed on the island, 20 that stop by seasonally, and 73 that visit occasionally. Look and listen carefully as you walk up the road to the cellhouse. You'll hear the fluting songs of house finches and sparrows in bushes, the doleful requiems of mourning doves on the ground, and buzzing of hummingbirds visiting red trumpet-shaped flowers. Chances are, though, that these songs will be drowned out by the loud caws of a family of ravens living in the Monterey cypress trees and the cacophony of western gulls that monopolize every last square inch of available ground for their nests.

In 2002, naturalist Christian Hellwig counted 850 pairs of western gulls living on Alcatraz, making it the second most important western gull nesting area after the Farallone Islands. After egg collecting during the Gold Rush era devastated populations, strong laws were created to protect nesting seabird colonies. On Alcatraz, the park service is responsible for enforcing these laws. The parade ground and Agave Trail are closed to visitors during mating and nesting season, usually January to August.

Western gulls are 24 to 27 inches long, with white breasts and gray top feathers, and a yellow bill with a red spot. The white breasts are a cooling mechanism; the birds can sit facing the sun and stay cool, while the gray feathers camouflage the gull when it is bobbing on seawater. When temperatures cool in winter, gulls fly south to fish, but return to Alcatraz to mate in January. Unattached males find an unoccupied territory and waiting until interested females approach. The male then goes into action, producing a delicious dinner of regurgitated fish for the female of his dreams. If she is impressed, the pair build a nest together and mate. The female lays a clutch of speckled eggs, which both male and female take turns protecting. The eggs start to hatch in May. Naturalists call gull chicks "precocious," meaning that when they hatch they already have speckled downy feathers, can stand and feed as soon as they are born, and start flying as early as four to six weeks, although they will retain their "baby feathers" until they are sexually mature—four years for males and three years for females.

Gulls coexist with one of the largest colonies of black-crowned night herons in the bay area. About 120 pairs nest in the rubble on the parade ground and stalk fish in the shallows at night. Four hundred pairs of cormorants nest on Alcatraz. Three different species can be seen diving off rocks below the West Road and spreading their wings to dry in the sun. Pelagic cormorants, the smallest of the three, are black with a red pouch beneath the bill and white patches on the sides of breeding birds. The largest and darkest are Brandt's cormorants, which have bands around their pouches that become bright blue in mating season. Double-crested cormorants are also black, with a patch of orange skin under their bills. Breeding adults have white tufted feathers behind each eye. Pigeon guillemots and snowy egrets can also be seen nesting on the island, but, contrary to myth, not pelicans, which are attacked by territorial gulls as they fly near the island. If the word *alcatraz* can refer to gulls, pelicans, cormorants, or guillemots, which birds do you think the Spanish had in mind when they named Alcatraz?

OPPOSITE: Cellhouse above Barker Beach. PHOTO ©JEFF GNASS

THE GARDENS OF ALCATRAZ

Pride-of-Madeira.   ©JEFF D. NICHOLAS

Agaves and foghorn along Agave Trail.   ©JEFF GNASS

Sedum.   ©JEFF D. NICHOLAS

In most national parks, the presence of exotic plants that crowd out endemic, or native, plants is undesirable. Fast-growing exotics able to grow in a variety of places take over specialized niches inhabited by plants with more delicate sensibilities, only able to survive under certain conditions. This is not a problem on Alcatraz. The original island was rocky and barren, clad only in lichens, mosses, and grasses that found their way here in the digestive tracts of birds. It's a rare situation when man alters an environment for the better, but such was the case on Alcatraz.

When the military added to fortifications around the island following the Civil War, they brought over soil from Angel Island to pack around gun batteries and landscape the island. Soldiers tried and generally failed to grow grass, alfalfa, honeysuckle, barley, ice plant, clover, and agave to stabilize the earthworks; only a few survived. But native plants did well. The seeds of hardy California poppy, coyote brush, and blackberry hitched a ride over in the soil transported to the island and blossomed into wild patches that revived the spirits of soldiers posted on the rugged island.

Small gardens of ornamental plants in front of officer's homes became showcases for family members with green thumbs, who coaxed roses, sweet peas, lupines, red hot pokers, and other plants to grow despite the lack of fresh water. The officers' obvious pride in their gardens is visible in photographs of the front of the Citadel taken by San Francisco photographer Eadweard Muybridge in 1869. Families gussied up in stiff formal Victorian clothing proudly sit amid their flowers, piles of shot in the background, as though they are being judged for the Chelsea Flower Show.

In the early 1900s, when the fort was officially decommissioned in favor of a military prison, gun batteries buried beneath the soil were taken over by new plantings. On February 7, 1924, the California Spring Blossom and Wildflower Association planted 300 trees and shrubs, including the mighty Monterey cypress and eucalyptus trees that provide much-needed shelter on the winding road to the top of the island. They also sowed 100 pounds of nasturtium and poppy seeds, which today spill out of every nook and cranny in the rocks. Prison labor was used to tend the extensive plantings.

Visiting dignitaries and reporters were charmed by Alcatraz's gardens and wrote glowingly of the transformation that had occurred on the Rock. "The visitor who comes here expects to find a barren rock, but as he strolls over it he is surprised to find roses in bloom, sweet peas, lilies, and a large variety of other flowers in all their beauty and fragrance," wrote one visitor in March 1918. "In this way barren wastes are converted into garden spots, and ugliness is transformed into beauty."

When the military left in 1933, incoming correctional officers took over the maintenance of the existing gardens. One additional garden was planted by Freddie Reichel, secretary to Warden Johnston from 1934 to 1941, on the steep west slope near the prison recreation yard. Tending daffodils, nasturtiums, fruit trees, roses, and artichokes offered staff and inmates a welcome respite from the rigid regime of the prison and undoubtedly soothed their souls.

The closure of the prison proved a boon for nature as well as the prisoners. Formal gardens made a bid for freedom and ran wild all over the island, reseeding themselves in cracked concrete and ruined buildings, cascading down walls, and exuberantly monopolizing entire slopes, surviving on fog and rain. When the National Park Service took over the island in 1972, the plants were protected along with the buildings and offer a reminder of the island's long human history.

Today, more than 145 species or varieties of plants in 105 known genera live on Alcatraz. Look for oxalis, pelargoniums, poppies, and fuschia along the dock and rambling roses near the Sally Port. Lupine, ferns, and succulents can be seen in walls next to Building 64, the old officer's apartment buildings. Red valerian seems to spurt from every wall, but is particularly dense in the ruins of the Post Exchange. Partway up the road to the cellhouse, the remains of gardens in the ruined foundations of officer's row include red and purple firecracker fuschia, white calla lilies, and English ivy. In the small private garden that adjoined the Warden's House, you can still see red tea roses, pale yellow rose hybrids, and fuschia. The old Citadel gardens were destroyed when the new cellhouse was built in 1908.

On the West Road, the remains of the potting shed and Reichel's gardens attract both songbirds and humans. Red hot pokers; magenta pelargoniums; hybrid and white roses; and apple, walnut, and fig trees grow here, along with yellow and orange nasturtiums and Japanese honeysuckle, which attracts hummingbirds and butterflies. A single blue Pride of Madeira has naturalized and spread. Large mirror plants clustered along the cliffs provide nesting habitat for black-crowned night herons. Great egrets sometimes nest in the cypress and eucalyptus near the top of the Agave Trail. Continuing along the trail to the shoreline, you can still see armies of sword-waving agave, or century plant. Planted as erosion control, they also served a useful purpose as a barrier to prisoners trying to escape. More than one escapee found himself bayoneted by these spikey plants as he tried to negotiate the rocky slopes leading to freedom.

OPPOSITE: Garden on south side of Alcatraz Island. PHOTO ©BRENDA THARP

GOLDEN GATE N.R.A.

Fort Point and Golden Gate Bridge, morning light.

Alcatraz is a unit of Golden Gate National Recreation Area (GGNRA), which was set aside in 1972 and has now grown to 75,500 acres and is the largest urban park in the world. Administered by the National Park Service, GGNRA is a park-in-progress, with new acreage being added all the time. Included in the park are woods, headlands, mountains, islands, wetlands, bays, bird sanctuaries, and seashores, as well as civil war forts and World War I and World War II installations; ancient Indian shellmounds; historic buildings, and lighthouses; theaters, museums, shops, and waterfronts.

GGNRA comprises seven different life zones and supports 1,000 types of plants and 23 rare and endangered species and 500 species of mammal, bird, reptile, and amphibian. It ranks third in the United States for endangered species and is part of UNESCO's Central California Coast Biosphere Reserve.

Among the park's units are:

PRESIDIO OF SAN FRANCISCO

Used by the Ohlone Indians, Spanish soldiers, and the U.S. Army, this 1,480-acre site was transferred to the park service in 1994. Highlights include: Presidio visitor center, Fort Point, red-bricked barracks, the officer's club, forested landscaping, the stables, San Francisco National Cemetery, Lobos Creek.

FORT MASON

Occupying the northernmost point of land in San Francisco, the bayfront promontory has been used by Spanish soldiers, the U.S. Army, earthquake refugees, port authorities, offices, and shops. A building in Upper Fort Mason houses GGNRA park headquarters. Highlights include: Fort Mason Center, The Great Meadow, Black Point Battery and Picnic Area, Aquatic Park.

GOLDEN GATE BRIDGE

Opened in 1937. Views include Fort Point, Fort Baker, USS San Francisco Memorial Lot, Conzelman Road, Hawk Hill, Bridge Vista Point.

OPPOSITE: Twilight surf, Marin Headlands, GGNRA
PHOTO ©GALEN ROWELL/MOUNTAIN LIGHT

PAGE 60/61: Alcatraz Island seen from East Bay. PHOTO ©STEVE MOHLENCAMP

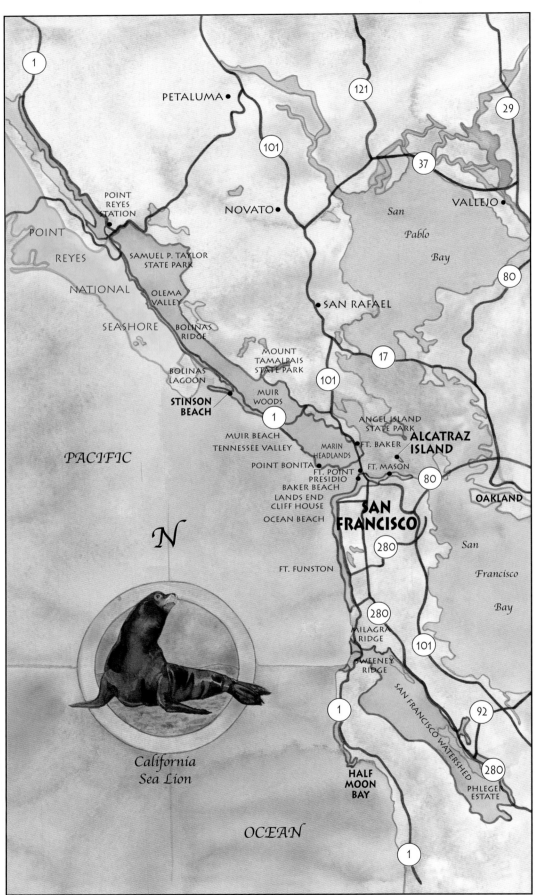

PETALUMA

POINT REYES STATION

POINT REYES NATIONAL SEASHORE

SAMUEL P. TAYLOR STATE PARK

OLEMA VALLEY

BOLINAS RIDGE

BOLINAS LAGOON

MOUNT TAMALPAIS STATE PARK

STINSON BEACH

MUIR WOODS

PACIFIC

MUIR BEACH
TENNESSEE VALLEY

POINT BONITA

MARIN HEADLANDS

FT. POINT
PRESIDIO
BAKER BEACH
LANDS END
CLIFF HOUSE
OCEAN BEACH

FT. FUNSTON

NOVATO

SAN RAFAEL

San Pablo Bay

VALLEJO

ANGEL ISLAND STATE PARK

FT. BAKER

ALCATRAZ ISLAND

FT. MASON

SAN FRANCISCO

OAKLAND

San Francisco Bay

MILAGRA RIDGE

SWEENEY RIDGE

SAN FRANCISCO WATERSHED

HALF MOON BAY

PHLEGER ESTATE

OCEAN

California Sea Lion

N

ILLUSTRATION BY DARLECE CLEVELAND

MARIN HEADLANDS

Located just north of the Golden Gate Bridge, highlights include scenic Conzelman Road and Hawk Hill, Kirby Cove, Seacoast Fortifications Tour, Battery Wallace Picnic Area, Point Bonita Lighthouse, and Fort Baker.

MUIR WOODS
NATIONAL MONUMENT

Set aside in 1908 to protect a remnant stand of virgin redwoods and named after famed environmentalist John Muir. Highlights include the redwoods, Redwood Creek, and trails within the woods and into adjoining valleys.

MOUNT TAMALPAIS
STATE PARK

Highlights include Mt. Tam, the tallest mountain in the Bay Area; Bootjack and East Peak Picnic Area, Ridge Road, loop trails, and Old Railroad Grade Trail.

BOLINAS LAGOON/
AUDUBON CANYON RANCH

One of the richest wetlands on GGNRA's shores. Highlights include birds, seals, and lagoon life; trails and overlooks; Audubon Canyon Ranch wildlife sanctuary.

ANGEL ISLAND
STATE PARK

A fishing site for Coastal Miwok Indians and later used by Spanish explorer Juan de Ayala, cattle ranchers, the U.S. Army, and as a government immigration station. Access is by ferry from San Francisco, Oakland, Vallejo, or Tiburon (call 435-2131).

For general GGNRA information, contact the National Park Service at Golden Gate National Recreation Area, Fort Mason, Building 201, San Francisco, CA 94123-0022; (415) 561-4700; www.nps.gov/goga.

FOR MORE INFORMATION

GOLDEN GATE NATIONAL PARKS CONSERVANCY is a nonprofit membership organization dedicated to the preservation and public enjoyment of Golden Gate National Recreation Area. It is funded by the contributions of members, corporations, and foundations, as well as income earned through park stores, educational materials, and interpretive tours. Since its formation in 1981, the Parks Association has provided the National Park Service with nearly $50 million for the Golden Gate National Parks. For more information about publications and becoming a member, contact:
Golden Gate National Parks Conservancy
Fort Mason, Building 201
San Francisco, CA 94123
(415)561-3000
www.parksconservancy.org

ALCATRAZ ISLAND and
GOLDEN GATE NATIONAL RECRE-
ATION AREA
Fort Mason, Building 201–Alcatraz
San Francisco, CA 94123
(415) 561-4900 (Visitor Information)
www.nps.gov/alca

GOLDEN GATE NATIONAL RECRE-
ATION AREA
Fort Mason, Building 201
San Francisco, CA 94123
(415) 561-4700
www.nps.gov/goga

NATIONAL PARKS ON THE INTERNET:
www.nps.gov

RESERVATIONS

BLUE & GOLD FLEET
(415) 705-5555
www.blueandgoldfleet.com
or www.nps.gov/alca

OTHER G.G.N.R.A. SITES

BOLINAS LAGOON and AUDUBON
CANYON RANCH
(415) 868-9244

CLIFF HOUSE VISITOR CENTER
(415) 556-8642

FORT POINT NATIONAL HISTORIC SITE
PO Box 29333
Presidio of San Francisco, CA 94129
(415) 556-1693
www.nps.gov/fopo

MARIN HEADLANDS VISITOR CENTER
(415) 331-1540

MOUNT TAMALPAIS STATE PARK
(415) 388-2070

MUIR WOODS NAT'L MONUMENT
Mill Valley, CA 94941
(415) 388-2595, 556-2766 (TTY)
www.nps.gov/muwo

PRESIDIO OF SAN FRANCISCO
(William Penn Mott, Jr. Visitor Center)
Write to: Golden Gate NRA

Building 201, Fort Mason
San Francisco, Ca 94123
(415) 561-4323, 561-4314 (TTY) www.nps.gov/prsf

OTHER REGIONAL SITES

ANGEL ISLAND STATE PARK
(415) 435-1915
www.parks.ca.gov/
NOTE: Access to Angel Island is by ferry from San Francisco, Vallejo, or Tiburon. For additional information call (415) 435-2131.

EUGENE O'NEILL NATIONAL HISTORIC SITE
PO Box 280
Danville, CA 94526
(925) 838-0249
www.nps.gov/euon

JOHN MUIR NATIONAL HISTORIC SITE
4202 Alhambra Avenue
Martinez, Ca 94553
(925) 228-8860
www.nps.gov/jomu

POINT REYES NATIONAL SEASHORE
Point Reyes, CA 94956
(415) 464-5100
www.nps.gov/pore

SAN FRANCISCO MARITIME NATIONAL
HISTORICAL PARK
Building E, Fort Mason Center

San Francisco, CA 94123
(415) 561-7100, 556-1843 (TDD)
www.nps.gov/safr

SUGGESTED READING

Babyak, Jolene. *Eyewitness of Alcatraz: Interviews of Guards, Families, and Prisoners Who Lived on the Rock.* Berkeley, CA: Ariel Vamp Press. 1988.

————————. *Bird Man: The Many Faces of Robert Stroud.* Berkeley, Ca: Ariel Vamp Press. 1994.

Delgado, James P. *Alcatraz: Island of Change.* San Francisco, CA: Golden Gate National Parks Association. 1991.

Fortunate Eagle, Adam. *Alcatraz! Alcatraz! The Indian Occupation of 1969-1971.* Foreward by Vine DeLoria, Jr. Berkeley, CA: Heyday Books. 1992.

Fortunate Eagle, Adam. *Heart of Rock: The Indian Invasion of Alcatraz.* In collaboration with Tim Findley. Foreword by Vine DeLoria, Jr. Norman, OK: University of Oklahoma Press. 2002.

Isom, Tara. *A Child Out of Alcatraz.* Boston and London: Faber and Faber. 1997.

Johnson, Troy. *We Hold the Rock: The Indian Occupation of Alcatraz, 1969-1970.* San Francisco, CA: Golden Gate National Parks Association. 2002.

Johnston, James A. *Alcatraz Island Prison and the Men Who Live There.* New York, NY: Charles A. Scribner. 1949.

Margolin, Malcolm. *The Ohlone Way: Indian Life in the San Francisco-Monterey Bay Area.* Berkeley, CA: Heyday Books. 1978.

Martini, John A. *Alcatraz at War.* San Francisco, CA: Golden Gate National Parks Association. 2002.

Martini, John A. *Fortress Alcatraz: Guardian of the Golden Gate.* Kailua, HI: Pacific Monograph. 1990.

Odier, Pierre. *Alcatraz: The Rock, A History of Alcatraz: The Fort/The Prison.* Eagle Rock, CA: L'Image Odier. 1982.

Okamoto, Ariel Rubissow. *Golden Gate National Recreation Area: Guide to the Parks.* San Francisco, CA: Golden Gate National Parks Association. 1995.

Quillen, James. *Alcatraz from Inside: The Hard Years, 1942-1952.* San Francisco, CA: Golden Gate National Parks Association. 1991.

Stuller, Jay. *Alcatraz: The Prison.* San Francisco, CA: Golden Gate National Parks Association. 1998.

Thompson, E.N. *The Rock: A History of Alcatraz Island 1847-1972.* Historic Resource Study, Golden Gate National Recreation Area, California. Denver, CO: US Dept of the Interior, National Park Service, Historic Preservation Division. 1979.

ABOVE: Alcatraz Island seen through the cables of the Golden Gate Bridge, sunrise. PHOTO ©JEFF D. NICHOLAS

ACKNOWLEDGMENTS

The publisher would like to extend a very special thank you to Clover Earl, Nicholette Phelps, and Susan Tasaki of the Golden Gate National Park Association for their encouragement and support; the staff of the G.G.N.R.A. Park Archives and Records Center; the staff of the National Archives and Records Administration in San Bruno, CA; The Bancroft Library at U.C. Berkeley; the San Francisco Public Library's History Center; the California Historical Society; and all the photographers who made their imagery available for this book! —JDN

PRODUCTION CREDITS

Publisher: Jeff D. Nicholas
Author: Nicky Leach
Consultant: John A. Martini
Production Assistant: Melissa Wass
Illustrations: Lawrence Ormsby/Carol Thickstun, and Darlece Cleveland
Printing Coordination: Sung In Printing America

All National Park Service photos courtesy of Park Archives and Records Center, Golden Gate National Recreation Area.
ISBN 1-58071-039-5 (Cl), 1-58071-040-9 (Pb)
©2003 Panorama International Productions, Inc. Sierra Press is an imprint of Panorama International Productions, Inc. All rights reserved. No part of this book may be reproduced in any form without written permission from the publisher.
Printed in the Republic of South Korea.
First printing, Spring 2003.

SIERRA PRESS

4988 Gold Leaf Drive, Mariposa, CA 95338
(209) 966-5071, 966-5073 (Fax)

BELOW:
Morning light in Cellblock D. PHOTO ©BRENDA THARP
OPPOSITE:
1862 Panorama of San Francisco Bay as seen from Russian Hill. LITHOGRAPH BY CHARLES B. GIFFORD, COURTESY HONEYMAN COLLECTION, THE BANCROFT LIBRARY
BACK COVER:
Cellblock crossover.
PHOTO ©JEFF GNASS
BACK COVER INSET:
Alcatraz Island and the East Bay Hills, dawn
PHOTO ©CHUCK PLACE

GIFFORD, Del & Lith.

| 21 Jones St. | 22 Lombard St. | 24 Angel Isld |
| A Arch Rock. | 23 Greenwich St. | 25 Alcatraz Isld & Fort |